JOURNAL FOR THE STUDY OF THE NEW TESTAMENT SUPPLEMENT SERIES

133

Executive Editor
Stanley E. Porter

Editorial Board
Richard Bauckham, David Catchpole, R. Alan Culpepper,
Margaret Davies, James D.G. Dunn, Craig A. Evans, Stephen Fowl,
Robert Fowler, Robert Jewett, Elizabeth Struthers Malbon

Sheffield Academic Press

Goulder and the Gospels

An Examination of a New Paradigm

Mark S. Goodacre

Journal for the Study of the New Testament
Supplement Series 133

Copyright © 1996 Sheffield Academic Press

Published by Sheffield Academic Press Ltd
Mansion House
19 Kingfield Road
Sheffield S11 9AS
England

Printed on acid-free paper in Great Britain
by Bookcraft Ltd
Midsomer Norton, Bath

British Library Cataloguing in Publication Data

A catalogue record for this book is available
from the British Library

ISBN 1-85075-631-7

CONTENTS

Part III
THE LECTIONARY THEORY

Half a dozen times a year, until my retirement in 1994, I used to organize a public disputation at the University of Birmingham. The topics were theological or biblical, and the format proved popular. Between seventy and two hundred people would attend, to hear two contrasting views of the same topic, in the hope of clearing their minds and deciding what was the better position. At first I would often be one of the disputants myself: I had new ideas to sell, and my services were free. Among those coming was an RE teacher from Burton-on-Trent, Janet Goodacre, and her teenage son Mark, who looked bright but was silent.

I was surprised in due course to be told by an Oxford friend, 'One of your students has got a scholarship here'; for I have no students in this sense. 'Well, his papers were full of your theories', was the comment. Three years later Mark Goodacre got the top First of his year, and he went on to do an MPhil on Lectionary Theories of the Gospels, under the then Dean Ireland Professor, Ed Sanders. I was happy to be shown the thesis on its way and to discover that in Mark's view all lectionary theories were flawed, with the sole exception of my own. He got the MPhil in 1990, and then he went on to a DPhil, the result of which is the present volume. Its flattering title masks some rather less flattering conclusions. It is a study of four of the hypotheses which I have advanced over the years about the Synoptic Gospels: on the Matthean vocabulary, the Minor Agreements, Lukan creativity and the lectionary background. I am afraid that the idol is shown to totter a good deal, even if, in the final issue, it is usually left standing.

The book has four enormous virtues (at least). It can discriminate a good argument from a bad one. It shows an enviable ability to think up tests for hypotheses, instead of merely finding them 'persuasive' or 'unconvincing'. It has a high standard of accuracy, often noticing examples (and counter-examples) which I had missed. And finally, despite the huge amount of detail, it is well-written and readable. My wife read the opening chapter and commented, 'Now for the first time I understand what you have been saying!'

Most scholars hope that through their PhD students their influence may be carried on to another generation. I have been fortunate enough to spend my University career in an Extramural Department, but this has meant that I have never had a PhD student. How marvellous then to have gone forth sowing for so many years, and at last to have found the seed giving fruit of itself, first the blade and then the ear! Blade is right in another sense, for there is some cutting of my proposals; and blessed is the scholar whose disciple can be critical as well as appreciative. But the fruitful ear lies before you, gentle reader: you will find it both satisfying and tasty. As for the full corn in the ear, I hope that will be forthcoming for many years.

Michael Goulder

PREFACE

Christopher Evans once suggested that one would need to live and work with Michael Goulder's ideas for some time before an adequate assessment of them could be made. I was lucky enough to be given time to do this when between 1990 and 1994 I worked on a DPhil thesis at the University of Oxford under Dr John Muddiman, the result of which is the present volume.

This book has been greatly enriched by interaction with both Dr Muddiman and Professor Goulder. Dr Muddiman's advice was always wise, insightful and, most importantly, right. My debt to Professor Goulder is obvious: he has done more to excite me about Biblical Studies than has any other, and if I have learnt to criticise his ideas, it is only because I have also learnt to think like him.

I am grateful to many: Dr John Ashton, my MPhil supervisor and my most restrained critic; Professor Ed Sanders who first encouraged me to write a thesis on Goulder's ideas; Mrs Barbara Shellard, close friend and ally; and Professor Christopher Rowland and Mr Ian Boxall, both inspirational. Other members of the Graduate New Testament seminar in Oxford showed kind interest and made useful criticisms of my ideas. I would also like to mention the staff of the Biblical Studies Department at Heythrop College where I greatly enjoyed and profited from my time as a part-time tutor.

My family and several friends have been blessings to me, not least Dr Matthew Brookes, Mr Paul Dryden, Dr Richard Grant, Mrs Kate Grant, Dr Gavin Holt and Mr Christopher Stanton. Most of all, though, I thank my wife Viola. Our beautiful daughter Emily Jane was born two weeks after the submission of my thesis and now I dedicate this book to Viola, with my love, as a token of how greatly I value both her and Emily.

University of Birmingham
February 1996

ABBREVIATIONS

R   On the assumption of Markan priority, a redactional insertion by Matthew or Luke into the 'Markan' material in their Gospels (cf. *LNP*, p. ix). A reference followed by 'R' (e.g. 'Lk. 5.17 R') signifies that the word, expression or feature under discussion is present in the verse in question in Matthew or Luke and absent from the parallel section in Mark.

QC   Words, expressions or features occurring in Q contexts which are common to Matthew and Luke (and not in Mark) (see *LNP*, pp. ix and 180 n. 22). A reference followed by 'QC' (e.g. 'Mt. 23.37 QC') signifies that the word, expression or feature under discussion occurs in the parallel section in Matthew or Luke.

QD   Words, expressions or features occurring in Q contexts which are different in Matthew and Luke (and are not in Mark) (see *LNP*, pp. ix and 180 n. 22). A reference followed by 'QD' (e.g. 'Mt. 5.47 QD') signifies that the word, expression or feature under discussion does not occur in the parallel section in Matthew or Luke.

L   Special Lukan material, or special Lukan source. A reference followed by 'L' (e.g. 'Lk. 16.20 L') signifies that the verse in question occurs in Luke's special material.

M   Special Matthean material, or special Matthean source. A reference followed by 'M' (e.g. 'Mt. 10.23 M') signifies that the verse in question occurs in Matthew's special material.

MK   A reference followed by 'MK' (e.g. 'Mt. 13.54 MK') signifies that the word, expression or feature under discussion also occurs in the parallel section in Mark.

MA   Minor Agreement between Matthew and Luke against Mark. A reference followed by 'MA' (e.g. 'Mt. 26.68 MA') signifies that the word, expression or feature under discussion occurs in both Matthew and Luke and not in the parallel section in Mark.

Numbers   Numbers listed in the collocation 2/3/4+5, etc., signify the number of times a word, expression or feature occurs in Matthew/Mark/Luke+Acts.

2ST   Two-Source Theory

4ST	Four-Source Theory
L–A	Luke–Acts
§	Refers to sections of *LNP*, chapter three, e.g., §4.1, Soliloquy
MLM	*Midrash and Lection in Matthew* (London: SPCK, 1974)
EC	*The Evangelists' Calendar: A Lectionary Explanation of the Development of Scripture* (London: SPCK, 1978)
LNP	*Luke—A New Paradigm* (2 vols.; JSNTSup, 20; Sheffield: JSOT Press, 1989)
TTM	*A Tale of Two Missions* (London: SCM, 1994)

OTHER ABBREVIATIONS

AB	Anchor Bible
ABD	D.N. Freedman *et al.* (eds.), *The Anchor Bible Dictionary*
AnBib	Analectica biblica
ATANT	Abhandlungen zur Theologie des Alten und Neuen Testaments
ATR	*Anglican Theological Review*
AusBR	*Australian Biblical Review*
BapQ	*Baptist Quarterly*
BAGD	W. Bauer, W.F. Arndt, F.W. Gingrich and F.W. Danker, *Greek-English Lexicon of the New Testament*
BETL	Bibliotheca ephemeridum theologicarum lovaniensium
BJRL	*Bulletin of the John Rylands University Library of Manchester*
BTB	*Biblical Theology Bulletin*
BT	*The Bible Translator*
CBQ	*Catholic Biblical Quarterly*
ConBNT	Coniectanea biblica, New Testament
CQR	*Church Quarterly Review*
CRINT	Compendia rerum iudaicarum ad Novum Testamentum
DBI	R.J. Coggins and J.L. Houlden (eds.), *A Dictionary of Biblical Interpretation*
EncJud	*Encyclopaedia Judaica*
EpRev	*Epworth Review*
ETL	*Ephemerides theologicae lovanienses*
EvQ	*Evangelical Quarterly*
ExpTim	*Expository Times*
FRLANT	Forschungen zur Religion und Literatur des Alten und Neuen Testaments
HeyJ	*Heythrop Journal*
HTKNT	Herders theologischer Kommentar zum Neuen Testament
ICC	International Critical Commentary
IDB	G. A. Buttrick (ed.), *Interpreter's Dictionary of the Bible*
IDBSup	*IDB*, Supplementary Volume

Int	*Interpretation*
JAAR	*Journal of the American Academy of Religion*
JBL	*Journal of Biblical Literature*
JETS	*Journal of the Evangelical Theology Society*
JJS	*Journal of Jewish Studies*
JQR	*Jewish Quarterly Review*
JSNT	*Journal for the Study of the New Testament*
JSNTSup	*Journal for the Study of the New Testament*, Supplement Series
JSOTSup	*Journal for the Study of the Old Testament*, Supplement Series
JSS	*Journal of Semitic Studies*
JTS	*Journal of Theological Studies*
KEK	Kritisch-exegetischer Kommentar
LCL	Loeb Classical Library
MillSt	*Milltown Studies*
MNTC	Moffatt New Testament Commentary
N-A^{26}	*Novum Testamentum Graece* (26th edn)
NCB	New Century Bible
NEB	New English Bible
NovT	*Novum Testamentum*
NovTSup	*Novum Testamentum* Supplements
NRSV	New Revised Standard Version
NTS	*New Testament Studies*
PRS	*Perspectives on Religious Studies*
PSTJ	*Perkins (School of Theology) Journal*
RB	*Revue biblique*
RelSRev	*Religious Studies Review*
RRT	*Reviews in Religion and Theology*
RSR	*Recherches de science religieuse*
RSV	Revised Standard Version
RTR	*Reformed Theological Review*
SBLDS	SBL Dissertation Series
SBLMS	SBL Monograph Series
Scr	*Scripture*
ScrB	*Scripture Bulletin*
SEÅ	*Svensk Exegetisk Årsbok*
SJT	*Scottish Journal of Theology*
SNTSMS	Society for New Testament Studies Monograph Series
SNTU	Studium zum Neuen Testament und seiner Umwelt
TDNT	G. Kittel and G. Friedrich (eds.), *Theological Dictionary of the New Testament*
TLS	*The Times Literary Supplement*
TNTC	Tyndale New Testament Commentaries
TS	*Theological Studies*

TU	Texte und Untersuchungen
UBS[3]	*The Greek New Testament* (United Bible Societies, 3rd edn, 1983)
USQR	*Union Seminary Quarterly Review*
WBC	Word Biblical Commentary
WUNT	Wissenschaftlich Untersuchungen zum Neuen Testament
ZNW	*Zeitschrift für die neutestamentliche Wissenschaft*
ZTK	*Zeitschrift für Theologie und Kirche*

Chapter 1

GOULDER AND HIS CRITICS

A. *Introduction: Goulder and Farrer*

Michael Goulder's biblical scholarship has grown from the roots laid down by his 'tutor and mentor', Austin Farrer, described by Goulder as 'a genius as well as a saint', whose biblical studies 'were to be the flame to set alight my life's major work'.[1]

Farrer wrote two important books on the Gospels, *A Study in St Mark* and *St Matthew and St Mark*, but his influence on Goulder is most clearly seen in his famous article, 'On Dispensing with Q', in which Farrer argues that since a serious case can be made for Luke's knowledge of Matthew, Q is unnecessary and so dispensable. This would have enormous consequences for Gospel studies, as Farrer says:

> Let us indulge ourselves a little here, and prophesy. The literary history of the Gospels will turn out to be a simpler matter than we had supposed. St Matthew will be seen to be an amplified version of St Mark, based on a decade of habitual preaching, and incorporating oral material, but presupposing no other literary source beside St Mark himself. St Luke, in turn, will be found to presuppose St Matthew and St Mark, and St John to presuppose the three others. The whole literary history of the canonical Gospel tradition will be found to be contained in the fourfold canon itself except in so far as it lies in the Old Testament, the Pseudepigrapha, and the other New Testament writings.[2]

---

1.   These quotations are from *Midrash and Lection in Matthew*, p. xv and *Why Believe in God?*, p. 16. But see Dennis Nineham, 'Michael Goulder—An Appreciation', p. xiii, 'It would be quite wrong to overdo the debt to Farrer: Michael is a professional, linguistically fully qualified, and widely recognized biblical scholar—indeed a major biblical scholar—in a way that Farrer never was.'

2.   'Dispensing', p. 85.

This is indeed prophetic. If Lukan knowledge of Matthew is the key for Farrer, for Goulder it is the cornerstone. Almost everything that Goulder has written on the Gospels builds from it.

First, dispensing with Q inevitably sheds new light on Matthew. Farrer's comment that his Gospel 'will be seen to be an amplified version of St Mark, based on a decade of habitual preaching...presupposing no other literary source beside St Mark himself' would make an excellent summary of the thesis of Goulder's first book on the Gospels, *Midrash and Lection in Matthew* (London: SPCK, 1974) (*MLM*) which was written up from the Speaker's Lectures in Biblical Studies, delivered at Trinity College, Oxford in the Hilary Terms of 1969–71, 'the seminal ideas' of which Goulder says he owes to Farrer (*MLM*, p. xv).

Second, dispensing with Q will involve making an account of Luke's use of both Matthew and Mark, and this Goulder attempts in his eight-hundred page *Luke—A New Paradigm* (2 vols.; JSNTSup, 20; Sheffield: JSOT Press, 1989) (*LNP*).

Further, the simplicity of the picture which Farrer paints has actually become the hallmark of Goulder's scholarship, with its appeals to Occam's Razor and its emphasis on economy. If anything, Goulder makes the picture simpler than does Farrer and dispenses not only with Q, M, L and any other lost document but also with 'oral material'. For both Farrer and Goulder, the study of the Gospels is an inter-Scriptural discipline. Matthew draws on Mark, Paul and the Old Testament and Luke on Matthew, Mark, Paul and the Old Testament.

Farrer interpreted Scripture from within Scripture by means of typological exegesis, and the article 'On Dispensing with Q', for example, proposes a Hexateuchal structure for both Matthew and Luke. Goulder's first book on the New Testament, *Type and History in Acts* (London: SPCK, 1964) is clearly indebted to Farrer's method, and the pattern is evident also in Goulder's earliest work on the Gospels. His first article, 'St Luke's Genesis', written jointly with M. L. Sanderson (*JTS* 8 [1957], pp. 12-30), is an attempt to expound Luke 1–2 as 'a pious meditation upon the birth of the Lord' (p. 28) by Luke himself, fulfilling Genesis and other Old Testament texts, with very little historical tradition.

In this article, Goulder and Sanderson comment in passing on Matthew and John:

Their methods are in each case the same: to follow the thread from the Torah where it leads, weaving in threads from the prophets and writings as they suggest themselves, and filling in the remaining gaps from their imaginations (p. 29).

This appeal to the evangelists' imaginations, and so to a marked degree of creativity, is a key feature of Goulder's thought, quite as important as the theory of Luke's knowledge of Matthew. It is evident in two other important articles written in the 1960s. First, in 'The Composition of the Lord's Prayer' (*JTS* 14 [1963], pp. 32-45), Goulder argues that the Lord's Prayer was not dominical in the usually accepted sense but rather it was written up by Matthew from hints found in Mark. Luke is then dependent on the Matthean version. Second, in 'Characteristics of the Parables in the Several Gospels' (*JTS* 19 [1968], pp. 51-69),[3] Goulder rejects the theory that all of the synoptic parables go back in some measure to the teaching of Jesus. Rather, Matthew's parables are substantially his own creation, featuring a noticeably high allegory-count with stock characters in an aristocratic setting. Likewise, Luke's parables are his own work, with a lower allegory-count and realistic characters in a middle-class setting.

These two articles encapsulate several of the traits for which Goulder has become well-known. Matthew builds from a base in Mark, and Luke from a base in Matthew and Mark. Q is dispensed with, simplicity reigns and the tendencies of each evangelist will explain the salient features of each Gospel.

In the early 1970s, however, Goulder developed one other important idea which was to dominate much of his writing, the lectionary hypothesis. This hypothesis is to some measure influenced by Farrer too, since it depends largely on the uncovering of Old Testament patterns in the Gospels, in particular the Hexateuchal structure which Farrer postulated for both Matthew and Luke. More specifically, though, Goulder is here indebted to G.D. Kilpatrick's *The Origins of the Gospel According to St Matthew*[4] which laid considerable stress on the liturgical character and background of Matthew's Gospel.

Goulder combines, then, in *MLM*, three theories which were to be at the heart of his life's work on the Gospels, Luke's knowledge of

---

3. 'One of the best pieces I have ever done', *Why Believe in God?*, p. 25. Goulder produced one other article on the Gospels in the 1960s, 'The Chiastic Structure of the Lucan Journey', but Goulder later dropped this idea.

4. Farrer compliments Kilpatrick in 'Dispensing', p. 85; cf. *MLM*, p. 9.

Matthew, the creativity of the evangelists and the lectionary theory. The latter is expounded more fully in the sequel, *The Evangelists' Calendar* (London: SPCK, 1978) (*EC*) which constitutes the Speaker's Lectures in Biblical Studies of 1972. This book is primarily about Luke, but it also expounds a lectionary origin for Mark and attempts to undergird the whole proposal with greater evidence of the antiquity of lectionary cycles.

In addition to these works, one key article should also be mentioned, 'On Putting Q to the Test' (*NTS* 24 [1978], pp. 218-34), one of the most important articles on the Synoptic Problem to appear in the last quarter-century, which attempts to go one step beyond Farrer and render the Q theory implausible as well as dispensable. Shortly after writing this, Goulder commented that Farrer's article 'was a vision' but, Goulder adds, 'the vision is for many days' ('Farrer on Q', *Theology* 83 [1980], pp. 190-95, p. 194). It might be said that Goulder has captured Farrer's vision, making the thesis of Luke's knowledge of Matthew his own, rather as Goulder's Matthew seizes Mark and makes it his own, expanding and completing it, with many dashes of originality and flashes of inspiration along the way.

B. *The New Paradigm*

Goulder's *Luke—A New Paradigm* was published in 1989 and marks both continuity and discontinuity with Goulder's earlier work. Although *EC* is the sequel to *MLM*, *LNP* is really its companion volume, expounding Luke as Goulder had earlier expounded Matthew, without recourse to any hypothetical documents. Two key elements of the argument of *MLM* are now played down, however, the one 'midrash' and the other 'lection', both in response to criticism.

A revised version of the lectionary theory is expounded in chapter five of *LNP*, stressing correspondences between the key liturgical occasions in the Jewish festal year and passages in all three Synoptics taken in order. The sister theory, that the Synoptics, especially Luke, are organized on the basis of an annual cycle of readings from the Old Testament which are fulfilled in sequence, week by week, is now shelved. This is a striking retraction since the greater part of *EC* is devoted to reconstructing an annual cycle of readings and demonstrating their fulfilments in each section of the Gospels.

The other important modification is that Goulder drops the term 'midrash' under fire from Philip Alexander who argues convincingly that the term should be reserved for a particular genre of rabbinic literature of the form biblical lemma + commentary.[5] Goulder abstains from using the word because 'he has no wish to offend purists' (*LNP*, p. 128), but he argues that the technique of embroidering sacred texts was indeed widespread, 'and that it should be allowed as a possible method of procedure for Luke also' (*LNP*, p. 128).

The title of Goulder's book relates to his attempt in its first chapter[6] to replace 'the standard position, or paradigm, of the Gospels' (*LNP*, p. 5) with 'an alternative paradigm' (pp. 22-23). The two paradigms have only one hypothesis in common, Markan priority. The standard position is wrong on almost everything else. It is doubtful that there are any reliable non-Markan traditions in Matthew and Luke; Q is a total error; M and L are dubious too; there is no reliable independent tradition behind John's Gospel and no serious attention should be given to the Gospel of Thomas. In place of the older theories, Goulder offers the thesis that 'some parts of Mark go back to the events and words of Jesus' lifetime', that Matthew used Mark, that Luke used Matthew and Mark and that John used all three. Each evangelist wrote creatively, elaborating the work of his predecessor(s).

Goulder does not, in *LNP*, defend each of the proposals of his alternative paradigm other than indirectly. The book is concerned, Goulder says, 'to press two novel conclusions' (p. 23), the invalidity of the Q hypothesis and the thesis of Luke's creation of the L material. The first of these is the subject of the second chapter of *LNP* and the second is the subject of chapter three. Both are defended throughout the commentary section of the book. An additional chapter (4) expounds the thesis that Luke knew both 1 Corinthians and 1 Thessalonians.

The difficulty with labelling anything 'new' is that nothing remains fresh for long. Nevertheless, one might ask how novel or how different, at present, Goulder's approach is. Others beside Goulder have dispensed with Q. Farrer is the most influential, of course, and he argues with greater energy and persuasiveness than anyone before him, but he was not the first.[7] E.W. Lummis, H.G. Jameson, A. Schlatter and

---

5. P.S. Alexander's 'Midrash and the Gospels', pp. 12-15 deals specifically with Goulder.

6. An earlier version is published as 'A House Built on Sand'.

7. As Goulder acknowledges, *LNP*, p. 181 n. 37.

J.H. Ropes all argued that Luke read Matthew and that there was no Q.[8] Further, several more scholars since Farrer have dispensed with Q, A.W. Argyle, R.T. Simpson, N. Turner and more influentially, H. Benedict Green, John Drury and Ed Sanders.[9]

If not the first to suggest that Luke knew Matthew, Goulder is, however, the leading exponent of the view, the scholar who has done more than any other to work out the argument in detail, so much so, that he has given his name to this solution to the synoptic problem.[10] Further, Goulder is likely to remain at the heart of the debate on the synoptic problem since at present his is the only substantial commentary on Luke's Gospel working with the thesis that Luke used both Mark and Matthew.[11]

The other important facet of the paradigm, substantial Lukan creativity in the L material, is more specific to Goulder and is quite new. The thesis was foreshadowed by Farrer who emphasized the creative freedom of all the evangelists, and it is a major theme in the work of John Drury whose *Tradition and Design in Luke's Gospel*[12] was written not long after Goulder's *MLM* and refers to it frequently. Drury, like Goulder, tended to use the term 'midrash' in the 1970s and he is often categorized together with Goulder[13]—scholars have even spoken of 'the Goulder-Drury hypothesis'.[14] Drury is as radical as Goulder, if not more so. His *The Parables in the Gospels* takes

8. A. Schlatter, *Matthäus*; J.H. Ropes, *Synoptic Gospels* (see p. 93); E.W. Lummis, *Luke*; and H.G. Jameson, *Origin*.

9. A.W. Argyle, 'Evidence'; R.T. Simpson, 'Major Agreements'; N. Turner, 'Minor Verbal Agreements'; H.B. Green, 'Credibility'; J. Drury, *Tradition and Design*; and E.P. Sanders and M. Davies, *Studying*. The view has become particularly prevalent in Oxford: cf. Goulder's review of *The Sermon on the Mount*, by G. Strecker, p. 329, Q 'is now hardly credited to any teacher at Oxford'.

10. For example, J. Wenham, *Redating*, p. xxvii.

11. David Catchpole, for example, inevitably deals with Goulder more than any other proponent of Luke's knowledge of Matthew in *The Quest for Q*.

12. Written while Drury was chaplain of Exeter College, Oxford, across the road from Trinity College where Goulder was delivering his Speaker's Lectures. His debt to Goulder is acknowledged on p. xi-xii.

13. For example by Michael Prior, 'Revisiting Luke', p. 5.

14. Brian McNeil, 'Midrash in Luke?', p. 403; cf. F. Gerald Downing who speaks of 'a hypothetical "school" of midrash and lection' with reference to both Drury and Goulder, 'Redaction Criticism', part 2, pp. 29, 47 n. 18, 46, 48 n. 32; cf. also C.F.D. Moule, *Birth*, p. 95; and C.A. Kimball, *Jesus' Exposition*, pp. 18-21.

Goulder's 'Characteristics' article one stage further and suggests that Mark, like Matthew and Luke, composed the parables in his Gospel.

The radical element in what both Goulder and Drury hypothesize is the thoroughgoing nature of the evangelists' creativity. Many scholars, after all, have pointed to a pericope here or a pericope there which is written up without any substantial additional sources. Goulder is keen to stress this, noting that Luke is often seen as more of an author than an editor in his Birth and Infancy Narratives and 'it seems arbitrary to allow Lukan creativity in ch. 1 and to deny it in ch. 7 or ch. 15 *a priori*' (*LNP*, p. 78). Throughout the commentary section of the book, Goulder looks at those who have postulated Lukan creativity for any given section, Wellhausen and Bultmann on the Catch of Fish in 5.1-11 (*LNP*, p. 321); Fuller on the Widow of Nain in 7.11-17 (*LNP*, pp. 385-86); Bultmann, Creed and Pesch on the Ten Lepers in 17.11-19 (*LNP*, pp. 646-47), to name just a few. The difference between Goulder and these scholars is that when one turns to a given section of his commentary, however original and exciting the argument, Goulder will always postulate Lukan creativity on the basis of his use of Matthew and/or Mark. The predictability could almost be compared to that of a conservative-evangelical commentary in which one will always find arguments for the historicity of a given incident.

Goulder's central theses are, then, to some extent, novel. The way in which he argues the thesis is, on the other hand, largely a matter of old methods with new twists. Most of Goulder's work falls broadly into a source-critical category and Goulder's argument runs on several of the traditional fronts, dealing with the question of order, the problem of the Minor Agreements between Matthew and Luke against Mark (MAs) and the issue of the priority of the Matthean or the Lukan forms of Q material. Goulder has a fresh perspective on each of these. The problem of order Goulder solved first by means of the lectionary theory (*EC*) and subsequently by suggesting that Luke is trying hard to provide a reconciliation of Matthew and Mark (*LNP*). Goulder suggests that the MAs are especially problematic for the Two-Source Theory (2ST) and in his 1978 article, he suggests that a number of them, which are both Matthean and non-Lukan in character, are explicable only on the basis of his theory. The issue of the priority of the Matthean or the Lukan forms of Q sayings is one of the repeated themes of *MLM* and particularly *LNP*. Just as one can always be sure that in a given L passage Goulder will argue for Lukan creativity, so one can also be

sure that in a given Q passage, Goulder will argue for the priority of the
Matthean form. In connection with this, Goulder attempts to expose
both 'the Matthean Vocabulary Fallacy' and 'the Lukan Priority
Fallacy' (*LNP*, pp. 15-17). The standard methods of argument are circular, Goulder claims, because they often infer Matthean secondariness
on the basis of Matthean vocabulary and Lukan priority on the basis
that the style is less Lukan than it is Matthean. Both tenets assume what
they are supposed to prove, the 2ST.

Just as most redaction-critics adopt a particular source-critical stance,
so too Goulder practises redaction-criticism in tandem with source-
criticism. Indeed, just as it has often been maintained that one of the
strongest arguments in favour of the 2ST is the convincing redactional-
critical studies which have been written on the basis of it,[15] so too
Goulder's work is largely an attempt to bolster his source-critical
conclusions with a convincing redaction-critical explanation of both
Matthew and Luke. Goulder even claims that one requires Lukan
authorship of the L material in order to see what he is doing with
Matthew (*LNP*, p. 181).

Goulder is in many ways the redaction-critic *par excellence*. Some of
the finest flourishes in *MLM* and *LNP* occur while he is in the process
of expounding a passage in terms of the evangelists' tendencies as
exemplified from elsewhere in their Gospels. Goulder does not, however, often refer explicitly to redaction-criticism as a discipline and at
times he shows suspicion of those who practise it. When discussing the
work of J.D. Kingsbury, he says that 'redaction-critics are tempted to
over-interpret',[16] and he speaks of Bornkamm's famous essay on the
storm-stilling in Matthew[17] as 'a piece of serious over-interpretation'
(*MLM*, p. 324 n. 34).

If, though, there is a little ambiguity over Goulder's attitude to
redaction-criticism, there is more still in his attitude to form-criticism.
On the one hand, he follows Farrer in so enhancing the roles of the
evangelists as authors that the form-critical enterprise becomes largely
superfluous.[18] On the other hand, Goulder attempts to play some of the

15. For example, G. Stanton, *Gospel for a New People*, p. 35.
16. Review of *The Parables of Jesus in Matthew 13*, by J.D. Kingsbury, p. 165;
cf. the more positive evaluation of redaction-criticism in his review of J. Rohde,
Rediscovering, p. 598.
17. 'The Stilling of the Storm in Matthew'.
18. For Farrer's view, see *A Study in St Mark*, pp. 21-29, for example, p. 24: 'If

axioms of form-criticism to his advantage. His lectionary theory reinter-prets the traditionally designated pericopae as lections and, more impor-tantly, Goulder in *LNP* ironically presses much of the terminology of form-criticism into the service of his own thesis. He uses classifications like *Beispielerzählungen* derived from Jülicher to suggest not that certain material was preserved in a particular way but rather to suggest that the distinctiveness of the type is evidence of Luke's creation of the parables of that type (*LNP*, p. 101). Similarly, one might discern a hidden agenda in Goulder's discussion of the introductions and conclu-sions to Lukan pericopae, attempting to demonstrate that matters which have been the very stuff of form-criticism are actually best explained by his hypothesis.

Goulder's work is actually quite consonant, though, with the developing discipline of literary-criticism applied to the Gospels, with its emphasis on the evangelists as authors, looking at their books as wholes. Farrer pointed the way forward for Goulder here since for him, dispensing with Q was a matter of letting Matthew 'write as he is moved',[19] and he taught Goulder 'to look at Matthew as an author, and at his Gospel as revelation' (*MLM*, p. xv). Literary-critics are already beginning to show interest in Goulder's work and the clearest sign of this is his contribution on the Pauline Epistles to Alter and Kermode's *The Literary Guide to the Bible* (Cambridge, MA: Harvard University Press, 1987, pp. 479-502). John Drury contributed an essay on the Gospels to the same volume, and when he reviews *LNP* he sees that literary-critics could be regarded as 'allies' who, like Goulder, are interested 'in the techniques of imagination'.[20]

Nevertheless, Goulder himself is probably a little too interested in some of the older techniques and goals of New Testament criticism to embrace wholeheartedly some of the modern forms of literary-criticism.[21] He is happy, for example, to use the old redaction-critical argument that when something demonstrably comes from a source, it may not reflect the evangelist's viewpoint as clearly as something

St Mark is in fact after all a living whole, then the work of the form-critics is, every line of it, called in doubt'.

19. 'Dispensing', p. 86, the concluding words of the essay.

20. J. Drury, Review of *LNP*, p. 91.

21. There is a little suspicion of 'modern literary theories' in Goulder's comments on Du Rand in his review of J. Beutler and R.T. Fortna (eds.), *Shepherd Discourse*, p. 24—such theories 'add nothing to our understanding'.

which does not come from a source. In his discussion of Matthew's view of the Law (*MLM*, pp. 9-21), for instance, Goulder's opinion is, broadly, that the material which is most radical about the Law comes in from Mark and the material which is most conservative about the Law is added by Matthew himself, which suggests that Matthew's own view is conservative.

More generally, though, Goulder often shows himself to be more the historian than the literary-critic. There is sometimes an explicit and often an underlying concern in what actually happened, not only at the level of the evangelists' desks but also at the level of the historical Jesus. Goulder has written only once, briefly, specifically on the historical Jesus ('Jesus, the Man of Universal Destiny' in John Hick [ed.], *The Myth of God Incarnate* [London: SCM Press, 1977], pp. 48-63),[22] but he acknowledges elsewhere, in passing, that 'the primary historical task of New Testament criticism' is 'the Quest of the Historical Jesus'.[23] Indeed, one might see behind his studies on Matthew and Luke the attempt to eliminate from consideration the chance that there is any historical, dominical material so that one can concentrate, in reconstructions of the life of Jesus, on the material from Mark's Gospel.

C. *Goulder's Critics*

Goulder's work has been welcomed in some quarters. Most importantly, Ed Sanders has presented Goulder's ideas to a wider audience in *Studying the Synoptic Gospels*[24] and has accepted, at least partially, Goulder's solution to the synoptic problem. Goulder responds to this by saying:

> I will not conceal from the reader my delight at this conclusion as it is the one for which I have been arguing virtually *contra mundum* for the past two decades.[25]

Further, reviews of Goulder's work are rarely stinting in their praise for his style and literary method. Harvey, when discussing *MLM*, speaks of

---

22. Cf. also Goulder's reviews of Ben F. Meyer, *The Aims of Jesus* and Geza Vermes, *Jesus and the World of Judaism*.

23. Review of J. Rohde, *Rediscovering*, p. 598.

24. E.P. Sanders and M. Davies, *Studying*, chapters six and seven.

25. Review of Sanders and Davies, *Studying*, p. 1166.

'the wealth of learning shown on every page, the lucidity of the argument' and 'the lively and elegant style which unmistakably shows the author to be a worthy disciple of his revered master, Austin Farrer'.[26] Similarly, Evans comments:

> The author possesses an enviable capacity for writing with lucidity, elegance and even wit on highly technical matters, and shows a rare gift for marrying seriousness of purpose with lightness of touch.[27]

Likewise, John Muddiman says that Goulder marshalls the arguments of *LNP* with 'rhetorically brilliant advocacy, commanding the facts, producing coherent explanations, and at the same time deriding the alternatives with logic, counter-evidence, and touches of wicked irony'.[28]

Praise is also frequently issued at the bold, courageous nature of Goulder's work, and his books have often been regarded as highly significant. Evans comments on *MLM* and *EC* that:

> Together they are probably one of the most important, as they are certainly one of the most remarkable, contributions to the study of the gospels for some years.[29]

James A. Sanders notes that *MLM* 'is apparently designed to be provocative' and in this, he says, 'it is certainly successful'.[30] Muddiman describes *LNP* as 'a landmark in scholarship' which all future work on Luke's Gospel will have to recognize.[31] Danker says that 'Goulder lays claim to having driven out all demons that have bedevilled synoptic criticism since 1830',[32] and he concludes his review by saying:

> After much shaking of the head has been done, instead of rushing back to the homestead, all members of our craft will do well to re-examine under Goulder's tutelage whatever they have done or plan to do under the banner of synoptic study. Goulder could not, given demonic homesickness, hope for more.[33]

---

26. A.E. Harvey, Review of *MLM*, p. 189.
27. C.F. Evans, 'Goulder and the Gospels', p. 426.
28. John Muddiman, Review of *LNP*, p. 176.
29. C.F. Evans, 'Goulder and the Gospels', p. 425.
30. James A. Sanders, Review of *MLM*, p. 92.
31. John Muddiman, Review of *LNP*, p. 176.
32. F.W. Danker, Review of *LNP*, p. 162.
33. F.W. Danker, Review of *LNP*, p. 164.

Such praise is salted, however, by the essentially negative reputation
which Goulder has attained over the years in other quarters as a maverick, an *enfant terrible*, even a member of the 'lunatic fringe' of Biblical
Studies.[34] The reputation is in some ways unjust, though in other ways
unsurprising. Because his work is difficult to categorize, some have
classed Goulder with others who are not easily classified.[35]

Goulder is also tainted, for some, by association with others who
have proposed lectionary theories. No established scholar[36] agrees with
the earlier theories of either Philip Carrington or Aileen Guilding and in
spite of Goulder's hope that his theory 'has not been expounded with
pride, and that it will not be received with prejudice' (*EC*, p. 306), many
have taken the easy option of ignoring it or summarily dismissing it.[37]

Most clearly, though, Goulder's reputation as an outsider is built on
the radical nature of his theories, theories of which he is not ashamed.
If his ideas are right, then much of what has been taken for granted in
Gospel criticism will have to be abandoned, especially the existence of
Q and the existence of reliable, historical tradition behind the non-
Markan sections of Matthew and Luke. Much of what Goulder says,
therefore, shocks the scholar and horrifies the lay-person: Jesus did not
teach the Lord's Prayer to the disciples; he taught few of the parables
attributed to him; the Sermon on the Mount is composed by Matthew
and, to cap it all, Jesus was not raised from the dead and the Empty
Tomb story was invented by Mark.

In the light of this observation, it is not surprising that some of
Goulder's most ardent critics have been conservative-evangelical
scholars like R.T. France and Leon Morris. France[38] attempts to show

34. This is not often said in print, though see Dale C. Allison, *The New Moses*,
p. 309: 'the author has the reputation of being something of a maverick'.

35. The clearest example of this is A.E. Harvey, 'Rabbis', pp. 246-47 dealing
with Goulder. The article deals with J. Duncan M. Derrett under the same heading,
'a small number of individual scholars usually regarded as outsiders (if not
eccentrics) by the rest of the profession' (p. 245).

36. With the possible exception of J. Duncan M. Derrett, see below.

37. J.D.G. Dunn, *Unity and Diversity*, pp. 147-48, for example, deals with
Guilding and Goulder in the same breath and is somewhat scathing about both.

38. R.T. France, 'Jewish Historiography'. The volume in which this appears,
R.T. France and D. Wenham (eds.), *Gospel Perspectives* III is largely a response to
the work of Goulder and Drury—see p. 11.

that the historicity of the Gospels need not be undermined by Goulder's (and others') claim that the evangelists use 'midrashic' techniques. Morris, in a less restrained fashion, delivers quite an onslaught on Goulder's lectionary theory.[39]

Others too have accepted some of the challenges Goulder has laid down and several have decided to meet him head-on. In particular, Christopher Tuckett and Franz Neirynck, both champions of the Q hypothesis, have replied to some of Goulder's claims, especially over the question of the MAs.[40] Most recently, David Catchpole in *The Quest for Q* contests what he describes as 'Goulder's argument that Q and Matthew are source-critically indistinguishable because they are theologically indistinguishable'.[41] In similar vein, F. Gerald Downing has recently attempted to defend the 2ST against Goulder by claiming that it, and not Goulder's theory, is most consonant with what we know about ancient techniques of writing using literary sources.[42]

Goulder, however, thrives on any controversy which his work provokes and has published responses to all of the scholars just mentioned.[43] Indeed, much of Goulder's scholarship uses the confrontational method. There are always two sides to any issue: Goulder's side and his opponents' side. With irony he says of Neirynck:

> In the fight over Q and L his formidable powers are, I fear, engaged on the side of the Dragon, but when it comes to John he is with St Michael, and for John's use of all three Synoptics (*LNP*, p. 25).

Goulder is constantly aware of the need to convince his opponents:

> In the long run, there will be some who will not be persuaded however great the evidence; and of them it is written, 'Neither will they believe though one should rise from the dead' (*LNP*, p. 26).

Sometimes, it is arguable, he carries this method a little too far. Nolland says that 'Goulder's argument frequently proceeds on the basis of insisting that we must make our choice between sharply polarized

---

39. See the full discussion below, Part Three.
40. See the full discussion below, Chapter Three.
41. D. Catchpole, *Quest*, pp. 7-8, referring to *LNP*, pp. 52-70.
42. F. Gerald Downing, 'A Paradigm Perplex'.
43. Especially Neirynck and Tuckett, see below. He replies to Catchpole in his review of *Quest* and to Downing, in a less friendly vein, in 'Luke's Compositional Options'.

opposites'.[44] This is mainly because Goulder usually takes a 'hard-line' or 'red-blooded' view,[45] and he tends to be more comfortable arguing against others who are hard-line or red-blooded in their opposition.

There is a difficulty here, though, in the fact that the genuine alternatives to Goulder's hard-line positions are not always themselves hard-line. In Goulder's 'Characteristics' article, for example, he distinguishes between his view on the one hand and what he calls 'the homogeneous pool hypothesis', whereby each evangelist selected from the pool according to his needs, on the other. Yet a nuanced redaction-critical viewpoint might well want to stand somewhere between these two opposites.[46] Likewise, in *MLM*, Goulder constantly distinguishes between two viewpoints, his own and the view that the non-Markan traditions are 'dominical'. This is particularly clear from Goulder's otherwise excellent chapter on Matthew's imagery:

> In so far, therefore, as the Gospels reveal a volume of images of various kinds similar in proportion to the volume of teaching, and a similar handling of them, we have evidence of one mind being behind all the Synoptic teaching, and that the mind of the Lord...*Per contra* in so far as any imbalance is revealed in any area, or a different style of handling imagery, there we have evidence for our hypothesis, and against the non-Markan traditions (*MLM*, pp. 96-97).

This is really to set up an Aunt Sally: few scholars, these days, think that 'one mind...and that the mind of the Lord' is 'behind all of the Synoptic teaching'.

Nevertheless, the confrontational, forensic manner common in Goulder's writing is actually one of the great similarities between the Goulder of the book and the Goulder of the classroom. He will invite scholars to wage battle with him at day-schools, each delivering a lecture or two and waiting on the large audience present to probe and question. Professor Goulder's skill in public debate is matched by no one: he can think on his feet, turn criticism of his view to his own advantage and can spot the weaknesses in his opponent's view in an instant. His ability to argue lucidly and persuasively can see Professor

---

44. J. Nolland, Review of *LNP*, p. 271.

45. This is to adopt the term used by Goulder of views of God in *Why Believe in God?*, for example, p. 18.

46. I will discuss this example in more detail below, pp. 287-90.

Goulder through to victory even when the odds might seem to be stacked against him.[47]

It is disappointing, given his popularity in Britain, that there is substantial ignorance of Goulder's work in Germany. His books are rarely reviewed there[48] and German-speaking scholars do not often refer to them.[49] This is largely, no doubt, because of the widespread source-critical orthodoxy of the *Zweiquellentheorie*. Although highly influential both in Britain[50] and in America,[51] Farrer's 'On Dispensing with Q' has made no discernible impact on German scholarship.[52] In addition to this, Goulder's lectionary hypothesis is a peculiarly British affair[53] and this has, no doubt, prejudiced many would-be German sympathizers against Goulder's work.

This ignorance is particularly disappointing given the development of Goulder's 'user-friendliness' to German Gospel critics. Goulder in *MLM* only engaged occasionally with relevant German criticism but in *LNP*, he constantly refers to and discusses important German material. As Drury sees, 'the change of strategy' between *MLM* and *LNP* 'shows Goulder's determination to get his new paradigm accepted by his colleagues if he possibly can'.[54] Further, in chapter three of *LNP*, Goulder makes some very useful criticisms of the methods used by Rehkopf, Jeremias and Schürmann to distinguish Lukan and pre-Lukan linguistic usages (*LNP*, pp. 79-84; cf. pp. 18-20), and scholars who continue to use such criteria without first reading and evaluating

---

47. Cf. *Why Believe in God?*, itself a product of a day school, chapter one, for some insight into this, for example: '"Your function", said John Hull, "is to point out that we are all wearing the Emperor's clothes"' (p. 26); cf. also Goulder's 'The Bible and Extramural Teaching'.

48. With the exception of *The Prayers of David* reviewed by H. Seidel in *Theologische Literaturzeitung* 117 (1992), pp. 348-50.

49. An exception is U. Luz, *Matthew 1–7*.

50. Although not all have been convinced by Farrer, many have felt the need to answer him. On the British side, for example, see Stephen Neill, *Interpretation*, p. 126. On the American side, see R.H. Fuller, *New Testament*, pp. 73-74.

51. For the American influence, see particularly the common appeal to Farrer by neo-Griesbachian scholars, especially W. Farmer, 'Certain Results', pp. 79-80.

52. An exception is R. Morgenthaler, *Statistische Synopse*, pp. 301-305.

53. Cf. R.E. Brown, Review of *MLM*, p. 298: 'We may reflect on the peculiar fascination of British scholars for such a lectionary approach'.

54. J. Drury, Review of *LNP*, p. 89.

Goulder's critique jeopardize the value of their own scholarship.[55]

On the other hand, however, Goulder appears relatively uninterested in some of the classic problems which have bedevilled Lukan scholarship over the last half-century and most particularly, he does not seem to grapple with Conzelmann[56] and the question of salvation-history. Indeed, Goulder's opinion of Luke as 'a thoroughly likable man' (*LNP*, p. 88) stands in stark contrast to Käsemann's reputed hatred for Luke. Goulder's view, though, is not based on any theological judgment about the evangelist but rather on theories about the kind of human being he was, imaginative and creative, kindly and conciliatory, bright but bumbling. This sympathetic view of Luke is symptomatic of a particular kind of British scholarship best represented by John Fenton's statement that Luke is 'the only one of the four evangelists that you could possibly have invited to a meal, and certainly the only one who would have enjoyed such an invitation had he accepted it'.[57]

Goulder does attempt a refutation of Conzelmann's salvation-historical view in *Type and History in Acts* (pp. 142-44) but in *LNP*, the references are limited. Goulder notes when commenting on 16.16 that 'the verse has been the lynch-pin of Hans Conzelmann's enormous hypothesis; but its position here seems too casual to carry such weight' (*LNP*, p. 633; cf. p. 458) and there is no detailed discussion.

Of course, this may be simply because Goulder does not have anything fresh to contribute to the debate, and he has quite enough to do in eight-hundred pages of *LNP* to relegate Q and L from consideration without engaging in extra, unnecessary battles on theological topics. He introduces his important discussion of Lukan stylistic features, for example, by noting that 'there are already some excellent works' dealing with Luke the theologian but the 'broader fields in which a writer lets himself be known...have lacked a systematic treatment' (*LNP*, p. 86). However, it may be that by playing down theological factors in his discussion, Goulder deprives himself of a potentially useful tool for arguing the case for Luke's knowledge of Matthew. Eric Franklin here offers a different perspective, claiming that Luke's dissatisfaction with Matthew went much deeper than

---

55. Cf. Danker, Review of *LNP*, p. 164.
56. H. Conzelmann, *The Theology of St Luke*.
57. John Fenton, Review of *Tradition and Design*, by Drury, pp. 65-66.

Goulder suggests,[58] providing a reason, on the Farrer hypothesis, for the severity of many of Luke's modifications to Matthew.

D. *A Tale of Two Missions*

Since the publication of *LNP* in 1989, Goulder has produced a series of articles united by the theme of 'the two missions hypothesis', an explanation of the development of early Christianity by means of a radical conflict between Peter, or more specifically James the brother of Jesus, and Paul. Then in 1994, the theory was expounded in a popular paperback, *A Tale of Two Missions* (London: SCM, 1994) (*TTM*).

Although there is no space here for a full critique of *TTM*, a few observations on the theory should shed some light on our topic. The fact that Goulder has chosen to write his theory up in popular form should do him no harm: indeed, it enables one of his great skills, as a communicator to a wider public, to come to the fore. The book is as accessible to the sixth-former as it is to the academic (cf. p. xi). This is a book which one could easily take to the sea-side. Even more than Goulder's other books it is filled with wit, warmth and some great moments.[59]

In *TTM*, Goulder is at his radical and ambitious best. He confesses himself to be looking for 'a single unitary hypothesis, one overarching theory that explain[s] the whole, a history, a tale of how our New Testament came to be'. Goulder is 'after the jackpot'[60] and 'the Two Missions hypothesis is a master-key to open every lock' (*TTM*, p. 157). Goulder has always attempted to be overarching, accounting for every detail, in his theories. Indeed Evans concludes his article on Goulder by saying:

> His object has been not to throw light here and there on the synoptic gospels but to account for all of them *in toto*, and it is this all or nothing character of his thesis which is its weakness.[61]

For Goulder, though, this is not a weakness but a strength and *TTM* is the culmination of three decades of work, explaining now not only

---

58. E. Franklin, *Luke*, particularly pp. 311-12.
59. See, for example, Goulder's use of the 'consider the lilies' passage in *TTM*, p. 72.
60. Quoted from Goulder's Inaugural Lecture, 'A Tale of Two Missions', p. 4.
61. C.F. Evans, 'Goulder and the Gospels', p. 432.

individual New Testament documents but also the origins of Christianity.

The theory is present in germ in Goulder's earlier work. In an article on 'The Liturgical Origin of St John's Gospel' (in E.A. Livingstone [ed.], *Studia Evangelica* VII [Berlin: Akademie Verlag, 1982], pp. 205-32), Goulder develops the theory of a Christian world split into two halves with Jewish Christians on the one side and Paulines on the other. 'The battle was particularly hard-fought', Goulder says, and for Paul the result was 'particularly disastrous in Asia Minor' ('Liturgical Origin', p. 208).

However, the real origin of the theory can perhaps be seen in *MLM*, chapter seven, where Goulder explains why it is, on *a priori* grounds, that we find reliable Jesus tradition only in Mark's Gospel. Peter, John and James the brother of Jesus, the pillars of the Church in Jerusalem, were 'the inner circle of the apostles, and the repositories of *the* authentic paradosis' (*MLM*, p. 140) and it is on them that Mark is dependent:

> Mark is a theological development of PJJ [the Peter–John–James paradosis], perhaps a reaction from it even, no doubt a selection of it: but ultimately it is from the community of the Three that it has come (*MLM*, p. 141).

For a number of reasons, not least that Matthew provides no convincing alternative version of any Markan story, Goulder believes that Matthew had no substantial alternative tradition outside Mark to turn to.

The knock-on effect of Goulder's 'midrashic' theory has been, then, a striking conservatism over Mark's Gospel. As Sanders observes, Goulder in *MLM* often takes Mark 'to represent Jesus with apparently complete accuracy' and when Goulder establishes the differences between Matthew's parables and Mark's, 'he understands himself to have established the difference between Matthew and Jesus'.[62] Goulder is now, in *TTM*, not quite so certain about the historical accuracy of Mark,[63] but he does carry forward the essential conservatism and develops the 'PJJ' theory in a startling way:

---

62. E.P. Sanders, Review of *MLM*, pp. 454-55, referring to *MLM*, pp. 112-13.

63. In particular, the thesis of 'A Pauline in a Jacobite Church' requires some degree of creativity. Also, Goulder has always maintained a creative element in Mark 16.

He knows the traditions about the disciples, and especially the Three, because they used to meet in his home; and he tells these stories with an edge on them because he ended up as a convinced disciple of Paul, their *bête noire* (*TTM*, p. 20).

It is arguable that Goulder's broad rejection of form-criticism actually requires a theory like this. If Matthew, Luke and John all creatively expand the material which has come to them, without recourse to oral traditions, one will want to know how to account for the material in Mark, especially if his Gospel is to be dated about 70 (*LNP*, p. 22), and here is the answer: Mark is John Mark, cousin of Barnabas, who received all the traditions first hand.

More generally, this combination of the conservative with the radical is an often repeated feature of Goulder's writing, and it may be designed partly to shock his readers to attention. Not only is Mark actually John Mark, but also some of the Psalms were written for David,[64] the so-called Deutero-Paulines are actually by Paul[65] and Luke the evangelist is indeed the companion of Paul (*LNP*, pp. 129-31).[66] It may well be, however, that the conservative-radical combination has the overall detrimental effect of making Goulder's work even harder to categorize, so adding to his reputation as a maverick.

Some of Goulder's other interests are reflected in *TTM*. As I observed earlier, Goulder shows a fascination with history and loves to do detective work, identifying clues here and hints there and inferring what lies behind the documents we have. Also important is the role of the imagination in attempting to reconstruct a plausible picture. As Goulder says in *MLM*, 'where we have no facts we must use our imaginations with as much control as we can' (p. 141). While some

64. Broadly speaking, this is the thesis of *The Prayers of David*. I do not have the space (or the competence) to deal with Goulder's ideas on the Old Testament, but Goulder is quite at home in Old Testament as well as New Testament studies.

65. 'The Visionaries of Laodicea', on Ephesians with comments too on Colossians; 'Silas in Thessalonica', on (1 and) 2 Thessalonians. Cf. Goulder's review of A.T. Lincoln's Word Commentary on *Ephesians*.

66. This is criticized by John Muddiman in his review of *LNP*: 'Goulder's old-fashionedness here prevents him from exploiting a valuable argument in favour of his basic thesis' (p. 180), that if one dates Luke late it becomes more likely still that Luke read Matthew. Cf. Drury, Review of *LNP*: 'Chapter 4 commits the logical mistake, astonishing in so exacting a critical logician as Goulder, of confusing knowledge of 1 Corinthians with personal acquaintance with Paul himself' (p. 90). I do not think Drury is right: see the distinction on *LNP*, p. 131.

might accuse Goulder of using his imagination with too little control, it could equally be argued that one of his important contributions to New Testament criticism, and one of the exciting features of *TTM*, is precisely that by using his imagination, he stimulates the imagination of the reader.

There is, further, a subtle feature of the argument of *TTM* which is common in Goulder's writing. Goulder turns from detective to lawyer, perceiving where his opponents might have a case against him and attempting to use their evidence in favour of his own thesis. An example is Goulder's discussion of Eph. 2.19-22 on 'the foundation of the apostles and prophets, Christ Jesus himself being the headstone'. Goulder has just expounded the theory that 'Petrines' thought of the Church as a Temple and Peter as the foundation stone (*TTM*, pp. 81-82), so the presence of the same image in Ephesians, especially if it is written by Paul, might cause a problem for the thesis. Goulder says, however, that 'Paul is light on his feet, and he can use other people's images when they are convenient' (*TTM*, p. 82), and he concludes the chapter by saying:

> You cannot but admire the apostle. Eighteen centuries before Disraeli, he perfected the art of stealing the opposition's clothes while they were bathing (*TTM*, p. 83).[67]

This is also precisely what Goulder himself has just done and often does.

Finally, on *TTM*, the appeal to simplicity is again made by Goulder. 'There are no anonymous hypothetical groups in it', Goulder says, and:

> I have kept to the documents we have, and have eschewed hypothetical sources (pre-Pauline hymns, Q, M, L, proto-Thomas, etc.), in whose existence I do not believe (*TTM*, p. x).

This strikes a note which has already resonated all the way through *LNP* where Goulder's appeal to simplicity is a matter of not postulating any lost documents.[68] This, Goulder claims, gives him the right of 'prior consideration' (*LNP*, p. 24). His position is 'exposed', he says, and 'readily falsifiable' (*LNP*, p. 24).

---

67. For another example of the phenomenon, see *TTM*, p. 178, on 1 Cor. 15.4, the detail 'that he was buried' as the basis for Mark's invention of the Empty Tomb story.

68. Cf. 'Luke's Compositional Options', p. 151: 'My claim to be "simple" is solely that I do not hypothesize any lost documents (Q, M, L)'.

TTM is in this respect, however, quite another proposition. Goulder's theory requires Paul to be the author of the 'hymn' in Phil. 2.6-11 since, for Goulder, the doctrine of the incarnation originated with Paul.[69] More seriously, though, Goulder does, for once, hypothesize a lost entity behind 'the documents we have':

> It looks as if we can descry behind our present *Pauline* Gospel of Mark a *pre-Pauline, Jerusalem* Gospel outline. Just as later Matthew was to re-write Mark to make it more Petrine, so Mark took over the earlier version of the Gospel (whether written or oral) and made it more Pauline (*TTM*, p. 129; Goulder's italics).

The difficulty is that Goulder's favourite virtue of falsifiability seems to have disappeared. Indeed, Goulder can always account for the data in the Synoptic Gospels on the basis of the Two Missions hypothesis since all three have, according to the theory, some elements of both Paul and Peter. Mark is a Paulinized Petrine, Matthew a Petrinized Pauline and Luke a reconciliation of Paul and Peter. The problem under such circumstances is that circularity becomes difficult to avoid.[70]

With this exception, then, *TTM* illustrates some of the important facets of Goulder's work and provides insights into some of his earlier arguments. In the book, as well as in his other writing, Goulder attributes to his subjects several of his own characteristics, working by imagination and inference, turning opponents' arguments to his own advantage and fighting the great battle with devotion and energy.

E. *Examining the New Paradigm*

One of the difficulties with assessing Goulder's work is its scope. His thesis is so wide-ranging and the implications so enormous that many have taken cover in ignorance or hasty dismissal. Sanders predicted this response when reviewing *MLM* and said it would be 'an unfortunate and unnecessary reaction'.[71] It is certainly worth the attempt to distinguish between 'the pearl of great price' and 'the light fantastic'.[72]

---

69. Unless, of course, one goes down Dunn's route in *Christology in the Making* but Goulder is convinced that Phil. 2.6-11 is incarnational (*TTM*, pp. 146-47).

70. Cf. A.E. Harvey, Review of *TTM*, p. 31, 'We shall never be able to catch Goulder out'.

71. E.P. Sanders, Review of *MLM*, p. 455.

72. R.E. Brown's image, Review of *MLM*, p. 299, though used by him negatively.

How would one, then, go about analysing Goulder and the Gospels? Sanders suggests working through *MLM* step by step[73] and I might add that the same steady work would be necessary with *EC* and *LNP* too. Clearly, though, everything cannot and should not be given equal weight and some distinctions need to be made. One might say that there are three central concerns in Goulder's work on the Gospels. The first is Luke's knowledge of Matthew, dispensing with Q; the second is the creativity of the evangelists, dispensing with M and L; the third is the lectionary theory.

A study of each of these three areas will make up the three parts of this book. Within each area I will attempt to isolate for special study not simply key propositions but also testable propositions. It is one of the great virtues of Goulder's work that he challenges the reader to attempt to falsify it. His method is largely an attempt to be scientific about Gospel studies and so to show that he has reason on his side.

In Part One, therefore, it will be worth looking at two of the pillars which support Goulder's hypothesis of Lukan knowledge of Matthew. First, in Chapter 2, I will examine Goulder's claim that Matthew's and Q's vocabulary are substantially the same (*LNP*, pp. 11-15 etc.) by looking for a control: to what extent do we see any of Luke's vocabulary in Q? Then, in Chapter 3, I will ask a similar question of the MAs and will discuss Goulder's treatment of the phenomenon.

In Part Two, I will focus on the issue of Lukan creativity and Goulder's rejection of L. This will take the form of an analysis of Goulder's isolation of Lukan stylistic features in *LNP*, chapter three and the use of the features in the commentary section of *LNP*. In particular, I will look at the extent to which each of the features is distinctively Lukan.

In Part Three I will turn to the lectionary theory and examine its presuppositions, its plausibility and its probability.

Part One, therefore, largely concerns *LNP*, chapters one and two; Part Two deals with *LNP*, chapter three and Part Three is an examination of *LNP*, chapter five.[74] It needs to be observed, nevertheless, that Goulder himself does not isolate these three facets in quite the way that I have. It is an aspect of the 'all or nothing' package

73. E.P. Sanders, Review of *MLM*, p. 453.
74. I do not look in detail at Luke's use of Paul which is the subject of *LNP*, chapter four. I do not have anything fresh to say about this, and it is not intrinsic to Goulder's paradigm in the way that the other three theories are.

deal which Goulder delivers to us that different parts of the thesis support and elucidate each other. In particular, he makes the creativity theory dependent on the source theory, and he feels that dispensing with L makes Luke's use of Matthew explicable. It will be important, therefore, to attempt to keep each part of the overall paradigm in mind throughout and where possible to look at how well the different parts cohere.

It should be added that while this attempts to be a comprehensive treatment of Goulder and the Gospels, it is not an exhaustive one. There will be no opportunity, for example, to deal with Goulder's excellent section on the history of the acceptance of the Q hypothesis (*LNP*, pp. 26-37) nor with several of Goulder's other arguments against Q. This need not be a weakness. There are facets of his thesis on which Goulder lays special emphasis and what follows is largely an attempt to see whether the Gospel data can actually take the stress at these key points.

Goulder describes the standard paradigm of Gospel studies as 'a house built on sand' (*LNP*, chapter one, and often). In building his house, Goulder has, by contrast, 'dug and deepened and laid a foundation'.[75] This book is an attempt to see whether Goulder's house stands firm after the wind and rain of analysis, scrutiny and counter-testing have been thrown against it; to see, in short, whether Goulder's house is built on the rock.

---

75. 'A House Built on Sand', p. 22.

PART I

TWO STUDIES IN THE SYNOPTIC PROBLEM

Chapter 2

QC WORDS AND CHARACTERISTIC VOCABULARY

A. *Introduction*

Throughout *Midrash and Lection in Matthew*, Goulder attempts to corroborate his thesis by looking at the language in each pericope. The high percentage of characteristic vocabulary in Q and M passages is held to be a factor showing that Matthew is the composer of both the Q material and the M material. After discussing each passage, Goulder gives a linguistic count. In an M passage, 25.31-46 (the Last Judgment), Goulder lists 'Matthean' and 'semi-Matthean' words: 'More than 100 out of 279 words are characteristic' and only three words are 'non-Matthean' (p. 444). On 6.25-34 (Earthly Cares), a Q passage, Goulder says: 'The linguistic evidence is strongly in favour of Matthean authorship—54 characteristic words out of 183' (p. 304). On 9.37-38 (Harvest is Plentiful), also Q, he says that there are 12 out of 20 words which are characteristic—'Only δέομαι is non-Matthean' (p. 328).

These are only examples. The reader is impressed by occasion after occasion on which both Q and M passages are apparently full of vocabulary characteristic of the evangelist. The method seems to be sound: Goulder's thesis in *MLM* is that 'the non-Markan passages are, over all, Matthew's midrash' (p. 475). When he does his word count, it would seem natural to look at all words extra to Mark, whether such words are R or Q or M.

But the method carries with it a problem. The word counts for Q passages are undertaken in the same way as are the word counts for M passages. Goulder does not, in *MLM*, distinguish between Q words which Matthew shares with Luke and Q words which are unique to Matthew. In one important respect, Goulder is assuming his thesis rather than attempting to prove it.

In his subsequent *Luke—A New Paradigm*, however, Goulder does distinguish between the two types of word in Q, and he calls them 'QC words' and 'QD words' respectively. The distinction is now important in making the case against Q. Goulder charges two-source theorists with 'the Matthean vocabulary fallacy' (pp. 11-15), the idea that Matthean vocabulary in Q passages demonstrates his secondariness. It is a fallacy because 'Matthew's style is to such an extent the same as Q's' (p. 15): for example, QC words like ὀλιγόπιστος; 'And it came to pass when Jesus had completed all these words...' and 'weeping and gnashing of teeth' have a Matthean stamp.

These are not special examples, Goulder says. Taking the first full paragraph of Q, John the Baptist's preaching, he shows how 20 per cent of the text is written in 'Matthew's preferred phrases'. Goulder then looks for a 'control' and finds just one Lukan phrase, ὁ θεός, and so the passage appears to be a problem for the 2ST:

> Either Matthew took over Q's phrases *en masse* for re-use in his own redaction—in which case the distinction between Matthew's style and Q's has broken down completely—or Matthew wrote the passage himself (p. 14).

Now if the same is true throughout, that 'Q's vocabulary and Matthew's seem to be the same' (p. 14), this would indeed be a weighty corroboration of Goulder's thesis.

A control test, then, is required. If Goulder is right, one will expect to find a greater proportion of Matthean vocabulary than of Lukan vocabulary among QC words. If one were to find a good number of characteristically Lukan words, the impressiveness of Goulder's case, on the basis of vocabulary at least, would be diminished.

To illustrate the principle, in the passage mentioned above, Mt. 9.37-38 // Lk. 10.2, 'only δέομαι is non-Matthean' becomes less impressive when one notes that δέομαι, in addition to being non-Matthean, is also characteristic of Luke, with figures of 1/0/8+7, occurring in Luke's redaction of Mark at 5.12 and 8.28. Further, a quick search will confirm that it is the only word among the QC words here which is markedly characteristic of either evangelist; the Matthean words are all congenial to Luke, for example οὖν (57/3/31), κυριός + genitive (24/4/16) and ἐργάτης (6/0/4).

This chapter will work through each Q passage and list the Matthean words and the Lukan words among the QC words. One would expect to see, on Goulder's thesis, a rump of Matthean words and not so many Lukan ones: Matthew is the composer of the material and Luke has taken over many of Matthew's own words. It would not be surprising to find some vocabulary characteristic of Luke: some of the words which Matthew has in his vocabulary but uses rarely might happen to be some of Luke's favourite words and in any case, Luke is likely to take over 'Luke-pleasing' words.[1] Clearly, though, a lot of characteristically Lukan vocabulary will be damaging to Goulder's case.

In order to list characteristic words and phrases, however, one requires criteria and the test will be fairer if the criteria Goulder uses are ours too. He uses those of Sir John Hawkins in *Horae Synopticae*, that a word should occur at least four times in a Gospel and at least twice as often in the one Gospel as in the other two Synoptic Gospels put together.[2] Goulder adds words which in *MLM* he calls 'semi-Matthean', those which either occur twice as often in Matthew as in Mark and more often than in Luke or which are inserted redactionally by Matthew into an agreed Markan context or Old Testament citation (pp. 122 and 476). In *LNP* (p. 800), a characteristic word is one which is introduced by Luke redactionally or which 'occurs with a markedly greater frequency in Luke than in Mark and Matthew' and in at least three different contexts.

Goulder's criteria are not quite as straightforward as Hawkins's, however, and his lists need to be treated with caution. While his vocabularies are supposed to be tools which provide help in the demonstration of his thesis, in one respect they take the thesis for granted: the redactional criterion assumes Lukan knowledge of Matthew. A word which has one or more QD occurrences is more likely to be on the Luke list than one which, when it occurs in Q passages, is QC. This is because for Goulder, QD words are Luke's additions to Matthew and QC words are those which Luke takes over from Matthew. Equally, because Goulder sees Matthew as the composer of Q, he makes no distinction in *MLM* between QC and QD.

Further, some of the words on Goulder's Matthew list actually occur in Mark-Q overlap passages, in passages where on the 2ST Matthew is conflating Mark and Q. The participle λαβών, for example, is listed as occurring redactionally at Mt. 13.31 // Mk 4.30, but the word also

---

1. For the term 'Luke-pleasing', see Farrer, 'Dispensing', p. 57; cf. Goulder's 'Farrer on Q', p. 192.

2. Hawkins, *Horae*, pp. 3, 15. His criteria for characteristic words in Mark are different (p. 10). For comments on Hawkins, see F. Neirynck, 'Hawkins's Additional Notes' and Lloyd Gaston, *Horae Synopticae Electronicae*.

occurs in the parallel Lk. 13.18. It is, on the 2ST, a word which comes from Q and so it is only inserted redactionally into Mark if one assumes Goulder's hypothesis.

This is not too serious a criticism, however, because there are only 18 words and phrases on the Matthew list on the redactional criterion alone, ἀναγινώσκω, ἀπαγγέλλω, βάλλω, γάρ, δαιμονίζομαι, δοκέω, ἐάν, εἰ...εἰ, θάπτω, θέλω, 'Ισραήλ, κάθημαι, μέλλω, νόμος, οὐκ...εἰ μή, πορεύομαι, συνίημι and ὧδε.[3]

More important is the criterion 'twice as often in Matthew as in Mark'. One difficulty with this is that Matthew is a good deal longer than Mark: the potential for any word to appear on the Matthew list is greater than the potential for it to appear on a (hypothetical) Mark one. The criteria really need to be adjusted in proportion to the Gospels' lengths. Several words would then drop out of the Matthew list, like ἀγρός (16/7/9), βάλλομαι (11/5/5) and δύο (40/19/28). It is also worth noting that as far as Matthew is concerned, Goulder's criteria assume Markan priority: a word needs to be twice as common in Matthew as in Mark but only more frequent in Matthew than in Luke. This is, no doubt, because the relation between Matthew and Mark is regarded as more significant than the relation between Matthew and Luke.

Another difficulty arises when one uses Goulder's Matthew list alongside his Luke list. In *LNP*, Goulder does not observe the strict distinction between Hawkins's words and his own—there is no mention of 'semi-Lukan' words.[4] However, Goulder does give asterisks to words which satisfy Hawkins's criteria and pretty well all of the remaining words one could call 'semi-Lukan' words since they satisfy the same conditions as the semi-Matthean words in *MLM*: they occur at

3. Most of these should not be on the list even on the redactional criterion since Goulder claims that 'where the word is included on the redactional criterion, two instances are given' (p. 476) and often only one is given. The full list is in *MLM*, pp. 477-85. The Lukan list is in *LNP*, pp. 800-809. Cf. Neirynck's comments on the Lucan list in his Review of *LNP*. Neirynck isolates and lists the items which Goulder has added to Hawkins's list. His comment that 'Goulder's criterium is merely numerical. Therefore *βοᾶν (1/2/4+3) should not be in the list' (p. 436) shows the weakness of Goulder's looser statement of the criteria for characteristic words in *LNP* as compared with *MLM*: βοᾶν does pass the *MLM* test of appearing twice as often in the one Gospel as in Mark and more often than in the other.

4. There is, however, a distinction between 'Lukan' and 'semi-Lukan' words in *MLM*, apparently with the same definition as for the 'semi-Matthean' words in Matthew, for the first time on p. 283 and thereafter frequently.

least twice as often in Luke as in Mark and more often than in Matthew. In order, then, to make the test fair, I will use these criteria for 'semi-Lukan' words and any words on Goulder's list not satisfying these criteria will not be regarded as characteristic.

Goulder's lists, however, are not unique in presenting such difficulties. Luz, for example, provides a Matthean vocabulary, and he says that it 'contains all vocables which result in significant redactional findings'.[5] His is not, therefore, a list of vocabulary characteristic of Matthew's Gospel, like Hawkins's and Goulder's, but rather it is, as he calls it, a list of 'vocabulary preferred by Matthew'. He admits that it is circular but claims that his attempt to state the number of redactional occurrences is new.[6]

As a result of the method, Luz has on his list words which come a huge number of times in all the Gospels, like κύριος (80/18/104) and δέ (495/164/543). Also odd is the fact that words like ὁμοίως (3/1/11) feature on Luz's list. This word, which is on Hawkins's and Goulder's Luke lists, is over three times as common in Luke as in Matthew but it is regarded as 'Matthew's preferred vocabulary' because he has it twice redactionally.[7] Such an enterprise is of limited usefulness for my purposes since I will be looking for QC words which are more characteristic of Luke than of Matthew or more characteristic of Matthew than of Luke in order to see if there is a bias in Matthew's favour. Further, Luz is looking for redactional occurrences in Matthew on the assumption of the 2ST, one of the tenets of which, Q, Goulder is putting to the test.

The vocabulary which Davies and Allison provide is not exempt from the same difficulties. They list Hawkins's words and then others which 'while they do not satisfy Hawkins's criteria for "characteristic", must nevertheless be regarded as very often editorial'.[8] In other words,

---

5. U. Luz, *Matthew 1–7*, this quotation, p. 52. The list is on pp. 54-72.

6. U. Luz, *Matthew 1–7*, p. 52. Actually it is not new; Lloyd Gaston's *Horae Synopticae Electronicae*, also working from the 2ST, is attempting to do same thing, and with Mark and Luke too. For Gundry's list, see his *Matthew*, pp. 641-49.

7. The redactional occurrences in Matthew are 22.26 and 26.35. Luke has it at 5.33 R; 6.31 QD; 17.28 QD; 17.31 R/QD and so, even on Luz's redactional criterion, Luke likes the word more than does Matthew. Goulder gives Hawkins's figures of 3/2/11+0 which presumably read ὁμοίως at Mk 4.16, like Greeven but unlike N-A[26].

8. W.D. Davies and D.C. Allison, *Matthew*. Their list is on pp. 75-79. This quotation, p. 76.

Davies and Allison are establishing certain words as characteristic by looking at Matthew's supposed editorial practice, the understanding of which depends on a certain source theory, in their case the 2ST. It is surprising then to find the claim just a few pages on that:

> These statistics are…helpful for determining to what extent a given passage has been moulded by the evangelist.[9]

Again this is circular.

More objectivity in the testing of hypotheses might be reached if scholars were to look at words which are undoubtedly characteristic of a Gospel rather than at words which may be, on a certain theory, characteristic of an evangelist. For my purposes, however, it will be advisable to use Goulder's list alone in order that I might have a reliable control, Goulder's thesis tested against itself.

I will not attempt to make direct comparisons between the numbers of characteristically Lukan and the numbers of characteristically Matthean words in QC. Goulder's own distinction between 'Matthean' and 'semi-Matthean' words shows that some words are more characteristic than others and one is going to be more impressed by words which are strongly characteristic of either Matthew or Luke than one is by words which are at the same time characteristic of one and congenial to the other. Most of all, then, one is looking for those words which, like δέομαι (1/0/8+7), are not only characteristic of one evangelist but also uncharacteristic of the other.

The passages will be taken in the order in which they come in Matthew; the numbering is my own. In each pericope, words satisfying Hawkins's criteria will be listed first and words satisfying Goulder's additional criteria will be listed afterwards. In each category, the words are listed in the order in which they come in the pericope. I will not take into account the 18 Matthean words listed above, those which are on Goulder's list on the redactional criterion alone, but I will take into account other words which do meet Hawkins's criteria and Goulder's additional criteria but which do not appear on their lists.[10]

---

9. Davies and Allison, *Matthew*, p. 79. Cf. Goulder's criticisms of Jeremias, Rehkopf and Schürmann in *LNP*, pp. 79-84, with the conclusion that their methods for finding characteristic vocabulary are circular.

10. The key work in the area has for some time been R. Morgenthaler's *Statistik* which Goulder himself uses (see *MLM*, p. 476 and *LNP*, p. 79). There are two important recent works, K. Aland, *Vollständige Konkordanz*, II, pp. 1-306,

I have used Goulder's and Hawkins's lists but have sometimes altered their figures for reasons given in the notes. My own figures are given in accordance with the text of N-A²⁶. Sometimes I have given different R and QD instances from those on Goulder's lists for reasons given in the notes.

B. *Analysis*

1. *John the Baptist: Matthew 3.1-12 // Luke 3.1-9, 15-17 (cf. Mark 1.1-8)*
One word among the QC words in this passaage satisfies Hawkins's criteria for Matthew: συνάγω (24/5/6+12, Mt. 27.27 R).[11]

There is one word which satisfies the Hawkins criteria for Luke: κεῖμαι (3/0/6, Lk. 23.53 R).

There are plenty of semi-Matthean words and phrases: γέννημα (3/0/1); ἔχιδνα (3/0/1);[12] καρπὸν ποιέω × 2 (11/0/6, Mt. 21.43 R; cf. καρπός, 19/5/12, Mt. 21.34 R);[13] οὖν × 2 (56/5/31, Mt. 12.26 R);[14] ἄξιος (9/0/8, Mt. 10.11 R); μή + aorist subjunctive[15] (28/9/18, Mt. 24.23 R); λέγω ὑμῖν ὅτι (21/4/12); δένδρον × 2 (12/1/7, Mt. 21.8 R); καλός, epithet (15/4/8); ἐκκόπτω (4/0/3, Mt. 18.8 R); πῦρ × 3 (12/4/7);[16] βάλλομαι (11/5/5, Mt. 9.2 R); μέν (20/5/10+48, Mt. 20.23 R)[17] and κατακαίω (3/0/1).

'Wortstatistik', and F. Neirynck and F. Van Segbroeck, *New Testament Vocabulary*.

11. Goulder does not give the number of occurrences in Acts (12). He gives Mt. 26.57 as R but this is a possible MA with Lk. 22.66. Mt. 27.27 is a better example.

12. It is the same 3/0/1 as γέννημα.

13. Goulder gives figures of 9/0/5 in his *MLM* list and 10/0/6 in *LNP*, p. 13. I find 11/0/6: Mt. 3.8 QC; 3.10 QC; 7.17 QD × 2; 7.18 QC × 2; 7.19 QD; 12.33 M × 2; 13.26 M; 21.43 R; Lk. 3.8 QC; 3.9 QC; 6.43 QC × 2; 8.8 R; 13.9 L. The discrepancy is either over Mt. 7.18 where N-A²⁶ reads ποιέω twice, or over Mt. 12.33 where the words occur together twice but not with the meaning 'bear fruit'.

14. Goulder gives 57/5/31 with Mt. 14.15 R but οὖν is not read here by either Greeven or N-A²⁶. Mt. 12.26 is a better example.

15. Matthew: μή δόξητε; Luke: μή ἄρξησθε.

16. Goulder gives Mt. 3.11 as R but this is QC (or MA). There are no R examples of πῦρ in Matthew.

17. On μέν...δέ Goulder gives figures of 20/6/10. H.J. Cadbury, *Style*, p. 145, gives figures of 20/5/10 and Davies-Allison, *Matthew*, and Luz, *Matthew 1–7*, both 20/3/8. The uncertainty is over the Markan and Lukan occurrences: Goulder's figures are actually for μέν and not μέν...δέ. On all twenty occasions in Matthew, μέν occurs with δέ (Mt. 3.11 QC; 9.37 QC; 10.13 QD; 13.4-5 R [cf. Mk 4.4-5,

The semi-Lukan words are: περίχωρος (2/1/5+1, Lk. 8.37 R); ὑποδείκνυμι ὑμῖν (1/0/3+1, Lk. 6.47 QD; 12.5 QD); μετάνοια (2/1/5+6, Lk. 5.32 R; 15.7 QD); ἑαυτόν (32/24/58+22, Lk. 9.47 R; 20.20 R); Ἀβραάμ × 2 (7/1/15+7); ὁ θεός (51/48/122+166, Lk. 6.12 R; 9.43 R).

Goulder isolates this pericope for special comment in *LNP* (pp. 13-15; see above) where he lists several phrases which are characteristic of Matthew, γεννήματα ἐχιδνῶν, καρπὸν ποιέω, ἐκκόπτω καὶ βάλλω (cf. 5.30; 18.8 R), εἰς πῦρ (cf. 13.42 M; 13.50 M), and κατακαίω / συνάγω τὸν σῖτον εἰς τὴν ἀποθήκην (cf. Mt. 13.30 M). He says that there is a control—one can look for Lukan characteristic phrases—and he finds just one, ὁ θεός, though he should have added ὑποδείκνυμι ὑμῖν.

Goulder adds that Mt. 3.7 // Lk. 3.7 follows the form offensive vocative followed by rhetorical question, in *MLM* labelled an *echidnic* (p. 79), adding that 'Such a combination does not seem to occur in Mark or L' (*LNP*, p. 13). However, Mk 9.19 ('O faithless generation, how long am I to be with you…?') looks very much like the same form and so do Lk. 11.40 QD (cf. *LNP*, p. 526); 12.56 QD; 13.15 L; 24.25-26 L and Acts 13.10.

Nevertheless, the evidence from this pericope is in Goulder's favour: there is a good deal more semi-Matthean vocabulary than there is semi-Lukan vocabulary and three of the words are un-Lukan, γέννημα, ἔχιδνα and κατακαίω. However, only one word satisfies Hawkins's criteria for Matthew alongside one for Luke and further, among the semi-Lukan words, ὑποδεικνύω is un-Matthean.[18]

μὲν…καί]; 13.8 R; 13.23 R; 13.32 R; 16.3 QD; 16.14 R; 17.11-12 R [cf. Mk 9.12-13, μὲν…ἀλλά]; 20.23 R [cf. Mk 10.39]; 21.35 R; 22.5 QD; 22.8 QD; 23.27 QD; 23.28 QD; 25.15 QD; 25.33 M; 26.24 MK; 26.41 MK). μὲν…δέ is found in Mark only at 12.5, 14.21 and 14.38, probably Davies-Allison and Luz's three. μέν comes in Mk 4.4-5 with καί and in 9.12-13 with ἀλλά, probably Cadbury's five. Goulder's six figure, shared with Aland, incorporates also Mk 16.19 (cf. also Neirynck and Van Segbroeck, *New Testament Vocabulary*, p. 284). Cf. also Mk 10.39, μὲν…καί in Greeven but not N-A²⁶. μὲν…δέ is in Lk. 3.16 QC; 3.18-19 R; 10.2 QC; 11.48 QD; 13.9 L; 23.33 R; 23.41 L; 23.56–24.1 R (this is Luz's and Davies-Allison's eight), μὲν…καί at Lk. 8.5 MK and μὲν…πλήν at Lk. 22.22 R (cf. Mk 14.21) (this makes up Goulder's ten).

    18. As Goulder himself points out in *MLM*, p. 244, without noting that it is also semi-Lukan. There are further comments on this pericope and Goulder's analysis of it in the conclusion, below, p. 83.

2. *The Baptism of Jesus: Matthew 3.13-17 // Luke 3.21-22 (// Mark 1.9-11)*[19]

There are no words which satisfy Hawkins's criteria.

There is one semi-Matthean word: ἀνοίγω (11/1/7+16, Mt. 20.33 R). There are no semi-Lukan words.

3. *Temptation: Matthew 4.1-11 // Luke 4.1-13 (// Mark 1.12-13)*

One word, twice in the passage (once LXX), is on the Hawkins list for Matthew: προσκυνέω (13/2/2, Mt. 15.25 R). Since the only two usages in Luke are in this passage, the word could be called un-Lukan.

There is one word which comes in Hawkins's subsidiary list for Luke, that is words which occur four times more often in Luke and Acts together than in Mark and Matthew together, that is, words which though not characteristic of Luke's Gospel are characteristic of Luke as a writer: λατρεύω (1/0/3+5). This word is in a LXX quotation, however, whereas Matthew's προσκυνέω, on one of the occasions, is not.[20]

Several words are semi-Matthean: διάβολος (6/0/5);[21] πεινάω (9/2/5, Mt. 12.1 R); εἰ × 2 (35/13/31, Mt. 8.31 R); γέγραπται γάρ (3/0/1, Mt. 26.31 R); ἐντέλλομαι (4/2/1, Mt. 17.9 R; LXX).

There are considerably more semi-Lukan words: εἶπον × 3 (182/84/294+124, Lk. 8.4 R; 9.49 R);[22] ὁ θεός × 2 (51/48/122+166, Lk. 6.12 R; 9.43 R); γίνομαι (75/55/129+124, Lk. 20.14 R; 20.16 R); γράφω × 3 (10/10/21+12, Lk. 18.31 R; 20.17 R);[23] ἐπί + dative (17/16/35+27, Lk. 9.43 R; 23.38 R); ζάω (6/2/9+13, Lk. 24.5 R);[24] περί + genitive (20/13/40+64, Lk. 4.37 R; 5.15 R); πούς (10/6/19+19, Lk. 8.35 R);[25] κύριος-ὁ-θεός × 2 (3/2/7+3, Lk. 20.37 R); δόξα (7/3/13+4, Lk. 9.31 R;

---

19. This is a classic case of Mark-Q overlap, and I take the QC words as being those which are common to Matthew and Luke and which are not in Mark. This will be my policy in other Mark-Q overlap passages. My criteria for identifying Mark-Q overlap are stated below, p. 109.

20. See here D. Catchpole, *Quest*, pp. 3-4.

21. The verse in which διάβολος occurs, Mt. 4.1, is listed by Goulder as R but this is really Mark-Q overlap. Cf. διάβολος in Lk. 4.3 QD.

22. Goulder also gives 20.34 as R, but this is a MA with Mt. 22.29. Lk. 9.49 is a clearer example.

23. One of these is γέγραπται γάρ, 3/0/1.

24. Goulder gives figures of 6/3/9+13 but one of the Markan occurrences is 16.11. Goulder also gives Lk. 10.28 as QD, but I have not treated Lk. 10.25-28 as a Mark-Q overlap passage.

25. Goulder also gives Lk. 8.41 as R, but πούς occurs in the parallel Mk 5.22.

9.32 R). Of these, several occur in quotations from the LXX: ἐπί + dative, ζάω, περί + genitive, κύριος-ὁ-θεός × 2.

The occurrence of λατρεύω, albeit in a LXX quotation, as a word on Hawkins's subsidiary list for Luke, does not quite balance the double occurrence of προσκυνέω which is strongly characteristic of Matthew, but at the same time there is a good deal more semi-characteristic Luke than there is semi-characteristic Matthew, probably enough in this passage to be considered problematic for Goulder's thesis.

4. *Introduction to the Sermon; The Beatitudes: Matthew 5.1-12 // Luke 6.17-23*[26]
There is one word characteristic of Matthew according to Hawkins's criteria: μισθός (10/1/3), and one characteristic of Luke: χαίρω = rejoice (3/1/11+5, Lk. 19.37 R).[27]

The semi-Matthean words are: πεινάω (9/2/5, Mt. 12.1 R); πονηρός (26/2/13, Mt. 9.4 R)[28] and οὐρανός (82/18/34, Mt. 28.2 R).

There is one semi-Lukan word: πτωχός (5/5/10, Lk. 14.21 QD).[29]

Since Matthew and Luke each have one strongly characteristic word, the evidence on Hawkins's criteria does not support Goulder. However, there are two more semi-Matthean words than there are semi-Lukan ones.

26. *LNP*, p. 357, 'Some of the words in QC are rather characteristic of Matthew...in other cases Luke and Matthew have different expressions, each of which is characteristic.'

27. Occurrences listed in Hawkins, *Horae*, p. 49.

28. Goulder marks this with an asterisk, but the word is not on Hawkins's list, nor does it qualify for it; cf. *MLM*, p. 295, where Goulder claims that πονηρός only occurs in Luke in Q contexts. This is not quite true. Although it occurs in Lk. 6.22, 35, 45 (x 2); 11.13, 26, 29, 34; 19.22 (all QC), and 7.21 (QD), it is also in Lk. 3.19 and 8.2 which are not in Q contexts. But even if it were always in Q contexts, this would be unimpressive given the importance of distinguishing between QC and QD. Further, Goulder's R example is Mt. 16.4 which is Mark-Q overlap or MA. A clearer instance is 9.4.

29. There are no R occurrences of πτωχός in either Matthew or Luke; Goulder does not give this QD occurrence, 14.21. Matthew never has πτωχός without a parallel in Mark or Luke: Mt. 5.3 QC; 11.5 QC; 19.21 MK; 26.9 MK; 26.11 MK; Luke often does: Lk. 4.18 L; 14.13 L; 14.21 QD; 16.20 L; 16.22 L; 19.8 L; cf. Lk. 6.20 QC; 7.22 QC; 18.22 MK; 21.3 MK.

5. *Salt and Light: Matthew 5.13-16 // Luke 14.34-35; 11.33 (cf. Mark 9.50; 4.21)*
There are no words here which are characteristic of either evangelist. The verb μωραίνω (1/0/1), however, has a related noun μωρός with figures of 6/0/0, Mt. 7.26 QD.

6. *The Law and the Prophets: Matthew 5.17-20 // Luke 16.17*[30]
No words appearing on Hawkins's list come in this passage; there is one word combination which does qualify, however, and it is characteristic of Matthew: οὐρανός/γῆ (14/2/5, 24.30 R; 6.10 QD; cf. γῆ: 43/19/25 and ἡ γῆ = the world: 22/6/14+14, Mt. 6.10 QD).[31]

Goulder lists νόμος as semi-Matthean but this is one of the words which appears on the list on the redactional criterion alone, and it occurs more often in Luke than in Matthew and more often in Acts than in either (8/0/9+17, Mt. 12.5 R).

There are no other semi-Matthean or semi-Lukan words.

With οὐρανός/γῆ, the evidence leans slightly in Goulder's direction.

7. *On Murder: Matthew 5.25-26 // Luke 12.58-59*
Just one word satisfies Hawkins's criteria, and it is Lukan: κριτής × 2 (3/0/6+4).

There are three semi-Matthean words: φυλακή = prison (8/2/6); ἐκεῖθεν (12/5/3, Mt. 9.9 R); and ἔσχατος (10/5/6).

There are no semi-Lukan words.

In spite of the presence of three semi-Matthean words and no semi-Lukan ones, the word κριτής means that the evidence is not entirely in Goulder's favour.

---

30. Cf. the similar passages, Mt. 24.34-36 // Mk 13.30-32 // Lk. 21.32-33. I do not treat this as Mark-Q overlap, however, because it does not meet the criteria below, p. 109.

31. These figures are mine. For οὐρανὸς/γῆ, Goulder gives figures of 15/1/6, Luz, *Matthew 1–7*, of 13/2/5 and Davies-Allison, *Matthew*, of 10/2/4-5. My figures comprise: Mt. 5.18 QC; 5.34-35 M; 6.10 QD; 6.19-20 QD; 11.25 QC; 16.19 M × 2; 18.18 × 2; 24.30 R (though cf. Mk 13.27); 24.35 MK; 28.18 M; Mk 13.27; 13.31; Lk. 10.21 QC; 12.56 QD; 16.17 QC; 21.33 MK. Two other possible occurrences in Matthew would bring the figure to 14: 18.19 M (γῆ with τοῦ πατρός μου τοῦ ἐν οὐρανοῖς) and 23.9 M (with ὁ πατὴρ ὁ οὐράνιος). Three more possible occurrences in Luke would bring his figure to 7: Lk. 2.13-14 L; 4.25 L and 21.25-26 R. Goulder does not give any redactional occurrences. For ἡ γῆ = the world, see p. 72 n. 112, below.

8. *On Divorce: Matthew 5.31-32 // Luke 16.18 (cf. Matthew 19.1-12; Mark 10.1-12)*
There are no words here which are characteristic of either evangelist.

9. *On Retaliation and Loving One's Enemies: Matthew 5.38-48 // Luke 6.27-36*
There is one word/phrase which comes on Hawkins's lists: ὁ πατήρ ὑμῶν/ἡμῶν, etc. (20/1/3, Mt. 26.29 R).[32]
    There is one semi-Matthean word: πονηρός (26/2/13, Mt. 9.4 R).
    One semi-Lukan word occurs three times, ἀγαπάω (8/5/13), and there is καί = also (60/36/124+91, Lk. 4.41 R; 5.33 R). Both of these words are congenial to Matthew, therefore this passage is not difficult for Goulder's thesis.

10. *The Lord's Prayer: Matthew 6.9-13 // Luke 11.2-4*
This passage is important for Goulder's theory: the Lord's Prayer did not stand in Q, M, L or oral tradition but it is:

> a prayer composed by the evangelist from the traditions of the prayers of Jesus in Mark and the teaching on prayer by Jesus in Mark, amplified from the Exodus context of the Sermon, and couched in Matthean language (*MLM*, p. 298; cf. 'Composition').

It is the last clause which concerns us here. An analysis of the QC words reveals no words which are characteristic of Matthew on Hawkins's criteria while there are two which are characteristic of Luke: πειρασμός (2/1/6+1, Lk. 4.13 R/QD; 8.13 R)[33] and εἰσφέρω (1/0/4+1, Lk. 5.18 R; 5.19 R).
    Goulder does not draw attention to εἰσφέρω as an un-Matthean word; indeed the usual word count is missing in the discussion of this passage. Instead, Goulder draws attention to the parallel charge by Jesus to his disciples in Gethsemane, to pray ἵνα μὴ εἰσέλθητε εἰς πειρασμόν. Matthew, Goulder claims, 'puts the words into *oratio recta*, μὴ εἰσενέγκῃς ἡμᾶς εἰς πειρασμόν, and supplies the converse, "but deliver us from the evil one". His εἰσενέγκῃς is merely a Greek Aphel...' (*MLM*, p. 299).

---

32. Listed by Hawkins, *Horae*, p. 31. See p. 69 n. 105 below.
33. Cf. Marion L. Soards, *Passion*, p. 46, for a good summary of the use of πειρασμός in Luke.

It is not so certain, however, that the dependence goes in this direction, from the saying in Gethsemane to the Lord's Prayer. The form of the saying in Gethsemane which Goulder quotes is from Matthew (26.41), not Mark, whose version reads: ἵνα μὴ ἔλθητε εἰς πειρασμόν (Mk 14.38). It could be argued that Matthew changed Mark's ἔλθητε εἰς to his own εἰσέλθητε εἰς under the influence of the presence of εἰσενέγκῃς (εἰς) in the Lord's prayer. Support for this view could be found in the fact that Matthew in 26.42 has γενηθήτω τὸ θέλημά σου (cf. Lk. 22.42; contrast Mk 14.36), identical to the wording of the Lord's Prayer in Mt. 6.10 but different from the wording of its parallel in Mk 14.36.

Further, Luke too has εἰσέλθητε εἰς and not ἔλθητε εἰς in 22.46, and Matthew and Luke both apparently correlate their addresses to God in the Lord's Prayer with the addresses in Gethsemane (Mt. 26.39, πάτερ μου, cf. 6.9, πάτερ ἡμῶν; Lk. 22.42, πάτερ, cf. Lk. 11.2, πάτερ).

There are a few semi-Matthean words: ἁγιάζω (3/0/1); ἀφίημι = forgive × 2 (17/8/15+1, Mt. 12.31 R);[34] μή + aorist subjunctive (28/9/18, Mt. 24.23 R).[35]

One word is semi-Lukan, ὄνομά (22/15/34+60, Lk. 5.27 R; 23.50 R).

ἁγιάζω is un-Lukan, though one might note that it comes in the passive (imperative, ἁγιασθήτω) only here in the Synoptic Gospels and there are no redactional occurrences in Matthew.

Goulder's case for the Lord's Prayer, on the basis of vocabulary at least, is not as strong as he claims. He says:

> All the Lukan variations of language can be (and most commonly are) accounted for as Luke's changes (*LNP*, p. 497).

---

34. Goulder's figures for ἀφίημι = to forgive, are 17/8/14 but if one includes Lk. 23.34 ('Father, forgive them'), there are 15 in Luke: Mt. 6.12 QC × 2; 6.14 MK × 2; 6.15 R × 2; 9.2 MK; 9.5 MK; 9.6 MK; 12.31a MK; 12.31b R; 12.32 QC × 2; 18.21 QC; 18.27 M; 18.32 M (these two on forgiving debt in a parable); 18.35 M; Mk 2.5, 7, 9, 10; 3.28; 4.12; 11.25 × 2; Lk. 5.20 MK; 5.21 MK; 5.23 MK; 5.24 MK; 7.47 L × 2; 7.48 L; 7.49 L; 11.4 QC × 2; 12.10 QC × 2; 17.3 QD; 17.4 QC; 23.34 L; Acts 14.17. On Luke's use of ἀφίημι, see Cadbury, *Style*, p. 180.

35. One could add ὀφειλ—words, 10/0/6+1. Goulder says, 'Luke leaves ὀφείλω in the second half of the verse to spoil the balance of the sentence' (*MLM*, p. 300). This is not completely accurate as Matthew has ὀφείλημα / ὀφειλέτης against Luke's ὀφείλω. The figures for these words are: ὀφείλω, 6/0/5+1 (Mt. 18.28 × 2; 18.30, 34; 23.16, 18, all M; Lk. 7.41 L; 11.4 QD; 16.5 L; 16.7 L; 17.10 L; Acts 17.29); ὀφειλέτης, 2/0/1 (Mt. 6.12 QD; 18.24 M; Lk. 13.4 L); ὀφειλή, 1/0/0 (Mt. 18.32 M); ὀφείλημα, 1/0/0 (Mt. 6.12 QD).

The difficulty with the argument is that Goulder only concerns himself with accounting for Luke's supposed changes to Matthew; he does not look at the presence of Lukan language among the QC words. Goulder is producing an account of Matthew's and Luke's procedure on the basis of his own thesis rather than examining the evidence for his theory from within this pericope.[36] εἰσφέρω is not listed among the Lukan words in the passage and one's attention is not drawn towards πειρασμός as it does not have the asterisk which would mark it out as one of Hawkins's words (*LNP*, p. 501).

11. *On Treasures: Matthew 6.19-21 // Luke 12.33-34*
There are no words which satisfy Hawkins's criteria.

θησαυρός × 2 (9/1/4, Mt. 12.35b QD) is semi-Matthean and comes close.[37] Other semi-Matthean words are: οὐρανός (82/18/34, Mt. 28.2 R); ἐκεῖ (28/11/16, Mt. 14.23 R) and ἔσται/ἔσονται (38/10/33, Mt. 19.27 R).

There is one semi-Lukan word (usage), καί = also (60/36/124+91, Lk. 4.41 R; 5.33 R).

Although the semi-Matthean words are congenial to Luke, the evidence here leans slightly in Goulder's direction.

12. *The Single Eye: Matthew 6.22-23 // Luke 11.34-36*
Just one word satisfies Hawkins's criteria and it is Lukan: λύχνος (2/1/6, Lk. 11.36 QD; 12.35 QD).[38]

There are, however, several semi-Matthean words: ὀφθαλμός × 2 (24/7/17, Mt. 17.8 R);[39] πονηρός (26/2/13, Mt. 9.4 R); οὖν (56/5/31, Mt. 12.26 R) and σκότος (6/1/4).[40]

There are no semi-Lukan words.

---

36. This is true of *LNP, MLM* and 'Composition' (p. 33). The same could be said for Matthew, that there are strong traces of his style where he differs from Luke: cf. Hawkins, *Horae*, p. 32.

37. Note that θησαυρός also comes in Matthew's v. 19 QD; i.e., Matthew has it three times in this passage.

38. λύχνος occurs again in this passage for Luke, in v. 36, given by Goulder as QD in his vocabulary list but not mentioned in *LNP*, p. 516.

39. Matthew has ὀφθαλμός again in v. 23 QD; i.e., he has it three times in the passage.

40. Matthew has σκότος twice here.

The prevalence of semi-Matthean words is good for Goulder's thesis, but the presence of the Lukan λύχνος is not so good.

13. *Two Masters: Matthew 6.24 // Luke 16.13*
One word, occurring twice, satisfies Hawkins's criteria and it is Lukan: ἕτερος × 2 (9/1/33+17, Lk. 3.18 R; 4.43 R).

There are a few semi-Matthean words: κύριος of a man (32/2/25, Mt. 15.27 R);[41] δύο (40/19/28, Mt. 22.40 R) and ἤ = or × 2 (59/28/36, Mt. 27.17 R).

The semi-Lukan words are: ἀγαπάω (8/5/13, Lk. 11.43 R/QD) and θεός anarthrous (6/2/10+3, Lk. 3.2 R; cf. θεός, 51/48/122+166, Lk. 6.12 R; 9.43 R).

The presence of the Lukan ἕτερος (× 2) alongside no words strongly characteristic of Matthew is unfavourable to Goulder's thesis.

14. *Earthly Cares: Matthew 6.25-34 // Luke 12.22-31*
Six words/word combinations, one occurring twice, are Matthean according to Hawkins's criteria. These are: σῶμα/ψυχή × 2 (4/0/2, Mt. 10.28 QD); τροφή (4/0/1+7, Mt. 3.4 R); ἔνδυμα (7/0/1, Mt. 28.3);[42] ὀλιγόπιστος (4/0/1, Mt. 8.26 R); πατήρ ἡμῶν etc., ὁ (20/1/3, Mt. 10.20 R; 6.45 QD);[43] εἷς τούτων (7/1/2, Mt. 10.42 R; 18.14 QD).[44] Of these,

41. Goulder gives figures for κύριος of a man of 32/3/24. I find one less case in Mark and one more in Luke: Mt. 6.24 QC; 9.38 QC; 10.24 QD; 10.25 QD; 13.27 M; 15.27 R; 18.25 M; 18.27 M; 18.31 M; 18.32 M; 18.34 M; 20.8 M; 21.30 M; 21.40 MK; 24.42 MK; 24.45 QC; 24.46 QC; 24.48 QC; 24.50 QC; 25.11 × 2 (one QC, one QD); 25.18 M; 25.19 M (or QD); 25.20 QC; 25.21 QD × 2; 25.22 QC; 25.23 QD × 2; 25.24 QC; 25.26 QD; 27.63 M; Mk 12.9; 13.35; Lk. 10.2 QC; 12.36 QD; 12.37 QD; 12.42 QC; 12.43 QC; 12.45 QC; 12.46 QC; 12.47 QD/L; 13.8 QC; 13.25 QC; 14.21 QD; 14.22 QD; 14.23 QD; 16.3 L; 16.5 L × 2; 16.8 L; 16.13 QC; 19.16 QC;19.18 QC; 19.20 QC; 19.25 QD; 19.33 R; 20.13 R; 20.15 MK. Possibly one should not include Mt. 24.42 where ὁ κύριος ὑμῶν is more literal than the more figurative parallel Mk 13.35, ὁ κύριος τῆς οἰκίας ἔρχεται.

42. In *LNP*, p. 546, Goulder points out that Mt. 3.4 contains a redactional combination of ἔνδυμα and τροφή.

43. Listed in Hawkins, *Horae*, p. 31. Goulder gives 26.29 as R but this is πατήρ μου, not included in Hawkins's 20/1/3 figures; 10.20 R is a better example. See further, p. 69 n. 105 below.

44. Not on Hawkins's list but added by Goulder, the occurrences of εἷς τούτων are Mt. 6.29 QC; 10.42 R; 18.6 MK; 18.10 QD; 18.14 QD; 25.40 M; 25.45 M; Mk 9.42 (cf. 9.37); Lk. 12.27 QC; 17.2 MK, 7/1/2. Four of the occurrences in Matthew

neither σῶμα/ψυχή nor τροφή are strong examples of characteristic Matthew, the former because it occurs in only two contexts in Matthew, here and 10.28 (× 2, QD) and the latter because it occurs twice as often in Luke–Acts as it does in Matthew.

There are three Lukan words/word combinations, one occurring twice, which satisfy the Hawkins criteria: τίς ἐξ ὑμῶν; (2/0/6, Lk. 15.4 QD);[45] ἐσθίω (φαγεῖν) + πίνω (4/0/14+3, Lk. 5.30 R; 5.33 R)[46] and προστίθημι × 2 (2/1/7+6, Lk. 3.20 R).

There are several semi-Matthean words: διὰ τοῦτο (10/3/4, Mt. 13.13 R);[47] μεριμνάω × 3 (7/0/5, Mt. 10.19 R); διαφέρω (3/1/2); Σολομών (5/0/3); περιβάλλω (5/2/2); εἰ (35/13/31, Mt. 8.31 R); ἀγρός (16/7/9, Mt. 13.31 R/QD); βάλλομαι (11/5/5, Mt. 9.2 R); οὕτως (32/10/21, Mt. 19.8 R) and ἔθνος (15/6/13, Mt. 21.43 R).[48]

The semi-Lukan words are: αὐξάνω (2/1/4+4); δόξα (7/3/13+4, Lk. 9.31 R; 9.32 R); σήμερον (7/1/11+9, Lk. 5.26 R); θεός (51/48/122 + 166, Lk. 6.12 R; 9.43 R) and ζητέω (14/10/25+10, Lk. 5.18 R; 6.19 R).

There are more characteristically Matthean words than there are characteristically Lukan words here, both of the kind that satisfy Hawkins's criteria and of the kind that do not. ἔνδυμα (7/0/1) and ὀλιγόπιστος (4/0/1) are particularly noticeable in that they are un-Lukan. Nevertheless, the very presence of characteristically Lukan words here, and especially of those which satisfy Hawkins's criteria, is uncomfortable for Goulder's thesis. It is worth noting that the only two occurrences of προστίθημι in Matthew (2/1/7+6) are in this passage

are in the phrase εἰς τῶν μικρῶν τούτων, 10.42; 18.6 (// Mk 9.42 // Lk. 17.2); 18.10; 18.14; i.e. 4/1/1.

45. τίς ἐξ ὑμῶν; is not on Goulder's list, but it is on Hawkins's with a breakdown of occurrences in *Horae*, p. 46. Hawkins gives figures of 2/0/5 which do not include Lk. 11.11, τίνα ἐξ ὑμῶν.

46. Goulder's figures are 5/0/14 but I find only four occurrences in Matthew, 6.31; 11.18; 11.19 and 24.49, all QC. Greeven (but not N-A[26]) reads καὶ πίνει in Mk 2.16 which would make the figures 4/1/14, and Lk. 5.30 would then not be R.

47. Goulder lists διὰ τοῦτο in *MLM* as 11/2/4 but adjusts it, rightly, to 10/3/4 in *LNP*, p. 546 (cf. Davies-Allison, *Matthew*, and Luz, *Matthew 1–7*). Mt. 23.13, presumably the eleventh occurrence, is not part of the N-A[26] text, and there are three clear examples in Mk, 6.14; 11.24; 12.24.

48. ὡς = like, is on Goulder's *MLM* list and with figures of 40/20/25, Mt. 17.2 R, it only just qualifies as semi-Matthean. However, if with most texts including N-A[26] and Greeven one does not read ὡς at Mt. 15.38, the figure for Matthew is 39.

and, further, that the four occurrences in Matthew of ἐσθίω + πίνω (4/0/14+3) are all QC, Mt. 6.31 // Lk. 12.29; Mt. 11.18 // Lk. 7.33; Mt. 11.19 // Lk. 7.34 and Mt. 24.49 // Lk. 12.45.

15. *Judging: Matthew 7.1-5 // Luke 6.37-42*

There are three words which satisfy Hawkins's criteria for Matthew, one of them occurring three times in the passage: ἀδελφός in a transferred sense × 3 (15/0/6, Mt. 28.10 R; 5.47 QD);[49] ὑποκριτής (13/1/3, Mt. 22.18 R) and τότε (90/6/14, Mt. 9.6 R).[50]

One Lukan word appears on the Hawkins list: κατανοέω (1/0/4+4, Lk. 12.24 QD; 20.23 R).[51]

There is one semi-Matthean word: ὀφθαλμός × 6 (24/7/17, Mt. 17.8 R).

There are no semi-Lukan words.

49. Although Goulder marks ἀδελφός in a transferred sense with an asterisk in his *MLM* list, when he distinguishes between Matthean and semi-Matthean words in the text he always refers to it as semi-Matthean (twice on p. 287; also pp. 295, 305, 403, cf. pp. 401 and 423). Goulder's figures are 14/0/5 and he does not give a redactional example; I find 15/0/6 including 28.10 R: Mt. 5.22 × 2 M; 5.23 R/M; 5.24 M; 5.47 QD; 7.3 QC; 7.4 QC; 7.5 QC; 18.15 × 2, one QC, one QD; 18.21 QD; 18.35 M; 23.8 M; 25.40 M; 28.10 R (cf. *MLM*, p. 449); Lk. 6.41 QC; 6.42 × 3, two QC, one QD; 17.3 QC; 22.32 R/L. Cf. also Mt. 12.46-50 and parallels in which there is a move from literal brothers to figurative ones.

50. Goulder also lists ἐκβάλλω = bring out as characteristic with figures of 5/0/2 (*MLM*, p. 479). There seems to be some confusion over these in *MLM*, however. Goulder has ἐκβάλλω = bring out here (x 3, *MLM*, p. 305), at 12.20 (p. 330 n.) and at 13.52 (p. 375). These could be the five occurrences in the list except that the three occurrences in 7.4-5 come × 3 in the Lukan parallel (Lk. 6.42, when ἐκβάλλω = bring out is supposed to come only twice in the Gospel) besides which 'bring out' would be an odd translation of ἐκβάλλω here (cf. NRSV 'take out'). Further, Goulder twice lists 'ἐκβάλλω = take out' as characteristic: Mt. 9.38 // Lk. 10.2 (p. 328; again 'take out' would be an odd translation; cf. NRSV 'send out'), 12.35 × 2 (QD, cf. Lk. 6.45, προφέρω, p. 333). It may be that Goulder is taking ἐκβάλλω = take out as semi-Matthean (3/0/1) which would leave ἐκβάλλω = bring out as 5/0/3. In *LNP*, p. 473, however, the 5/0/2 figures are clarified: 'ἐκβάλλειν = *hôtsí'*, without hostile meaning, Mt. 9.38 (= Lk. 10.2); 12.20 R; 12.35 × 2 QD; 13.52; MK - , Lk. 10.35, Acts -.'

51. Although it is not in the strictly parallel verse, one could add ὁ + phrase + noun, 1/3/7+20, Lk. 9.37 R; 19.30 R (Hawkins's figures, subsidiary list, cf. *Horae*, p. 50; Goulder's are 2/3/7+19), Mt. 7.3: τὴν δέ ἐν τῷ σῷ ὀφθαλμῷ; Lk. 6.42, τὴν ἐν τῷ ὀφθαλμῷ σου δοκόν.

The evidence here is in favour of Goulder's thesis. Although κατανοέω is a *hapax* in Matthew and therefore striking,[52] there are three words strongly characteristic of Matthew, one of which, ἀδελφός in a transferred sense, occurs three times.

16. *Answer to Prayer: Matthew 7.7-11 // Luke 11.9-13*
One word combination satisfies Hawkins's criteria for Matthew: ἀγαθὸς/πονηρός (10/0/4, Mt. 5.45 QD; 7.17 QD).[53]

Three Lukan words/phrases, one occurring twice, satisfy Hawkins's criteria: κρούω (2/0/4, Lk. 12.36 QD; 13.25 QD);[54] τίς ἐξ ὑμῶν; (2/0/6, Lk. 15.4 QD)[55] and ἐπιδίδωμι (2/0/5+2).

The semi-Matthean words are: ἀνοίγω × 2 (11/1/7+16, Mt. 20.33 R); λαμβάνω (57/21/22, Mt. 16.7 R); ἤ = or[56] (59/28/36, Mt. 27.17 R); εἰ (35/13/31, Mt. 8.31 R); οὖν (56/5/31, Mt. 12.26 R); πονηρός (26/2/13, Mt. 9.4 R) and οὐρανός (82/18/34, Mt. 28.2 R).

The semi-Lukan words are: ζητέω × 2 (14/10/25+10, Lk. 5.18 R; 6.19 R); εὑρίσκω × 2 (27/11/45+35, Lk. 5.19 R; 6.7 R) and καί = also (60/36/124+91, Lk. 4.41 R, 5.33 R).[57]

The presence of three words/phrases strongly characteristic of Luke with just the one strongly characteristic of Matthew is not in favour of Goulder's thesis.

---

52. In *MLM*, p. 305, Goulder points to κατανοέω as un-Matthean without saying that it is Lukan.

53. Goulder's figures for ἀγαθὸς/πονηρός are 8/0/4. The occurrences I find are: Mt. 5.45 QD; 7.11 QC; 7.17 QD; 7.18 QD; 12.34 QD; 12.35 QC × 3; 20.15 M; 22.10 QD; Lk. 6.45 QC × 3; 11.13 QC. This is 10/0/4 if one counts Mt. 12.35 // Lk. 6.45 as × 3 or 8/0/2 if one counts it once.

54. κρούω is one of Hawkins's words 'on which little stress can be laid' (*Horae*, p. 2). There are only four uses and they are not all in different contexts. It is not listed in *LNP*, p. 501.

55. Cf. p. 57 n. 45 above.

56. Taking the ἤ καί of Mt. 7.10 as parallel to the ἤ καί of Lk. 11.12 with N-A[26] (and Greeven), not reading ἤ καί at Lk. 11.11.

57. Though not on his list, Goulder mentions μή interrogative × 2 in *LNP*, p. 501. However, a couple of Luke's six are the two dubious occurrences here (11.11 and 12), neither of which is read by N-A[26] (though both are read by Greeven).

17. *The Golden Rule: Matthew 7.12 // Luke 6.31*
There are no words here which are characteristic of either evangelist.[58]

18. *The Two Ways: Matthew 7.13-14 // Luke 13.24*
There are no words which satisfy the Hawkins criteria.
     There is one semi-Matthean phrase: διά + genitive (26/11/13, Mt. 3.3 R).
There are no semi-Lukan words.

19. *False Prophets: Matthew 7.15-20 // Luke 6.43-44*
There are two words which satisfy the Hawkins criteria and they are both Matthean: συλλέγω (7/0/1) and σαπρός (5/0/2).[59]
     There are several semi-Matthean words/phrases: καρπός × 3 (19/5/12, Mt. 21.34 R, including καρπὸν ποιέω × 2, 11/0/6, Mt. 21.43 R); δένδρον × 2 (12/1/7, Mt. 21.8 R); καλός, epithet (15/4/8).
There are no semi-Lukan words.
     The evidence of this passage runs in favour of Goulder's thesis; there are no words characteristic of Luke at all and among the Matthean words, συλλέγω is un-Lukan. Nevertheless, the evidence may look a little more impressive than it is: neither σαπρός nor συλλέγω have redactional occurrences in Matthew and συλλέγω is one of the words bracketed by Hawkins: six of the seven occurrences are in Mt. 13.28-48, five of these in the Parable of the Talents and its interpretation.

20. *Warning Against Self-Deception: Matthew 7.21-23 // Luke 6.46; 13.26-27*
There are no words which satisfy Hawkins's criteria.
     There is just one semi-Matthean word, κύριε, but with figures of 29/1/28, it is almost equally characteristic of Luke (cf. Mt. 8.25 R;[60] Lk. 22.33 R). The phrase κύριε κύριε comes three times in Matthew

58. Goulder lists οἱ ἄνθρωποι = men, with figures of 27/5/10, Mt. 9.8 R. I am not sure how he arrives at these figures, so I have omitted reference to this here and elsewhere where οἱ ἄνθρωποι occurs.
     59. There are two occurrences of σαπρός here in Matthew, vv. 17 and 18, and two in Luke, both v. 43, so it might be thought to be × 2 QC. However, the first occurrence in Luke, 6.43a, is directly parallel to πονηρός in Matthew. It is only in three contexts in Matthew's Gospel, here × 2, 12.33 × 2 (a doublet with Mt. 7.18 // Lk. 6.43) and 13.48 M.
     60. Goulder lists 8.2 as R but this is a MA, so I have replaced it with 8.25.

(here twice and 25.11, κύριε κύριε ἄνοιξον ἡμῖν // Lk. 13.25, κύριε ἄνοιξον ἡμῖν), however, against just this one occurrence here in Luke.[61]

There are no semi-Lukan words.

21. *Hearers and Doers of the Word: Matthew 7.24-27 // Luke 6.47-49*
There are no words which satisfy Hawkins's criteria.

There are two semi-Matthean words: πέτρα (5/1/3, Mt. 27.51 R) and ἐκεῖνος (54/23/33, Mt. 14.1 R).

There are two semi-Lukan words, one occurring twice: πᾶς pleonastic (common, Lk. 4.37 R; 5.17 R) and οἰκοδομέω × 2 (8/4/12+4).

The evidence in this pericope is neither strongly in favour of nor strongly against Goulder's thesis.

22. *The Centurion's Servant: Matthew 8.5-13 // Luke 7.1-10; 13.28-29*[62]
Goulder claims:

> The pericope is one of the most embarrassing for the Q hypothesis because of its characteristic Matthean phrases (*LNP*, p. 380).

Not all of these phrases occur among the QC words, however, and there are some Lukan words and phrases too.

There are two words/phrases characteristic of Matthew according to Hawkins's criteria: ἀνατολή (5/0/2) and ὁ κλαυθμὸς καὶ ὁ βρυγμὸς τῶν ὀδόντων (6/0/1).[63]

There is one word characteristic of Luke according to Hawkins's criteria: ἰάομαι (4/1/11+4, Lk. 6.19 R; 9.2 R). Three words qualify for the subsidiary list: ἑκατοντάρχης/ἑκατόνταρχος (4/0/3+13, Lk. 23.47 MA);[64] ἱκανός (3/3/9+18, Lk. 8.27 R; 8.32 R) and ἄγω (4/3/13+26, Lk. 4.40 R).[65]

---

61. The doubled vocative is common in Luke, however (see below, p. 79).

62. I have not taken the end of the Sermon (Mt. 7.28 // Lk. 7.1) into account in a separate section because there are no actual words in common here, even though the similar content means that one could call it a Q passage.

63. κλαυθμός occurs once additionally in Mt. 2.18 i.e. it is 7/0/1. βρυγμός is 6/0/1 and ὀδούς 7/1/1+1.

64. ἑκατόνταρχος is on Goulder's Matthew list which does not take into account the number of occurrences in Acts. Cf. BAGD, p. 237, on the different spellings. Further, κεντυρίων is 0/3/0. There is some textual evidence also for χιλίαρχος here: see G. Zuntz, 'Centurion'.

65. Goulder gives Lk. 19.30 and 19.35 as R examples but these are both MAs, with Mt. 21.2 and 21.7. 4.40 is a clearer instance.

There are several semi-Matthean words/phrases: κύριε (29/1/28, Mt. 8.25 R); δοῦλος (30/5/26); ἐκεῖ (28/11/16, Mt. 14.23 R) and ἔσται /ἔσονται (38/10/33, Mt. 19.27 R).

There are also several semi-Lukan words and phrases: εἶπον × 2 (182/84/294+124, Lk. 8.4 R; 9.49 R); καὶ γάρ (3/2/7+1, Lk. 6.32 QD; 11.4 QD);[66] πορεύομαι × 2 (29/0/51+37, Lk. 4.42 R; 5.24 R); ἀκούω part. + δέ (7/1/8+15, Lk. 18.22 R; 18.36 R);[67] θαυμάζω (7/4/13+5, Lk. 9.43 R);[68] εὑρίσκω (27/11/45+35, Lk. 5.19 R; 6.7 R) and Ἀβραάμ (7/1/15+7).

An analysis of the QC words here does not provide strong support for Goulder. Although the most impressive of the characteristic words/phrases is Matthean, ὁ κλαυθμὸς καὶ ὁ βρυγμὸς τῶν ὀδόντων (6/0/1), there is a good number of words characteristic of Luke, on both Hawkins's and Goulder's criteria.

23. *Two Claimants to Discipleship: Matthew 8.19-22 // Luke 9.57-60*
There are no words in this pericope which for Matthew satisfy Hawkins's criteria. For Luke there are three: κλίνω (1/0/4, Lk. 9.12 R; 24.5 R); ἕτερος (9/1/33+17, Lk. 3.18 R; 4.43 R) and ἑαυτοῦ, sandwiched (1/0/6, 11.21 QD).[69]

---

66. Goulder's figures for καὶ γάρ are 2/2/8+1 so that it would qualify as characteristic on Hawkins's criteria. My figures, however, are 3/2/7+1: Mt. 8.9 QC; 15.27 R; 26.73 MK; Mk 10.45; 14.70; Lk. 1.66 L; 6.32 QD; 6.33 QD (but γάρ is in square brackets in N-A[26] and not read by Greeven); 7.8 QC; 11.4 QD; 22.37 L; 22.59 MK; Acts 19.40.

67. Goulder's figures for ἀκούσας (etc.) δέ are 5/0/9+16: this would then qualify for Hawkins's subsidiary list. However, I am unsure how he arrives at these figures. Mine of 7/1/8+15 (cf. also Luz, *Matthew 1–7*) are for any participle of ἀκούω with δέ directly following on: Mt. 2.3 M; 2.22 M; 4.12 R; 8.10 QC; 14.13 R; 19.22 R; 19.25 R (all with aorist participle); Mk 6.16; Lk. 7.3 QD; 7.9 QC; 14.15 QD; 18.22 R; 18.36 R; 19.11 QD; 20.16 R; 20.45 R (all with aorist participle except 19.11 and 20.45, present participle); Acts 1.37; 5.21; 7.12; 7.54; 8.14; 11.18; 13.48; 14.14; 17.32; 18.26; 19.5; 19.28; 22.2; 22.26; 23.16 (all with aorist participle except 13.48, present participle). The figures for ἀκούω aorist participle + δέ would be 7/1/8. Lk. 9.7 and 16.14 (cf. Acts 11.1, 7, 22 and 22.22) have other forms of ἀκούω + δέ which would make the figures 7/1/10+19. Cf. *LNP*, p. 632 on 16.14 (ἤκουον δέ) which lists 'ἀκούειν-δέ in transition' as characteristic.

68. Goulder also gives Lk. 8.25 as R but this is a MA with Mt. 8.27. Goulder's figures for θαυμάζω are 7/4/12+5, but this does not take into account Lk. 24.12 which Goulder does read (see *LNP*, pp. 776-77).

69. Goulder lists ἑαυτοῦ sandwiched here, Lk. 9.60, as QD but the phrase τοὺς

There is only one semi-Matthean word: οὐρανός (82/18/34, Mt. 28.2 R).

There are by contrast several semi-Lukan words: εἶπον (182/84/294 +124, Lk. 8.4 R; 9.49 R); οὐ/μὴ ἔχω + noun clause (3/2/6+3, Lk. 12.4 QD);[70] ποῦ (4/3/7, Lk. 8.25 R; 17.37 QD)[71] and ἐπιτρέπω (2/2/4+5, Lk. 8.32 R).

The evidence of characteristic vocabulary for this pericope goes markedly against Goulder's thesis. Not only are there three words/ phrases strongly characteristic of Luke but also there are several more semi-Lukan words than there are semi-Matthean ones.

In *MLM* (p. 323), Goulder mentions that 'κλίνω is non-Matthean' though he does not note that it is Lukan. Further, he says that 'there are 6 characteristic words out of 69'. Of these six, four, however, are QD, προσελθών, εἰς = τις, 'a good γραμμάτευς' and κύριε. The only QC word Goulder mentions is θάπτω, twice in the passage, which is about as characteristic of Luke as it is of Matthew (3/0/3+4, Mt. 14.12 R).[72]

24. *Mission: Matthew 9.35–10.16 // Luke 8.1; 9.1-6; 10.1-12 (cf. Mark 1.39 etc.; 6.6b-13)*
One Matthean word satisfies Hawkins's criteria: ὅπως (17/1/7+14, Mt. 8.34 R).[73]

Two Lukan words satisfy Hawkins's criteria: δέομαι (1/0/8+7, Lk. 5.12 R; 8.28 R)[74] and εἰρήνη (4/1/13+7, Lk. 11.21 R/QD; 19.38 R).

The semi-Matthean words are: μέν (20/5/10+48, Mt. 20.23 R);

ἑαυτῶν νεκρούς is identical in the parallel Mt. 8.22 and so QC. Goulder's figures are 1/0/5 but I count six Lukan occurrences, 2.3 L; 9.60 QC; 11.21 QD; 13.34 (ἑαυτῆς, QD); 14.26 QD; 14.33 L.

70. Goulder gives figures for οὐ/μὴ ἔχω + noun clause of 3/3/6+3. I am unsure where the third Markan instance comes from; the others are probably taken as Mt. 8.20 QC; 15.32 MK; 18.25 M (or QC, cf. Lk. 7.42); Mk 8.1, 2; Lk. 7.42 L; 9.58 QC; 11.6 L; 12.4 QD; 12.17 L; 14.14 L; Acts 4.14; 25.26; 28.19.

71. Goulder gives 17.31 as QD, an error for 17.37.

72. Goulder does not mention οὐρανός as semi-Matthean, nor ἐάν (56/29/26, Mt. 21.21 R) which is on his list but is excluded from consideration here because it does not occur more than twice as often in Matthew as in Mark.

73. Goulder also lists ἐκβάλλω = take out; but see p. 58 n. 50 above.

74. Cadbury, *Style*, p. 175, lists four occasions on which δέομαι comes redactionally in Luke, 5.12; 8.28, 38 and 9.40.

θερισμός × 3 (6/1/3);[75] πολύς/ὀλίγος (5/0/3, 25.21 QD);[76] οὖν (56/5/31, Mt. 12.26 R); κύριος + gen. (24/4/16, Mt. 15.27 R; cf. κύριος of a man, 32/2/25, Mt. 15.27 R);[77] ἐργάτης × 3 (6/0/4);[78] νόσος (5/1/4, Mt. 4.23 R); ἰδού (62/17/57, Mt. 28.2 R);[79] θεραπεύω × 2[80] (16/5/14, Mt. 4.23 R); ἄξιος (9/0/8, Mt. 10.11 R/QD); ἄν (40/20/32, Mt. 15.5 R);[81] Σόδομα (3/0/2); ἐκεῖνος (54/23/33, Mt. 14.1 R) and ἔσται/ἔσονται (38/10/33, Mt. 19.27 R).

The semi-Lukan words are: πόλις × 3[82] (26/8/39+42, Lk. 4.31 R; 4.43 R); ἐν μέσῳ (3/2/7+6, Lk. 8.7 R; 21.21 R; cf. μέσος: 7/5/14+10, Lk. 4.35 R); ἐγγίζω (7/3/18+6, Lk. 19.37 R; 22.1 R); ὑπόδημα (2/1/4+2)[83] and ἡμέρα (45/27/83+94, Lk. 4.42 R; 5.17 R).

Although there are several more semi-Matthean words than there are semi-Lukan ones, on the Hawkins criteria there are two words/phrases characteristic of Luke against the one characteristic of Matthew. One of the Lukan words, δέομαι, is also un-Matthean whereas the Matthean

75. θερισμός looks more characteristic of Matthew when one notes that all three Lukan occurrences are here, that it is + 0 (Acts) and that θεριστής is 2/0/0.

76. In *MLM*, Goulder's figures for πολύς/ὀλίγος are 4/0/3 but in *LNP* (p. 473), he lists five in Matthew, three in Luke and one in Acts: Mt. 7.14 QD; 9.37 (= Lk. 10.2); 22.14; 25.21 QD; 25.23 QD; Lk. 7.47 and 12.48; Acts 26.29. I do not see πολύς/ὀλίγος in Acts 26.29. If, with Greeven, one reads ὀλίγος in Lk. 10.42, then the figures would be 5/0/4 (incorporating Lk. 10.41-42). Cf. also, parallel to Mt. 7.13-14, Lk. 13.23-24: ὀλίγος/πολύς.

77. For κύριος of a man, see p. 56 n. 41 above. Goulder's figures in *MLM* for κύριος with genitive are 25/5/18; I find one fewer in Matthew, one fewer in Mark and two fewer in Luke: Mt. 9.38 QC; 10.24 QD; 10.25 QD; 11.25 QD; 12.8 MK; 15.27 R; 18.27 M; 18.31 M; 18.32 M; 18.34 M; 20.8 M; 21.40 MK; 22.44 MK; 24.42 MK; 24.46 QC; 24.48 QC; 24.50 QC; 25.18 QD; 25.19 QD; 25.21 QD × 2; 25.23 QD × 2; 25.26 QD; Mk 2.28; 12.9; 12.36; 13.35; Lk. 1.43 L; 6.5 MK; 10.2 QC; 10.21 QC; 12.36 QD; 12.43 QC; 12.45 QC; 12.46 QC; 14.21 QD; 16.3 L; 16.5 L × 2; 19.33 R (οἱ κύριοι αὐτοῦ); 20.13 R; 20.15 MK; 20.42 MK.

78. Cf. *LNP*, p. 473, ἐργάτης = a literal worker: 6/0/3 QC + 0, removing Lk. 13.27 from consideration.

79. Goulder gives Mt. 9.2 as R but this is a MA with Lk. 5.18, so I have replaced it with Mt. 28.2 R.

80. Mt. 10.1 // Lk. 9.1 and Mt. 10.8 // Lk. 10.9.

81. Goulder gives Mt. 21.44 as R but even if one reads this verse (N-A[26] places it in brackets), it is a MA with Lk. 20.18. I have replaced it with Mt. 15.5 R.

82. Mt. 9.35 // Lk. 8.1 (Mark-Q overlap); Mt. 10.14 // Lk. 10.11 and Mt. 10.15 // Lk. 10.12.

83. Not on Goulder's list but in *LNP*, p. 473.

word, ὅπως, is congenial to Luke (× 7, with plenty of occurrences in Acts) so the evidence does not support Goulder's thesis.

25. *Affliction of the Disciples: Matthew 10.19-20 // Luke 12.11-12 (cf. Mark 13.11-12 // Luke 21.14-15)*

There are no words here which are characteristic by Hawkins's criteria.

There are two semi-Matthean words: μή with aor. subj. (28/9/18, Mt. 24.23 R) and ἤ = or (59/28/36, Mt. 27.17 R).

There are no semi-Lukan words.

26. *Disciple and Master: Matthew 10.24-25 // Luke 6.40*

There is one word which is characteristic according to Hawkins's criteria and it is Matthean: ὑπέρ + acc. (4/0/2+1).

There are no semi-Matthean words.

There are no semi-Lukan words.

27. *Exhortation to Fearless Confession: Matthew 10.26-33 // Luke 12.2-9 (cf. Mark 4.22 // Luke 8.17; Luke 21.18)*

On this pericope Goulder comments:

> The difficulty [for the Q hypothesis] is that the sentence structure as well as the vocabulary in the QC words is so strongly reminiscent of Matthew (*LNP*, p. 532).

Our evidence here will partly bear this out: there are three words/ phrases characteristic of Matthew according to Hawkins's criteria, one occurring twice: εἷς ἐξ αὐτῶν (4/0/2+1, Mt. 22.35 R);[84] ὁμολογέω × 2 (4/0/2, Mt. 14.7 R) and ἔμπροσθεν τῶν ἀνθρώπων (5/0/1, Mt. 10.33 QD; 23.13 QD;[85] cf. ἔμπροσθεν, 18/2/10, Mt. 27.11 R).

There is one Lukan word which satisfies the Hawkins criteria, φοβέομαι, of God (1/0/6+5).[86]

---

84. εἷς ἐξ αὐτῶν is not on the *MLM* list but in *LNP*, p. 532. Goulder lists Mt. 18.12 QD; 22.35 R and 27.48 R; the other Lukan occurrence is 17.15 L but cf. 22.50 R; also Acts 11.28.

85. Goulder's figures for ἔμπροσθεν τῶν ἀνθρώπων are 6/0/1 (*LNP*, p. 533), and he lists 5.16 M; 6.1 M; 6.2 M; 10.32 QC; 10.33 QD and 23.14 QD. However, 6.2 does not contain the actual phrase ἔμπροσθεν τῶν ἀνθρώπων, so I have adjusted the figures to 5/0/1. Further, most modern editions (including N-A[26] and Greeven) would read the phrase in Mt. 23.13 rather than 23.14.

86. Occurrences of φοβέομαι of God are listed by Hawkins, *Horae*, p. 49.

The semi-Matthean words are: κρυπτός (5/1/2);[87] γέεννα (7/3/1, Mt. 23.33 QD); διαφέρω (3/1/2) and ἔμπροσθεν (18/2/10, Mt. 27.11 R).[88]

The semi-Lukan words are: εἶναι + part. (16/31/62+46, Lk. 4.31 R; 23.51 R); εἶπον (182/84/294+124, Lk. 8.4 R; 9.49 R); οὐχί (9/0/17+3, Lk. 6.39 QD; 12.51 QD) and καί = also (60/36/124+91, Lk. 4.41 R; 5.33 R).

The trend here is in favour of Goulder's thesis with three words strongly characteristic of Matthew against one strongly characteristic of Luke and a similar number of semi-Matthean/semi-Lukan words. ἔμπροσθεν τῶν ἀνθρώπων is un-Lukan and φοβέομαι of God is un-Matthean.

28. *Division in Households: Matthew 10.34-36 // Luke 12.51-53*

There are no words which satisfy the Hawkins criteria for Matthew, but there is one which does for Luke: εἰρήνη (4/1/13+7, Lk. 11.21 QD; 19.38 R).[89]

There is one semi-Matthean word: γῆ (43/19/25; cf. ἡ γῆ = the world, 22/6/14+14, Mt. 6.10 QD).[90]

There are no semi-Lukan words.

The presence of εἰρήνη is not favourable to Goulder's thesis.

29. *Conditions of Discipleship: Matthew 10.37-39 // Luke 14.26-27; 17.33 (cf. Matthew 16.24-25 // Mark 8.34-35 // Luke 9.23-24)*

There are no words here which are characteristic of either evangelist.

30. *Receiving and Hearing: Matthew 10.40 // Luke 10.16 (cf. Matthew 18.5 // Mark 9.37 // Luke 9.48)*

There are no words here which are characteristic of either evangelist.

31. *The Baptist's Question and Jesus' Testimony to John: Matthew 11.2-19 // Luke 7.18-35; 16.16*[91]

---

87. κρυπτός might be taken as a Markan word rather than as Q—it is in the first clause in Mk 4.22 // Lk. 8.17, cf. Mt. 10.26 and Lk. 12.2. Luke's two uses of the word are both here—Lk. 8.17 and 12.2.

88. This is in addition to the ἔμπροσθεν τῶν ἀνθρώπων listed above.

89. Note, however, that Matthew also has the word on his own in the same verse.

90. On ἡ γῆ = the world, see p. 72 n. 112, below.

91. This is often taken as two pericopae, for example, by Greeven, Mt. 11.2-6 // Lk. 7.18-23 and Mt. 11.7-19 // Lk. 7.24-35 (and 16.16), but I will take the two parts

There are four words/phrases characteristic of Matthew according to the Hawkins criteria: σκανδαλίζομαι ἐν (4/1/1, Mt. 26.31 R);[92] οὗτος ἐστιν (14/2/4, Mt. 13.19 R);[93] ὁμοιόω (8/1/3) and ἄνθρωπος (ἄνηρ) + noun (7/0/3, Mt. 21.33 R).[94]

There are more words/phrases, seven with one occurring twice, characteristic of Luke according to the Hawkins critera: πέμπω (4/1/10+11, Lk. 20.11 R; 20.12 R); προσδοκάω (2/0/6+5, Lk. 3.15 R; 8.40 R); εὐαγγελίζομαι (1/0/10+15, Lk. 3.18 R; 20.1 R); προσφωνέω (1/0/4+2, Lk. 6.13 R; 23.20 R); ἐσθίω + πίνω × 2 (4/0/14+3, Lk. 5.30 R; 5.33 R); φίλος (1/0/15+3, Lk. 21.16 R; 12.4 QD) and δικαιόω (2/0/5+2, Lk. 7.29 QD).

The semi-Matthean words are: ἤ = or (59/28/36, Mt. 27.17 R); ἀποκριθεὶς εἶπεν (45/14/34, Mt. 13.11 R); τυφλός (LXX, 17/5/8, Mt. 15.30 R); χωλός (5/1/3, Mt. 15.30 R); κωφός (7/3/4);[95] ἐγείρομαι (30/10/14, Mt. 9.25 R); μή + aor. subj. (28/9/18, Mt. 24.23 R); οἱ ὄχλοί (33/2/15, Mt. 9.8 R);[96] θεάομαι (4/2/3); κάλαμος (5/2/1); ἰδού × 2 (62/17/57, Mt. 28.2 R); ναί (9/1/4, Mt. 9.28 R); ἔμπροσθεν (18/2/10, Mt. 27.11 R);[97] μείζων × 2 (10/3/7, Mt. 20.31 R) and ὁ υἱὸς τοῦ

together since the second passage is directly related to the first and for a two source theorist they will have to have stood together in Q.

92. Listed by Hawkins, *Horae*, p. 33.

93. Goulder does not list οὗτος ἐστιν; Luz, *Matthew 1–7*, has 13/2/3 and Davies-Allison, *Matthew*, 17/5/7. My examples are οὗτος (masc. nom. only) with ἐστιν (pres. only) immediately following (with the exception of conjunctions like γάρ) at the beginning of a sentence or clause: Mt. 3.3, 17; 7.12; 11.10; 13.19, 20, 22, 23; 14.2; 17.5; 18.4; 21.11, 38; 27.37; Mk 9.7; 12.7; Lk. 7.27; 9.35, 48; 20.14. Luke's other three uses of the expression all have parallels, 7.27 QC; 9.35 MK; 20.14 MK.

94. Goulder's figures are 7/0/1 but there are three clear Lukan occurrences: here; Mt. 12.41 // Lk. 11.32, ἄνδρες Νινευῖται; and Lk. 24.19, ἀνὴρ προφήτης. ἄνθρωπος + noun is 6/0/1.

95. Goulder lists Mt. 15.30 as R but κωφός does appear in the parallel Mk 7.32; cf. it occurs again in Mt. 15.31 // Mk 7.37.

96. Goulder has an asterisk with οἱ ὄχλοι but it is not on Hawkins's list nor does it qualify for it. He gives 7.28 as R but 9.8 is a clearer R example.

97. This is one of the agreements between Matthew and Luke against Mark (1.2) in the form of this citation from Exod. 23.20 and Mal. 3.1, so it might be regarded as a MA rather than as QC. See, for example, E.P. Sanders and M. Davies, *Studying*, pp. 95-96; see also below, p. 95.

ἀνθρώπου ἔρχεται (7/2/5, Mt. 16.28 R).[98]

The following are semi-Lukan: εἶναι + part. (16/31/62+46, Lk. 4.31 R; 23.51 R); πορεύομαι (29/0/51+37, Lk. 4.42 R; 5.24 R); ἀπαγγέλλω (8/4/11+15, Lk. 8.36 R; 18.37 R);[99] πτωχός (LXX; 5/5/10); ἄρχομαι-λέγω (2/4/9, Lk. 3.8 QD; 12.1 QD); περί + gen. × 2 (20/13/40+64, Lk. 4.37 R; 5.15 R); σαλεύω (2/1/4+4, Lk. 6.38 QD; 6.48 QD); εἶναι + part. (16/31/62+46, Lk. 4.41 R; 23.51 R); γράφω (10/10/21+12, Lk. 20.17 R; 21.22 R); νόμος (8/0/9+17);[100] δαιμόνιον (11/11/23+1, Lk. 4.33 R; 4.35 R); τελώνης (8/3/10, Lk. 7.29 QD);[101] ἁμαρτωλός (5/6/18, Lk. 24.7 R) and σοφία (3/1/6+4, Lk. 21.15 R; 11.49 QD).

There are many words and phrases characteristic of Luke in this pericope, and it is, therefore, problematic for Goulder's thesis. Several words are strongly characteristic of Luke; εὐαγγελίζομαι (1/0/10+15), προσφωνέω (1/0/4+2) and φίλος (1/0/15+3) are all un-Matthean. Indeed Goulder lists εὐαγγελίζομαι and προσφωνέω (but not φίλος) as un-Matthean, but he does not note that they are Lukan. He talks about

98. Goulder's figures for ὁ υἱὸς τοῦ ἀνθρώπου ἔρχεται are 7/2/3 but I find five in Luke: Mt. 10.23 QD/M; 11.19 QC; 16.28 R; 20.28 MK; 24.30 MK; 24.44 QC; 25.31 M; Mk 10.45; 13.26; Lk. 7.34 QC; 21.27 MK; 12.40 QC; 18.8 L; 19.10 L; cf. Mk 8.38 // Mt. 16.27 // Lk. 9.26. Goulder also lists 'theological ἦλθον' (9/3/4), but this designation is a little vague and many of the occurrences are open to different interpretations. Two further expressions might be added to the semi-Matthean list: πορευθείς (pleonastic) + finite verb (11.4 // Lk. 7.22, Davies-Allison, *Matthew*, p. 83; but cf. Fitzmyer, *Luke I–IX*, p. 115) and γεννητοῖς γυναικῶν (11.11 // Lk. 7.28), genitive + substantive verbal adjective of agent with the passive (Davies-Allison, *Matthew*, p. 84).

99. ἀπαγγέλλω does not appear on Goulder's *LNP* list but is on his *MLM* list because of Mt. 12.8 R (probably a misprint for 12.18 R) and 28.8 R (actually a MA with Lk. 24.9).

100. νόμος is not on Goulder's *LNP* list but is on the *MLM* list because of redactional occurrences at Mt. 12.5 and 22.36. Mt. 22.40 would be a better R example as 22.36, ἐν τῷ νόμῳ, is a MA/Q agreement with Lk. 10.26. There are no R or QD examples in Luke.

101. Goulder lists 'τελώνης, approvingly' (or *LNP*, pp. 396-97, 'τελώνης, friendly') as 6/2/10 which withdraws Mt. 5.46 and 18.17 from the list, both clearly negative. My Markan figure is 3, Mk 2.15 and 2.16 × 2; Goulder is probably not counting one of the occurrences in Mk 2.16 which, however, N-A[26] (and Greeven) does read. Goulder's 'approvingly' really applies only to Jesus's speech since statements like 'Why does he eat with tax collectors and sinners?' are included in the 6/2/10 figures.

Luke's supposed changes to Matthew, the methodological problem whereby Goulder is assuming his own thesis rather than attempting to prove it. He says that 'in almost every respect the Lukan version is seen to be secondary' (*MLM*, p. 359) but this cannot be shown from analysis of the QC words.

32. *Woes on the Cities of Galilee: Matthew 11.20-24 // Luke 10.12-15*
One Matthean word qualifies as characteristic according to the Hawkins criteria: κρίσις (12/0/4). One Lukan word qualifies: πλήν (5/1/15+4, Lk. 22.22 R).

The semi-Matthean words are: εἰ (35/13/31, Mt. 8.31 R); δύναμις = miracle (6/3/2+3, Mt. 7.22 QD);[102] ἄν (40/20/32, Mt. 15.5 R); ἔσται /ἔσονται × 2 (38/10/33, Mt. 19.27 R); ἕως as prep. × 2 (LXX; 28/10/13, Mt. 22.26 R; cf. ἕως, 48/15/28, Mt. 17.9 R); οὐρανός (LXX; 82/18/34, Mt. 28.2 R); λέγω ὑμῖν ὅτι (21/4/12) and Σόδομα (3/0/2).

The semi-Lukan words are: γίνομαι × 2 (75/55/129+124, Lk. 20.14 R; 20.16 R); μετανοέω (5/2/9+5, Lk. 15.7 QD; 17.3 QD)[103] and ἡμέρα (45/27/83+94, Lk. 4.42 R; 5.17 R).

Since there are several more semi-Matthean words than there are semi-Lukan ones, the evidence might seem to be in Goulder's favour. However, there is only the one word strongly characteristic of Matthew and alongside this there is one strongly characteristic of Luke.

33. *Thanksgiving: Matthew 11.25-27 // Luke 10.21-22*
There are two words/phrases here which are characteristic of Matthew according to Hawkins's criteria: οὐρανός/γῆ (14/2/5, cf. οὐρανός, 82/18/34, Mt. 28.2 R; γῆ, 43/19/25 and ἡ γῆ = the world: 22/6/14+14, Mt. 6.10 QD)[104] and ὁ πατήρ μου (16/0/4, Mt. 12.50 R).[105]

---

102. Goulder gives figures of 7/3/2 but I find only six in Matthew: Mt. 7.22 QD; 11.20 QD; 11.21 QC; 11.23 QD; 13.54 MK; 13.58 MK; Mk 6.2, 5; 9.39; Lk. 10.13 QC; 19.37 R; Acts 2.22; 8.13; 19.11.

103. Goulder gives 17.2 as QD, an error for 17.3.

104. See p. 72 n. 112, below.

105. ὁ πατήρ μου is not in the *MLM* list but appears in the text of *LNP*, p. 480. Davies-Allison, *Matthew*, also give figures of 16/0/4. Oddly, Hawkins does not list this phrase though he has ὁ πατὴρ ἡμῶν, ὑμῶν, σου, αὐτῶν with figures 20/1/3 (listed in *Horae*, p. 31). Goulder in *MLM* has these figures of 20/1/3 for 'πατὴρ ἡμῶν, etc., ὁ' but he gives 26.29 as R, an example of ὁ πατὴρ μου, not included in Hawkins's 20/1/3 figures. Luz gives figures of 34/2/7 for 'πατὴρ, μου, ὑμῶν' but I cannot work out how he arrives at these. This is a breakdown of the occurrences:

There is one Lukan word which satisfies the Hawkins criteria: πάτερ abs. (1/0/9, Lk. 22.42 R; 23.46 R).[106]

The semi-Matthean words are: κύριε (29/1/28, Mt. 8.25 R); ναί (9/1/4, Mt. 9.28 R); οὕτως (32/10/21, Mt. 19.8 R); ἔμπροσθέν (18/2/10, Mt. 27.11 R) and εἰ × 2 (35/13/31, Mt. 8.31 R).

Semi-Lukan are: εἶπον (182/84/294+124, 8.4 R; 9.49 R); ταῦτα abs. (25/15/55+37, Lk. 19.28 R; 23.49 R) and γίνομαι (75/55/129+124, Lk. 20.14 R; 20.16 R).

There are several more semi-Matthean words and phrases than there are semi-Lukan words and phrases and there are two words strongly characteristic of Matthew against one strongly characteristic of Luke. However, the Lukan word, πάτερ abs. (1/0/9), is particularly striking as it occurs only here in Matthew. It is a word readily recognisable as Lukan, occurring in his version of the Lord's Prayer (11.2 QD) and his version of the Gethsemane prayer (22.42 R) as well as twice in Jesus' prayers on the cross (23.34 L, 'Father forgive them...', 23.46 L, 'Father into your hands...') Further, it is markedly un-Matthean—he prefers πάτερ with the genitive (3/0/0) which he has in his versions of the prayers of Jesus: the Lord's Prayer, Mt. 6.9 QD, and twice in the Gethsemane prayer, Mt. 26.39 R; 26.42 R. This point is quite strongly against Goulder's thesis.

34. *Beelzebul Controversy: Matthew 12.22-37 // Luke 11.14-23; 6.45 and 12.10 (// Mark 3.22-30; Matthew 9.32-34)*

There are two words/phrases characteristic of Matthew according to the

---

ὁ πατὴρ ὑμῶν: Mt. 5.16, 45, 48; 6.1, 8, 14, 15, 26, 32; 7.11; 10.20, 29; 23.9; Mk 11.25; Lk. 6.36; 12.30, 32 (13/1/3); ὁ πατὴρ σου: Mt. 6.4; 6.6 × 2; 6.18 × 2 (5/0/0); ὁ πατὴρ ἡμῶν: Mt. 6.9 (1/0/0); ὁ πατὴρ αὐτῶν: Mt. 13.43 (1/0/0); ὁ πατὴρ μου: Mt. 7.21; 10.32, 33; 11.27; 12.50; 15.13; 16.17; 18.10, 19, 35; 20.23; 25.34; 26.29, 39, 42, 53; Lk. 2.49; 10.22; 22.29; 24.49 (16/0/4); the Son of Man and ὁ πατὴρ αὐτοῦ: Mt. 16.27 // Mk 8.38, cf. Lk. 9.26 (1/1/0).

106. In Goulder's list, πάτερ abs. is 0/0/7 (*LNP*, p. 805, cf. p. 765) but in *LNP*, p. 496 it is 1/0/8, taking into account this QC occurrence. But these figures do not take into account Lk. 23.34 on which the MS evidence is divided (it is bracketed by N-A[26]; Goulder does read it, *LNP*, p. 765). Including Lk. 23.34, the figures are 1/0/9: here (Mt. 11.25 // Lk. 10.21); Lk. 11.2 QD; 15.12 L; 15.18 L; 15.21 L (these all the Prodigal Son); 16.27 L (of Abraham); 22.42 R (Mark αββα ὁ πατήρ, Matthew πάτερ μου); 23.34 L; 23.46 L. πάτερ overall (i.e. including cases with the genitive and with names) is 4/0/11. πάτερ overall of God is 4/0/5. πάτερ abs. of God is 1/0/5.

Hawkins criteria: ἀγαθὸς/πονηρός (10/0/4, Mt. 5.45 QD; 7.17 QD) and συνάγω (24/5/6+12, Mt. 27.27 R).

There are two words/phrases characteristic of Luke according to the Hawkins criteria: κριτής (3/0/6+4) and ἐφ᾽ ὑμᾶς (2/1/7+2, Lk. 10.9 QD; 21.12 QD).

The semi-Matthean words are: κωφός (7/3/4);[107] οἱ ὄχλοι (33/2/15, Mt. 9.8 R); εἰ × 2 (35/13/31, Mt. 8.31 R); διὰ τοῦτο (11/2/4, Mt. 13.13 R); ἔσται/ἔσονται (38/10/33, Mt. 19.27 R); ἄρα (7/2/6, Mt. 18.1 R); ἀφίημι = forgive × 2 (17/8/15, Mt. 12.31 R);[108] θησαυρός (9/1/4); πονηρός × 3 (26/2/13, Mt. 9.4 R); περισσεύω (5/1/4, Mt. 13.12 R)[109] and στόμα (11/0/9, Mt. 15.11 R).[110]

The semi-Lukan words are: δαιμόνιον × 3 (11/11/23+1, Lk. 4.33 R; 4.35 R); θαυμάζω (7/4/13+5, Lk. 9.43 R); εἶπον × 2 (182/84/294+124, Lk. 8.4 R; 9.49 R); θεός anarthrous (6/2/10+3, Lk. 3.2 R; cf. θεός: 51/48/122+166, Lk. 6.12 R; 9.43 R); θεός (in addition to θεός anarthrous); ὤν (5/7/15+32, Lk. 20.36 R; 24.6 R) and μή + part. × 2 (16/4/24+12, Lk. 9.33 R; 7.30 QD).

Goulder says:

> The weakness with the QD words is not so damaging as with the QC words, where Matthean authorship looks so plausible (*LNP*, p. 507).

This overestimates the evidence for Matthew's authorship on the basis of vocabulary. There are two Lukan words/phrases which satisfy Hawkins's criteria just as there are two Matthean words/phrases. There are more semi-Matthean words/phrases than there are semi-Lukan ones but it is not many more. The distribution of characteristic words differs, moreover, with a greater concentration of Matthean words in Mt. 12.35 // Lk. 6.45 than in the rest of the material.

The difficulty in methodology is that Goulder has searched the QC words for characteristic Matthew and the QD words for characteristic

---

107. Mt. 12.22 and 9.32 // Lk. 11.14.

108. Mt. 12.32 // Lk. 12.10. For the first occurrence cf. ἀφίημι in Mk 3.28 // Mt. 12.31, not in Luke. For the second occurrence cf. ἔχει ἄφεσιν in the parallel Mk 3.29.

109. Goulder gives Mt. 14.20 as R, but this is a MA with Lk. 9.17. 13.12 is a clearer instance.

110. These last four words are all in Mt. 12.35 // Lk. 6.45 and there are no words characteristic of Luke here. Cf. ἀγαθὸς/πονηρός listed above is here too.

Luke. To search the QC words for Lukan vocabulary provides a reliable control here.

35. *Sign of Jonah: Matthew 12.38-42 // Luke 11.16, 29-32 (cf. Matthew 16.1-2, 4; Mark 8.11-12)*

There are two words/phrases, one occurring twice, characteristic of Matthew according to Hawkins's criteria: κρίσις × 2 (12/0/4+1) and ἄνθρωπος / ἀνήρ + noun (7/0/3, Mt. 21.33 R). The latter phrase (ἄνδρες Νινευῖται) is a little uncertain as a word strongly characteristic of Matthew, however, because ἀνήρ + noun is 1/0/3, none of the six occurrences of ἄνθρωπος + noun in Matthew are plural and ἀνήρ is a word strongly characteristic of Luke.

ἀνήρ is the one word characteristic of Luke according to the Hawkins criteria (8/4/27+100, Lk. 5.12 R; 5.18 R).

The semi-Matthean words are: πονηρός (26/2/13, Mt. 9.4 R); εἰ (35/13/31, Mt. 8.31 R; Ἰωνᾶς × 4 (5/0/4); οὕτως εἶναι (13/4/4);[111] ἔσται/ἔσονται (30/10/33, Mt. 19.27 R); ἰδού × 2 (62/17/57, Mt. 28.2 R); ἐγείρομαι (30/10/14, Mt. 9.25 R); γῆ (43/19/25; cf. ἡ γῆ = the world: 22/6/14+14, Mt. 6.10 QD);[112] Σολομών × 2 (5/0/3) and ἦλθον + inf. of purpose (11/4/7, Mt. 28.1 R).[113]

---

111. οὕτως εἶναι is listed by Goulder as 12/2/2 in *MLM* and 13/2/3 in *LNP*, p. 514, but I count four occurrences in Mark, 4.26; 7.18; 10.43 and 14.59 and four in Luke, 11.30; 15.7; 17.24 and 17.26.

112. ἡ γῆ = the world does not appear in the *MLM* list but Goulder gives figures of 22/4/14+10, Mt. 6.10 R; 16.19 R in *LNP*, p. 514. My figures comprise: Mt. 5.5 M; 5.13 R/QD; 5.18 QC; 5.35 M; 6.10 QD; 6.19 QD; 9.6 MK; 10.34 QC; 11.25 QC; 12.40 QD; 12.42 QC; 16.19 M × 2; 17.25 M; 18.18 M × 2; 18.19 M; 23.9 M; 24.30 R; 24.35 MK; 27.45 MK; 28.18 M; Mk 2.10; 4.31; 9.3; 13.27, 31; 15.33; Lk. 2.14 L; 5.24 MK; 10.21 QC; 11.31 QC; 12.49 L; 12.51 QC; 12.56 QD; 16.17 QC; 18.8 L; 21.23 R; 21.25 R; 21.33 MK; 21.35 L; 23.44 MK; Acts 1.8; 2.19; 3.25; 4.24, 26; 8.33; 10.11, 12; 11.6; 13.47; 14.15; 17.24, 26; 22.22. Goulder's Mt.6.10 R should read 6.10 QD. Included in these figures is Mt. 27.45 // Mk 15.33 // Lk. 23.44, darkness coming over either 'the earth' or 'the land'. Not included is Mt. 23.35 QD, 'all the righteous blood shed on earth'.

113. ἦλθον + infinitive of purpose does not appear in the *MLM* list but Goulder gives figures of 11/4/6 in *LNP*, p. 514. Goulder lists occurrences in Matthew but 8.29 should read R, not MK. I also find four in Mark, but seven in Luke: Mk 1.24; 2.17; 5.14; 10.45; Lk. 1.59 L; 3.12 L; 4.34 MK; 6.18 R; 11.31 QC; 12.49 L; 19.10 L. Also cf. Mk 15.36 (ἔρχεται), Lk. 5.32 (ἐλήλυθα) and Lk. 8.35 (ἐξῆλθον). It is + 0 (Acts). Cf. Luz gives figures for ἔρχομαι + infinitive of purpose of 12/5/8.

Semi-Lukan are: μετανοέω (5/2/9+5, Lk. 15.7 QD; 17.3 QD) and σοφία (3/1/6+4, Lk. 21.15 R; 11.49 QD).

With just one word strongly characteristic of Luke and two semi-Lukan words, the evidence is in Goulder's favour. There are a good few semi-Matthean words and at least one word is strongly characteristic of Matthew.

36. *Return of the Evil Spirit: Matthew 12.43-45 // Luke 11.24-26*
Three words/phrases are characteristic of Matthew according to Hawkins's criteria: ὅθεν (4/0/1); τότε (90/6/14, Mt. 9.6 R)[114] and κατοικέω (4/0/2, Mt. 4.13 R).

There are three words/phrases characteristic of Luke according to Hawkins's criteria: ἐξέρχομαι ἀπό (5/1/13+3, Lk. 4.35 R; 4.41 R);[115] διέρχομαι (1/2/10+21, Lk. 5.15 R; 9.6 R) and ἕτερος (9/1/33+17, Lk. 3.18 R; 4.43 R).

The semi-Matthean words are: διά + gen. (26/11/13, Mt. 3.3 R); ἐλθών, -όντες (30/11/11, Mt. 4.13 R; cf. ἐλθών immediately before a verb, 14/5/4+1, Mt. 4.13 R; 9.10 R);[116] παραλαμβάνω (16/6/6, Mt. 27.27 R); πονηρός (26/2/13, Mt. 9.4 R); ἐκεῖ (28/11/16, Mt. 14.23 R); ἔσχατος (10/5/6+3) and ἐκεῖνος (54/23/33, Mt. 14.1 R).

The semi-Lukan words are: ζητέω (14/10/25+10, Lk. 5.18 R; 6.19 R); εὑρίσκω × 2 (27/11/45+35, Lk. 5.19 R; 6.7 R); εἰς τὸν οἶκον + gen. (4/6/15+5, Lk. 8.41 R;[117] cf. οἶκος: 10/12/33+25, Lk. 7.10 QD; 10.5 QD); πορεύομαι (29/0/51+37, Lk. 4.42 R; 5.24 R); ἑαυτόν (32/24/58 +22, Lk. 9.47 R; 20.20 R) and γίνομαι (75/55/129+124, Lk. 20.14 R; 20.16 R).

---

114. There are possibly two occurrences of τότε, but the reading in Lk. 11.24 is uncertain—N-A[26] places it in square brackets and it is not read by Greeven.

115. The occurrences of ἐξέρχομαι ἀπό are: Mt. 12.43 QC; 15.22 R; 17.18 R; 24.1 R; 24.27 QD; Mk 11.12; Lk. 4.35 × 2 R; 4.41 R; 5.8 L; 8.2 L; 8.29 R; 8.33 R; 8.35 R; 8.38 R; 8.46 R; 9.5 R/QD; 11.24 QC; 17.29 L. Goulder gives + 1 for Acts but I find 3: Acts 16.18, 40; 28.3.

116. Goulder's figures for ἐλθών immediately before a verb are 16/5/3 (not on the *MLM* list but in *LNP*, p. 507). I find, however, 14/5/4+1: Mt. 2.8 M; 2.9 M; 2.23 M; 4.13 R; 5.24 M; 8.7 QD; 9.10 R; 9.18 MK; 9.18 R; 12.44 QC; 14.12 R; 15.25 MK; 18.31 M; 28.13 M; Mk 5.23; 7.25; 12.14; 14.40; 16.1; Lk. 5.7 L; 7.3 QD; 11.25 QC; 15.17 L; Acts 16.39. Cf. Lk. 10.32; 13.14; 15.25; 16.21; 18.5.

117. Goulder also gives 5.28 as R. This is an error either for 5.25 or 5.29, but 5.29 is ἐν τῇ οἰκίᾳ αὐτοῦ (not εἰς)—and is in Mk 5.15 in any case—and 5.25 is a MA with Mt. 9.7. See further below, p. 155.

The even balance of words strongly characteristic of Matthew and of words strongly characteristic of Luke, as well as of words semi-Matthean and semi-Lukan, means that the evidence here does not support Goulder. Among the strongly characteristic words there is one word which is un-Matthean, διέρχομαι (1/2/10+21) and one which is un-Lukan, ὅθεν (4/0/1).

37. *Blessedness of the Disciples: Matthew 13.16-17 // Luke 10.23-24*
There are no words characteristic of either evangelist according to the Hawkins criteria.

There are two semi-Matthean words: ὀφθαλμός (24/7/17, Mt. 17.8 R) and λέγω ὑμῖν ὅτι (21/4/12).

There are no semi-Lukan words.

38. *Mustard Seed: Matthew 13.31-32 // Luke 13.18-19 (// Mark 4.30-32)*
There is one word/phrase which satisfies Hawkins's criteria and it is Matthean: ὁμοία ἐστίν (7/0/3, Mt. 11.16 QD).[118]

There are two semi-Matthean words: λαβών (22/7/8, Mt. 27.48 R;[119] cf. λαμβάνω, 57/21/22, Mt. 16.7 R) and δένδρον (12/1/7, Mt. 21.8 R).

There is one semi-Lukan word: αὐξάνω (2/1/4+4).

The evidence here is in Goulder's favour.

39. *Leaven: Matthew 13.33 // Luke 13.20-21*
There are two words/phrases which satisfy Hawkins's criteria, and they are both Matthean: ὁμοία ἐστίν (7/0/3, Mt. 11.16 QD) and ἕως + ind. (4/0/1+1, Mt. 24.39 QD; cf. ἕως, 48/15/28, Mt. 17.9 R).[120]

---

118. Goulder's figures for ὁμοία ἐστίν are 8/0/3 but I find only seven occurrences in Matthew, Mt. 11.16 QD; 13.31 QC; 13.33 QC; 13.44 M; 13.45 M; 13.47 M; 20.1 M; Lk. 13.18 QD; 13.19 QC; 13.21 QC. Goulder gives the QC occurrence in Mt. 13.31 as R.

119. Goulder gives 13.31, this verse, as a redactional instance of λαβών, a QC word in a Mark-Q overlap passage. Better examples are 27.48 R and 27.59 R. Cf. Davies and Allison, *Matthew*, p. 83: λαμβάνω as auxilliary is in the list of Semitisms in Matthew.

120. Goulder gives figures for ἕως + indicative of 4/0/2 in the *MLM* list yet he says on p. 370, 'Significantly, Luke has ἕως + indicative here alone' and similarly *LNP*, p. 569, 'ἕως (οὗ) is normally found with the subjunctive in the Gospels: the only other exceptions are at Mt. 1.25 ἕως οὗ ἔτεκεν υἱόν, 2.9 and 24.39 QD'. One could add Mt. 5.25 and Mk 6.45 to the list though here ἕως = while. ἕως +

There are two semi-Matthean words: ζύμη (4/2/2) and λαβών (22/7/8, Mt. 27.48 R; cf. λαμβάνω, 57/21/22, Mt. 16.7 R).
There are no semi-Lukan words.
The evidence here is in Goulder's favour.

40. *Sign in the Heavens: Matthew 16.2-3 // Luke 12.54-56*[121]
There are no words characteristic of either evangelist according to the Hawkins criteria.
There is one semi-Matthean word: ούρανός (82/18/34, Mt. 28.2 R).
There are no semi-Lukan words.

41. *Leaven of the Pharisees: Matthew 16.6 // Luke 12.1 (cf. Mark 8.14-21 // Matthew 16.5-12)*
There are no words characteristic of either evangelist according to the Hawkins criteria.
There is one semi-Matthean word: προσέχω (6/0/4, Mt. 10.17 R).[122]
There are no semi-Lukan words.

42. *Faith, Mountain and Mustard Seed: Matthew 17.20 // Luke 17.6 (// Mark 11.22-23 // Matthew 21.21)*
There are no words which are characteristic of either evangelist according to either Hawkins's or Goulder's criteria.

43. *About Offences: Matthew 18.6-7 // Luke 17.1-2*
There are two words/phrases which satisfy Hawkins's criteria and they are both Matthean: εἷς τούτων (7/1/2, Mt. 10.42 R; 18.14 QD) and σκάνδαλον (5/0/1, Mt. 16.23 R).[123]
There are no semi-Matthean or semi-Lukan words or phrases.
Here the evidence is in Goulder's favour.

indicative is also found in Acts 21.26. Cf. Luz, *Matthew 1–7*, ἕως conjunction 20/5/15; ἕως οὗ 7/0/7.
121. Mt. 16.2b-3 is textually uncertain, placed in square brackets in N-A[26]. Goulder says that he was inclined to omit it in *MLM* (p. 381) but argues in its favour, partly on linguistic grounds, in *LNP*, p. 557.
122. This is parallel to Mark's βλέπω (Mk 8.15). Matthew has προσέχω again in v. 11. Note also that Luke has προσέχετε ἑαυτοῖς, 0/0/3+2, here QD.
123. σκάνδαλον occurs three times (of its five) in Matthew here, and perhaps for this reason Goulder does not give the word an asterisk on his list. He gives this verse (18.7) as R, but although it comes in a Markan context (Mt. 18.6-9 // Mk 9.42-48), the Q element complicates the matter and Mt. 16.23 is a clearer R example.

44. *The Lost Sheep: Matthew 18.10-14 // Luke 15.3-7*
One word satisfies the Hawkins criteria for Matthew: πρόβατον (11/2/2, Mt. 15.24 R).

There is one word which satisfies Hawkins's criteria also for Luke: χαίρω = rejoice (3/1/11+5, Lk. 19.37 R).

There is one semi-Matthean word: οὐρανός (82/18/34, Mt. 28.2 R).

There are two semi-Lukan words: πορεύομαι (29/0/51+37, Lk. 4.42 R; 5.24 R) and εὑρίσκω (27/11/45+35, Lk. 5.19 R; 6.7 R).

The evidence here runs against Goulder's thesis since there is more characteristic Luke than there is characteristic Matthew, and, in particular, there is the one word strongly characteristic of Luke alongside the one strongly characteristic of Matthew.

45. *Reproving and Reconciling: Matthew 18.15, 21-22 // Luke 17.3-4*
There is one word here which satisfies Hawkins's criteria, and it is Matthean: ἀδελφός in a transferred sense (15/0/6, Mt. 28.10 R; 5.47 QD).

There is one semi-Matthean word: ἀφίημι = forgive (17/8/15+1, Mt. 12.31 R).

There are no semi-Lukan words.

The evidence here is in favour of Goulder's thesis.

46. *Twelve on Thrones: Matthew 19.28 // Luke 22.28-30*
There are no words which satisfy Hawkins's criteria.

There is one semi-Matthean word: θρόνος (5/0/3+2).[124]

There are no semi-Lukan words.

47. *First and Last: Matthew 20.16 // Luke 13.30 (cf. Matthew 19.30 // Mark 10.31)*[125]
There are no words which satisfy Hawkins's criteria.

There are two semi-Matthean words, one occurring twice: ἔσχατος × 2 (10/5/6+3) and ἔσται / ἔσονται (38/10/33, Mt. 19.27 R).

There are no semi-Lukan words.

---

124. Goulder gives this verse (Mt. 19.28) as a redactional example of θρόνος—it comes once again in the verse in addition to this QC occurrence.

125. Although Luke's only parallel to Mk 10.31 is here (Lk. 13.30), I have counted it as a Q passage on the basis of context.

48. *Parable of the Great Supper: Matthew 22.1-10 // Luke 14.15-24*
There are no words which satisfy Hawkins's criteria.

There are three semi-Matthean words: δοῦλος (30/5/26+3, Mt. 21.35 R), ἕτοιμος (4/1/3+2, Mt. 22.8 QD) and ἀγρός (16/8/9+1, Mt. 24.40 QD).[126]

There is one semi-Lukan word: καλέω × 2 (26/4/43+18, Lk. 19.29 R; 21.37 R).

49. *Discourse against the Scribes and the Pharisees: Matthew 23.1-36 // Luke 11.39-52; 14.11; 18.14; 22.26 (// Mark 12.37b-40 // Luke 20.45-47; cf. Matthew 18.4)*
There are four words/phrases which for Matthew satisfy the Hawkins criteria: φιλέω = love (not kiss) (4/0/1, Mt. 10.37 QD; cf. φιλέω 5/1/2);[127] κρίσις (12/0/4); ἀπό... ἕως (8/1/1+3, Mt. 27.45 R) and θυσιαστήριον (6/0/2).

There are also four words/phrases which for Luke satisfy the Hawkins criteria: ἀσπασμός (1/1/5); A καὶ-μή non-A (3/0/8+5;[128] cf. κἀκεῖνος, 2/2/4+3, Lk. 22.12 R); ἔδει (3/0/6+4, Lk. 22.7 R; cf. δεῖ, 8/6/18+22, Lk. 4.43 R) and οἱ πατέρες ἡμῶν/ὑμῶν (2/0/7+18, Lk. 6.23 QD; 11.47 QD).

Semi-Matthean are: μείζων (10/3/7, Mt. 20.31 R),[129] καθαρός (3/0/1, Mt. 27.59 R), διὰ τοῦτο (11/2/4, Mt. 13.13 R) and αἷμα = life taken × 3 (10/1/5, Mt. 27.24 R).[130]

---

126. Goulder's figures for ἀγρός are 16/7/9; cf. Luz, *Matthew 1–7*: 17/9/10 and Gundry, *Matthew*, and Davies-Allison, *Matthew*: 17/9/9. I agree with Goulder's 16 figure for Matthew and 9 for Luke but find 8 in Mark: 5.14; 6.36, 56; 10.29, 30; 11.8; 13.16; 15.21. Luz, Davies-Allison and Gundry's count of 9 no doubt includes Mk 16.12.

127. φιλέω = love is not on Goulder's list, but he refers to it in *LNP*, p. 701, on Lk. 20.46 where it occurs in parallel to Mt. 23.6. 11.43 QD, also parallel, has ἀγαπάω.

128. Goulder's figures for A καὶ-μή non-A are 2/0/6. The six occurrences in Luke are probably taken as 1.20 (*LNP*, p. 220), 11.42 (p. 526), 12.21 (p. 539), 13.11 and 13.14 (p. 570, cf. p. 565) and 18.1 (p. 662). However, 14.29 provides another possible example (cf. *LNP*, p. 597) and 18.16 another certain example. The latter is a MA with Mt. 19.14 and there are two other examples in Matthew, 1.19 and 23.23. There are five in Acts, 1.20 (LXX); 12.19; 15.38; 18.9 and 27.15. Goulder gives Lk. 12.21 as QD but this is really L.

129. Mt. 23.11 // Lk. 22.26.

130. αἷμα = life taken: Mt. 23.30, 35 × 3; 26.28; 27.4, 6, 8, 24, 25; Mk 14.24; Lk. 11.50, 51 × 2; 13.1; 22.20.

Semi-Lukan are: δάκτυλος (1/1/3, Lk. 11.20 QD); ἑαυτόν (32/24/58 +22, Lk. 9.47 QD; 20.20 R);[131] ταῦτα abs. (25/15/55+37, Lk. 19.28 R; 23.49 R); καί = also (60/36/124+91, Lk. 4.41 R; 5.33 R)[132] and οἰκοδομέω (8/4/12+4, Lk. 7.5 QD; 17.28 QD).

This evidence stands against Goulder's thesis. He says: 'With a limited amount of QC words, the Mattheanisms are limited' (*LNP*, p. 525) but among the limited number of QC words, there are as many words and phrases (four) strongly characteristic of Luke as there are of Matthew. One of the words, ἀσπασμός (1/1/5+0), is also un-Matthean. Moreover, there are as many semi-Lukan words as there are semi-Matthean ones.

50. *Lament over Jerusalem: Matthew 23.37-39 // Luke 13.34-35*
There are no words characteristic of Matthew according to the Hawkins criteria, but there are two words characteristic of Luke, one occurring twice: Ἰερουσαλημ × 2 (2/0/27+36, Lk. 5.17 R; 6.17 R) and ἀποστέλλομαι, pass. (2/0/5+4, Lk. 4.43 R; 19.32 R).[133]

There are two semi-Matthean words: ἰδού (62/17/57, Mt. 28.2 R) and ἕως (48/15/28, Mt. 17.9 R).

Semi-Lukan are: οἶκος (10/12/33+25, Lk. 7.10 QD; 10.5 QD); εἶπον (182/84/294+124, Lk. 8.4 R; 9.49 R); εὐλογέω (5/5/13+2, Lk. 6.28 QD) and ὄνομα (22/15/34+60, Lk. 5.27 R; 23.50 R).[134]

The analysis of the characteristic vocabulary in the QC words here is markedly against Goulder's thesis. There are no words characteristic of Matthew according to the Hawkins criteria while there are two characteristic of Luke and Ἰερουσαλημ Ἰερουσαλημ is striking. Matthew on every other occasion has the spelling Ἰεροσόλυμα[135]

---

131. Mt. 23.12 // Lk. 14.11 // Lk. 18.14, cf. Mt. 18.4.

132. Mt. 23.26: καὶ τὸ ἐκτός // Lk. 11.40: καὶ τὸ ἔσωθεν.

133. ἀποστέλλομαι pass.: Mt. 15.24 R; 23.37 QC; Lk. 1.19 L; 1.26 L; 4.43 R; 13.34 QC; 19.32 R; Acts 10.17; 11.11; 15.33; 28.28.

134. The dative ὀνόματι which occurs here is given in the *LNP* list as 1/1/7+22 but '= by name' is missing (cf. Hawkins, *Horae*, p. 44). Goulder's *LNP* list also features 'κύριος anarth = God', but I am not sure how Goulder reaches the figures of 18/4/15+11—there are many more than this. *LNP*, p. 580, on this passage, presents some oddities: Ἰερουσαλημ, ἀποστέλλομαι pass., εἶπον and εὐλογέω are all missing from the list of characteristic words for 13.34-35 and οἶκος and ὄνομα, which are listed, should be in brackets since they are QC.

135. BAGD (p. 373) notes that Ἰεροσόλυμα is the form always found in

(11/10/4+23) and further, the doubled vocative is characteristic of Luke, 8.24 R 'Master Master', 10.41 L 'Martha Martha', 22.31 R 'Simon Simon', Acts 9.4, 22.7, 26.14 'Saul Saul'.[136] The only occurrence in Mark is at 14.45, 'Rabbi Rabbi' (Matthew and Luke different) and in Matthew 'Lord Lord' comes three times (Mt. 7.21 // Lk. 6.46; Mt. 7.22; 25.11).

Goulder says:

> The doubled Jerusalem is a rabbinic device...or in Matthew, 'Yea, Yea,
> Nay, Nay', 'Not everyone who says to me, Lord, Lord' (*MLM*, p. 429).

Goulder does not, however, note that the doubled vocative is characteristic of Luke. In *LNP* (p. 579), where Goulder even says that 'we may notice the usual Matthean features', the doubled vocative is explained by reference to Mt. 4.15, 'Land of Zabulon and land of Naphtali', imposed by Matthew on the text of Isa. 8.23, and he refers also to 2.6, 'And thou, Bethlehem, land of Judah'. Neither text, however, provides an exact parallel for the repeated 'Jerusalem'; the clause 'land of Naphtali' poetically qualifies 'land of Zabulon', just as 'Land of Judah' adds to 'Bethlehem'. Goulder also refers to 2.6 to explain the spelling Ἰερουσαλημ:

> The Semitic Judah is preferred to the normal Judea as Ἰερουσαλημ is
> here to Ἰεροσόλυμα (*LNP*, p. 579).

Mt. 2.6, however, is a quotation from Mic. 5.2 and although γῆ Ἰούδα is Matthew's redactional insertion, it is unlikely that he would have used the spelling 'Judea' when 'Judah' appears in the next clause (οὐδαμῶς ἐλαχίστη εἶ ἐν τοῖς ἡγεμόσιν Ἰούδα).[137]

51. *Days of the Son of Man: Matthew 24.26-28 // Luke 17.23-24, 37*
There is one word which is characteristic of Matthew according to Hawkins's criteria: ὥσπερ (10/0/2, Mt. 20.28 R).

There are no words which for Luke satisfy Hawkins's criteria.

There are three semi-Matthean words/phrases: ἰδού × 2 (62/17/57,

---

Matthew, adding that 'the sole exception 23.37 is obviously from a quotation'. In *LNP*, p. 17, the figures for Ἰεροσόλυμα are given as 11/0/4, a printing error. Cf. I. de la Potterie, 'Les deux noms'; J. Jeremias, 'ΙΕΡΟΥΣΑΛΗΜ'; D.D. Sylva, '*Ierousalem*' and R. Schütz, ''Ιερουσαλημ'.

136. Cf. Cadbury, *Making*, p. 218.

137. It is perhaps worth adding that Luke here has Ἰερουσαλημ three times together since Ἰερουσαλημ is the last word in 13.33.

Mt. 28.2 R); οὕτως εἶναι (13/4/4; cf. οὕτως, 32/10/21, Mt. 19.8 R) and ἐκεῖ (28/11/16, Mt. 14.23 R).

There are no semi-Lukan words.

The analysis of characteristic vocabulary here provides no problems for Goulder's thesis.

52. *Unexpected Judgment: Matthew 24.37-41 // Luke 17.26-27, 34-35*

There are no words which are characteristic of Matthew according to Hawkins's criteria.

There are two words/phrases which for Luke satisfy Hawkins's criteria: ἄχρι (1/0/4+15, Lk. 21.24 R) and ὅς in attraction (4/1/16+25, Lk. 3.19 R; 9.36 R).[138]

Semi-Matthean are: οὕτως εἶναι (13/4/4; cf. οὕτως, 32/10/21, Mt. 19.8 R); ἔσται/ἔσονται (38/10/33, Mt. 19.27 R); δύο × 2 (40/19/28, Mt. 22.40 R) and παραλαμβάνω × 2 (16/6/6, Mt. 27.27 R).

Semi-Lukan is: ἡμέρα × 2 (45/27/83+94, Lk. 4.42 R; 5.17 R).

Although there are more semi-Matthean words than there are semi-Lukan words, the analysis here does not lend support to Goulder; there are two words strongly characteristic of Luke while there are not any strongly characteristic of Matthew; ἄχρι is un-Matthean.

53. *Watchfulness and Faithfulness: Matthew 24.43-51 // Luke 12.35-46*

There are two words/phrases which for Matthew satisfy the Hawkins criteria: φρόνιμος (7/0/2, Mt. 7.24 QD) and ὁ κύριος αὐτοῦ (10/0/4, Mt. 10.24 QD; 15.27 R; cf. κύριος of a man, 32/2/25 and κύριος with gen., 24/4/16).[139]

---

138. Goulder gives Hawkins's figures for ὅς in attraction of 2/1/11+23, listed by Hawkins on *Horae*, pp. 44-45. Goulder, however, 14 times (viz. *LNP*, pp. 204, 220, 255, 281, 327, 445, 451, 616, 656, 657 × 2, 688, 769 and 788) gives ὅς in attraction as characteristic of Luke, including here, 17.27, not one of Hawkins's 11. Under Hawkins's own definition, 'the only "attraction" here considered is that of the relative pronoun to a noun (expressed or understood)' (*Horae*, p. 45). I find 4/1/16+25: Mt. 18.19 M; 24.38 QC; 24.50 × 2 QC; Mk 7.13; Lk. 1.4 L; 1.20 L; 2.20 L; 3.19 R; 5.9 L; 9.36 R; 9.43 R; 12.46 × 2 QC; 15.16 L (or partitive genitive); 17.27 QC; 17.29 QD; 17.30 QD; 19.37 R; 23.41 L; 24.25 L; Acts 1.1, 2, 22; 2.22; 3.21, 25; 7.16, 17, 45; 8.24; 9.36; 10.39; 13.39; 17.31; 20.38; 21.19, 24; 22.10, 15; 24.21; 25.18; 26.2, 16, 22; 27.25. Cf. also J. M. Creed, *St Luke*, p. lxxxii and Fitzmyer, *Luke 1-IX*, p. 108.

139. For κύριος of a man, see p. 56 n. 41 above. For κύριος with genitive, see p. 64 n. 77 above. ὁ κύριος αὐτοῦ is not on the *MLM* list but is in *LNP*, p. 554,

For Luke there are several words and phrases which satisfy Hawkins's criteria: τοῦ + infinitive (7/0/26+24, Lk. 21.22 R; 22.6 R);[140] ὑπάρχω (3/0/15+25, Lk. 8.41 R; 9.48 R; cf. τὰ ὑπάρχοντα, 3/0/8+1, Lk. 8.3 R; 11.21 R/QD); ἐσθίω + πίνω (4/0/14+3, Lk. 5.30 R; 5.33 R); προσδοκάω (2/0/6+5, Lk. 3.15 R; 8.40 R) and ὅς in attraction × 2 (4/1/16+25, Lk. 3.19 R; 9.36 R).

Semi-Matthean are: ἄν (40/20/32, Mt. 15.5 R); εἰ (35/13/31, Mt. 8.31 R); οἰκοδεσπότης (7/1/4, Mt. 21.33 R); ἕτοιμος (4/1/3+2, Mt. 22.8 QD); ὁ υἱὸς τοῦ ἀνθρώπου ἔρχεται (7/2/5, Mt. 16.28 R); ἄρα (7/2/6, Mt. 18.1 R); καθίστημι × 2 (4/0/3); κύριος of a man × 4 (32/2/25, Mt. 15.27 R; cf. for three of these κύριος with gen., 24/4/16, Mt. 15.27 R);[141] δοῦλος × 3 (30/5/26, Mt. 21.35 R); ἐκεῖνος × 3 (54/23/33, Mt. 14.1 R); ἐλθών (-όντες) (30/11/11, Mt. 4.13 R); οὕτως (32/10/21, Mt. 19.8 R);[142] λέγω ὑμῖν ὅτι (21/4/12) and ἀμὴν λέγω ὑμιν (σοι) (31/13/6, Mt. 19.23 R; cf. λέγω ὑμῖν ὅτι).

Semi-Lukan are: γνῶτε / γινώσκετε—ὅτι (3/2/5+1, Lk. 21.20 R; 10.11 QD);[143] γίνομαι (75/55/129+124, Lk. 20.14 R; 20.16 R); εὑρίσκω (27/11/45+35, Lk. 5.19 R; 6.7 R);[144] ποιέω + adv. (2/3/9+2, Lk. 9.15 R; 6.27 QD); ἐπί + dative (17/16/35+25, Lk. 9.43 R; 23.38 R); εἶπον (182/84/294+124, Lk. 8.4 R; 9.49 R); τύπτω (2/1/4+5, Lk. 6.29 QD) and ἡμέρα (45/27/83+94, Lk. 4.42 R; 5.17 R).

Although there are several more semi-Matthean words than there are semi-Lukan ones, some of them occurring more than once in the

with figures of 11/0/2. I find 10/0/4: Mt. 10.24 QD; 10.25 QD; 15.27 R (τῶν κυρίων αὐτῶν); 18.32 M; 18.34 M; 24.46 QC; 25.18 QD; 25.21 QD; 25.23 QD; 25.26 QD; Lk. 12.43 QC; 12.47 L; 14.21 QD and 19.33 R (οἱ κύριοι αὐτοῦ).

140. For τοῦ + infinitive, Goulder gives Hawkins's figures of 6/0/20+18 (listed in Hawkins, *Horae*, p. 48). In my figures of 7/0/26+24, I have included examples excluded by Hawkins where τοῦ is governed by a preposition or when the genitive is dependent on the previous noun or verb (see Hawkins, *Horae*, p. 48).

141. This κύριος of a man × 4 includes the ὁ κύριος αὐτοῦ already listed among words and phrases strongly characteristic of Matthew.

142. Mt. 24.46 is paralleled in both Lk. 12.37 and Lk. 12.43. The words which occur twice in Luke, i.e. in both of these verses, but only once in Matthew, I have only counted once. They are δοῦλος, ἐκεῖνος, ἐλθών, -όντες and κύριος of a man.

143. Goulder gives figures of 2/1/4 for γνῶτε / γινώσκετε—ὅτι but I find 3/2/5+1: Mt. 24.32 // Mk 13.28 // Lk. 21.30; Mt. 24.33 // Mk 13.29 // Lk. 21.31; Mt. 24.43 // Lk. 12.39; Lk. 10.11 QD; Lk. 21.20 R; Acts 20.34. Goulder gives Lk. 21.31 as R, but the word combination is in the parallels in Mark and Matthew.

144. In Mt. 24.46 and in both Lk. 12.37 and Lk. 12.43.

passage, the strongly characteristic words and phrases are mainly Lukan, τοῦ + infinitive, τὰ ὑπάρχοντα, ἐσθίω + πίνω, προσδοκάω and ὅς in attraction. Only φρόνιμος and ὁ κύριος αὐτοῦ are strongly Matthean.[145] The evidence here is, therefore, against Goulder's hypothesis. He says in *LNP* :

> Again the QC block in vv. 42-46, and Luke's visible secondariness over most of the differences, expose the weakness of the Q theory; for so much of the language echoes Matthew elsewhere (p. 554).

This does not take into account the Lukan words among the QC words. Further, of the words Goulder lists as being characteristic of Matthew (*LNP*, p. 554; cf. *MLM*, p. 437), τρόφη (Mt. 24.45, 4/0/1) is QD and ἀμὴν λέγω ὑμῖν (Mt. 24.47) is partially QD (Luke has ἀληθῶς λέγω ὑμῖν (Lk. 12.44, contrast v. 37).

54. *Lamps Lit: Matthew 25.1-13 // Luke 12.35-36 (cf. Luke 13.25)*
One word satisfies Hawkins's criteria, and it is Matthean: γάμος (8/0/2). However, of Matthew's eight uses of this word, seven are in the same context, 22.1-12, and for this reason Hawkins brackets the word.

There are two semi-Matthean words: ἀνοίγω (11/1/7+16, Mt. 20.33 R) and κύριε (29/1/28, Mt. 8.25 R; cf. κύριος of a man, 32/2/25, Mt. 15.27 R).

There are no semi-Lukan words.

There are no problems here for Goulder's thesis.

55. *Parable of the Talents / Pounds: Matthew 25.14-30 // Luke 19.11-27*
There are no words characteristic of Matthew according to Hawkins's criteria but there are two characteristic of Luke: σύν (4/6/23+52, Lk. 5.19 R; 8.1 R) and δέκα (3/1/11+1, Lk. 19.13 QD).[146]

Semi-Matthean are: δοῦλος × 3 (30/5/26, Mt. 21.35 R); λέγων (-οντες) (142/42/96, Mt. 8.3 R); κύριε × 3 (29/1/28, Mt. 8.25 R; cf. κύριος of a man, 32/2/25, Mt. 15.27 R); πέντε × 2 (12/3/9);[147] πονηρός (26/2/13, Mt. 9.4 R) and ἐλθών (-όντες) (30/11/11, Mt. 4.13 R).

Semi-Lukan are: καλέω (26/4/43+18, Lk. 19.29 R; 21.37 R); μή +

---

145. Further, four of the seven occurrences of φρόνιμος are in the same context, Mt. 25.1-13.

146. Note, however, that six of the eleven Lukan usages of δέκα are here.

147. Mt. 25.20 × 4; Lk. 19.18-19 × 2.

part. (16/4/24+12, Lk. 9.33 R; 7.30 QD) and πᾶς pleonastic (common, Lk. 4.37 R; 5.17 R).

Although there are more semi-Matthean words and phrases than there are semi-Lukan ones, the difficulty for Goulder's thesis is the presence of two words strongly characteristic of Luke when there are none strongly characteristic of Matthew.

C. *Conclusion*

Earlier, we looked at the Preaching of John the Baptist (Mt. 3.1-12 // Lk. 3.1-9, 15-17) which forms part of Goulder's discussion of 'the Matthean vocabulary fallacy':

> Of the 89 words in John's sermon, 18 form part of Matthew's vocabu-
> lary elsewhere... That 20% of an alien text should happen by sheer
> accident to have been written in Matthew's preferred phrases would
> rather strain belief; but it may reasonably be asked if there is any
> control... The answer is that... Luke, on the same basis I have taken for
> Matthew, would have written ὁ θεός on his own. So it seems clear
> (subject always to counter-demonstration) that 20% of the phrases is
> indeed problematical (*LNP*, p. 14).

The evidence here appears more impressive than it need be. Goulder has limited this case study to characteristic phrases (though even here he misses the Lukan ὑποδεικνύμι–ὑμῖν) but an analysis of all the characteristic vocabulary in the passage gives a reasonable number of Lukan words, less than half the number of Matthean words, but still more than a handful.

More importantly, Goulder has chosen the right example. It is not always the case that the evidence goes in his favour. The other pericope about John the Baptist in Q, Mt. 11.2-19 // Lk. 7.18-35, where wording is again very close between the two evangelists, provides a good example of a pericope which has more characteristic Luke than it has characteristic Matthew. On Hawkins's criteria there are three words/ phrases characteristic of Matthew against seven characteristic of Luke and they include words which occur only here in Matthew, εὐαγγελίζομαι (1/0/10+15), προσφωνέω (1/0/4+2) and φίλος (1/0/ 15+3). On Goulder's criteria too there are more words characteristic of Luke.

It was stated at the outset that we should not be surprised to find some Lukan vocabulary. If Luke did use Matthew, one would expect him to have taken over some 'Luke-pleasing' words. But clearly to discover a large number of characteristically Lukan words and phrases among QC words would not be satisfactory for Goulder's thesis. This study has shown that there is a large number of Lukan words and phrases in Q, frequently in individual pericopae as much characteristic of Luke as there is characteristic of Matthew.

The equation Q = Matthew begins to look less certain in pericopae like the Lament over Jerusalem (Mt. 23.37-39 // Lk. 13.34-35). 'Jerusalem' occurs only here in Q, and it has the spelling Ἰερουσαλημ. Q shares this spelling with Luke (2/0/27+36), against Matthew's preferred Ἰεροσόλυμα (11/10/4+23), and, further, it is Luke among the evangelists who shows a preference for the doubled vocative. Nor are there any Matthean words on Hawkins's criteria here.

To give one more example, the study of characteristic vocabulary in the Lord's Prayer does not bear out Goulder's conclusions: on Hawkins's criteria there are indeed words characteristic of Matthew among QD words but among the QC words, the only words passing Hawkins's test are Lukan, εἰσφέρω (1/0/4+1) and πειρασμός (2/1/6+1).

One of the difficulties with this data is, however, that the 'Matthean vocabulary fallacy', as Goulder presents it, does not rest on the odd word here and the odd one there in QC. Rather, memorable Matthean phrases and formulas like 'brood of vipers', 'weeping and gnashing of teeth' and 'Ye of little faith' seem to crop up regularly in Q; memorable Lukan phrases do not: Matthean authorship of Q can look persuasive. The difficulty, though, is that memorable Lukan phrases are difficult to come by in general; Luke is a little more subtle than Matthew. Goulder himself says:

> Matthew has a somewhat stereotyped style: he uses formulas, and is fairly regular in his vocabulary, as he is also in his doctrinal tendencies. Luke, however, has a rich vocabulary, and a dismaying habit of varying his synonyms. It is therefore much easier to pick out the charac-teristically Matthean than the characteristically Lukan expression (*LNP*, p. 17).

Goulder says that the danger is 'to jump to the conclusion that in such cases Luke has the Q form, which Matthew has amended' (*LNP*, p. 17). There is an equal danger, however, that if in general it is easier to spot Mattheanisms, Lukanisms among QC words could go unnoticed and one could, on Goulder's thesis, jump to the conclusion that Matthew composed a passage and Luke amended it.

We should be placed on our guard by the fact that memorable Mattheanisms also crop up in Mark, 'your Father who is in heaven' at 11.25 and 'hypocrites' at 7.6 among them.[148] Goulder has, in any case, dissociated himself from any simple form of the argument that a characteristic phrase of one writer, when it appears in another's work, necessarily demonstrates that the latter is dependent on the former. Matthean phrases like 'you generation of vipers' which occur just once in Luke 'might just be Q phrases that Matthew liked very much'.[149]

Is, then, 'the Matthean vocabulary fallacy' not a fallacy after all? As Goulder presents it, the basis of the fallacy is that, contrary to the realization of most two source theorists, Q's vocabulary and Matthew's are actually the same. This aspect of the 'fallacy' does not stand up to scrutiny. Goulder is right, nevertheless, to criticise those who attempt to use Matthean language in a Q passage to prove Matthew's secondariness to Luke. This can indeed assume what needs to proved.

Goulder says that:

> All arguments of the form, 'This expression is Matthean, so the Lukan version of a QD phrase will be earlier' are invalid (*LNP*, p. 15).

In the light of this study, one could perhaps refine this to:

> All arguments of the form, 'This expression is Matthean, so the Lukan version of a QD phrase will necessarily be earlier' are invalid.

If, on other grounds, a scholar was convinced of the existence of Q, it would be legitimate to use arguments of the form, 'This expression is Matthean, so the Lukan form of a QD phrase may be earlier'. The strength of Goulder's case is in pointing to the circularity involved in using Matthean vocabulary in Q passages as an argument for occasional Lukan priority and so for the Q hypothesis.

However, this study has import not just in relation to 'the Matthean vocabulary fallacy'. Where in *LNP* Goulder is concentrating on Mattheanisms in Q in order to demonstrate Luke's dependence on Matthew, in *MLM* he is pointing to the same phenomena to prove

---

148. Farmer takes this type of argument further in 'Certain Results'. He concentrates more on formulas than on short phrases and uses the whole as an argument for the Griesbach Hypothesis.

149. 'Some Observations', p. 100. See also Farmer's 'Reply to Michael Goulder'.

Matthean authorship of all the non-Markan material in his Gospel. The Q material is like R and M, so resonant with Matthew's language that it must have been composed by him. But since we have seen a good deal of Lukan vocabulary as well as Matthean vocabulary in QC, one key factor is taken away from the argument.

Nevertheless, at the conclusion of *MLM*, Goulder presents what he claims to be 'statistical proof' of Matthew's own creation of the non-Markan pieces, based on a study of vocabulary. Goulder sets up the test earlier in the book where, largely to show the soundness of the method, he attempts to demonstrate Markan priority (pp. 122-23). He gives three percentages: a) the number of characteristically Matthean words in Matthew's Markan passages (MK + R), about 15 per cent; b) the number of characteristically Matthean words among the Markan words in these passages (MK), 3 per cent and c) the number of characteristically Matthean words among Matthew's supposed additions (R), 28 per cent. Figure b) is low and c) is high, just as one would expect—'therefore', Goulder says, 'the Markan priority theory is true' (p. 123).

Then, in his conclusion (pp. 474-75), Goulder gives the rest of the figures.[150] If his theory is correct, he says, one will expect the percentage of characteristic words in Q and in M to be similar to figure c) above, around 28 per cent:

> In the Q-passages there are, on my computation, 3,561 words, of which 965 are characteristic—27 per cent. In the M-passages there are 4,346 words, of which 1,351 are characteristic—31 per cent...the overall percentage in the non-Markan passages is 29 per cent: therefore, the non-Markan passages are, over all, Matthew's midrash (p. 475).[151]

---

150. When Goulder sets up the test in the earlier chapter, he says 'there is a statement of the results in Chapter 23' (*MLM*, p. 123). Clearly this should read 'Chapter 22'. It is odd though that by the time we reach chapter 22, some of the percentage figures are different. The 28 per cent figure is the same, but I do not understand why Goulder gives for the number of Matthean words in the Markan passages overall a 15 per cent figure in the earlier chapter (p. 123) against 18 per cent in the later chapter (p. 474). The figures which Goulder gives, 1,668 characteristic words among the 9,280 words in the Markan passages provide a percentage of 17.97. But also the 3 per cent figure quoted in the earlier chapter for characteristically Matthean words among the Markan words in MK passages is wrong according to Goulder's figures in the later chapter, 539 words out of 9,280, making 5.8 per cent, almost twice Goulder's percentage.

151. R.T. France, 'Infancy Narratives', p. 249, comments on Goulder's

The evidence looks impressive but, unfortunately, the argument is fallacious. Goulder's figures are all calculated using his own Matthean vocabulary list, but it is illegitimate to do this because his criteria for establishing characteristic words involved Mark. One criterion was that:

> They are inserted redactionally by Matthew into an agreed Markan context or Old Testament citation (p. 476).

Goulder has given a figure for the percentage of characteristic words among Matthew's redactional words when one of the criteria for defining a characteristic word is that it should be inserted redactionally into Mark. This is a perfect circle.

This criticism is not too serious because there are only 18 words on the list on the redactional criterion alone (see above) but the other criterion for characteristic words was that:

> They occur twice as often in Matthew as in Mark *and* more often than in Luke (p. 476).

This loads the test in Goulder's favour. The percentage figure of characteristically Matthean words in Markan passages (MK) is bound to be comparatively low, but not necessarily because Matthew is following a source here. Rather, where Matthew and Mark share a word, the very fact that they share that word greatly reduces the probability that that word will come overall 'twice as often in Matthew as in Mark'. Conversely, where Matthew and Mark do not share words, viz. in R, Q and M, the probability that any word here will come overall 'twice as often in Matthew as in Mark' is greater.[152]

The difficulty is, simply, that Goulder's vocabulary lists take Markan priority for granted. For our study on QC words this was not a problem:

conclusion to *MLM,* but he does not see the fallacy as he says he has no reason to doubt Goulder's statistics.

152. The point Goulder is attempting to make is actually similar to one which Hawkins makes in *Horae,* pp. 10, 15 and 25, that Matthew's, Mark's and Luke's characteristic vocabulary is all more thickly spread in the peculiar parts than in the common parts. But this is obvious: one of the ways in which we identify common parts is common vocabulary and this common vocabulary will necessarily reduce the number of words characteristic of an evangelist in these sections. Hawkins's lists also define characteristic words by means of their relation with the other Gospels.

Matthean vocabulary was played off against Lukan vocabulary and the criteria used for defining each were the same. In Goulder's test, though, it is a problem—one cannot prove Markan priority by using lists of characteristic vocabulary which take it for granted,[153] nor can one legitimately make calculations about source material, or the lack of it, in non-Markan sections in Matthew, using lists which unfairly bias the test.

It needs to be said, then, that if Goulder's thesis is right, the analysis of vocabulary in Q passages does not prove it to be so. Matters like style (other than vocabulary) and content may turn out to be more reliable indicators in arguing a case on the relationship between the gospels, and Goulder does of course place some emphasis on such things. The attraction which analysis of vocabulary has at first sight is that it is, apparently, more concrete. One can actually count words and compare numbers and one might seem to have proof for a case—things look more scientific.[154] The danger is that the concrete nature of vocabulary analysis opens up the possibility of a control test, a control test which diminishes the impressiveness of Goulder's claims.

153. A control test could be done on Goulder's claims for Markan priority in an attempt to break the circle. The same calculations could be made on Mark in passages which he shares with Matthew, i.e. a) the overall percentage of words characteristic of Mark in such passages; b) the percentage of characteristic words among the words they share; c) the percentage of characteristic words among words unique to Mark. But this would be a big task as the conditions for a Markan word list would have to be identical to the conditions for Goulder's Matthean one. One would have to look for words which come twice as often in Mark as in Matthew in proportion to the relative lengths of the gospels. Words like διδαχή (3/5/1+4) would qualify since Mark is about 63 per cent of the length of Matthew.

154. Lloyd Gaston comes to a similar conclusion in his *Horae Synopticae Electronicae*, saying of his own statistics, 'perhaps the very preciseness of the tables will encourage us to rely more on considerations of style and content. These latter criteria, while superficially not as "objective", are really much more important' (p. 12).

Chapter 3

THE MINOR AGREEMENTS AND CHARACTERISTIC LANGUAGE

A. *Introduction: Goulder on the Minor Agreements*

In *Midrash and Lection in Matthew* Goulder was already following Farrer's lead[1] in drawing attention to the Minor Agreements (MAs) as a problem for the Two-Source Theory (p. 8; cf. pp. 450-51 and 453 n. 3). The argument was then worked out in detail in 'On Putting Q to the Test', a seminal article in the ongoing scholarly debate over the MAs.[2] In this article, Goulder says that in order to demonstrate Luke's knowledge of Matthew, it is necessary to find instances among the MAs where words or phrases are either characteristic of Matthew or uncharacteristic of Luke or, preferably, both. This is the lynchpin of Goulder's thesis:

> The minor agreements in fact provide the most important test of the 4ST ('On Putting Q to the Test', p. 218).

Goulder says that Luke will often make the same changes as Matthew, 'at the especially aramaizing, vulgar and primitive points of Mark' and 'he will tend to use those words and phrases which are congenial to him, some of which, whether by accident or not, are also congenial to Matthew'. Goulder continues:

1. A. Farrer, 'Dispensing', p. 61, 'Small Matthean echoes keep appearing because St Luke is after all acquainted with St Matthew'.
2. For a history of the discussion of the MAs and a bibliography, see F. Neirynck, *Minor Agreements* and T.A. Friedrichsen, 'Survey'. The bibliography of the latter article is updated further in F. Neirynck, 'Minor Agreements and the Two-Source Theory', particularly pp. 28-29; pp. for this article will be cited from G. Strecker (ed.), *Symposium Göttingen 1991*. This article earlier appeared in F. Van Segbroeck (ed.), *Evangelica II*, Part One of which (pp. 1-138) deals with the MAs. For a good bibliography on the MAs see also *Symposium Göttingen 1991*, pp. 231-40.

So what we are looking for, in order to test the 4ST, is a rump of cases where it appears that Luke agrees with Matthew against Mark in expressions which he, Luke, never uses elsewhere, or to which he shows a marked aversion; or which are unnatural; or in matters of order... However, it is possible to refine our test further, for it might be that out of the non-Lukan rump among the agreements there was included a number of words and phrases that were typical of, or plainly redacted by, Matthew; and if so this would tell...that Luke knew Matthew ('On Putting Q to the Test', p. 219).

Goulder then proceeds to give twelve examples in which, he says, 'these criteria are met' and his conclusion is characteristically forthright:

The evidence from the agreements shows that Luke knew Matthew, and that Q is therefore no longer a valid hypothesis ('On Putting Q to the Test', p. 234).

B. *Tuckett's Response: Towards a Control*

In a subsequent article, 'Farrer on Q', Goulder reflected on his 12 examples of Mattheanisms in Luke and said:

It will be interesting to see whether it is possible to make a convincing reply to them (p. 95).

The challenge was taken up by Christopher Tuckett, one of the most staunch defenders of the 2ST. In his 1984 article, 'On the Relationship Between Matthew and Luke', he says:

Goulder's methodology is admirable; if examples satisfying these conditions can be found, then they will show Luke's knowledge of Matthew. Moreover, only one such case needs to be established for the conclusion to follow. (Goulder has produced twelve; hence he could be wrong in eleven cases and his overall conclusion would still be established.)[3]

Tuckett feels that not one of Goulder's twelve examples is successful. He points out that some of the words or phrases uncharacteristic of Luke in the MAs are equally as uncharacteristic of Matthew. 'The Matthew-Luke agreement', he stresses, 'must be both positively Matthean, and positively un-Lukan'.[4]

---

3.   C.M. Tuckett, 'Relationship', p. 130. The article is cited with favour by Neirynck, 'The Two-Source Theory: Introduction', p. 11.
4.   C.M. Tuckett, 'Relationship', p. 130.

Tuckett's claim that one example alone would be sufficient is not, however, persuasive. If Matthew and Luke were independent of one another, it would be possible, perhaps even likely, that there would be the odd example of a MA with characteristically Matthean wording by coincidence. Equally, one would expect to find the odd example which by coincidence featured a characteristically Lukan expression. Further, it is at least possible that one MA with Matthean wording might occur by means of textual corruption which left no trace in the manuscript tradition—indeed, this could even be the case on the theory that Luke had read Matthew.[5]

Tuckett's point that one Matthean, un-Lukan MA would be enough, the logic of which is accepted by Goulder,[6] does, however, help to focus the issue. The question arises: how many examples of Mattheanisms among the MAs would be required to establish the case that Luke read Matthew? If one is not enough, are Goulder's twelve examples sufficient?[7]

Both Goulder and Tuckett are arguing as if they are in the law-court. Goulder is the prosecutor; Tuckett is the defence-lawyer; Q is on trial. Goulder will hear nothing in favour of the 2ST, Tuckett nothing against it. Goulder responds to Tuckett in both *LNP* and 'Luke's Knowledge of Matthew', a paper given at the Göttingen Symposium on the MAs in 1991 and, to extend the law-court metaphor, Timothy Friedrichsen, in an article published in 1989,[8] does a judge-like summing-up of Goulder's and Tuckett's arguments, with the readers left to make their own verdict.

---

5. Further, Tuckett does not object to the idea of conjectural emendation of the text—he thinks it explains the key MA at Mk 14.65 (though he does not think that Goulder's argument from Matthew's style is convincing). See his discussion of the phenomenon in 'The Minor Agreements and Textual Criticism'.

6. 'Luke's Knowledge of Matthew', hereinafter called 'Knowledge', pp. 143-44.

7. R.H. Gundry lists 33 examples of MAs which, he thinks, show Matthew's hand enough to make the case: 'It becomes a matter of individual judgment whether these Matthean foreign bodies among Luke's agreements with Matthew against Mark are of sufficient number and weight to clinch the arguments from these agreements as a whole that Luke used Matthew as well as Mark. It seems to me that they are'('Matthean Foreign Bodies', p. 1493). For a recent comment on this article, see E. Franklin, *Luke*, pp. 302-303 n. 2.

8. T.A. Friedrichsen, 'Survey', pp. 378-80.

Much of Goulder's scholarship is conducted in the same way, the case presented forcefully and argued boldly with difficulties admitted only in order that they might be dispensed with. In the analysis of his thesis, however, the sciences provide us with a model preferable to the law-court one. Any useful experiment requires a good, reliable control and here, as with the analysis of the QC words, one could look for Lukanisms as well as for Mattheanisms.

If Goulder is right, one will expect to find a good number more MAs featuring language positively Matthean and positively un-Lukan than one finds of MAs with language positively Lukan and positively un-Matthean.

Before looking at examples of MAs which feature Mattheanisms or Lukanisms, however, it is necessary to look more closely at the way in which Goulder argues the case. It might be said that Goulder uses five different (though overlapping) arguments on the MAs, of which that from wording characteristic of Matthew and uncharacteristic of Luke is only the first.

C. *Goulder's Arguments*

1. *Matthean, Un-Lukan Wording*
When Tuckett says that in order for Goulder's case to be established, MAs 'must be both positively Matthean and positively un-Lukan',[9] he is going a little further than Goulder does in 'On Putting Q to the Test'. In this article it is certainly the case that the MA must be 'positively un-Lukan': Goulder is looking for 'expressions which he, Luke, never uses elsewhere, or to which he shows a marked aversion; or which are unnatural' ('On Putting Q to the Test', p. 219). It is not so clear that MAs must be 'positively Matthean'. Rather, Goulder speaks of 'words and phrases' that are 'typical of, or plainly redacted by Matthew' ('On Putting Q to the Test', p. 219) and when he concludes, he says:

> So much agreement in detail against Luke's normal ways cannot be an accident; and in each case there is reason to think that Matthew himself is responsible for the redactions to Mark which have then been taken over into Luke ('On Putting Q to the Test', p. 234).

9. C.M. Tuckett, 'Relationship', p. 130.

The stress is on the 'un-Lukan' criterion. The 'Matthean' criterion is comparatively weak: Goulder is only attempting to show that MAs which feature un-Lukan words or expressions can plausibly be regarded as Matthew's own additions to Mark.[10]

This observation is an important one because several of Tuckett's replies to Goulder centre on the 'Matthean' criterion. Twice Tuckett admits the un-Lukan nature of Goulder's examples without agreeing with Goulder that the wording is Matthean. Goulder's first case largely concerns the spelling Ναζαρά in Mt. 4.13 // Lk. 4.16. Tuckett agrees that 'it is certainly untypical of Luke' but adds: 'However, it appears to be equally untypical of Matthew'.[11] Goulder, though, had not even attempted to demonstrate that the spelling is Matthean; he only comments that the whole verse in Matthew 'is redactional' ('On Putting Q to the Test', p. 222).[12]

Second, when discussing Goulder's sixth example, Mt. 10.1 // Mk 6.7 // Lk. 9.1, Tuckett says:

> The use of νόσος as the direct object of θεραπεύειν is unique in Luke-Acts and is un-Lukan. But it appears to be equally un-Matthean.[13]

Here, though, Goulder had not argued that the use of θεραπεύω with νόσος is particularly Matthean; he only comments that in this verse, 'Matthew amplifies Mark in typical fashion' ('On Putting Q to the Test', p. 226).[14] Here, and throughout most of 'On Putting Q to the Test', Goulder's argument is that Matthew is 'plainly redacting' Mark and that since the expression in question is un-Lukan, Luke must be dependent on Matthew.

The distinction between this argument and the more straightforward one that an agreement needs to be 'both positively Matthean and positively un-Lukan' is subtle but important. Goulder is not as forthright in 'On Putting Q to the Test' as Tuckett portrays him and this fact often

---

10. This argument is also used by R. T. Simpson, 'Major Agreements', for example on the MA at Mk 12.28-31 (Great Commandment), p. 280. The same kind of argument is basic to Gundry's 'Matthean Foreign Bodies'.

11. C.M. Tuckett, 'Relationship', p. 131.

12. See further on this example below, pp. 101-102.

13. C.M. Tuckett, 'Relationship', p. 135.

14. Goulder does add that 'the completely characteristic wording of Matt. 10.1 excludes a Q-overlap' but this is part of the same underlying argument, attempting to demonstrate only that the verse must have been redacted by Matthew. This is one of the examples which drops out of consideration in 'Knowledge'.

appears to give Tuckett the edge in the debate between them.

The issue is complicated further, however, by Goulder's own later statements of the argument, in which he becomes steadily more forthright. In 'Farrer on Q' in 1980, Goulder says that the relevant MAs 'must be in some way characteristic of Matthew' and 'in some way uncharacteristic of Luke' (p. 195).[15] This is already a stronger statement of the necessary condition for Matthew[16] but Goulder goes further still in 'Luke's Knowledge of Matthew', in which the qualification 'in some way' is not added. Rather, he says simply that 'the wording in Matthew should be characteristic of Matthew' and 'the same words in Luke should be uncharacteristic of Luke' ('Knowledge', p. 144). Even here, though, in Goulder's most recent statement of the argument from the MAs, it is important to note that the stress is still on the 'un-Lukan' tenet. In his conclusion, Goulder says:

> Can it really be maintained that it [the 2ST] is plausible when it has to excuse so many occasions when Luke agrees with Matthew in locutions which are unnatural to him—κλίνη, ἔμπροσθεν, ἐπιφώσκειν? ('Knowledge', p. 160)

Although it is important to be clear about Goulder's argument, it is also necessary to see that the ideal for Goulder is indeed to isolate MAs which feature language which is strongly characteristic of Matthew and markedly uncharacteristic of Luke. On several occasions, as we shall see below, Goulder does isolate MAs which satisfy these conditions strictly. Curiously, however, only one of them occurs in 'On Putting Q to the Test' (pp. 219-21, Mk 6.2 and parallels, E.2. (below) and none occur in the restatement in 1993. The rest occur in *LNP* where Goulder draws attention in particular to the use of ὕστερον in the MA at Mk 12.22 (E.2.e below).

2. *Order*

There is actually a second kind of argument in 'On Putting Q to the Test', one which receives a little less stress, the argument from order.

15. Cf. T.A. Friedrichsen's review of Victor Seung-Ku Yoon's thesis in 'New Dissertations', in particular pp. 391-92 where Friedrichsen criticizes Yoon's uneven application of Goulder's methodology. In defence of Yoon it needs to be noticed that Goulder's own statements of his methodology have been a little ambiguous.

16. In the short general section on the MAs in *LNP* (pp. 47-50), however, Goulder is more circumspect, stressing only the un-Lukan criterion (particularly p. 50). See further on the argument in *LNP* below.

In his introductory comments to the article, Goulder briefly mentions that 'matters of order' will help 'to test the 4ST'.[17] Goulder appeals to this criterion four times, for the MAs at Mk 6.2 ('On Putting Q to the Test', pp. 219-21; cf. 'Knowledge', pp. 144-46; *LNP*, pp. 299-310); Mk 1.16-39 and 3.7-19 ('On Putting Q to the Test', pp. 221-22; cf. 'Knowledge', pp. 148-50; *LNP*, pp. 311-28); Mk 3.16-17 ('On Putting Q to the Test', pp. 222-23; cf. 'Knowledge', pp. 150-51; *LNP*, pp. 341-43); and Mk 1.2 ('On Putting Q to the Test', pp. 224-25; cf. 'Knowledge', pp. 151-53; *LNP*, pp. 392-93).

On only one of these four occasions, however, does the argument from order stand on its own in 'On Putting Q to the Test', the second of these cases, the postponement of the Call of the First Disciples, and even here Goulder attempts to show that it is to some degree unnatural: 'the Markan order would be logical in Luke also, for in Lk. 4.38 Jesus enters Simon's house without Simon being mentioned before' ('On Putting Q to the Test', p. 221).

On the other occasions, the argument from order is used either as a form of, or to add strength to, the overall case from Matthean, un-Lukan features. Goulder points out, for example, that 'Andrew his brother' comes forward in Lk. 6.14 MA but not in the parallel list in Acts 1.13 (p. 224)—this change in order is, then, 'un-Lukan'. On the Mal. 3.1–Exod. 23.20 text, the argument from order is combined with arguments on Matthean redaction—ἔμπροσθεν comes in Mt. 11.10 // Lk. 7.27 and has figures of 18/2/10+2, for example.[18]

The argument from order is, then, in the context of Goulder's discussion of the MAs, a subsidiary one. It surfaces, no doubt, because Goulder is conscious of Streeter's argument that Luke would have been a crank to destroy Matthew's fine order (particularly in 'On Putting Q

17. See the full quotation above, p. 90.
18. The argument from order here is actually quite weak since for a two-source theorist, the quotation will have come from Q so it is in the Q order. Also figures of 18/2/10+2 for ἔμπροσθεν are not particularly impressive—see above for the greater number of strongly Lukan words in this pericope. The greater difficulty here for the 2ST is the problem of Mark-Q overlap which involves explaining how Q and Mark have the same five alterations to the Mal. 3.1–Exod. 23.20 quotation, see 'Knowledge', pp. 151-53 and Sanders and Davies, *Studying*, pp. 95-96, who also, however, overstress the importance of ἔμπροσθεν.

to the Test', p. 234). If Goulder can show that Luke actually follows Matthew's order on several occasions in triple tradition passages, then he is already part of the way to defeating Streeter's argument.

The attempt to explain Luke's order is a key concern in Goulder's work: it is one of the most important themes of *LNP* and is represented in summary form in his article 'The Order of a Crank'. Here, though, the argument has moved away from concentrating on the MAs towards explaining the whole of Luke's Gospel as a reconciliation of Mark and Matthew.[19] When in *LNP* Goulder draws attention to the MAs as a problem for the 2ST, he does not mention the question of order.[20]

3. Clusters of not very Lukan Words

In *LNP*, chapter two, on Q, Goulder presents two arguments from the MAs.[21] The first is that of 'On Putting Q to the Test', 'the accumulation of uncharacteristic Lukan changes in a limited number of texts where Matthew has made the same change' (*LNP*, p. 48). The second is new and it is summarized by Goulder as:

> The presence of a large number of less notable MAs, for any one of which parallel Lukan use can be advanced; but whose combined improbability is enormous (*LNP*, p. 50).

The example Goulder gives is Mt. 16.21 // Mk 8.31 // Lk. 9.22 (First Passion Prediction) where Matthew and Luke coincide in making four changes to Mark, three of which are in language which is 'not very Lukan'. Goulder works out figures for the likelihood of each of the changes occurring by accident—ἀπό = 'by' occurs five times elsewhere in Luke–Acts whereas ὑπό with the genitive occurs 61 times, so the chance of ἀπό occurring here by accident would be 5 in 66. Then, by multiplying together such figures for each word or expression, Goulder ends up with odds of 333:1 against this verse occurring in Luke by accident.

Neirynck and Friedrichsen have replied to this argument[22] by stressing the case for independent redaction by Luke. The overall thrust

---

19. I discuss Lukan order in this context below, pp. 258-59.

20. The argument resurfaces, however, in relation to the MAs in 'Knowledge', probably because it is a restatement of 'On Putting Q to the Test'.

21. The arguments are summarized in 'Knowledge', p. 144.

22. F. Neirynck and T.A. Friedrichsen, 'Note On Luke 9.22'; the pages below are cited from *ETL* 65.

of their short article is to reduce considerably Goulder's odds of 333:1. Goulder's second point, for example, concerns Matthew's and Luke's omission of Mark's second two articles in the phrase ἀπό τῶν πρεσβυτέρων καί ἀρχιερέων καί γραμματέων (*LNP*, p. 49). Goulder points to three other occasions on which Luke omits a second article in a short list of groups (like Lk. 14.3, πρὸς τοὺς νομικοὺς καί Φαρισαίους) against sixteen cases where Luke retains the second article in such a list (like Lk. 5.21, οἱ γραμματεῖς καί οἱ Φαρισαῖοι), thus the chances of Luke omitting Mark's second and third articles by accident would be 3 in 19. Neirynck and Friedrichsen attempt to correct this picture, however, by saying that 'all instances where Luke repeats the article are in the nominative, and in the four cases without repetition of the article, (indirect) objects are involved'.[23] Therefore, they feel that Luke would have written ἀπὸ τῶν πρεσβυτέρων καί γραμματέων in 9.22 on his own.[24]

Neirynck and Friedrichsen are not as successful with each of Goulder's points. On the use of ἐγερθῆναι instead of Mark's ἀναστῆναι (*LNP*, pp. 49-50), for example, they show that Luke's use is explicable especially in relation to parallels in Acts,[25] but they do not deal with Goulder's point that Luke keeps Mark's ἀναστήσεται in 18.33 and writes ἀναστῆναι in an identical context in 24.7. It could probably be said that after the exchange between Goulder and Neirynck—Friedrichsen on Lk. 9.22, the chips are shared out evenly.

Neirynck and Friedrichsen do not, however, reply to Goulder's general argument from this kind of data. They do not discuss Goulder's notion that the accumulation of 'not very Lukan' words in single verse MAs can be impressive; they only deal with the specific example which Goulder provides. Since, however, as Goulder says, there is a 'rarity of straightforward instances like Lk. 9.22' (*LNP*, p. 185 n. 51) and since Neirynck and Friedrichsen have reduced the impressiveness of this,

---

23. Neirynck and Friedrichsen, 'Note', p. 393.

24. See, however, Gundry's response to this point, 'The suggestion does not pass muster, however, for Luke–Acts contains some twenty-one instances of Luke's repeating the definite article in an oblique case' ('Matthean Foreign Bodies', p. 1476). It is particularly noticeable from Gundry's list that Neirynck and Friedrichsen would have had a different picture if they had considered the instances from Acts, and some of these are listed by Goulder (Acts 4.5; 6.12 and 23.14, *LNP*, p. 49).

25. Neirynck and Friedrichsen, 'Note', pp. 393-94.

Goulder's choice example, it is clear that on this argument Goulder has not yet made his case.[26]

4. *Luke's Dependence on Matthew's Redaction*

Two arguments, then, are spelt out clearly in *LNP*, chapter two, the first from 'un-Lukan' words in some of the MAs and the second from clusters of 'not very Lukan' words. Two further arguments emerge in the commentary section of the book. First, where Matthew and Luke agree in differing from Mark but do not agree on precisely the same words, Goulder will sometimes attempt to show that Matthew is redacting Mark and that Luke is to some degree dependent on the Matthean redaction. In such cases Goulder feels that it is sufficient simply to demonstrate that Matthew is adding to Mark in his own characteristic style so that Luke, being secondary, must be relying on the Matthean redaction. This argument is like the first outlined above but focuses on MAs in which the wording in Matthew is characteristic of Matthew and in Luke is characteristic of Luke. There is no appeal in cases like these to the 'un-Lukan' tenet of the other argument.

When commenting on Lk. 9.11b (καὶ τοὺς χρείαν ἔχοντας θεραπείας ἰᾶτο, Feeding of the Five Thousand // Mt. 14.14 // Mk 6.34), for example, Goulder says that Luke has agreed with Matthew in three ways—'in interpreting Mark's ἐσπλαγχνίσθη as implying healing', in placing this at the end of the verse and in structuring the clause in the same way. He then adds:

> It is no use objecting that the words are different. Luke regularly changes ἄρρωστος, and this requires different wording; he likes χρεία (6/4/7+5...) and adapts θεραπεία (cf. 12.42) from Matthew's θεραπεύειν. He then needs a different verb, and uses his preferred ἰᾶσθαι (*LNP*, p. 434).

The difficulty here is that although this makes a plausible account of Luke's procedure on the basis of his knowledge of Matthew, it is not a strong argument for Lukan knowledge of Matthew. The argument is reversible—with such characteristic Lukan wording the same data

---

26. Goulder responds to Neirynck and Friedrichsen in his Review of Neirynck's *Evangelica II*, 'I was rash enough to argue that Lk. 9.22 alone contained four Minor Agreements so striking as to give three chances in a thousand of being coincidental. Neirynck effectively weakens the argument; but perhaps coincidence now stands at only 3 chances in 100, and that is still uncomfortable odds' (p. 201).

could support an argument that Matthew used Luke. Further, more seriously, cases like this are conducive to the independent redaction hypothesis.[27]

This phenomenon is actually quite common among the MAs: there are several occasions on which Matthew uses words characteristically and Luke has a parallel characteristic expression. In Mt. 26.14 // Mk 14.10 // Lk. 22.3, for example, Matthew has 'The one called (ὁ λεγόμενος) Judas Iscariot' and Luke has 'Judas, the one called (τὸν καλούμενον) Iscariot'. λεγόμενος with names is common in Matthew (13/1/2, Mt. 26.14 R; 27.33 R) just as καλούμενος is common in Luke (0/0/10+13, Lk. 6.15 R; 22.3 R). This is the kind of clarifying addition in their own style which one could easily imagine the evangelists making independently. Goulder speaks about this as a 'rather striking Minor Agreement' (*LNP*, p. 720), but it needs to be noticed that in cases like this, there are no real difficulties for the 2ST.[28]

5. *Undoubtable Links and Coincidence of* Hapax

The second additional argument which emerges in *LNP* is an underlying one whereby Goulder simply attempts to show that there is an undoubtable link between Matthew and Luke in a given MA. This is usually done by observing that the words in question are *hapax legomena*, the point being that it is highly unlikely that Matthew and Luke would make the same change to Mark independently. It is an argument from the unlikeliness of coincidence.

When discussing Mt. 26.16 // Mk 14.11 // Lk. 22.6 ('he sought an opportunity to betray him') where Matthew and Luke have εὐκαιρίαν instead of Mark's εὐκαίρως, for example, Goulder says:

> Matthew and Luke have agreed here in changing Mark's adverb into an accusative of the related noun, which is a hapax in both Matthew and L– A… The coincidence of hapax is due to Luke's reminiscence of Matthew (*LNP*, p. 721).

27. On the argument for independent redaction in this MA see F. Neirynck, 'The Matthew-Luke Agreements in Matt. 14.13-14 / Luke 9.10-11' (pp. below are cited from *Evangelica II*; pp. 89-90 on this MA). See further below, p. 113 n. 58. Neirynck also discusses Lk. 9.11 which features a noticeable Mattheanism, οἱ ὄχλοι…ἠκολούθησαν on which, see further below, pp. 113-15.

28. Matthew and Luke both also have the spelling Ἰσκαριώτης(ν) against Mark's Ἰσκαριώθ. Goulder points out that at Mt. 10.4 // Mk 3.19 // Lk. 6.16, Mark and Luke have Ἰσκαριώθ against Matthew's Ἰσκαριώτης (*LNP*, p. 720).

Like this is Mt. 9.26 // Mk 1.28 // Lk. 4.14 (a 'report' on Jesus goes around), where Matthew and Luke agree in their use of the word φήμη. Goulder says:

> φήμη is a Lukan hapax, and the agreement with Mt. 9.26 is almost word-for-word: if, as Delobel thinks, Mt. 9.26 is Mt. R, drawing on διαφημίζειν in Mk 1.45, is it not very remarkable that Luke should also have decided to make use of Mk 1.45 here, and to change it in the identical way (p. 306)?[29]

In such cases Goulder has the 2ST clearly in view; it becomes the only opponent which needs to be eliminated. The sole alternative to it is Lukan knowledge of Matthew. Consequently, any time that Goulder thinks that he can show that there is a strong link between Matthew and Luke which can be ascribed to neither Q nor coincidence, he feels that he has hammered a sizeable nail into Q's coffin. Every time, then, that he sees a MA which he thinks two-source theorists would have difficulties with, he feels that the MA supports his solution to the synoptic problem.

Since the 2ST is indeed the major competitor to the hypothesis of Luke's knowledge of Matthew, it is quite legitimate for Goulder to count shots fired against the 2ST as shots fired for his own theory. There are, however, difficulties with this kind of argument. Like the previous argument, this one is reversible: the same data could be used to support Matthew's knowledge of Luke. In both of the examples quoted above, the words in question are *hapax*es in Matthew as well as in Luke.

Further, even if one accepts the logic of Goulder's argument on such MAs, the logic only works against a 'hardline' 2ST. Goulder may be right that it will not do to ascribe MAs of this kind, featuring rare words, to independent redaction by Matthew and Luke. If he is right, though, it does not necessarily follow from this that Luke knew Matthew. Hardline two-source theorists could lose the argument over

---

29. Goulder is referring here to J. Delobel, 'La rédaction'; pp. 211-13 are on φήμη. (The article is a response to the Schürmann article cited in p. 102 n. 33.) The 'true' parallels to Mk 1.28 are Mt. 4.24 and Lk. 4.37. Neirynck lists this MA with both Mt. 9.26 and Lk. 4.14 in brackets, *Minor Agreements*, p. 62. Goulder treats this MA together with two others in Lk. 4.14-16, Ναζαρά and 'their' synagogues. See further on these MAs above, p. 93, and below, pp. 101-102 and pp. 111-13.

the MAs but someone other than Goulder might take the spoils.[30]

D. *Key Minor Agreements*

It is important to stress that the previous two arguments specified are underlying and only emerge in the commentary section of *LNP*. The argument which Goulder emphasizes is the one from Matthean, un-Lukan language among some MAs, an argument which is methodologically strong in that it does not just attempt to undermine the 2ST and the hypothesis of independent redaction by Matthew and Luke, but also attempts specifically to demonstrate Luke's knowledge of Matthew.

The difficulty, however, is that several of the most extraordinary MAs, including some of those listed in 'On Putting Q to the Test', do not actually feature Matthew's characteristic style, even when the wording is, indeed, un-Lukan. One of Goulder's favourite examples is like this. In Mt. 4.13 // Mk 1.14 // Lk. 4.16 ('On Putting Q to the Test', pp. 219-21; *LNP*, pp. 299-301 and 306-307; 'Knowledge', pp. 144-48), there is a MA not only over order (see above, p. 95) but also over the spelling Ναζαρά. Goulder points out that the spelling is a *hapax legomenon* in Luke, and it is, therefore, uncharacteristic and shows Luke's knowledge of Matthew. Goulder responds to Tuckett's point that it is equally uncharacteristic in Matthew[31] by saying,

> We do have evidence in Mt. 2.23 of Matthew's own adjectival coinage Ναζωραῖος. He is working here from Mark 1, with Ναζαρηνός at 1.24 and could have formed Ναζαρά on the analogy of Γαδαρηνός/Γαδαρα, Μαγδαληνός/Μαγδαλα. It may well be Matthew who introduced the variant spelling (*LNP*, p. 307; cf. 'Knowledge', pp. 147-48).

The argument is, then, that Matthew can plausibly be seen to have added Ναζαρά to Mark himself and that since the spelling is un-Lukan, this provides evidence of Lukan knowledge of Matthew. Goulder summarizes:

> If Matthew inserted it redactionally, we have a very striking Minor Agreement (*LNP*, p. 306).

---

30. Cf. 'Knowledge', pp. 143-44, where Goulder defends his approach of treating the 2ST as the major competitor to his theory and *LNP*, chapter one, where he mentions the 'variety of softlines' (p. 10). See further on this below, pp. 125-29.

31. C.M. Tuckett, 'Relationship', p. 131. The spelling comes only here in the New Testament.

This kind of argument on this kind of MA is not as strong as one which points to language which is clearly identifiable as characteristic of Matthew and uncharacteristic of Luke. It is the value of Tuckett's response to Goulder that he draws attention to this methodological point, showing that several of Goulder's examples do not satisfy stringently applied criteria.

Mt. 26.68 // Mk 14.65 // Lk. 22.64 (τίς ἐστιν ὁ παίσας σε;) is like this example. Much has been written about this MA, some of it in response to Goulder,[32] but it will be worth dwelling on it at a little more length for it is vital in Goulder's thesis, his key MA, and not simply because it is a five consecutive word MA featuring a *hapax* in Luke (παίω), but more particularly because it occurs in the Passion Narrative. Goulder makes a great deal of this in his attempt to demonstrate that the 2ST is a 'house built on sand' (*LNP*, chapter one; cf. 'On Putting Q to the Test', p. 228).

The argument which Goulder uses is an acute form of argument 5 outlined above, that there is too much agreement between Matthew and Luke to ascribe to coincidence or independent redaction, acute because the MA occurs in the Passion Narrative:

> This is the saving grace in the paradigm: if there were one significant and clear MA in the Passion story, then we should know that Luke was following Matthew; and Q, and with it the whole structure, would be undermined (*LNP*, p. 6).[33]

The argument functions by opposing Goulder's thesis of Lukan knowledge of Matthew with a hardline 2ST which always supposes independent redaction by Matthew and Luke. In this Goulder is successful, since no 'hardliner', Schmid, Streeter, Tuckett or Neirynck, does suppose independent redaction here. Rather, they all resort to

---

32. The literature includes: C.H. Turner, *Study*, p. 47; Streeter, *Four Gospels*, pp. 325-28; Josef Schmid, *Matthäus und Lukas*, pp. 157-59. The key modern defence from a hardline 2ST perspective is F. Neirynck, ΤΙΣ ΕΣΤΙΝ; the pp. below are cited from *Evangelica II*. See also 'Minor Agreements and the Two-Source Theory', pp. 49-50; Tuckett, 'Relationship', pp. 136-37 and 'Minor Agreements and Textual Criticism', pp. 135-41.

33. Contrast Ναζαρά, which Streeter (*Four Gospels*, pp. 206-207), Schürmann (*Das Lukasevangelium I*, pp. 227-28 and 'Der «Bericht von Anfang»'), Tuckett ('Relationship', p. 131 and 'Lk. 4.16-30') and now Catchpole ('Anointed One', pp. 235-36) place in some form of Q; cf. also Schweizer (*Matthew*, pp. 67-68).

some form of textual argument.[34] It remains one of the greatest strengths of Goulder's thesis that he can explain the MA at Mk 14.65 using the text as it stands. Likewise, it is perhaps the greatest single problem for the 2ST that recourse to theories of conjectural emendation is necessary to save it.[35]

Nevertheless, it is important to notice that on all three occasions on which Goulder discusses this MA, he is not satisfied in using simply this plain argument that the link between Matthew and Luke is too great for coincidence or independent redaction. Rather, he attempts also to show that the wording of the MA is characteristic of Matthew but uncharacteristic of Luke, so it shows specifically that Luke has read Matthew ('On Putting Q to the Test', p. 227; *LNP*, p. 7; 'Knowledge', p. 153).

Goulder says that Matthew redacts the Markan narrative in the following characteristic ways: 1) just as Matthew in 27.29 specifies that when the soldiers mocked Jesus they put a crown of thorns 'on his head' and a rod 'in his right hand', so here he presses the detail: the soldiers spat 'in his face'; 2) then, by omitting the blindfolding of Jesus' 'face', Matthew involves himself in a muddle, as often; and 3) Matthew frames the question by adding a sarcastic Χριστέ (cf. 27.40), by writing τίς ἐστιν as at Mt. 9.13 R; 12.7 R; 12.11 R and 21.10 R, by writing ὁ with a participle as at 10.4 R; 19.28 R; 26.25 R; 26.52 R and 27.3 R and by using the verb παίω.[36]

Some of these points are strong; some are less so. All of them require

---

34. See p. 102 n. 32. I do not have space to look at their arguments in detail, but it needs to be noted that they all choose not to read τίς ἐστιν ὁ παίσας σε; in Mt. 26.68.

35. The objection is not to the idea of conjectural emendation as such but to the notion of emending the text in order to save a synoptic theory. Cf. Goulder, 'Knowledge', p. 155, 'Neirynck's appeal to Synoptic parallels is the end of rational discussion'. Neirynck, however, is keen to stress that his appeal to conjectural emendation here is a one-off ('Minor Agreements and the Two-Source Theory', p. 49).

36. These points are listed from 'Knowledge', p. 153. Cf. *LNP*, p. 7 where Goulder also makes the point that Matthew is 'adding a few words of oratio recta as often'. This claim is common in *MLM*, see below, p. 242 n. 13. Goulder also notes in 'On Putting Q to the Test' that it is a rhetorical question. Here cf. Cadbury who claims that 'Luke to some extent avoids' rhetorical questions (*Style*, p. 81) but contrast J.G.F. Collison who observes that they come 55 times in Luke against 31 times in Matthew ('Linguistic Usages', p. 247 n. 12).

qualification. With point two, Goulder may be attempting to read a potential weakness for his thesis as a strength. It is a key part of both Tuckett's and Neirynck's theses on this verse that since the blindfolding is omitted in Matthew, the story in his Gospel does not make sense as it stands, therefore, τίς ἐστιν ὁ παίσας σε; is unlikely to have been in the original text of Matthew.[37] Goulder deals with this difficulty by saying that the omission of the blindfolding is actually best explained by his thesis: it is characteristic of Matthew to 'muddle' his sources, therefore, the 'oversight' here is evidence that Matthew himself redacted the verse. This is a brilliant move but acceptance of Goulder's point will depend on acceptance of his general argument about 'muddle' among all the evangelists.[38]

Goulder's first point is really part of the same 'muddle' argument: if Goulder can demonstrate that it is in some way characteristic of Matthew to have the soldiers spitting 'in his face', then there is more reason to accept the notion that Matthew has omitted the blindfolding of Jesus' 'face' by accident. Now, since at Mt. 27.28-29 // Mk 15.19-20, Matthew makes two similar clarifying additions, the crown of thorns 'on his head' and the rod 'in his right hand', Goulder's point here is sound. Mt. 27.28-29 // Mk 15.19-20 are closely parallel to the verse being discussed since both depict the mocking of Jesus.[39]

Goulder's third point is actually several points about Matthew's style. The addition of Χριστέ may well show Matthew's hand in redacting Mark, but it is not particularly helpful since the word does not occur in

37. C.M. Tuckett, 'Relationship', pp. 136-37 and particularly 'The Minor Agreements and Textual Criticism', pp. 140-41; Neirynck, ΤΙΣ ΕΣΤΙΝ, particularly pp. 119-22, and 'The Minor Agreements and the Two-Source Theory', pp. 49-50.

38. Cf. the full discussion below, chapter eleven. In G. Strecker (ed.), *Symposium Göttingen 1991* the question of 'oversight' here is dealt with three times, by Goulder (p. 153), by Neirynck (pp. 49-50) and by Tuckett (pp. 140-41). The debate turns on whether Matthew redacts Mark 'sensibly' (Tuckett) or 'characteristically' (Goulder). Neirynck objects that Mt. 26.68 is unlike Goulder's analogy Mt. 14.3-12. It is worth noting that Farmer makes sense of Matthew without the 'oversight' theory, *The Synoptic Problem*, p. 149; for comment, see Tuckett, *Revival*, pp. 72-75. See also Franklin, *Luke*, p. 304 which is, however, circular: 'Surprisingly, he omits Mark's reference to their blindfolding of Jesus, but he knows that it has happened for he is following Mark's narrative'.

39. The point might apply more naturally to Luke who, according to Goulder, commonly makes matters more concrete or specific (cf. *LNP*, pp. 97 and 107-108).

Luke.[40] The most important points concern the five consecutive words in common to Matthew and Luke but not Mark, τίς ἐστιν ὁ παίσας σε;.

Among the words in this question, παίω is a *hapax* in both Matthew and Luke therefore it is unhelpful for establishing Matthean redaction.[41] Goulder is right that 'questions beginning τίς/τί ἐστιν' (*LNP*, p. 7) are Matthean. Of Goulder's list,[42] though, both Mt. 9.13 and Mt. 12.7 should be omitted: neither of these are questions beginning τίς/τί ἐστιν. 12.11 R and 21.10 R are legitimate examples and to them could be added 7.9 QD; 8.26 MK; 9.5 MK; 12.48a MK; 12.48b R; 18.1 R; 19.27 R; 23.17 M and 24.45 QC. Questions beginning τίς/τί ἐστιν, therefore, come twelve times in Matthew including five times R (12.11; 12.48b; 18.1; 19.27 and 21.10). This, however, is not the whole picture; questions beginning τίς/τί ἐστιν also come five times in Mark (1.27; 2.9; 3.33; 4.40 and 4.41) and significantly, thirteen times in Luke including five times R: Lk. 1.66 L; 5.21 R; 5.23 MK; 7.49 L; 8.25 MK; 8.30 R; 9.9 R; 10.29 L; 12.42 QC; 20.2 R; 20.17 R; 24.38 L (and here, 22.64 MA).[43] Clearly, then, this part of the question is far from being un-Lukan.

Goulder is also right that ὁ with a participle often comes in Matthew, though three of his examples (10.4, 26.25 and 27.3) are in the phrase ὁ παραδιδούς/παραδούς of Judas. Again, however, this can be qualified by noticing that ὁ with a participle is also common in Luke and is at 8.45 R; 9.48 R; 20.2 R and 22.23 R.

On both counts, then, τίς/τί ἐστιν and ὁ with a participle, the style is just as Lukan as it is Matthean. In addition, though, Goulder does not ask the important question whether τίς/τί ἐστιν ever occurs together with ὁ and a participle outside of this MA. Unfortunately for Goulder's thesis, there is one occasion and it is in Luke, in a redactional rephrasing of Mark:

40. Cf. Tuckett, 'Relationship', p. 136.

41. παίω comes once also in Mark, 14.47, the striking of the servant of the High Priest, and once in John, 18.10 (parallel to Mk 14.47). Elsewhere it is only at Rev. 9.5. Goulder thinks that in Matthew it is a reminiscence of Mk 14.47 ('On Putting Q to the Test', p. 227).

42. *LNP*, p. 7, and 'Knowledge', p. 153, have the same list which I discuss here; there is a different list in 'On Putting Q to the Test'.

43. I have included only examples of τίς/τί nominative singular or plural with any tense or person of εἶναι in direct questions where εἶναι is the main verb.

Mk 11.28:   Ἐν ποίᾳ ἐξουσίᾳ ταῦτα ποιεῖς; ἢ τίς σοι ἔδωκεν τὴν
              ἐξουσίαν ταύτην ἵνα ταῦτα ποιῇς; (cf. Mt. 21.23).
Lk. 20.2:   Εἰπὸν ἡμῖν ἐν ποίᾳ ἐξουσίᾳ ταῦτα ποιεῖς, ἢ <u>τίς ἐστιν</u>
              <u>ὁ δούς</u> σοι τὴν ἐξουσίαν ταύτην;

Further, Luke phrases a question similarly on two other occasions, Lk. 8.45 R, τίς ὁ ἁψάμενός μου; for Mark's τίς μου ἥψατο τῶν ἱματίων; (Mk 5.30) and Lk. 20.17 R, τί οὖν ἐστιν τὸ γεγραμμένον τοῦτο...; for Mark's οὐδὲ τὴν γραφὴν ταύτην ἀνέγνωτε...; (Mk 12.10).[44]

The MA τίς ἐστιν ὁ παίσας σε; is then, if anything, a little more Lukan in style than it is Matthean. This is difficult for Goulder in two ways. First, this state of affairs is conducive to the theses of both Neirynck and Tuckett, that Luke himself was responsible for the question which was later interpolated into Matthew. Second, if the question is just as Lukan as it is Matthean, it is clear that this MA does not satisfy the criteria that 'the wording in Matthew should be characteristic of Matthew, and that the same words in Luke should be uncharacteristic of Luke' ('Knowledge', p. 144). There is an un-Lukan word—παίω—but it is also un-Matthean. There are Matthean words— τίς ἐστιν and ὁ plus participle—but these expressions are just as Lukan. Since the MA at Mk 14.65 is Goulder's key MA, this is an important observation.[45]

The argument from Matthean, un-Lukan language on this MA could, however, be revised rather than discarded. As we have seen, the great problem for hardline two-source theorists is the unanimous witness to the reading τίς ἐστιν ὁ παίσας σε; in Matthew. As Goulder stresses, 'there is no manuscript, version or patristic citation for the omission from Matthew here' ('Knowledge', p. 156). He argues against Neirynck's thesis by saying:

> We cannot exclude the *possibility* of errors in all our witnesses, but we are justified in positing such only when we cannot make sense of our texts without them. This is by no means the case here, as I have shown when expounding Matthew above ('Knowledge', pp. 154-55).

44. Cadbury also draws attention to Lk. 8.45 R and 20.2 R and compares them with the MA here. He suggests that Luke composed the question which was later, by assimilation, added to Matthew (*Style*, p. 136).

45. Cf. Tuckett, 'Relationship', p. 137, comes to a similar conclusion but from observation of the context rather than the language, 'The question is neither Matthean nor un-Lukan. (In fact it fits Luke's context and not Matthew's, and hence could be used to show Matthew's knowledge of Luke.)'

This is a strong argument. Goulder has shown that it is quite possible to imagine Matthew adding τίς ἐστιν ὁ παίσας σε; to Mark, largely because the language (with the exception of παίω) is congenial to Matthew. It follows from this that arguments like Neirynck's are unnecessary. The fact that the language is a little more congenial to Luke than it is to Matthew (again with the exception of παίω) is a problem for the pure form of Goulder's argument. In a revised form of the argument one could say that the congeniality of the language to Luke might have encouraged him to take over the five consecutive words without changing them.

To summarize, then, Goulder's general argument from wording characteristic of Matthew but uncharacteristic of Luke is unsatisfactory for the MA at Mk 14.65. Although the language is congenial to Matthew, it is also, if anything, more congenial to Luke. Nevertheless, Goulder's underlying argument about the unlikelihood of coincidence or independent redaction is valid here, particularly as both Matthew and Luke coincide in using the *hapax* παίω. This argument, from the unlikelihood of coincidence, is accepted by two-source theorists like Neirynck and Tuckett in that they conjecturally emend the text at Mt. 26.68 to remove the MA. Such a solution is problematic because there is no manuscript evidence for the omission in Matthew and because, as Goulder has shown, it is at least possible to regard the addition of τίς ἐστιν ὁ παίσας σε; as Matthew's own.[46]

E. *Minor Agreements Featuring Language Characteristic of Matthew and Uncharacteristic of Luke*

1. *Preliminary Comments*

Unfortunately, then, for Goulder's thesis, the wording of some of the most striking MAs does not satisfy the criteria of being both characteristic of Matthew and uncharacteristic of Luke. Although this is not the only argument used by Goulder, it is the most important one

---

46. Throughout, I have assumed for the purposes of argument that Matthew's knowledge of Luke is not a viable option. Also I have mentioned only Goulder's key contemporary opponents (on this MA) Tuckett and Neirynck. There are, of course, other opinions on the verse, for example Fitzmyer (*Luke X–XXIV*, p. 1458) who thinks that Luke took the words from L, criticized by Goulder in *LNP*, p. 752. The view that these two MAs are due to oral traditions is defended by Marion Soards, *Passion*. For further bibliography, see Neirynck, ΤΙΣ ΕΣΤΙΝ.

and also, as Tuckett observes, it is strong methodologically. A question naturally arises from this: do any of the thousand or so MAs listed by Neirynck satisfy these criteria? Further, do any satisfy the reverse criteria whereby the wording would be both characteristic of Luke and uncharacteristic of Matthew?[47]

A large part of the debate between Goulder and Tuckett centres on definition of terms. In the examples that follow, I will count as characteristic words those which satisfy Hawkins's criteria (see previous chapter) or I will give reasons. Where necessary I will show how an evangelist uses the word/phrase in question elsewhere in the Gospel.

The term 'uncharacteristic' or 'un-Lukan' is less straightforward. Goulder tends to treat as uncharacteristic words those which are *hapax legomena* in a gospel; or words where the evangelist could have used a favourite word with a similar meaning; or words which an evangelist uses in an unnatural or unusual way. Some of these criteria will be used below. A word of qualification should be added on the *hapax* criterion. Of course any writer will use the odd word or expression from his or her vocabulary only once in a given document: the word or expression in question may not be uncharacteristic of that writer even when it is uncharacteristic of the given document. As Goulder points out, we should be put on our guard by the fact that the odd word which is a *hapax* in Luke can be very common in Acts (*LNP*, pp. 20-21). Therefore, wherever one sees a *hapax*, it does not necessarily follow that the evangelist will be taking it over from a source, even if that potential source is in Matthew.

If on a number of occasions, however, one sees words or expressions which are *hapaxes* in Luke, which are at the same time characteristic of Matthew, it will become steadily less likely that Luke does not know Matthew. This is one of the values of Goulder's stress on attempting to find a 'rump' of such cases. The more times it happens, the more likely it will become that the 'un-Lukan' word or expression will have been taken over by Luke, perhaps inadvertently, from Matthew.[48]

---

47. With one exception, the examples cited below are taken from Neirynck's *Minor Agreements*.

48. Further, in the examples which follow I will concentrate on characteristic language rather than, say, theology or history. Cf. Cadbury, *Style*, p. vi, 'As a rule the linguistic study should precede rather than follow the theological and historical study. Instead of explaining a writer's language in the light of a theory about his

None of the following MAs are among those sometimes seen as Mark-Q overlap. It is worth remembering, however, that there is a fine line between a Mark-Q overlap and a MA and that for Goulder there is no line at all, rather a sliding scale of influence on Luke from Matthew. I have counted as Mark-Q overlap and so excluded from consideration the following: a) passages where there are six or more new words in agreement between Matthew and Luke against Mark, or b) passages in which there is agreement between Matthew and Luke against Mark with parallel passages in either Matthew or Luke or both or c) passages in which there is agreement between Matthew and Luke against Mark which occurs in Q contexts in Luke.

I will list six examples which satisfy the relevant criteria, MAs which are both positively Matthean and positively un-Lukan.

2. *The Examples*
a. *Matthew 12.15 // Mark 3.10 // Luke 6.19*[49]

Mt. 12.15:   καὶ ἠκολούθησαν αὐτῷ [ὄχλοι] πολλοί, καὶ
ἐθεράπευσεν αὐτοὺς <u>πάντας</u>.

Mk 3.7:   καὶ πολὺ πλῆθος ἀπὸ τῆς Γαλιλαίας
[ἠκολούθησεν]...10. πολλοὺς γὰρ ἐθεράπευσεν, ὥστε
ἐπιπίπτειν αὐτῷ ἵνα αὐτοῦ ἅψωνται ὅσοι εἶχον
μάστιγας.

Lk. 6.17:   καὶ πλῆθος πολὺ τοῦ λαοῦ...18. οἳ ἦλθον ἀκοῦσαι
αὐτοῦ καὶ ἰαθῆναι ἀπὸ τῶν νόσων αὐτῶν· καὶ οἱ
ἐνοχλούμενοι ἀπὸ πνευμάτων ἀκαθάρτων
ἐθεραπεύοντο, 19. καὶ πᾶς ὁ ὄχλος ἐζήτουν ἅπτεσθαι
αὐτοῦ, ὅτι δύναμις παρ' αὐτοῦ ἐξήρχετο καὶ ἰᾶτο
<u>πάντας</u>.

Matthew regularly uses πᾶς of sick people and it is particularly common in summary passages like this one and it is usually R. πᾶς is used of the sick in Matthew in 4.23 R (θεραπεύων πᾶσαν νόσον καὶ πᾶσαν μαλακίαν), 4.24 MK (καὶ προσήνεγκαν αὐτῷ πάντας τοὺς κακῶς ἔχοντας ποικίλαις νόσοις...), 8.16 R (πάντας τοὺς κακῶς ἔχοντας ἐθεράπευσεν), 9.35 R (θεραπεύων πᾶσαν νόσον καὶ πᾶσαν

identity and interests, we should test the theory by an independent study of the language.'

49. Neirynck, *Minor Agreements*, p. 79. Hawkins, *Horae*, p. 117, refers to this MA as an example of Matthew and Luke (independently) altering a passage 'seeming to limit the power of Jesus' (more particularly relevant to Mk 1.32, 34).

μαλακίαν), 10.1 R (θεραπεύειν πᾶσαν νόσον καὶ πᾶσαν μαλακίαν), 14.35 R (προσήνεγκαν αὐτῷ πάντας τοὺς κακῶς ἔχοντας) and here.[50]

πᾶς with the sick comes only once in Mark, at 1.32 // Mt. 4.24. In his parallel to Mk 1.32, Luke uses ἅπας (Lk. 4.40) and Luke uses this again in the same way in Acts 5.16. Elsewhere, πᾶς of the sick comes only once in Luke and it is here in this MA. Figures, then, are 7/1/1+0 and the combination would appear to be strongly characteristic of Matthew and markedly uncharacteristic of Luke. Goulder does not comment on this MA.

b. *Matthew 8.27 // Mark 4.41 // Luke 8.25*[51]

Mt. 8.27:	Ποταπός ἐστιν οὗτος ὅτι καὶ <u>οἱ</u> ἄνε<u>μοι</u> καὶ ἡ θάλασσα αὐτῷ ὑπακού<u>ουσιν;</u>
Mk 4.41:	Τίς ἄρα οὗτός ἐστιν ὅτι καὶ ὁ ἄνεμος καὶ ἡ θάλασσα ὑπακούει αὐτῷ;
Lk. 8.25:	Τίς ἄρα οὗτός ἐστιν ὅτι καὶ <u>τοῖς</u> ἀνέμ<u>οις</u> ἐπιτάσσει καὶ τῷ ὕδατι, καὶ ὑπακού<u>ουσιν</u> αὐτῷ;

Goulder here comments:

> Luke retains Mark's singular ἄνεμος till here, and uses the singular throughout the storm scene in Acts 27; he has the plural here = Mt., and at Acts 27.4, where the sense requires it. Neirynck (*MA*, p. 286) gives a list of six such Agreements, and Schürmann suggests independent change; but Luke shows that he is not interested in a plural for its own sake by καὶ τῷ ὕδατι (*LNP*, p. 421).[52]

The figures for ἄνεμος singular are 4/6/3+3 (Mt. 11.7 // Lk. 7.24; Mt. 14.24 // Mk 6.48; Mt. 14.30 R; Mt. 14.32 // Mk 6.51; Mk 4.37 // Lk.

---

50. Luz lists the occurrences in Matthew in his list, *Matthew 1–7*, p. 65, but he does not point out how rare it is in Mark and Luke.

51. Neirynck, *Minor Agreements*, pp. 97 and 286; Schmid, *Matthäus und Lukas*, p. 110.

52. There are several MAs in this pericope (Mt. 8.23-27 // Mk 4.35-41 // Lk. 8.22-25), and they are discussed by Goulder in *LNP*, pp. 419-22. Albert Fuchs makes a good deal of this pericope in his attempt to demonstrate a Deutero-Marcus in *Sprachliche Untersuchungen*. When Goulder reviews this book, the argument from Mattheanisms among the MAs emerges for the first time. See also more recently by Fuchs, 'Die „Seesturmperikope"'; pp. 83-84 on this MA. Although he refers briefly to Goulder on p. 90 n. 93, Fuchs does not engage with Goulder's claim that Deutero-Marcus is Matthäus. Cf. also the response to Fuchs by Schenk in the same volume, G. Strecker (ed.), *Symposium Göttingen*, pp. 93-117.

8.23; Mk 4.39a // Lk. 8.24; Mk 4.39b; Mk 4.41; Acts 27.7, 14, 15). For ἄνεμος plural the figures are 5/1/1+1, Mt. 7.25 QD; 7.27 QD; 8.26 R; 8.27 MA // Lk. 8.25, here; Mt. 24.31 // Mk 13.27; Acts 27.4.

ἄνεμος plural is, then, strongly characteristic of Matthew. It satisfies Hawkins's criteria; there are two QD occurrences; there is a redactional occurrence in the sense that Matthew has the plural where Mark has the singular and ἄνεμος singular recedes in the Gospel. It is uncharacteristic of Luke and comes only here in his Gospel. Luke shows a marginal preference for the singular which comes twice in this passage (Lk. 8.22-25) following Mark and it comes also in Lk. 7.24 QC.[53]

c. *Matthew 13.54 // Mark 6.2 // (Luke 4.15-16)*[54]

Mt. 13.54: καὶ ἐλθὼν εἰς τὴν πατρίδα αὐτοῦ ἐδίδασκεν αὐτοὺς ἐν τῇ συναγωγῇ <u>αὐτῶν</u>.

Mk 6.2: καὶ γενομένου σαββάτου ἤρξατο διδάσκειν ἐν τῇ συναγωγῇ.

Lk. 4.15-16: καὶ αὐτὸς ἐδίδασκεν ἐν ταῖς συναγωγαῖς <u>αὐτῶν</u> δοξαζόμενος ὑπὸ πάντων. καὶ ἦλθεν εἰς Ναζαρά, οὗ ἦν τεθραμμένος, καὶ εἰσῆλθεν κατὰ τὸ εἰωθὸς αὐτῷ ἐν τῇ ἡμέρᾳ τῶν σαββάτων εἰς τὴν συναγωγὴν...

This parallel forms part of the first of Goulder's list of examples in 'On Putting Q to the Test' (pp. 219-21; cf. *LNP*, pp. 299-301 and 306-307),[55] the other points being the spelling of Ναζαρά which is common to Lk. 4.16 and Mt. 4.13, together with the agreement in order (see above, pp. 95 and 101-102). Goulder writes,

> There are two places in Mark where the word αὐτῶν is used without the antecedent, meaning 'the Jews'. This use is congenial to Matthew, who has it in all seven times in his Gospel, this being one: 'their scribes',

53. This is Gundry's sixth example of a MA which is a 'foreign body' in Luke, 'Matthean Foreign Bodies', pp. 1472-73.

54. This MA is not listed by Neirynck and it is rarely, if ever, discussed as a MA. Tuckett is discussing it in response to Goulder. Delobel, 'La rédaction', p. 214, does draw attention to αὐτῶν in Mt. 13.54, noting that this is Matthew's style, but he thinks that Luke's αὐτῶν in 4.15 comes not from here but from Mk 1.39.

55. This MA drops out of the discussion in 'Knowledge' (pp. 144-48) without comment, perhaps because Goulder wants to stress the MA between Mt. 4.13 and Lk. 4.16 without drawing in the additional parallel Mt. 13.54 // Mk 6.2 // Lk. 4.15 Unfortunately, however, this is at the expense of the only aspect in Lk. 4.15-16 which is demonstrable as Matthean and un-Lukan.

'their synagogues' are tacitly contrasted with 'our scribes', 'our syna-gogues' in a Jewish-Christian community. It is not so congenial to Luke who, as a Gentile Christian, did not have a synagogue, or scribes in his Church: and Luke has the expression only once in the Gospel and Acts, here. I do not know of any response to this point ('On Putting Q to the Test', p. 221).

Tuckett does respond to the point and agrees that 'This is often recognized as a feature of Mt. R', but he adds that 'it is not clear that this is also un-Lukan':

Certainly it is not exclusively Matthean, since Mark can also refer to 'their' synagogues (Mk 1.23, 39). Further, Luke refers to the 'synagogues of the Jews' in Acts (Acts 13.5; 14.1; 17.1)... Do we know that Matthew's church had synagogues? Matthew's language here only shows a self-conscious differentiation between the Christian and Jewish communities of his day; but in this Luke is not very different (cf. the programmatic statements in Acts 13.46; 18.6; 28.28). The use of αὐτῶν here is not necessarily un-Lukan, and it therefore fails to satisfy the second of Goulder's conditions.[56]

These points are contestable. The qualification 'not exclusively Matthean' is not very helpful. αὐτῶν occurs without antecedent in reference to synagogues five times in Matthew, three times redaction-ally (4.23 MK; 9.35 R; 10.17 R; 12.9 R and here). It is, then, twice as common in Matthew as it is in Mark (1.23, 39) and, more importantly, it is five times as common in Matthew as it is in Luke in which it occurs only here. Further, Matthew has οἱ γραμματεῖς αὐτῶν at 7.29 R and ἐν ταῖς πόλεσιν αὐτῶν at 11.1 R, hence Goulder's figures of 7/2/1+0 for 'αὐτῶν = the Jews' (*MLM*, p. 477). This usage, then, satis-fies Hawkins's criteria. It is worth noting also that the occurrences are distributed evenly over Matthew's Gospel.

Further, the two usages in Mark in one important way add to Goulder's case in that Luke has parallels to both in which he does not have αὐτῶν. Where Mark in 1.23 has καὶ εὐθὺς ἦν ἐν τῇ συναγωγῇ αὐτῶν ἄνθρωπος ἐν πνεύματι ἀκαθάρτῳ, Luke in 4.33 has καὶ ἐν τῇ συναγωγῇ ἦν ἄνθρωπος ἔχων πνεῦμα δαιμονίου ἀκαθάρτου. Where Mark in 1.39 has καὶ ἦλθεν κηρύσσων εἰς τὰς συναγωγὰς αὐτῶν εἰς ὅλην τὴν Γαλιλαίαν, Luke in 4.44 has καὶ ἦν κηρύσσων εἰς τὰς συναγωγὰς τῆς Ἰουδαίας.

---

56. C. M. Tuckett, 'Relationship', p. 131.

Tuckett's second point about 'synagogues of the Jews' in Acts and the differentiation between Christian and Jewish communities does not really address the issue. Goulder's point is that αὐτῶν of the Jews is Matthew's own characteristic style, albeit influenced by his church situation. The analogies Tuckett draws from Acts deal only with similar content: the expressions are different. Other than in this MA, there is no place in Luke–Acts where the usage is found.

This, then, is a striking MA. The wording is both Matthean and un-Lukan. The only difficulty for Goulder is the question of the legitimacy of reading the parallel, an issue not addressed by Tuckett. Mt. 13.54 // Mk 6.2, in which Jesus teaches in the synagogue at his home town, is parallel to Lk. 4.16. Mark and Luke here both have 'the synagogue'; only Matthew has 'their synagogue'. Luke's αὐτῶν is in his previous verse, 4.15, in a slightly different context, with 'synagogues' plural, and more obviously parallel to Mk 1.14b-15 // Mt. 4.17.[57]

d. *Matthew 14.13 // Mark 6.33 // Luke 9.11*[58]

Mt. 14.13:   καὶ ἀκούσαντες <u>οἱ ὄχλοι ἠκολούθησαν</u> αὐτῷ πεζῇ
             ἀπὸ τῶν πόλεων.

Mk 6.33:   καὶ εἶδον αὐτοὺς ὑπάγοντας καὶ ἐπέγνωσαν πολλοί
             καὶ πεζῇ ἀπὸ πασῶν τῶν πόλεων συνέδραμον ἐκεῖ
             καὶ προῆλθον αὐτούς.

Lk. 9.11:   <u>οἱ</u> δὲ <u>ὄχλοι</u> γνόντες <u>ἠκολούθησαν</u> αὐτῷ.

There are three differences between Matthew/Luke and Mark here: οἱ ὄχλοι, an aorist participle (ἀκούσαντες/γνόντες) and ἠκολούθησαν,

---

57. Neither Huck-Greeven, Aland, Orchard nor Sparks read the parallel here. Farmer, in his *Synopticon*, marks ἐν ταῖς συναγωγαῖς αὐτῶν in Lk. 4.15 as 'complete verbatim agreement between Matthew and Luke' but it is unclear where he sees the agreement; if it is with either Mt. 13.54 or with Mt. 4.23 // Mk 1.39, then the colouring is not consistent. Cf. Tuckett, 'The Minor Agreements and Textual Criticism', 'Perhaps one should reserve the term "MA" for texts where there is no doubt about the existence of a literary relationship between all three gospels' (p. 121).

58. Neirynck, *Minor Agreements*, p. 112. This MA is the fifth of Hawkins's list of twenty difficult MAs, *Horae*, pp. 210-11. Hawkins is followed by Lagrange, *Saint Luc*, p. lxxxi. It is part of Gundry's ninth example, 'Matthean Foreign Bodies', pp. 1474-75. This is one of several MAs in the pericope detailed by M.-E. Boismard in 'Two-Source Theory at an Impasse', cited with favour by Goulder (*LNP*, p. 434). Neirynck responds to the argument in the article cited in, p. 99 n. 27. Cf. Boismard's subsequent 'Introduction' and F. Neirynck, 'Response'.

among which οἱ ὄχλοι is semi-Matthean with figures of 33/2/15. Goulder says,

> Luke rarely writes οἱ ὄχλοι in the way that Matthew does without introducing them (11.14 is another example, but again with a Matthean parallel, Mt. 9.33) (*LNP*, p. 434).

It might be added that whereas Matthew, in his account of the Feeding of the Five Thousand (Mt. 14.13-21 // Mk 6.30-44 // Lk. 9.10-17), four times speaks about οἱ ὄχλοι plural, Luke has the plural only here.[59] These are the other usages in the pericope:

Mt. 14.14:	καὶ ἐξελθὼν εἶδεν πολὺν ὄχλον // Mk 6.34: καὶ ἐξελθὼν εἶδεν πολὺν ὄχλον.
Mt. 14.15:	ἀπόλυσον <u>τοὺς ὄχλους</u> // Mk 6.36: ἀπόλυσον αὐτούς // Lk. 9.12: ἀπόλυσον τὸν ὄχλον.
Mt. 14.19a:	καὶ κελεύσας <u>τοὺς ὄχλους</u> ἀνακλιθῆναι ἐπὶ τοῦ χόρτου // Mk 6.39: ἐπέταξεν αὐτοῖς // Lk. 9.14: κατακλίνατε αὐτοῖς.
Mt. 14.19b:	ἔδωκεν τοῖς μαθηταῖς τοὺς ἄρτους, οἱ δὲ μαθηταὶ <u>τοῖς ὄχλοις</u> // Mk 6.41: ἵνα παρατιθῶσιν αὐτοῖς // Lk. 9.16: παραθεῖναι τῷ ὄχλῳ.

On each occasion, then, οἱ ὄχλοι plural is a redactional change to Mark.[60]

Moreover, outside of this context, the combination ἀκολουθέω + ὄχλοι comes only in Matthew, and always redactionally.[61] It is at Mt. 4.25 R (cf. Mk 3.7-8; Lk. 6.17); 8.1 R; 19.2 R and 21.9 R, so the combination has figures of 5/0/1+0:[62] four times Matthew R, never in

---

59. Elsewhere Luke has ὄχλοι plural at 3.7 QD; 3.10 L; 4.42 R; 5.3 L; 5.15 R (or MA); 7.24 QC; 8.42 R; 8.45 R; 9.18 R; 11.14 QC; 12.54 QD; 14.25 L (or QD); 23.4 R (or L) and 23.48 R. It is certainly not uncharacteristic of Luke and οἱ ὄχλοι on its own in this MA is not sufficient to excite attention.

60. Streeter, *Four Gospels*, p. 314: 'As the unexpressed subject is people, described in the next sentence of Mark as πολὺν ὄχλον, Matthew and Luke naturally supply οἱ ὄχλοι'. Streeter has not seen the force of the agreement over the plural οἱ ὄχλοι. Cf. *LNP*, p. 434 and Cadbury, *Style*, p. 93.

61. Boismard, 'Impasse', p. 8, claims that the expression is 'foreign to Luke's style' and adds: 'When Luke describes a crowd that follows Jesus, he prefers to use the verb συνπορεύεσθαι. When he wishes to describe a crowd gathering around Jesus, as here, he more often uses the verb συνερχεσθαι.' Cf. Neirynck, 'The Matthew–Luke Agreements in Matt. 14.13-14', pp. 85-86.

62. It may be 6/0/1+0 if ὄχλοι is read at Mt. 12.15. It is not read by Greeven, and N-A[26] places it in square brackets. Cf. ἀκολουθέω with ὄχλος πολύς

Mark and only in Luke–Acts in this MA. Here, then, is a combination of words strongly characteristic of Matthew and uncharacteristic of Luke.[63]

e. *Matthew 22.27 // Mark 12.22 // Luke 20.32*[64]

Mt. 22.27: ὕστερον δὲ πάντων ἀπέθανεν ἡ γυνή.
Mk 12.22: ἔσχατον πάντων καὶ ἡ γυνὴ ἀπέθανεν.
Lk. 20.32: ὕστερον καὶ ἡ γυνὴ ἀπέθανεν.

Goulder draws attention to this example when he discusses the MAs in *LNP*, chapter two:

> Matthew never has the adverb ἔσχατον, but has ὕστερον x 7, including 21.37 R, 26.60 R. Luke also writes ὕστερον; but he never uses the word elsewhere, either in Gospel or Acts (*LNP*, p. 48).[65]

The figures for ὕστερον are 7/0/1+0[66] and one might add that in Mt. 21.37 (ὕστερον δὲ ἀπέστειλεν πρὸς αὐτοὺς τὸν υἱὸν αὐτοῦ), the same substitution, ὕστερον for ἔσχατον, occurs in a similar context. ὕστερον appears to be Matthew's word for representing the last in a series. Similar again is 26.60-61, ὕστερον δὲ προσελθόντες δύο εἶπαν, Οὗτος ἔφη, Δύναμαι καταλῦσαι τὸν ναὸν...[67] The language in this MA is,

Mt. 20.29 R; Mk 5.24 ἀκολουθέω with ὄχλος πολύς; Lk. 7.9 QD ἀκολουθέω with ὄχλος. Cf. Luz, *Matthew 1–7*, p. 54, says that ἀκολουθέω occurs with ὄχλοι four times redactionally in Matthew. See further Neirynck, 'The Matthew–Luke Agreements in Matt. 14.13-14', pp. 85-88.

63. Neirynck responds to Goulder (and others) on this MA in 'The Minor Agreements and the Two-Source Theory', pp. 51-55. In particular he draws attention to the fact that Luke uses the singular ὁ ὄχλος in 8.40 (MK) and then the plural in vv. 42 and 45 against the singular in Mark (p. 53).

64. Neirynck, *Minor Agreements*, p. 156; also listed on p. 284 among 'changes in vocabulary'.

65. In context, Goulder is criticizing Schmid's approach to the MAs.

66. Goulder variously gives the figures as 7/0/1 and 7/1/1; the Markan instance is Mk 16.14. Elsewhere in the New Testament, ὕστερον occurs only in Jn 13.26 and Heb. 12.11.

67. Hawkins, *Horae*, p. 209, places this in the category of MAs which 'consist of words so ordinary and colourless and so nearly synonymous with Mark's that the use of them may be merely accidental' but he also notes (p. 209 n. 2) that ὕστερον is characteristic of Matthew. Schmid claims that the adverbial ἔσχατον is little used (*Matthäus und Lukas*, p. 142-43), but Goulder notes that the same phrase ἔσχατον πάντων comes in 1 Cor. 15.8 (*LNP*, p. 699) and, further, ὕστερον is uncommon in the New Testament outside Matthew (see previous note).

then, as Goulder says, 'characteristic of Matthew' and 'not characteristic of Luke at all' (*LNP*, p. 48).

f. *Matthew 26.47 // Mark 14.43 // Luke 22.47*[68]

Mt. 26.47:	Καὶ ἔτι αὐτοῦ λαλοῦντος <u>ἰδοὺ</u> Ἰούδας εἷς τῶν
			δώδεκα <u>ἦλθεν</u>.
Mk 14.43:	Καὶ εὐθὺς ἔτι αὐτοῦ λαλοῦντος παραγίνεται Ἰούδας
			εἷς τῶν δώδεκα.
Lk. 22.47:	Ἔτι αὐτοῦ λαλοῦντος <u>ἰδοὺ</u> ὄχλος, καὶ ὁ λεγόμενος
			Ἰούδας εἷς τῶν δώδεκα <u>προήρχετο</u> αὐτούς.

ἰδού is common in both Matthew and Luke (62/17/57), and they both
often insert it into Mark—they agree, for example, in having ἰδού
against Mark in the Healing of the Paralytic (Mt. 9.2 // Mk 2.3 // Lk.
5.18) and in the Healing of the Leper (Mt. 8.2 // Mk 1.40 // Lk. 5.12).
Luke, however, never outside of this MA inserts ἰδού after a genitive
absolute. Matthew, on the other hand, regularly does this.[69] He has the
construction eleven times in all, at least four times redactionally: 9.10
R; 9.18 R; 9.32 (?R); 12.46 R and 17.5 R. It is noticeable further that
on three of these occasions, as in this MA, the ἰδού interrupts people
speaking:

Mt. 9.18:	Ταῦτα αὐτοῦ λαλοῦντος αὐτοῖς ἰδοὺ ἄρχων εἷς
			ἐλθὼν προσεκύνει αὐτῷ λέγων... (// Mk 5.21 // Lk.
			8.40-41).[70]
Mt. 12.46:	Ἔτι αὐτοῦ λαλοῦντος τοῖς ὄχλοις ἰδοὺ ἡ μήτηρ καὶ
			οἱ ἀδελφοὶ αὐτοῦ εἱστήκεισαν ἔξω... (// Mk 3.31 //
			Lk. 8.19).
Mt. 17.5:	ἔτι αὐτοῦ λαλοῦντος ἰδοὺ νεφέλη φωτεινὴ
			ἐπεσκίασεν αὐτούς... (// Mk 9.7 // Lk. 9.34).[71]

The expression is, then, markedly characteristic of Matthew and it is
un-Lukan.[72]

68. Neirynck, *Minor Agreements*, p. 175; listed also on p. 273 with instances of
the introduction of καὶ ἰδού into Mark.

69. Occurrences are listed by Hawkins, *Horae*, p. 31.

70. Note also that Luke agrees with Matthew against Mark here in using ἰδού
but not in using a genitive absolute beforehand (Lk. 8.40-41).

71. Here Luke agrees with Matthew against Mark in using a genitive absolute
but not in using ἰδού.

72. Goulder mentions that Luke agrees with Matthew in inserting ἰδού here
(*LNP*, p. 746) but does not comment on the genitive absolute + ἰδού construction.

3. *Conclusion*

There are, then, at least six MAs which feature language which is at the same time both characteristic of Matthew and un-Lukan. That is to say, in at least six different MAs, Goulder's criteria are satisfied. In each of these six MAs, at Mk 3.10; 4.41; 6.2, 33; 12.22 and 14.43, the words or expressions in question satisfy Hawkins's criteria for characteristic Matthew and also occur only once in Luke. In five of the examples (the exception being Mk 4.41 where ἄνεμος plural comes once in Acts), the word or expression comes only once in the whole of Luke–Acts. In five of the examples (the exception being Mk 6.2), the MA is in a 'genuine' parallel and not in a verse bracketed by Neirynck.

For each example, arguments for independent redaction by Matthew and Luke could no doubt be adduced. Independent redaction has been posited by Tuckett for the MA at Mk 6.2 and has been strongly urged by Neirynck for the MA at Mk 6.33. The question which arises, however, is whether or not one can envisage Luke on all these occasions writing using words or expressions which are not only un-Lukan but are also characteristic of Matthew.

It is worth remembering that, as Goulder says, 'we all use, when writing on our own, a grade of frequency of expressions, from once up to many times' (*LNP*, p. 20) and, clearly, an 'un-Lukan' word or expression will not necessarily be the sign of a source. Among the MAs, a *hapax* in Luke will not necessarily be a sign that he is following Matthew, even if the expression happens also to be one of Matthew's favourites. Perhaps out of a thousand or so MAs one would expect on the 2ST to find a handful which do satisfy Goulder's criteria. What is required, then, is some sort of control test: is it possible to point to MAs which feature language which is both characteristic of Luke and also un-Matthean?

F. *Minor Agreements Featuring Language Characteristic of*
Luke and Uncharacteristic of Matthew

1. *Preliminary Comments*

For Sanders and Davies, the point that 'there are Mattheanisms in Luke' provides the most important indicator that Luke knew

In *MLM*, p. 451, however, in Goulder's critique of Dahl's *Die Passionsgeschichte bei Matthäus*, it is listed among words and expressions in the Passion Narrative 'characteristic of Matthew' and 'definitely non-Lukan'.

Matthew.[73] When they briefly consider the opposite case, they say:
'there have been no successful attempts to find "Lukanisms" in
Matthew'.[74] Few, if any, attempts have actually been made, however, to
look for Lukanisms in Matthew and this is probably because of the
difficulty of imagining the idea that Matthew knew Luke.[75] There is,
however, another reason for looking for Lukanisms in Matthew and
that is to provide a control test for Goulder's claims. We have already
seen a good number of striking Lukanisms in the Q material. The
question now arises: are there similar striking Lukanisms among the
MAs?

Although a couple of MAs come close,[76] there are, I think, only two
MAs which clearly satisfy the converse of Goulder's criteria and there
is a textual question mark against the second of these.

2. *The Examples*
a. *Matthew 14.21 // Mark 6.44 // Luke (9.14)*[77]

Mt. 14.21:	οἱ δὲ ἐσθίοντες ἦσαν ἄνδρες <u>ὡσεὶ</u> πεντακισχίλιοι χωρὶς γυναικῶν καὶ παιδίων...
Mk 6.44:	καὶ ἦσαν οἱ φαγόντες [τοὺς ἄρτους] πεντακισχίλιοι ἄνδρες.
Lk. 9.14:	ἦσαν γὰρ <u>ὡσεὶ</u> ἄνδρες πεντακισχίλιοι.

73. Sanders and Davies, *Studying*, pp. 93 and 96.

74. Sanders and Davies, *Studying*, p. 97.

75. See Neirynck, *Minor Agreements*, p. 28 n. 85, for scholars who have argued
for some form of Matthean dependence on Luke and cf. Schmid, *Matthäus und
Lukas*, p. 3 n. 1 and p. 6 n. 4. See also Ronald V. Huggins, 'Matthean Posteriority'.
It is astonishing that Huggins does not refer to Goulder, especially as, on p. 5 n. 11,
he lists scholars who have argued Luke's use of Matthew.

76. Those which come close are: 1) Mt. 9.7-8 // Mk 2.12 // Lk. 5.25-26
(Neirynck, *Minor Agreements*, p. 70): the addition of εἰς τὸν οἶκον + genitive
(4/6/15+5, Lk. 8.41 R); cf. Lk. 1.23, the identical clause, ἀπῆλθεν εἰς τὸν οἶκον
αὐτοῦ; and cf. *LNP*, pp. 91-92 and below, pp. 155. 2) Mt. 21.2 // Mk 11.2 // Lk.
19.30 and Mt. 21.7 // Mk 11.7 // Lk. 19.35 (Neirynck, *Minor Agreements*, pp. 144-
45): the substitution of ἄγω (4/3/13+26) for φέρω; cf. Matthew's preference for
προσφέρω (14/3/4+3).

77. Neirynck, *Minor Agreements*, p. 116. Lk. 9.14 is bracketed by Neirynck
because Luke has the statement of the size of the crowd earlier in his account than
do Matthew and Mark. Streeter, *Four Gospels*, p. 315, explains ὡσεί in Matthew as
a scribal addition, pointing out that 'this is omitted in Matthew by W, the uncial
fragment 0106, Old Lat. Syr. C. (hiat. S.) Orig.[Mt.]; and ὡς is substituted in Δ 33, D,
Θ 1'. Most, however, read ὡσεί here without question.

The word ὡσεί is strongly characteristic of Luke—it is on Hawkins's list and has figures of 3/1/9+6.[78] Luke often uses it with numbers, and usually redactionally:

3.23:   καὶ αὐτὸς ἦν Ἰησοῦς ἀρχόμενος <u>ὡσεὶ</u> ἐτῶν
                  τριάκοντα...

9.28 R: ἐγένετο δὲ μετὰ τοὺς λόγους τούτους <u>ὡσεὶ</u> ἡμέραι
                  ὀκτώ... (cf. Mk 9.2 // Mt. 17.1).

22.41 R: καὶ αὐτὸς ἀπεσπάσθη ἀπ᾽ αὐτῶν <u>ὡσεὶ</u> λίθου
                  βολήν... (cf. Mk 14.35 // Mt. 26.39).

22.59 R: καὶ διαστάσης <u>ὡσεὶ</u> ὥρας μιᾶς ἄλλος τις
                  διϊσχυρίζετο λέγων... (cf. Mk 14.70 // Mt. 26.73).

23.44 R: καὶ ἦν <u>ὡσεὶ</u> ὥρα ἕκτη καὶ σκότος ἐγένετο ἐφ᾽ ὅλην
                  τὴν γῆν... (cf. Mk 15.33 // Mt. 27.45).

With numbers and measures, ὡσεί has figures of 1/0/7+4, the other occurrences being Lk. 22.44, 24.11; Acts 1.15, 2.41, 10.3 and 19.7.[79] It actually occurs twice in Lk. 9.14. This is the second occasion:

Lk. 9.14b R: κατακλίνατε αὐτοὺς κλισίας <u>ὡσεὶ</u> ἀνὰ πεντήκοντα
                    (cf. Mk 6.39 // Mt. 14.19).[80]

By contrast, in Matthew ὡσεί occurs with numbers or measures only here. On the two other occasions on which he uses the word, he uses it with images, both times in places where Mark has ὡς. In Mt. 3.16 the spirit descends like, ὡσεί, a dove, where Mark (1.10) and Luke (3.22) have ὡς περιστεράν. In Mt. 9.36 the crowds are like, ὡσεί, sheep without a shepherd, where Mark (6.34) has ὡς.

It is surprising then to find the word here in Matthew, and the point is all the more striking when one notes that Matthew has the almost identical wording with only the ὡσεί missing in his account of the Four Thousand where there is no Lukan parallel:

78. If, unlike N-A[26], one reads ὡσεί at Acts 19.34, there are seven occurrences in Acts.

79. Cf. Cadbury, *Style*, p. 129, 'This use of ὡσεί is found elsewhere in the NT only in Luke's writings...with the solitary exception of Mt. 14.21...which is thus under suspicion of having been assimilated to Luke 9.14'. It is worth noting that whereas Matthew here has the number immediately after ὡσεί, Luke here, and always, has a noun between ὡσεί and the numeral. I am grateful to Professor Goulder for this observation.

80. ὡσεί is, however, placed in square brackets here by N-A[26].

Mt. 15.38: οἱ δὲ ἐσθίοντες ἦσαν ( ) τετρακισχίλιοι ἄνδρες χωρὶς γυναικῶν καὶ παιδίων.

Here, then, there is a word in a MA used in a way which is strongly characteristic of Luke but which is at the same time clearly un-Matthean.

b. *Matthew 22.35 // Mark 12.28 // Luke 10.25*[81]

Mt. 22.35: καὶ ἐπηρώτησεν εἷς ἐξ αὐτῶν [νομικὸς] πειράζων αὐτόν, 36. Διδάσκαλε, ποία ἐντολὴ μεγάλη...

Mk 12.28: καὶ προσελθὼν εἷς τῶν γραμματέων...ἐπηρώτησεν αὐτόν, Ποία ἐστὶν ἐντολὴ πρώτη πάντων;

Lk. 10.25: καὶ ἰδοὺ νομικός τις ἀνέστη ἐκπειράζων αὐτὸν λέγων, Διδάσκαλε, τί ποιήσας...

νομικός is strongly characteristic of Luke with figures of 1/0/6+0 (7.30 QD; 11.45 QD; 11.46 QD; 11.52 QD; 14.3 L and here).[82] Luke apparently uses it with little distinction in meaning from γραμματεύς. At 11.53, for example, after a discourse directed at Pharisees and νομικοί, Luke concludes with a comment on Pharisees and γραμματεῖς.[83] Matthew, on the other hand, never uses it elsewhere. His usual word for a scribe is γραμματεύς (23/21/14+4).

81. Neirynck, *Minor Agreements*, p. 157; on p. 284 this MA is listed with other 'changes in vocabulary'. Some scholars, like Crossan (see below, p. 215 n. 39) attribute the pericope in Luke to Q. It does not, however, satisfy any of the criteria outlined above (p. 110) for Mark-Q overlap. Schweizer, *Matthew*, p. 425, suggests that the MAs here are due to oral traditions. He reads νομικός without question. Sanders and Davies, *Studying*, pp. 84-86 discuss the pericope as an example of Matthew as the middle term and so a problem for the 2ST. They also read νομικός without question. See also Lagrange, *Saint Luc*, p. 310, 'νομικός est un terme de Luc (encore cinq fois)...Il est possible que le Matt. grec ait fait ici un emprunt à Luc.'

82. For Rehkopf, however, νομικός is 'illustrative of pre-Lukan speech usage' (*Die lukanische Sonderquelle*, p. 95). νομικός is also at Titus 3.9 and 13 and νομοδιδάσκαλος at Lk. 5.17, Acts 5.34 and 1 Tim. 1.7. There is a possible seventh occurrence in Luke, in 11.53, not read by either N-A[26] or Greeven but read by Gundry ('Matthean Foreign Bodies', p. 1480) and by Kilpatrick in 'Scribes, Lawyers and Lukan Origins' (p. 57). Kilpatrick does not read it in Mt. 22.35 but his reasoning is a little circular. Similar is Streeter, *Four Gospels*, p. 320.

83. Cf. Creed, *St Luke*, p. 152, 'The word is found not infreq. in papyri and inscrr. for "a lawyer"...The Gentile Luke tends to substitute it for the Jewish γραμματεύς.' With Streeter, Creed questions the reading in Matthew.

The word is characteristic of Luke but uncharacteristic of Matthew and would, therefore, be a weighty counter-example, but it is not straightforward because some MSS of Matthew lack the word. Goulder writes:

> νομικός has been suspected at Mt. 22.35 by a long line of text-critics, including Streeter, Hawkins, Burkitt and Kilpatrick; and it is now bracketed by N-A[26]. Metzger says, 'its absence from family 1 as well as from widely scattered versional (e syr[s] arm) and patristic (Orig.) witnesses takes on additional significance when...Matthew nowhere else uses the word' and thinks scribal introduction from Luke 'not unlikely'. We may further agree with Schmid that the phrase εἷς ἐξ αὐτῶν νομικός is 'remarkably overladen' (*LNP*, p. 486).[84]

Goulder, for once, sides with the two-source theorists, but the textual question is actually finely balanced. As Goulder points out, N-A[26] brackets νομικός, but one might add that Greeven reads it. The arguments used by Goulder are not conclusive: some of the scholars he cites are attempting to reduce the impact which this MA might make, especially as there are two more agreements in the same verse ([ἐκ]πειράζων and διδάσκαλε). That Matthew nowhere else uses the word is an uneasy criterion. It comes close to assuming what needs to be proved and begs the question why Matthean scribes do not introduce νομικός anywhere else.

Many scholars do read νομικός here in Matthew.[85] The fact that the phrase εἷς ἐξ αὐτῶν νομικός in Matthew is 'remarkably overladen' could tell in favour of the reading rather than against it.[86] If Matthew

---

84. Goulder actually talks about Mt. 22.34 but this is an error for 22.35. I have omitted Goulder's references from the quotation: Hawkins, from W. Sanday (ed.), *Oxford Studies*, p. 44 n. 2; Kilpatrick, see p. 120 n. 82 (above); Metzger, *Textual Commentary*, p. 59 but cf. *Text*, p. 64; the reference to Burkitt, *JTS* (o.s.) 26, p. 283 is an error (I do not know what the reference should be); Schmid, *Matthäus und Lukas*, pp. 143-47 (pp. 146-47 on νομικός).

85. For example p. 120 n. 81, above; also Fitzmyer, *Luke X-XXIV*, pp. 879-80 and Gundry, 'Matthean Foreign Bodies', p. 1480.

86. This is Gundry's view, 'Matthean Foreign Bodies', p. 1480. This MA sits oddly, however, as Gundry's thirteenth example of 'Matthean foreign bodies' among the MAs. γραμματεύς in Gundry's n. 27 on the same page is an error for νομικός.

wrote the overladen phrase, a scribe might well have omitted νομικός, especially as the resulting account makes perfect sense.[87]

This possible MA could, then, provide a second counter-example to Goulder's theory.

3. *Conclusion*

There is, therefore, at least one MA which satisfies the converse of Goulder's criteria, at Mk 6.44. This example is a striking one. Matthew does not use ὡσεί in his account of the Feeding of the Four Thousand where there is no Lukan parallel and when he uses the word elsewhere, it is with images. Luke, on the other hand, uses ὡσεί nine times in the Gospel including seven times with numbers and measures, often redactionally, including once again in the same verse. The usage is markedly Lukan and is quite un-Matthean. It is surprising to find ὡσεί in Mt. 14.21 on the assumptions both of the 2ST and of the hypothesis of Luke's knowledge of Matthew.

A second possible example, νομικός in the MA at Mk 12.28, also clearly satisfies the converse of Goulder's criteria. The word comes only here in Matthew. He prefers γραμματεύς of scribes. Luke, on the other hand, uses νομικός interchangeably with γραμματεύς. Goulder does not read νομικός in Mt. 22.35, but the textual evidence is inconclusive.

Since there is not a rump of cases like these ones, the six cases listed above of MAs with Matthean, un-Lukan language take on greater significance.

G. *Conclusion*

Goulder claims that 'the Minor Agreements in fact provide the most important test of the 4ST' ('On Putting Q to the Test', p. 218). In his two articles on the MAs and in *LNP*, Goulder sets out three arguments on the MAs which, he thinks, establish his thesis. The first (C.1) is the

---

87. πειράζω / ἐκπειράζω is not particularly enlightening. πειράζω is common enough in Matthew (6/4/2+5) and ἐκπειράζω occurs again in the citation of Deut. 6.16 at Lk. 4.12 QC (i.e. 1/0/2+0). διδασκαλέ is common in all three Synoptics (10/6/11). Cf. also, however, *LNP*, p. 486, suggesting influence of Matthew on Luke in the quotation of the Shema because of Matthew's knowledge of the Hebrew.

key one and looks for words in the MAs characteristic of Matthew which are also un-Lukan. The second (C.2) is an argument from order. The third (C.3) concerns clusters of 'not very Lukan' words or expressions in a single verse, words which on their own would not be impressive but together take on importance.

The second of these arguments (C.2), from order, recedes in relation to the MAs in *LNP*, and Goulder has not yet made his case on the third argument (C.3) in the light of Neirynck and Friedrichsen's critique.

Two underlying arguments then emerge in the course of *LNP*. First (C.4), where Matthew has a characteristic expression in a MA and Luke has a parallel characteristic expression, Goulder often argues that Luke is dependent on Matthew's redaction. This is relatively weak, partly because it is reversible but more importantly because it is conducive to the theory of independent redaction. The other argument (C.5) works from MAs where the link between Matthew and Luke, usually clear from the coincidence of *hapax*, is undoubtable.

The latter argument (C.5) is a good one, but it is not as strong methodologically as the first (C.1). Where a MA features an expression characteristic of Matthew but uncharacteristic of Luke, there is some indication that Luke may have known Matthew. Where there is simply an undoubtable link because of the coincidence of *hapax*, the MA may be problematic for a 'hardline' 2ST without providing clear evidence of Luke's knowledge of Matthew.

Several difficulties for Goulder's thesis emerge. Tuckett's response to 'On Putting Q to the Test' (B) attempts to show that Goulder's examples are either not clearly Matthean or not clearly un-Lukan. Tuckett, however, makes the conditions for 'Matthean' and 'un-Lukan' more stringent than does Goulder, for whom the stress was on the 'un-Lukan' criterion.

A particular difficulty for Goulder is that several of the most well-known and striking MAs do not feature language characteristic of Matthew (D). Ναζαρά (Mt. 4.13 // Lk. 4.16) is a *hapax* in both Matthew and Luke. Likewise, the MA at Mk 14.65 features a word, παίω, which is a *hapax* in both Matthew and Luke. Further, the question (τίς ἐστιν ὁ παίσας σε;) is framed in language which is no more characteristic of Matthew than it is of Luke.

Goulder's argument on such MAs could, however, be revised rather than discarded. His discussion of the MA at Mk 14.65 is couched in the terms of the argument from Matthean, un-Lukan language (C.1) but underlying this is the argument from the unlikeliness of coincidence or independent redaction (C.5). The alternative solution of hardline two-source theorists like Neirynck and Tuckett, conjectural emendation of the text at Mt. 26.68 to remove the MA, is problematic because there is no manuscript evidence for the omission in Matthew and because, as Goulder has shown, it is at least possible to regard the addition of τίς ἐστιν ὁ παίσας σε; as Matthew's own. Explanation of the MA at Mk 14.65 remains a difficulty for the 2ST and one of the strengths of Goulder's hypothesis.

Several MAs do, however, satisfy the criteria of having language both positively Matthean and positively un-Lukan. I have identified six. One of these forms part of one of Goulder's examples in 'On Putting Q to the Test', Mt. 13.54 // Mk 6.2 // Lk. 4.15-16 (E.2.c), αὐτῶν with συναγωγή occurring five times in Matthew, including three times R, but only here in Luke. The MA is not, though, in the 'true' parallel to the passage in Luke.

Three other examples from *LNP* are pertinent. Mt. 8.27 // Mk 4.41 // Lk. 8.25 (E.2.b) features ἄνεμος plural in Matthew and Luke against the singular in Mark. The plural comes only here in Luke (and once in Acts) but Matthew uses it five times including once elsewhere, redactionally, in this passage.

Similarly, at Mt. 14.13 // Mk 6.33 // Lk. 9.11 (E.2.d), Matthew and Luke agree against Mark in the combination οἱ ὄχλοι + ἀκολουθέω which outside of this MA comes four times in Matthew, each time redactionally, and never in Luke. Further, ὄχλος plural comes four times in Matthew's account (Mt. 14.13-21) but only here in Luke's.

In Mt. 22.27 // Mk 12.22 // Lk. 20.32 (E.2.e), Matthew and Luke agree in using ὕστερον (Matthew + πάντων) where Mark has ἔσχατον πάντων. Matthew uses ὕστερον six times elsewhere, twice redactionally, including Mt. 21.37 where it is again parallel to ἔσχατον in Mark (12.6) and used to represent the last in a series, as also at Mt. 26.60 R. Luke has the word only here.

Two noticeable MAs are not discussed by Goulder, Mt. 12.15 // Mk 3.10 // Lk. 6.19, the addition of πᾶς (E.2.a), and Mt. 26.47 // Mk 14.43 // Lk. 22.47, the addition of ἰδού (E.2.f). The first of these is significant because Matthew uses πᾶς of the sick six times elsewhere, often redactionally, but Luke never does. The second of these is important because Matthew has ἰδού ten times elsewhere after a genitive absolute; Luke never does. Matthew has ἰδού with the genitive absolute at least four times redactionally and on three of these occasions, as here, the ἰδού interrupts people speaking (Mt. 9.18 R; 12.46 R and 17.5 R).

In order to determine the importance of these six Matthean, un-Lukan MAs, I looked, as a control, for examples of MAs which satisfy the reverse criteria, language both Lukan and un-Matthean. I find only one certain example, an impressive one, Mt. 14.21 // Mk 6.44 // Lk. 9.14, where both Matthew and Luke qualify the number πεντακισχίλιοι with ὡσεί. ὡσεί with numbers or measures comes only here in Matthew, for whom ὡσεί is twice elsewhere used with images. Luke often uses ὡσεί in this way (1/0/7+4), often redactionally, including in the same verse, Lk. 9.14b R. Further, where Matthew has the nearly identical wording in 15.38, he does not use ὡσεί.

The existence of these counter-examples demonstrates how much care is necessary in using the argument from characteristic language. Tuckett says that one example alone of a MA which is both positively Matthean and positively un-Lukan would be enough to establish that Luke knew Matthew.[88] If this is the case, then it could be argued both that Luke knew Matthew and that Matthew knew Luke. These MAs, then, provide a sober warning that the argument from characteristic language among the MAs can at best only take us part of the way towards a solution to the synoptic problem.

The value of Goulder's approach is that he has attempted to demonstrate that there is a 'rump' of examples of this type of MA. Presumably the independent redaction hypothesis becomes steadily more difficult to maintain the more MAs with Matthean, un-Lukan language are pointed out. The problem with Goulder's approach is that several of his examples are not clearly Matthean and un-Lukan so his 'test' has not proved entirely convincing.

Our six examples of MAs which do satisfy the relevant criteria are not enough, then, to demonstrate that Luke knew Matthew. These are striking examples but there are not enough of them and there is at least one impressive counter instance. They may, however, provide some indication of the way the wind is blowing and could add evidence to a cumulative argument for Lukan knowledge of Matthew.

Finally, a further comment should be added about the relevance of Goulder's work to the contemporary debate about the MAs. Goulder's

---

88. C.M. Tuckett, 'Relationship', p. 130.

general argument has been criticized in two ways, first with regard to the quality of the majority of the MAs and second with regard to their relevance to the Q hypothesis. On the first matter, Tuckett says:

> Goulder's theory has to explain why the vast number of MAs are so *minor*. The very isolation of Mk 14.65 and 14.72 as MAs involving some substance in the texts of Matthew and Luke is itself a problem. Some substantive influence of Matthew's text on Luke (as at Mk 14.65 and 72) is relatively easy to conceive if Luke knew Matthew; but the theory that Luke's knowledge of Matthew has mostly led to changes at the level of καί becoming δέ, of ὑπό becoming ἀπό, or of λέγει becoming εἶπεν etc. is much harder to envisage.[89]

This perspective may, however, be the result of a trick of the light. Goulder's point is that 'the Two-Source hypothesis is in difficulty over the minor agreements' ('Knowledge', p. 144). They are 'a thorn in the side of the standard theory' (*LNP*, p. 50) and Goulder focuses on them in an attempt to undermine his main competitor, the 2ST. There is no difficulty for Goulder's thesis in the fact that many of them are δέ for καί or εἶπεν for λέγει. The greater influence of Matthew on Luke in triple tradition passages comes in passages which two-source theorists would assign to Mark-Q overlap which Goulder does not discuss in this context.[90] It is important to remember that Goulder's thesis is that Luke has reconciled Mark and Matthew and that this results in a sliding scale of Matthean influence on Luke, from pure triple tradition passages which feature MAs, to Mark-Q overlap passages which feature more Mattheanisms, to double tradition passages where Luke is dependent solely on Matthew.

In his earlier article, Tuckett makes another point, claiming that Goulder's twelve MAs cannot really put Q to the test:

> If one of his examples were established, this would indicate that Luke knew Matthew, but this would not of itself prove that the whole Q

---

89. Tuckett, 'Minor Agreements and Textual Criticism', p. 140; cf. 'The Synoptic Problem', *ABD* 6, p. 267.

90. For a good discussion of the problems which the theory of Mark-Q overlap raises, see E.P. Sanders, 'Overlaps' and Sanders and Davies, *Studying*, pp. 78-83. See also, however, Tuckett's treatment of both the MAs and the Mark-Q overlaps in *Revival*, chapters seven and eight. He stresses that one of the conditions for seeing Mark-Q overlap is evidence of another source underlying the Matthean and Lukan version, i.e. the Matthean version will not be explicable as a Mt. R rewriting of Mark; cf. 'The Synoptic Problem', *ABD* 6, p. 269.

hypothesis was invalid. It might be that Luke used Q for most of the 'double tradition', but that he also knew Matthew's gospel and used it occasionally.[91]

Similarly, Neirynck comments on Goulder's 1978 article:

> If Lukan knowledge of Matthew would be the conclusion to be drawn from the MAs, then Luke would have used Mark notwithstanding his knowledge of Matthew, and the inference could only be that elsewhere, where Luke is using another source, a similar subsidiary influence of Matthean reminiscences can be expected.[92]

Neirynck calls Goulder's conclusion, that Lukan knowledge of Matthew entails the end of Q, 'the Farrer fallacy'.[93]

It is in an attempt to deal with this kind of criticism that Goulder distinguishes between the 'hardline' and 'softline' versions of the 2ST in the first chapter of *LNP*, making Neirynck and Tuckett hardliners and those who postulate Lukan knowledge of Q and Matthew, like Gundry and Morgenthaler, softliners. Goulder says that the hardline is respectable because it is falsifiable. He then attempts to falsify it by drawing attention to the MA at Mk 14.65. The softline is less respectable because 'we can never know that we are wrong' (*LNP*, p. 10). Because of Occam's Razor, however, and because of 'the philosophical priority of consideration for the simple before the complex' (*LNP*, p. 24), Goulder feels that his hypothesis is preferable to any of the softlines like Lukan knowledge of Q as well as of Matthew.

It might be added that if Goulder is right about the MAs, it does not necessarily follow, as Neirynck suggests, that Luke will have used 'another source' in the same way, with 'similar subsidiary influence of Matthean reminiscences'. Neirynck assumes that one would expect

---

91. C.M. Tuckett, 'Relationship', p. 130. Gundry's 'Matthean Foreign Bodies' is the clearest recent illustration of this perspective, in an article using the same kind of arguments that Goulder uses on the MAs, ostensibly from Mattheanisms in Luke.

92. F. Neirynck, 'Recent Developments', p. 34. Cf. ΤΙΣ ΕΣΤΙΝ, p. 115 n. 116, where Neirynck quotes this and adds: 'Let us take it more simply: the reasoning from analogy cannot go beyond the limits of the similarity. If there is any subsidiary dependence upon Matthew in the triple tradition, how can this prove that there is anything more than subsidiary dependence in the double tradition?'

93. F. Neirynck, 'Recent Developments', p. 34, referring to Morgenthaler, *Statistische Synopse*, pp. 301-305.

Luke to have used Matthew in the same way that he used Mark. This would be a possible inference but not the only possible inference. Goulder's argument works quite legitimately by attempting to demonstrate that the MAs show Lukan knowledge of Matthew, and that this knowledge makes the theory of primary Lukan dependence on Matthew in double tradition material likely.

Friedrichsen adds to the similar criticisms of Tuckett and Neirynck, and comments on the second chapter of *LNP*:

> To place his treatment of the MAs in the section 'The Arguments Against Q' (pp. 46-51) is logically flawed. Goulder would do his position more good if he were to rightfully place the study of the MAs in a section entitled 'The Arguments Against the Independence of Matthew and Luke'.[94]

Friedrichsen is probably a little too forthright here. Dealing with the MAs among arguments against Q is certainly not 'logically flawed'. Goulder's argument in the section to which Friedrichsen is referring is that the presence of MAs has always been an 'aberrant factor', a 'major difficulty' for the 2ST 'for it might cast doubt on either of the *Zwei Quellen*' (*LNP*, p. 47). Goulder concludes that 'some of the considerations which caused hesitation in its acceptance' like the MAs 'seemed... still valid, and perhaps more damaging than had been supposed' (*LNP*, p. 69). The argument is that the MAs suggest that Luke read Matthew and that this takes away the primary reason for believing in Q, or, to turn the argument around: for Goulder, Luke's dependence on Matthew in double tradition is made more likely by the demonstrable (subsidiary) dependence on Matthew in the triple tradition.

Goulder responds directly to Tuckett and Friedrichsen in 'Luke's Knowledge of Matthew' and reiterates his argument of *LNP*. When faced with the MAs, Goulder says, 'the proper reaction...is to bestir oneself and ask whether the earlier hypothesis', that is the Q hypothesis, 'should not be dispensed with'. Referring once more to 'Occams's principle', Goulder adds:

> Of course it might turn out that we need Q as well as Matthew; but the apparent ignorance of Matthew by Luke in the triple tradition required

---

94. T.A. Friedrichsen, 'Survey', p. 384. He adds 'the MAs cannot bear all the weight (φορτία δυσβάστακτα!) put on them'. Cf. also D. Catchpole, *Quest*, pp. 1-3, for further comment on this methodological question.

Q—once the minor agreements are seen to be best explained by Lukan knowledge of Matthew, there is a very different complexion on the situation ('Knowledge', p. 159).

If, however, these criticisms by Tuckett, Neirynck and Friedrichsen require some qualification, Goulder's response to them helps to focus a key issue. Perhaps the most interesting point in what Goulder says is his use of the language of 'dispensing' with Q. This represents a return to Farrer, significant in the light of Goulder's earlier statement about Farrer's work:

Q is not going to collapse: it has the highest vested interest of any New Testament hypothesis in that virtually every scholar has written a book assuming its truth. It will have to be hunted from the field, and this can only be done by disproving it, not dispensing with it ('Farrer on Q', p. 194).

The shift is subtle but it is important methodologically and represents a partial concession to his critics. In this article, 'Farrer on Q', Goulder asks, 'Is Q then incapable of disproof?' and answers, 'Not quite', urging the twelve MAs discussed in 'On Putting Q to the Test' ('Farrer on Q', p. 194). In the recent article, however, Goulder says:

In matters of this kind we cannot hope for proof. The four hypotheses[95] are in competition with one another in *plausibility*...The Two-Source hypothesis starts with the tremendous advantage of having been widely taught as *the* solution for at least fifty years; but the extent and seriousness of the minor agreements threaten this plausibility ('Knowledge', pp. 144-45; Goulder's italics).

Goulder will probably not lose any ground by restating his thesis in this way. If 'On Putting Q to the Test' does disprove Q, it is clear that not many scholars have read or understood the disproof. Goulder's less forthright stance here is likely to add to the persuasiveness of his case.

Goulder's case might be more persuasive still if it were modified in other ways. The MA at Mk 14.65, for example, stands out as a 'serious difficulty' for the 2ST but not because its wording is Matthean and un-Lukan. Rather, it is difficult because independent redaction is almost impossible to imagine and because conjectural emendation of the text of Matthew is the standard current defence.

Goulder's argument from MAs featuring language characteristic of Matthew and uncharacteristic of Luke does not, then, prove Luke's

95. Namely the 2ST, Goulder's, Griesbach and Deutero-Marcus.

knowledge of Matthew. At best it adds to the plausibility of the hypothesis though even here we are put on our guard both by the fact that there are only a handful of such examples and by the existence of at least one counter-instance. If the MAs still prove to be the death of Q, it will not be just because of 'Mattheanisms' among them.

Part II

Luke's Special Material

Chapter 4

INTRODUCTION TO PART II: DISTINCTIVE FEATURES IN L

In chapter three of *Luke: A New Paradigm*, Goulder attempts to isolate some distinctive stylistic features in Luke's Gospel with a view to demonstrating that their presence in the Special Material is due to the evangelist's own creative hand. Goulder objects that much discussion on the topic of Luke's Special Material 'has been strangled by being limited so largely to linguistic phenomena' (*LNP*, p. 84), and after discussing what he regards as being the pitfalls of scholars like Rehkopf, Schürmann and Jeremias,[1] he broadens the scope of the argument, partly by making a plea for returning to Hawkins-type criteria for linguistic study (see Chapter Two above) but more importantly by isolating twenty-four features, covering both 'the Lukan story' and 'Lukan poetry' by which the author 'lets himself be known' (p. 86).

Goulder's discussion of such features, in the introduction to the book and in the commentary, is of undoubted value. Book after book and article after article discuss Luke's theology but by contrast, although some of the things Goulder points out have been noticed before, rarely do scholars give these Lukan features systematic treatment. Further, Goulder often draws out features from Luke and gives them names, like 'Guillotine Questions' or 'Oratio Recta Repetitions', and the very isolation and naming of them is a useful contribution to scholarship on Luke.[2]

---

1. F. Rehkopf, *Sonderquelle*; H. Schürmann, *Lukasevangelium*; J. Jeremias, *Sprache*. See also from the English side B.H. Easton's seminal article, 'Linguistic Evidence'. For other discussions of the linguistic analysis of L, see Cadbury, *Making*, particularly pp. 67-68 and 214-30; V. Taylor, *Behind*, chapters 21-24 and for a recent comment, see C.F. Evans, *Saint Luke*, pp. 27ff.

2. Cf. J. Fenton, Review of *LNP*, p. 68, 'Chapter 3 is crucially important'; John Muddiman, Review of *LNP*, p. 177, 'Many of these brief observations are

Nevertheless, the important question is whether or not the isolation of these features adds weight to Goulder's thesis. All the way through the commentary he uses them to demonstrate Lukan creation of material. On the Unjust Judge (Lk. 18.1-8), for example, Goulder counts nine Lukan features, including the hortatory nature of the parable, the disreputable hero, his soliloquy, his two-sidedness and the oratio recta repetition of the key words. Goulder says:

> One can shunt off the Lukan phrasing (which is also extensive), and suppose an earlier form without it: but what is left of the parable if one removed the nine points of its mode (p. 662)?

Arguments of this kind pervade the text, pushing the study of language very much into second place in the L sections.[3] Goulder says something similar on the Good Samaritan (Lk. 10.25-37):

> Not only is the language substantially Luke's own: the stylistic features which I have just listed make up the very stuff of the parable. If we took them away there would be nothing left (p. 491).

And on the Rich Fool (Lk. 12.13-21), Goulder says:

> Some of the...details could, of course, have been added in by Luke: but others concern the whole mode of the parable—the illustrative story, imperative point, the rich man as a horror figure, the animus against wealth, death rather than parousia, the run up to 12.22-34, and even the soliloquy. What sort of parable is left if we take all these features away? (pp. 537-38).

The argument, although simple, seems to be a strong one: if the L material is packed with these features and if the features are indeed distinctive of Luke, there would be little reason to avoid Goulder's conclusion that Luke is responsible for the creation of the L material, albeit using hints from here and there in Matthew and Mark. It is the primary means by which Goulder attempts to argue one of the most important aspects of his new paradigm, namely:

> Luke wrote his Gospel about 90 for a more Gentile church [than Matthew's], combining Mark and Matthew. He re-wrote Matthew's birth narratives with the aid of the Old Testament, and he added new material

highly original and controversial; Lucan researchers of the future will find a wealth of material for further development or critique.'

3.   If anything, Goulder has overstated his view on the language here; contrast *LNP*, pp. 636-37 on Dives.

of his own creation, largely parables, where his genius lay. The new
material can almost always be understood as a Lukan development of
matter in Matthew. There was hardly any L (*Sondergut*) (pp. 22-23).

It is vital, therefore, to examine Goulder's argument on Lukan style.
This can be done by looking, where possible, at the extent to which the
features occur in the L material, looking also at how distinctive of Luke
the features are. The latter point is particularly important. For Goulder's
case to be corroborated, the features should be difficult to find in
Matthew and Mark. If they are present there, albeit to a markedly lesser
degree than in Luke, this could be a signal that they are characteristic
not only of Luke, but also, to some degree, of pre-Lukan traditions.

First, then, I will look to see to what extent, if at all, the features are
present in Matthew and Mark. Goulder does this only occasionally in
his introduction. Second, I will look to see how far features are characteristic of Luke as a writer, looking for instances not only in L material
but also in his (supposed) redaction of Mark and Matthew. If I find a
feature present in L and not in R or QD, the possibility arises that the
feature is characteristic of Luke's source rather than of Luke himself.

The ideal for Goulder's thesis would be to see a feature to be scarce
in Matthew and Mark and at the same time present in Luke R, QD and
L. This is perhaps something of a tall order; the second approach needs
to be done with caution since it is possible that a feature may come in L
material alone but still be from Luke's own hand. Certainly it will be
helpful if features crop up in R and QD as well as in L, but if Goulder
is right, Luke is a good deal freer in the L material than he is in his
Mark and Q material, working small hints into great structures, and this
greater degree of freedom might in itself be a reason for the presence of
extra features in L.

Not all of Goulder's features work in the way that they do in the
above quoted examples of the Good Samaritan, the Rich Fool and the
Unjust Judge. In the case of Introductions (§1), Conclusions (§2) and
Allegory (§6), Goulder is largely looking for peculiarly Lukan traits
within the general category. Here, then, I will look for the Lukan tendencies within the category and see if they are reflected in R and QD as
well as L; and I will look for the same things in Matthew and Mark. In
other cases Goulder is not so much picking something out from the text
as looking at what lies behind it, at Luke's compositional procedure:
Muddle (§9), Inference of Setting (§13), Combination of Sources (§15),
Splitting of Sources (§16) and Transfer of Elements (§17). These

categories need to be treated with a little more caution, and I will comment on them in due course.

For the sake of clarity, it will be worth defining three important terms. To say that a feature is exclusive to Luke will mean that it occurs only in Luke and not in Matthew or Mark at all. A distinctive feature will be one which is common in Luke but scarce in Matthew and Mark. A characteristic feature will be one which occurs in Luke to a markedly greater degree than it occurs in Matthew and Mark.

Several of the features overlap with, and some of the features mirror, matters to which Goulder draws attention in *MLM*. In the course of the discussion, it will often be helpful to cross refer to, and deal with, Goulder's earlier argument for extensive Matthean creativity. Also relevant in this context will be Goulder's article 'Characteristics of the Parables in the Several Gospels'.

In order to keep the study to a manageable length, however, it will be concentrated in two ways. First, it will be limited primarily to Goulder's 'Lukan story' section (*LNP*, pp. 89-107). Although Goulder also deals with 'Lukan poetry' and 'Luke's background', his main interest and emphasis lies in Luke's creative genius as a storyteller. Second, Goulder sometimes refers in the commentary to stylistic features not listed in chapter 3. On the Good Samaritan, for example (see *LNP*, p. 491), 'philo-Samaritan sympathies' and 'positive emotions' are not treated in Goulder's 'Lukan Story' section. Likewise, eschatology creeps in to Goulder's discussions of both the Rich Fool (see above, p. 133) and Dives and Lazarus (*LNP*, p. 636).[4] If, though, other factors are sometimes drawn into the argument for Lukan creativity, the value of the chapter 3 analysis is that Goulder has given the features systematic treatment, a treatment which, valuably, lends itself to being tested.

---

4. Cf. Muddiman, Review of *LNP*, p. 177, 'There is one notable omission here; Goulder says nothing about distinctively Lucan eschatology'. Goulder does not really discuss any 'theological' topics in chapter three, however.

Chapter 5

INTRODUCTIONS AND CONCLUSIONS TO PERICOPAE (§1 AND §2)

A. *Preliminary Comments: Difficulties over Divisions*

Goulder isolates several facets of Luke's introductions to pericopae: sometimes introductions are elaborate and they often specify time and place (§1.1); he takes care over audience (§1.2); there is sometimes a comment from the evangelist (§1.3); there are foil questions, requests and comments from the audience (§1.4), often of a 'cloying piety' (§1.5); there are synagogue meals to which Jesus has been invited by a Pharisee (§1.6) and he sometimes re-introduces in mid-pericope (§1.7). Goulder says that 'all the evangelists naturally also provide a suitable close to any pericope' (*LNP*, p. 91) and he points specifically to the return home of characters (§2.1), notes of progress in chapters one and two (§2.2) and inclusio (§2.3).

Each of these subheadings will be taken in turn. First, though, one needs to establish where the introductions and conclusions to pericopae are: it is not always certain where one pericope ends and another one starts. Goulder speaks of Luke's 'liking for ornate openings and closures' (p. 170) but regularly Goulder uses other criteria for dividing pericopae. Length is certainly one factor influencing his division, especially as there is the need to produce the right number of sections for the calendar. Lk. 4.16, for example, looks very much like an ornate introduction to the Rejection at Nazareth (4.16-30), with indications of time (the sabbath day) and place ('Nazara where he was brought up...the synagogue') but Goulder makes his break at 4.14, so that the section is 4.14-30. This is presumably because 4.14-15 (summary section) is too short on its own for lectionary purposes.[1]

---

1. On the problems of dividing the text into appropriately-sized lections, see further below, pp. 308-309.

Another odd division is at 6.39, where the rubric is just εἶπεν δὲ καὶ παραβολήν. This is because Goulder needs a division somewhere in the Sermon on the Plain to make it into two sections, for reasons of length. Even odder is a division at 8.49, halfway through the Jairus / Woman with Flux complex, the new section marked by the statement that: 'While he was still speaking, a man from the ruler's house came...'

The most difficult of Goulder's divisions, however, is the following:

12.41: Εἶπεν δὲ ὁ Πέτρος, Κύριε, πρὸς ἡμᾶς τὴν παραβολὴν ταύτην
        λέγεις ἢ καὶ πρὸς πάντας;

Not only is this the beginning of a new section for Goulder but also the beginning of one of his triplets, apparently introducing the new theme of 'Coming Judgment'. It comes in the middle of the material about the Watchful Servant and the rubric in v. 41 is the only thing that interrupts the oratio recta which is directly parallel to Matthew. Both continue with τίς ἄρα ἐστὶν ὁ πιστός...(v. 42, Mt. 24.45). Goulder speaks of the pericope opening with 'the familiar foil question' (§1.4, p. 549; see further below) but his own list of Lukan traits in his §1 gives a much more obvious category in which 12.41 would fit, that of §1.7, re-introduction in mid-pericope.

Goulder speaks of 12.41 as featuring 'the Lukan rubric' for introducing a pericope, yet there are places where one might see more obvious examples of Lukan rubrics where Goulder does not subdivide, like 13.1; 18.15 and 18.35,[2] all of which look like elaborate introductions.[3]

It will be worth being at least a little wary, therefore, about Goulder's confidence over Luke's division into pericopae. The confidence is probably due not only to the constraints of the lectionary theory but also to Goulder's desire to see Luke as an author, writing freely as he is

2.   Although 18.35 looks like the beginning of a new pericope, especially with the characteristic ἐγένετο δέ, Goulder makes the section run from 18.31-43, and he quotes an article by Jan Lambrecht to defend his position (*LNP*, p. 674), citing 16.22; 17.14 and 19.15 as cases where ἐγένετο δέ does not begin a pericope. However, these verses are all so obviously mid-story that they will not do as evidence. These are all cases where a turning point in the story has been reached: 16.22: Dives dies; 17.14: the lepers are cleansed; 19.15: the nobleman returns.

3.   Other places where we might expect to see divisions and do not are 8.4, 9.46, 49, 57; 10.21; 11.29; 13.31. Finding divisions in the travel narrative is a particular difficulty—cf. Craig Blomberg, 'Midrash', p. 220.

moved rather than editing units which have come to him from oral tradition. This aspect of Goulder's presentation, attempting to steal the form-critics' clothes while they are still bathing, is arguably an underlying concern through much of this material on introductions and conclusions to pericopae.

B. *Elaborate Introductions (§1.1)*

1. *Preliminary Comment*
As Goulder admits, sometimes the introductions are quite feeble, as in his own example (p. 89):

16.1:   And he also said to the disciples...

Other examples of the same variety include 12.22, 54 and 17.1. There are also short introductions in sections not recognized as fresh pericopae by Goulder, like 11.5; 13.18 and 14.7.

2. *R*
Nevertheless, there are elaborate introductions and Luke does often specify time and place, especially in chs. 1–2. As Goulder points out, 3.1-2 R, the sevenfold dating of the ministry, is particularly long[4] but there are plenty of other occasions on which Luke apparently makes more elaborate an introduction which he finds in Mark. These are two examples:

5.12:   καὶ ἐγένετο ἐν τῷ εἶναι αὐτὸν ἐν μιᾷ τῶν πόλεων καὶ ἰδοὺ
               ἀνὴρ πλήρης λέπρας.
cf. Mk 1.40:   καὶ ἔρχεται πρὸς αὐτὸν λεπρός...(cf. Mt. 8.1, a little fuller,
               after the Sermon on the Mount).

20.20-21:   καὶ παρατηρήσαντες ἀπέστειλαν ἐγκαθέτους
               ὑποκρινομένους ἑαυτοὺς δικαίους εἶναι, ἵνα ἐπιλάβωνται
               αὐτοῦ λόγου, ὥστε παραδοῦναι αὐτὸν τῇ ἀρχῇ καὶ τῇ
               ἐξουσίᾳ τοῦ ἡγεμόνος. καὶ ἐπηρώτησαν αὐτὸν λέγοντες,
               Διδάσκαλε...
cf. Mk 12.13-14: καὶ ἀποστέλλουσιν πρὸς αὐτόν τινας τῶν Φαρισαίων καὶ
               τῶν Ἡρῳδιανῶν ἵνα αὐτὸν ἀγρεύσωσιν λόγῳ. καὶ

---

4.   But this is also the introduction to Jesus' ministry and to the Gospel proper. According to Streeter, these verses mark the beginning of Proto-Luke (*Four Gospels*, p. 209).

ἐλθόντες λέγουσιν αὐτῷ, Διδάσκαλε...(cf. Mt. 22.15, a little fuller).

3. *QD and L*

It is difficult to say whether or not Luke makes more elaborate the introductions to pericopae which he finds in Q / Matthew since the order is different. Much of the material consists of sayings which will appear without introductions or with different introductions in the different contexts in the two gospels, as at Matthew 10 // Luke 10, for example. Nevertheless, there are examples of Luke giving an elaborate introduction to Q material, most famously at 11.1-2, the introduction to the Lord's Prayer, contrasting with οὕτως οὖν προσεύχεσθε ὑμεῖς in Mt. 6.9. Another example would be the introductions to the parable of the Great Feast in each Gospel (Mt. 22.1 // Lk. 14.15-16).[5]

Likewise, there are occasions in both Q and L material where Luke makes explicit reference to time and place. Goulder draws attention to 9.51 particularly (*LNP*, p. 89) and explains it as marking a move in source, from Mark to Matthew. Other clear examples include:

7.11-12:	Καὶ ἐγένετο ἐν τῷ ἐξῆς ἐπορεύθη εἰς πόλιν καλουμένην Ναΐν, καὶ συνεπορεύοντο αὐτῷ οἱ μαθηταὶ αὐτοῦ καὶ ὄχλος πολύς. ὡς δὲ ἤγγισεν τῇ πύλῃ τῆς πόλεως...
17.11-12:	Καὶ ἐγένετο ἐν τῷ πορεύεσθαι εἰς Ἰερουσαλὴμ, καὶ αὐτὸς διήρχετο διὰ μέσον Σαμαρείας καὶ Γαλιλαίας. καὶ εἰσερχομένου αὐτοῦ εἴς τινα κώμην ἀπήντησαν [αὐτῷ] δέκα λεπροὶ ἄνδρες...[6]

Clearest of all, though, are chs. 1–2 where, as Goulder says, 'time is almost invariable, place normal' (*LNP*, p. 89).

Although there are some elaborate introductions, references to time and place can be quite vague, as in 11.37, 12.1 or 16.14, and one can go for long stretches through the travel narrative without specific time or place references, throughout ch. 12, or through most of 14.25–17.11, for example, even when the audience and the subject matter changes. Some of the time references are simply linking passages, making the connection with a previous pericope clear ('When they heard these things' etc.).

---

5.   Cf. also Mt. 8.5 // Lk. 7.1 where the evangelists share a reference to location (Capernaum) and Mt. 11.25 // Lk. 10.21 where they have a similar reference to time.

6.   Cf. also Lk. 10.1, 38; 13.1, 10, 22-23; 13.31; 14.1; 19.1 and 19.11.

When Luke has a long introduction in 15.1-3 to set the parable material which follows, there is no reference to either time or place. Indeed, it is more common for there to be no reference to time or place in the Q and L material as in 10.25; 11.14, 27, 29; 12.13, 22, 41, 54; 14.25; 15.1; 16.1, 19; 17.1, 20; 18.1, 9.

4. *Mark*

Regularly, a comparison of Mark and Luke in individual parallel pericopae will show Luke's introductions to pericopae to be shorter than Mark's. Indeed there are a good many more examples of Luke apparently diminishing the material found in Mark than there are of Luke enhancing it, and the difference is not always one of wording but is often one of content. Sometimes Mark has references to time and place which Luke lacks. These are examples:

Mk 10.17:   καὶ ἐκπορευομένου αὐτοῦ εἰς ὁδὸν προσδραμὼν εἷς καὶ
                γονυπετήσας αὐτὸν ἐπηρώτα αὐτόν, Διδάσκαλε ἀγαθέ...
cf. Lk. 18.18: καὶ ἐπηρώτησέν τις αὐτὸν ἄρχων λέγων, Διδάσκαλε
                ἀγαθέ... (cf. Mt. 19.16).

Mk 10.32:   ἦσαν δὲ ἐν τῇ ὁδῷ ἀναβαίνοντες εἰς Ἱεροσόλυμα, καὶ ἦν
                προάγων αὐτοὺς ὁ Ἰησοῦς, καὶ ἐθαμβοῦντο, οἱ δὲ
                ἀκολουθοῦντες ἐφοβοῦντο. καὶ παραλαβὼν πάλιν τοὺς
                δώδεκα ἤρξατο αὐτοῖς λέγειν τὰ μέλλοντα αὐτῷ
                συμβαίνειν ὅτι Ἰδοὺ ἀναβαίνομεν εἰς Ἱεροσόλυμα...
cf. Lk. 18.31: παραλαβὼν δὲ τοὺς δώδεκα εἶπεν πρὸς αὐτούς, Ἰδοὺ
                ἀναβαίνομεν εἰς Ἱερουσαλήμ... (cf. Mt. 20.17).[7]

5. *Conclusion*

Sometimes Luke's introductions to pericopae are very short. Sometimes they are more elaborate and feature reference to time and place. There are many long introductions to pericopae in both QD and L material. In material which Luke has in common with Mark, sometimes his introductions are demonstrably fuller than Mark's and sometimes they are shorter. It is not distinctive of Luke, then, to have

7.   Cf. also Mk 1.9 // Lk. 3.21; Mk 1.29 // Lk. 4.38; Mk 2.13-14 // Lk. 5.27; Mk 2.18 // Lk. 5.33; Mk 4.10-11 // Lk. 8.9-10; Mk 4.35-36 // Lk. 8.22; Mk 5.21-22 // Lk. 8.40-41; Mk 6.30-33 // Lk. 9.10-11; Mk 8.27 // Lk. 9.18; Mk 9.30-31 // Lk. 9.43b; Mk 9.33 // Lk. 9.46; Mk 10.46 // Lk. 18.35; and Mk 11.15 // Lk. 19.45. This is not to deny, of course, that context and other factors often explain the differences between the lengths of Mark's and Luke's introductions.

elaborate introductions to pericopae though it can be, on occasion, characteristic of his writing. Chapters 1–2 do, however, stand out from the rest of the Gospel in that they team with references to time and place, as Goulder stresses.[8]

C. *Those Addressed in Teaching Sections (§1.2)*

1. *Preliminary Comment*
Goulder claims that Luke often takes special care to distinguish those addressed in teaching sections (*LNP*, p. 89). This feature of Luke is observed also by Cadbury who gives it a comprehensive treatment.[9] Goulder's examples all feature in L material (with the possible exception of 5.1) and he draws attention particularly to the distinction between 'the crowds' and 'the disciples' (*LNP*, p. 89).[10]

2. *R*
Sometimes Luke agrees, or nearly agrees, with the setting which Mark gives to material. At the beginning of the parable chapter, for example, both Mark and Luke have teaching addressed to a crowd (Mk 4.1 // Lk. 8.4; Mt. 13.2, 'great crowds') and at Mk 6.7 // Lk. 9.1, teaching is addressed to 'the twelve', in Luke called 'apostles' (cf. Mt. 10.1).[11] On other occasions, Luke changes the setting a little. Mk 8.34 has 'the crowd with his disciples' whereas Lk. 9.23 has 'all' (cf. Mt. 16.24, 'the disciples'). Mk 12.1 // Lk. 20.9 (cf. Mt. 21.33) provides an example of Luke in his redaction of Mark distinguishing the audience with greater clarity than Mark, but it is the only possible example. Here Mark has 'them', probably 'the chief priests and the scribes and the elders' from Mk 11.27 and Luke has 'the people'.[12]

---

8. See further Bultmann, *History*, p. 360. The only difficulty with what Bultmann says is the notion that Luke uses καὶ ἐγένετο especially in his editing of Mark; καὶ ἐγένετο and ἐγένετο δέ are just as common in non-Markan sections (7.11; 9.51; 11.1, 27; 14.1; 17.11; 22.24).

9. *Style*, p. 120: 'Luke takes an especial interest in the nature of the audience to whom words of Jesus are addressed' with examples on pp. 120-26. Also useful is Paul S. Minear's article 'Jesus' Audiences, According to Luke', arguing that there are important and intended distinctions between ὁ λαός, ὁ ὄχλος and οἱ μαθηταί.

10. This idea is present in germ in 'Chiastic Structure', p. 200.

11. Other places where there is agreement or near agreement are Mk 4.10 // Mt. 13.10 // Lk. 8.9 and Mk 10.32 // Mt. 20.17 // Lk. 18.31.

12. By being more specific than Mark and Matthew, however, Luke may have

It is not clear, in general, from Luke's redaction of Mark, that Luke distinguishes the audience addressed with any greater clarity than does Mark, or for the most part Matthew.

3. *Q and L*

It is not easy to compare material from Matthew and Luke in the double tradition, but on at least two occasions, it is clear that the audience in Luke is the same as the audience for the same material in Matthew. The Sermon on the Plain is addressed to the disciples (6.20) in the hearing of the people (7.1) just as the Sermon on the Mount is addressed to the disciples (Mt. 5.1-2) and the crowds (Mt. 7.28-29). Likewise, after the messengers from John have left, Jesus addresses 'the crowds' in both Matthew and Luke (Mt. 11.7 // Lk. 7.24).

On another occasion, the audience in Luke is different from the audience in Matthew for the same material. John the Baptist's preaching is addressed to 'crowds' in Lk. 3.7 but in Mt. 3.7 to 'Pharisees and Sadducees'.[13] The Beelzebub Controversy (Mt. 12.22-30 // Mk 3.20-27 // Lk. 11.14-23) is similar. In Mark (3.22), the discourse is spoken to 'scribes from Jerusalem' and in Matthew (12.24), it is 'the Pharisees'. Luke, on the other hand, has the more general 'the crowds...some of them...others' (11.14-16).[14]

On other occasions, Luke and Matthew both have the same audience in parallel material where it is not so easy to compare the two Gospels. Lk. 12.22-31, the Ravens and the Lilies, for example, is addressed 'to his disciples' and the parallel section in Matthew is part of the Sermon on the Mount, Mt. 6.25-33, also addressed to the disciples (5.1, though crowds hear too, 7.28-29).

Even when clear comparison with Matthew is not possible, though, it is evident from Q and L material that Luke is regularly specific about

---

spoiled the flow of the story a little. The conclusion in Mark (12.12) arguably makes better sense than it does in Luke (20.19). Other places where Mark and Luke differ are Mk 12.38 // Mt. 23.1 // Lk. 20.45 and Mk 13.1-5 // Mt. 24.1-4 // Lk. 21.5-8.

13. Goulder argues (*LNP*, p. 273) that the Baptist's raillery is inappropriate against 'crowds' but quite appropriate against Matthean Pharisees and Sadducees, so it provides evidence for Lukan knowledge of Matthew. Catchpole (*Quest*, pp. 7-8) argues precisely the opposite.

14. It is arguable that Luke's audience is less appropriate than Matthew's since Luke shares with Matthew the saying about 'your sons' (Mt. 12.27 // Lk. 11.19); perhaps the saying has lost its relevance in Luke because the audience has been generalized.

those addressed in teaching sections. Often it is simply the disciples (6.20; 10.23; 11.1-2; 12.1, 22; 16.1; 17.1); or the crowd(s) (7.24; 11.14-15; 11.29; 12.13-16, 54; 14.25) but on other occasions, Luke designates different groups, 10.1: the seventy; 11.37-39: a Pharisee; 11.45-46: a lawyer; 13.1: some present from Galilee; 14.15-16: someone at table with Jesus; 15.1-3: Scribes and Pharisees; 17.20: Pharisees; 18.9: some who trusted in themselves that they were righteous.

On a couple of occasions, the references to audience are vague. 13.22-24 has 'someone' (τις) asking Jesus a question and Jesus responding to 'them' (αὐτούς). In 18.1, Jesus again addresses αὐτοῖς, though this may simply be the disciples (from 17.22). On a couple of other occasions, Luke does not tell us who is being addressed: 12.41-42 and 13.18. The relative scarcity of such examples, however, suggests that for Q and L material at least, Luke does take care to distinguish between those addressed in teaching sections.

4. *Mark*

Sometimes Mark is more specific than Luke about audience in triple tradition material. In Mk 8.34 // Lk. 9.23 (cf. Mt. 16.24), Mark's 'the crowd with his disciples' is more specific than Luke's 'all', although both are distinguishing between the disciples to whom Jesus has just given the first Passion prediction and the crowd who are all exhorted to take up their cross and follow Jesus. This is an interesting example of the interleaving of the two publics which Goulder lists as distinctive of Luke (p. 89), interesting because it is an example of the phenomenon in Mark.

In Mk 13.1-5 // Lk. 21.5-8 (cf. Mt. 24.1-4), Luke, who has the teaching addressed to 'some' (cf. v. 10, 'them'), is less specific than Mark who has the teaching addressed to Peter, James, John and Andrew (cf. 'the disciples' in Matthew). Mark's setting might be thought to be superior—the eschatological discourse makes better sense if spoken not to interested hangers-on but to the disciples or the inner circle of disciples.

Over triple tradition material, therefore, sometimes Mark and sometimes Luke is more specific about those addressed in teaching sections.

5. *Conclusion*

Luke sometimes takes care to distinguish audience, especially in Q and L material. He is sometimes more specific than Mark (as in 20.9) and sometimes less so (as in 21.5-8). Goulder's general position, therefore, is partially corroborated.

Goulder's more specific claim is that Luke sometimes 'interleaves' the two publics, crowds and disciples (*LNP*, p. 89). He gives examples from ch. 12: in 12.1 he speaks 'to his disciples first' with the multitude being addressed in 12.13, the disciples again in 12.22 and the multitude again in 12.54. To these examples one could add 6.20-49 where Jesus apparently addresses the disciples in the hearing of a large crowd (6.17-19; 7.1); and in 15.1-3, the Scribes and Pharisees are addressed but the tax-collectors and sinners are drawing near. Most clear is 20.45 R:

> And in the hearing of all the people he said to his disciples...

It is worth noting also that there is a counter-example of this phenomenon from Mark, in 8.34.

Goulder explains this feature by suggesting that 'Luke wished sometimes to address his committed church members, and sometimes the visiting, unbaptized adherents' (p. 89). This explanation is a little difficult to sustain when one looks at the subject matter in the relevant sections. In ch. 12, for example, the parable of the Rich Fool (vv. 13-21) is addressed to the crowd, and it preaches a similar message to vv. 22-31, the Ravens and the Lilies, which is spoken to the disciples and begins with 'therefore...'

If, though, Goulder's explanation of the 'interleaving' is uncertain, he is probably right, more generally, that Luke has his church audience in mind when describing Jesus's audiences. One might compare Cadbury's judgment:

> By giving to Christ's teachings a more definite setting, Luke does not intend to limit their scope and application. The audience is neither historically reproduced nor artistically delimited, but rather taken as typical and suggestive. Luke has really in mind the Christian Church of his own time.[15]

D. *The Evangelist's Comment (§1.3)*

Goulder (*LNP*, p. 90) lists three occasions on which 'opportunity is taken for the evangelist's comment', 18.1; 19.11 and 3.15 R, the latter not in an introduction but in mid-story. In the commentary (p. 389) he adds another example which he calls a 'clarifying introduction':

15. *Style*, p. 122.

SPCK was founded in 1698. The third oldest publisher in England and with over 200 years of bookselling experience, we have a well-deserved reputation for quality and scholarship. Now our expertise is available to you wherever you are, 24 hours a day.

As well as searching our database, you can browse our 'shelves' by category for a selection of books to suit all tastes and interests.

FREE COLLECTION

No delivery charge if you collect from any of our 32 bookshops. Or, if you prefer, order books for delivery direct to your home.

SPCK ONLINE BOOKSELLER

By e-mailing our online bookseller, your query will be answered by one of the many experts among our 250 staff.

NOT JUST BOOKS!

You can also order a wide range of music, software, gifts and cards.

JOIN OUR BOOK CLUB

Keep up-to-date with the latest new books and bargains.

We look forward to welcoming you to spckonline!

7.29-30: καὶ πᾶς ὁ λαὸς ἀκούσας καὶ οἱ τελῶναι ἐδικαίωσαν τὸν θεὸν βαπτισθέντες τὸ βάπτισμα Ἰωάννου· οἱ δὲ Φαρισαῖοι καὶ οἱ νομικοὶ τὴν βουλὴν τοῦ θεοῦ ἠθέτησαν εἰς ἑαυτοὺς μὴ βαπτισθέντες ὑπ᾽ αὐτοῦ.

This is in mid-pericope rather than in an introduction, but it is a QD example of the phenomenon. 19.11, introducing the parable of the Pounds, is also QD, whereas 18.1 is L.

Certainly the feature is present in Luke but it is not common—only twice in introductions, once L, once QD.[16] There is one possible occurrence of the feature in an introduction in Mark, in 7.1-4, the Tradition of the Elders, where Mark explains why the Pharisees and Scribes complain at the disciples eating with hands defiled, in parenthesis:

Mk 7.3-4: οἱ γὰρ Φαρισαῖοι καὶ πάντες οἱ Ἰουδαῖοι ἐὰν μὴ πυγμῇ νίψωνται τὰς χεῖρας οὐκ ἐσθίουσιν, κρατοῦντες τὴν παράδοσιν τῶν πρεσβυτέρων...

This could happily be described as a 'clarifying introduction', the phrase which Goulder applies to Lk. 7.29-30.

Elsewhere, Mark has comments in mid-pericope of the same kind:

11.32: ἐφοβοῦντο τὸν ὄχλον· ἅπαντες γὰρ εἶχον τὸν Ἰωάννην ὄντως ὅτι προφήτης ἦν. (Contrast Mt. 21.26 and Lk. 20.6).

12.12: καὶ ἐζήτουν αὐτὸν κρατῆσαι, καὶ ἐφοβήθησαν τὸν ὄχλον, ἔγνωσαν γὰρ ὅτι πρὸς αὐτοὺς τὴν παραβολὴν εἶπεν (cf. Mt. 21.46, Lk. 20.19).

One might also compare Mk 16.4, ἦν γὰρ μέγας σφόδρα (contrast Mt. 28 and Lk. 24), mid-way through the Empty Tomb story.

Matthew too has his own comments in the narrative, in one case in an introduction:

11.20 QD: τότε ἤρξατο ὀνειδίζειν τὰς πόλεις ἐν αἷς ἐγένοντο αἱ πλεῖσται δυνάμεις αὐτοῦ, ὅτι οὐ μετενόησαν· Οὐαί σοι, Χοραζίν... (Contrast Lk. 10.13 which goes into the speech without further introduction).

16. There are other places where one might see 'an evangelist's comment'. Fitzmyer, *Luke I-IX*, p. 382, describes 1.66 as 'a comment of the evangelist'. Most comprehensive is S. M. Sheeley, *Narrative Asides*.

More commonly, he has explanatory comments at the conclusions of pericopae, at 16.12 R; 17.13 R and 28.15. Matthew's regular citations from the Scripture are also the evangelist's characteristic comments on events (4.14-17; 8.17; 12.17-21; 21.4-5; 27.8-10).[17]

All the evangelists, then, provide comments at points during their narrative—it is not distinctive of Luke. Further, although Luke has two strong examples of such a comment in introductions to pericopae, 18.1 and 19.11, there is also an example of one in an introduction in Matthew, 11.20 QD, and possibly one in Mark, 7.1-4. In introductions, then, the feature is neither common nor distinctive of Luke.

E. *Foil Questions, Requests and Comments, and Cloying Piety (§1.4 and §1.5)*

1. *Preliminary Comment*
Goulder lists a good number of examples of questions, requests or comments leading up to teaching, 'in which another speaker acts as a foil to Jesus or John' (*LNP*, p. 90).[18]

2. *R*
There are few, if any, redactional examples of questions, requests or comments leading up to teaching in Luke. Goulder lists 20.16b as R in *LNP*, chapter three (p. 90 and also p. 694) but this half-verse, 'And when they heard, they said, God forbid', is not at the beginning of a pericope and really belongs to the section on re-introducing in mid-pericope.[19] Goulder also lists:

21.5:   καί τινων λεγόντων περὶ τοῦ ἱεροῦ ὅτι λίθοις καλοῖς καὶ ἀναθήμασιν κεκόσμηται εἶπεν...

---

17. Cf. Davies-Allison, *Matthew*, p. 96, listing several 'authorial comments' which 'make known to the reader what the literary critic would call the implied author', inserted by Matthew 'more regularly than his predecessors Mark and Q'.

18. Goulder's observations here are anticipated by Bultmann (*History*, pp. 335-37), who lists this feature as characteristic of Luke's editorial activity when he is working with speech material. For a recent treatment of the question and answer framework, see J. Navone, 'Dynamic'.

19. Cf. Bultmann, *History*, p. 337, 'Something peculiar to Luke is that in two places there is interruption of a speech, which Luke has inserted to give the reader a sense of the concrete situation'. The two places are here (20.16b) and 11.45.

It is a little misleading to speak of this as a redactional example, however, as the parallel section in Mark (13.1) has a foil question in direct speech.

3. *QD*

The distinction between QD and L is, once more, a little blurred here but, nevertheless, one can see some examples of this feature in Q material. In *LNP*, chapter three, Goulder lists 11.1-2 (cf. Mt. 6.9; also p. 496); 12.41 (cf. Mt. 24.45; also p. 549); 13.23 (cf. Mt. 7.13; also p. 572); 14.15 ('cloying piety'; cf. Mt. 22.1; also p. 589), 15.1-2 (cf. Mt. 18.12); 17.20 (cf. Mt. 24.23); 17.37 (cf. Mt. 24.28; also p. 655) and 19.25 (cf. Mt. 25.29; also p. 685). In the commentary, Goulder also treats 11.45 as an example of the phenomenon (p. 521, cf. Mt. 23).

Three of these examples, 11.45; 17.37 and 19.25, are probably not in introductions to pericopae (recognized by Goulder for 11.45 and 19.25 on *LNP*, pp. 521 and 685) and one, 12.41, is really mid-pericope. Even without these examples, however, this is clearly a feature of Luke in QD material.

4. *L*

Such foil questions, requests and comments are also clearly a feature of L material. In *LNP*, chapter three (pp. 90-91), Goulder gives several examples, 3.10; 11.27 ('cloying piety'; also p. 510); 12.13 (also p. 535); 16.14 (also p. 629) and 17.5 (also p. 641). In the commentary, Goulder also treats 13.1 as an example of the phenomenon (p. 560) but, although many would break the text up here, it is not, for Goulder, in the introduction to a pericope. 19.39, also given as an example in the commentary (p. 688), goes the other way: it is the beginning of a new pericope for Goulder, but for some (cf. p. 689), it would be mid-pericope. Further, 3.10 is clearly mid-pericope.

Goulder also appeals to this category when discussing the parables of the Lost Sheep and the Lost Coin at the beginning of Luke 15. The 'foil introduction', Goulder says, 'also takes the form of a pair of sayings of the Lord himself...and here Luke prepares the way for his Two Sons by the artfully contrasted Lost Sheep and Lost Coin' (*LNP*, p. 604). This is an oddity. To include a pair of parables which span seven verses in a category called 'foil introduction' can only make the category so general in its applicability as to make it unhelpful.

One possible example not considered by Goulder is:

13.31:   ἐν αὐτῇ τῇ ὥρᾳ προσῆλθάν τινες Φαρισαῖοι λέγοντες
                αὐτῷ, Ἔξελθε καὶ πορεύου ἐντεῦθεν, ὅτι Ἡρῴδης θέλει
                σε ἀποκτεῖναι.

Another one is in mid-pericope:

10.29:   ὁ δὲ θέλων δικαιῶσαι ἑαυτὸν εἶπεν πρὸς τὸν Ἰησοῦν, Καὶ
                τίς ἐστίν μου πλησίον;

One should, perhaps, allow the following example too:

4.22:   καὶ πάντες ἐμαρτύρουν αὐτῷ καὶ ἐθαύμαζον ἐπὶ τοῖς
                λόγοις τῆς χάριτος τοῖς ἐκπορευομένοις ἐκ τοῦ στόματος
                αὐτοῦ καὶ ἔλεγον, Οὐχὶ υἱός ἐστιν Ἰωσὴφ οὗτος;

One might add that there are a couple of striking features which cover both the QD and the L material. First, there are two examples, one QD (14.15) and one L (11.27) of the 'cloying piety' to which Goulder refers (§1.5, p. 91). Second, it is striking that Luke sometimes has one speaker asking a question or making a request with Jesus then responding to a wider audience: in 11.1-2 QD, 'one of his disciples' spoke to Jesus and 'he said to them...' In 13.23-24 QD, 'someone said to him...and he said to them'. One can compare 12.13-15 L, 'One of the multitude said to him...but he said to him...and he said to them... and he told them a parable'. Also 12.41-42 QD may be an example of the same feature, 'Peter said...and the Lord said'.

5. *Mark and Matthew*

If, however, this is clearly a feature of Luke, it is not so clear that it is distinctive of his Gospel.[20] There is a good number of foil questions, remarks and comments in Mark. These are examples:

Mk 2.18b: καὶ ἔρχονται καὶ λέγουσιν αὐτῷ, Διὰ τί οἱ μαθηταὶ
                Ἰωάννου καὶ οἱ μαθηταὶ τῶν Φαρισαίων νηστεύουσιν, οἱ
                δὲ σοὶ μαθηταὶ οὐ νηστεύουσιν; (cf. Mt. 9.14 and Lk.
                5.33).

Mk 8.11:   καὶ ἐξῆλθον οἱ Φαρισαῖοι καὶ ἤρξαντο συζητεῖν αὐτῷ,
                ζητοῦντες παρ' αὐτοῦ σημεῖον ἀπὸ τοῦ οὐρανοῦ,
                πειράζοντες αὐτόν. (cf. Mt. 12.38 where there is a question
                in direct speech).

20. Cadbury treats this question, with some useful examples, in *Style*, p. 122.

It is worth noting that in Luke's parallel to Mk 8.11, Jesus goes into the teaching without a question, remark or comment (Lk. 11.29, though in a Q context). Another interesting example is Mk 13.3-4 where the evangelist has the eschatological discourse introduced by a direct question from Peter, Andrew, James and John (cf. Mt. 24.3-4 and Lk. 21.7).[21]

The same feature is present in Matthew too. It is arguable that in his redaction of Mark, he sometimes transforms foil questions, requests and comments from indirect speech into direct speech (Mt. 12.24 // Mk 3.22 but Luke has the direct speech too, 11.15; Mt. 12.38 // Mk 8.11, see above; Mt. 13.10 // Mk 4.10, cf. Lk. 8.9 with the optative). There are, however, no clear redactional examples in the sense of Matthew having a foil request, comment or question where Mark does not have one. There is one QD example of the phenomenon in Matthew:

Mt. 18.21 QD: τότε προσελθὼν ὁ Πέτρος εἶπεν αὐτῷ, Κύριε, ποσάκις ἁμαρτήσει εἰς ἐμὲ ὁ ἀδελφός μου καὶ ἀφήσω αὐτῷ; ἕως ἑπτάκις; (cf. Lk. 17.3-4 where there is no question).

It is not such a marked feature of M material as it is of L material (cf. 13.36b M and 19.10 M). It is worth noting, nevertheless, that the teaching discourses in Matthew are sometimes broken up by foil questions, remarks or comments: in ch. 13 at vv. 10 and 36, in ch. 18 at v. 21 and in ch. 24 at vv. 3-4.

Several of the foil questions, requests and comments in Matthew and Mark come from opponents, usually Pharisees (Mk 2.18, 24; 3.22; 8.11 and parallels in Matthew and Luke; cf. non-teaching sections in Mark). In this respect, they do not differ from Luke (10.29; 11.45; 13.31; 15.2; 17.20; 19.39).

In contrast with Luke, though, Mark and Matthew do not have examples of 'cloying piety'. Further, where Mark and Matthew have foil questions, requests and comments, Jesus always responds to the speakers themselves. Even where it is a single speaker, as in Mk 12.28 and 13.1, and Matthew 18.21, Jesus responds directly to the person and not to a wider audience.

21. Other examples are Mk 2.24 (cf. Mt. 12.2 and Lk. 6.2); 3.22 (cf. Mt. 12.24 and Lk. 11.15); 4.10 (cf. Mt. 13.10 and Lk. 8.9); 11.21 (cf. Mt. 21.20); 12.28 (cf. Mt. 22.34; cf. also Lk. 10.25-29); and 13.1 (cf. Mt. 24.1 and Lk. 21.5, above). Also possible are Mk 2.16 (cf. Mt. 9.11 and Lk. 5.30) and 3.32 (cf. Mt. 12.47 and Lk. 8.20).

6. *Conclusion*

The Lukan examples of foil questions, remarks and comments introducing teaching span QD, L and possibly R material. The phenomenon
is widespread and is certainly characteristic of the evangelist.

However, all the evangelists employ the device, and it is a feature
found regularly in Mark and in parallel sections in Matthew and Luke.
On one occasion Mark has a request leading up to teaching where Luke
lacks it (Mk 8.11 // Lk. 11.39, Sign). There are a couple of M examples
and one possible Matthean QD case.

Therefore, although Luke uses the device more than do the other
evangelists, it is by no means distinctive of his writing. Within the
category, however, one can draw out two features which may be
distinctive of Luke's Gospel. The first is Goulder's sub-category §1.5,
'cloying piety' (p. 91). His two examples of this, 11.27 L and 14.15 QD
are the only examples of this in the Gospels. One should not make a
great deal of this, however, since there are only the two cases.

More impressively, it is striking that Luke sometimes has speakers
acting as a genuine foil to Jesus, asking a question or making a request
and Jesus then responding by teaching a wider audience. Not only are
there a handful of examples of this feature in Luke (11.1-2, 12.13-15;
13.23-24 and perhaps 12.41-42), but also the feature is lacking in both
Matthew and Mark, where Jesus always responds directly to the
speakers.

F. *Controversial Teaching Set in Synagogues or Meals to which Jesus
Has Been Invited by a Pharisee (§1.6)*

1. *Synagogue*

It is necessary to divide Goulder's category into two because the
evidence goes in different directions for the two aspects, synagogue and
meals with Pharisees. Goulder (*LNP*, p. 91) lists 4.16 QD; 4.33 MK;
6.6 MK and 13.10 L as examples of controversial teaching set in a
synagogue. Some qualifications and reservations are required here.
First, it is not clear that these verses all introduce teaching. 4.16-30
(Rejection at Nazareth) is a story which features teaching; 4.31-37
(Capernaum Synagogue) is the story of an exorcism; and 6.6-11
(Withered Hand) and 13.10-17 (Bent Woman) are both miracle stories.

Second, the feature is clearly not distinctive of Luke. Two of the examples are from Mark and although the reference to Nazara in 4.16 is parallel to Mt. 4.13, the story and the synagogue setting are parallel to Mk 6.1-6. Therefore, of Goulder's four examples, only 13.10 is not from Mark and there are no R or QD occurrences.

There are three examples of the feature in Mark (1.21; 3.1; 6.1-2), and two in Matthew (12.9 // Mk 3.1; 13.33-34 // Mk 6.1-2), against the four in Luke. The feature is not particularly characteristic of Luke.

2. *Meals to which Jesus is invited by a Pharisee*

Goulder lists three meals to which Jesus is invited by a Pharisee as a setting for controversial teaching, 7.36; 11.37 QD and 14.1 (*LNP*, p. 91).[22] Again it is not clear that these verses lead up to 'controversial teaching'. 14.1 leads up to the Healing of the Dropsical Man (14.1-6) but, on the other hand, it is also the scene for the teaching material of 14.7-24. Luke 7.36-50 (Simon the Pharisee), however, is not so much teaching material as a story with an element of teaching.

On the other hand, it is clearer here that we have a feature which is distinctive of Luke. Some basis for it might be found in texts like Mk 2.15-17 where Scribes and Pharisees comment on Jesus's eating with tax-collectors and sinners and Mk 7.1-2 where Pharisees observe that the disciples eat with hands defiled (cf. Lk. 11.37) but there are no cases in Mark or Matthew of Jesus being invited by a Pharisee to a meal.

Further, 7.36 could almost be thought of as an R example, if Lk. 7.36-50 is taken as his version of Mk 14.3-9. In this case, there would be an R example, a QD example and an L example so that the feature could be seen as being distinctive of Luke as a writer.[23]

G. *Re-introduction in Mid-pericope (§1.7)*

1. *Preliminary Comments*

In this category, the problem of the division of the text into pericopae becomes sharply focused. If one takes, for example, 12.54–13.9 as one long pericope, as does Goulder, there is no problem in seeing 13.1 as a

---

22. See Cadbury, *Style*, p. 120, which also lists 7.36; 11.37 and 14.1 and compares them with 5.29-32; 19.1-10 and 15.1-2.

23. See further below, pp. 248-49.

re-introduction in mid-pericope (*LNP*, p. 91; cf. above). Similarly, if one takes 10.17-24 as a unit, v. 21 can also be a re-introduction (*LNP*, p. 91; cf. also 13.31 as part of 13.22-35). The category is partly used, therefore, to help support some of Goulder's odder divisions of the text. This means that there is some arbitrariness about the way in which Goulder appeals to the feature. Not only do Goulder's re-introductions sometimes look like simple introductions, but also some of Goulder's simple introductions look like re-introductions, especially 12.41.

2. *R*

Goulder lists Lk. 5.36 as R, 'And he said this parable to them also...' and, indeed, these seven introductory words are lacking in both Mk 2.21 and Mt. 9.16. There are several other possible R examples, 3.15-16, interrupting John the Baptist's teaching (contrast Mk 1.7 // Mt. 3.11); and 21.10 and 21.29, both interrupting the Eschatological Discourse (contrast Mk 13.8 and 13.28, and Mt. 24.7 and 24.32).[24]

3. *QD*

Goulder gives one QD example, 10.21, ἐν αὐτῇ τῇ ὥρᾳ ἠγαλλιάσατο [ἐν] τῷ πνεύματι τῷ ἁγίῳ καὶ εἶπεν...(p. 91). This is really QC, however, in that Matthew too has a new introduction before Jesus' prayer of thanksgiving, in similar words to Luke's, Mt. 11.25, ἐν ἐκείνῳ τῷ καιρῷ ἀποκριθεὶς ὁ 'Ιησοῦς εἶπεν...Similar to this is Lk. 13.20, καὶ πάλιν εἶπεν, Τίνι ὁμοιώσω τὴν βασιλείαν τοῦ θεοῦ; introducing the parable of the Leaven. Goulder describes this as Luke re-opening with a pleonastic question, referring to this section in chapter 3 (p. 567), but although Luke has the question which Matthew lacks (Mt. 13.33), Matthew does have the same technique here of re-opening in mid-pericope, with ἄλλην παραβολὴν ἐλάλησεν αὐτοῖς...

Nevertheless, there are several QD examples of the phenomenon. At 6.39, midway through the Sermon on the Plain, the oratio recta is interrupted with εἶπεν δὲ καὶ παραβολὴν αὐτοῖς...For Goulder, though, this marks the beginning of the second half of the Sermon (pp. 346 and 348), assigned to a different week from the first half. A second example, 12.41 (contrast Mt. 24.45), also looks like a re-introduction in mid-

24. Cf. Streeter in W. Sanday (ed.), *Oxford Studies*, p. 207, and Cadbury, *Style*, p. 123, comparing this with Lk. 5.36.

pericope but Goulder makes it the beginning of a new pericope (p. 549, see above).

There are at least three additional examples which do work on Goulder's division of the text. At 7.29-30 there is a break in Jesus' teaching on John the Baptist (7.18-35); this contrasts with the parallel Mt. 11.7-19 which is uninterrupted oratio recta. Second, at 10.23 Jesus's thanksgiving to the Father (10.21-22 // Mt. 11.25-27) merges into a saying to the disciples (10.23-24 // Mt. 13.16-17) by means of a short re-introduction. Third, at 11.45-46 a lawyer interrupts Jesus' denunciation of the Pharisees and Lawyers (contrast Mt. 23 where there is no such break).

4. *L*

Distinguishing between Q and L material is, once more, a difficulty. In any one pericope, especially on Goulder's division of the text, there is a mixture of Q and L material. Nevertheless, re-introduction in mid-pericope is a feature found in L material as well as in Markan and Q sections of Luke and, interestingly, the re-introduction often marks the point at which Luke moves from Q to L material or vice versa.

Goulder gives three examples which are not QD or R, 13.1, 31 and 14.7 (*LNP*, p. 91). Goulder compares 13.1 and 13.31 with 10.21, noting the tendency to continue a pericope with 'in the same hour' or 'at the same time'. 13.1 and 13.31, however, are both examples of places in which Goulder does not divide the text where others might (see above). 14.7, on the other hand, ἔλεγεν δὲ πρὸς τοὺς κεκλημένους παραβολήν, ἐπέχων πῶς τὰς πρωτοκλισίας ἐξελέγοντο…, works well as a re-introduction in mid-pericope (14.1-14) and so does, one might add, 14.12, in the same pericope, ἔλεγεν δὲ καὶ τῷ κεκληκότι αὐτόν…

On Goulder's division of the text, other L examples could be seen at 13.6 (leading to the Fig Tree) and 15.11 (leading to the Prodigal Son). Also on Goulder's divisions, at 9.57 Luke turns from L material (Samaritan Village) to Q material (Would-be Followers); at 11.5 Luke turns from Q (Lord's Prayer) to L (Friend); at 11.29 Luke turns from L (True Blessedness) to Q / MK (Demand for a Sign); at 13.18 Luke turns from L (Bent Woman) to Q / MK (Mustard Seed); at 17.5 Luke turns from Q / MK (Repentance etc.) to L (Servant of all Work); at 17.22 Luke turns from L to Q (Coming Days); and at 18.15 Luke turns from L (Pharisee and Publican) to Mark (Little Children).

With Goulder's division of the text, therefore, this is a common feature in L. On most other divisions of the text, it will still be present in L (for example 11.5 and 17.5) though it will not be as common.

5. *Mark and Matthew*

Re-introductions in mid-pericope are common also in Mark and especially so if one works with Goulder's division of the text (*LNP*, pp. 175-77). A good example, present on a natural division of the text, is Mk 7.1-23 (Traditions of the Elders), with re-introductions at v. 9, καὶ ἔλεγεν αὐτοῖς..., v. 14, καὶ προσκαλεσάμενος πάλιν τὸν ὄχλον ἔλεγεν αὐτοῖς..., and v. 20, ἔλεγεν δὲ ὅτι...[25]

In Mk 4.13, 24 and 9.1, Mark has re-introductions in mid-pericope which Luke lacks in his parallels (see Lk. 8.9-15, 16-18 and 9.18-27). These would be cases where Luke suppresses the feature in his redaction of Mark.

Goulder does not give a statement of his division of the text of Matthew in *LNP* but even without this help, re-introductions are certainly a feature of Matthew on any reasonable division into pericopae. An obvious example is Mt. 11.7 QC, τούτων δὲ πορευομένων ἤρξατο ὁ Ἰησοῦς λέγειν τοῖς ὄχλοις περὶ Ἰωάννου (cf. Lk. 7.24). Another possible example is Mt. 18.21 QD, τότε προσελθὼν ὁ Πέτρος εἶπεν αὐτῷ· Κύριε, ποσάκις ἁμαρτήσει εἰς ἐμὲ ὁ ἀδελφός μου καὶ ἀφήσω αὐτῷ;. The feature is less common in Matthew than in Mark and Luke, however, particularly as Matthew has long sections of oratio recta, most famously the Sermon on the Mount, but also Mt. 24–25.

6. *Conclusion*

Re-introductions in mid-pericope are common in Luke and are found in all types of material, R, QD and L. They are particularly common if one works with Goulder's divisions but they are still present if one does

25. Other examples on Goulder's division of the text are Mk 1.29 and 32 (in 1.21-34), cf. Lk. 4.38, 40 and 42 (in 4.31-44); Mk 2.15 and 18 (in 2.13-22), cf. Lk. 5.29, 33 and 36 R (in 5.27-39); Mk 3.1 (in 2.23–3.6); Mk 3.13 (in 3.7-19), cf. Lk. 6.17 (in 6.12-19); Mk 4.13 (in 4.10-20); Mk 4.24 (in 4.21-25); Mk 4.33 (in 4.30-34); Mk 5.35 (in 5.21-43); Mk 6.6b-7 (in 6.1-13); Mk 6.53 (in 6.45-56); Mk 7.31 (in 7.24-37); Mk 8.14 and 22 (in 8.11-26); Mk 8.34 and 9.1 (in 8.27–9.1), cf. Lk. 9.23 (in 9.18-27); Mk 9.9 (in 9.2-13); Mk 9.33 and 38 (in 9.30-50), cf. Lk. 9.46 and 49 (in Lk. 9.43b-50); Mk 10.10 and 13 (in 10.1-16); Mk 10.35 and 46 (in 10.32-52), cf. Lk. 18.35 (in 18.31-43); Mk 11.15 and 20 (in 11.12-26); Mk 12.1 (in 11.27–12.12); Mk 12.18 (in 12.13-27); Mk 12.35, 38 and 41 (in 12.28-44).

not. They are not, however, distinctive of Luke since they are found regularly in Mark—particularly common if one works with Goulder's divisions but still present if one does not. They are also present in Matthew.

H. *The Return Home of Characters (§2.1)*

In Goulder's second section, on closes to pericopae, he gives ten examples of characters returning home at the end of a pericope (*LNP*, pp. 91-92). Of these, it is immediately noticeable that five are from chs. 1–2 and three from ch. 24. Of the remaining two, one is Markan (Lk. 8.39); the other (7.10) is QD, so if one were to take only the occurrences listed by Goulder, the distribution of the feature would not be even. This is not the complete picture, however. Goulder does not list all the occurrences and there are at least three others, 5.25 MA (cf. Mt. 9.7) in the Paralytic, 15.6 QD in the Lost Sheep (contrast Mt. 18.13) and 18.14 L in the Pharisee and the Publican. These occurrences are all towards the end of pericopae rather than right at the end. In the same category one should note the Prodigal Son (15.11-32) in which the return of the hero is the climax of the parable.

Other examples almost fit into the category, 19.5 L (Zacchaeus), 23.48 R (Crucifixion) and 24.52-53 L (end of the Gospel).

The feature is, then, characteristic of Luke but it is not quite distinctive. Goulder lists Mk 5.19 // Lk. 8.39 (Gerasene) but one might add reference to Mk 7.30 in which the Syro-Phoenician woman goes home (contrast Mt. 15.28) and 8.26 in which the blind man of Bethsaida is sent home. The only example in Matthew is the MA listed above (though cf. also Mt. 12.44 // Lk. 11.24 QC at the beginning of a pericope).

Within this category, it is characteristic of Luke to combine going home with rejoicing or praising God: in 2.20, the shepherds 'returned rejoicing and praising God'; in 5.25 R, the paralytic goes home glorifying God (contrast Mk 2.12 and Mt. 9.7-8); in 15.6 QD the shepherd returns home and calls together friends to rejoice with him and similarly in the Prodigal Son, the return home is accompanied by great rejoicing. One example from Mark is 5.19 // Lk. 8.39 where the Gerasene returns home and tells of what God has done for him.

I. *Notes of Progress in Chapters 1–2 (§2.2)*

Goulder lists three notes of progress, all from the first two chapters and all in comments which summarize several years of progress, 1.80; 2.40 and 2.52. Not surprisingly, the feature is only present here, where Luke is summarizing the childhood and growth of John and Jesus. The only other place in the Gospels in which the feature could occur, where there is a gap of many years, is between the end of Matthew 2 and the beginning of Matthew 3 but here it is not present. It is, then, distinctive of Luke's Birth and Infancy Narrative but since the feature is not evenly distributed, one cannot really say that it is characteristic of the Gospel as a whole.

J. *Inclusio (§2.3)*

Goulder says that inclusio 'was widely used' and that it is 'common without being specific to Luke' (*LNP*, p. 92). This contrasts somewhat with Goulder's earlier statement that 'Matthew's favourite *inclusio* is a rabbinic habit, and one rarely if ever to be found in the other two synoptics' (*MLM*, p. 27; cf. pp. 87 and 449).[26] Further, this is a feature which, like chiasmus, is difficult to isolate. One scholar will see it in one place and another in another; some will not see it at all.

Once more there is the danger of circularity in that the spotting of inclusio depends upon where one begins and ends pericopae. One of Goulder's examples is 3.22, 'You are my beloved son' with 3.38, 'the Son of God' at the end of the Genealogy, but this only works if one takes 3.21-38 as a unit as Goulder does. 3.21-22 could be taken as one pericope and 3.23-38 as another. In this example, in any case, there is no verbal connection between v. 22, Σὺ εἶ ὁ υἱός μου ὁ ἀγαπητός, and v. 38,...τοῦ Ἀδὰμ τοῦ θεοῦ.

Goulder has two other examples in his introduction, 3.1-20 and 4.1-13. In the commentary he lists 2.22-40 (p. 261); 6.30-35 (p. 365); 6.39-49 (p. 369); 13.22-35 (p. 572) and 22.1-23 (p. 727).

---

26. On this topic, see J.C. Fenton, 'Inclusio' and the summary in Davies and Allison, *Matthew*, 92-93.

K. *Conclusion*

The study of Luke's introductions and conclusions to pericopae is complicated because some of Goulder's divisions are uncertain (A. above). He divides the text where others would not and does not divide the text where others would.

Luke often has elaborate introductions to pericopae and sometimes he refers to time and place (B.), but it is not distinctive or even particularly characteristic of Luke to have elaborate introductions or references to time and place. Sometimes Mark will have a more elaborate introduction than Luke in a parallel passage and sometimes Mark will have references to time and place where Luke lacks them in parallel passages. In Q and L material Luke more often than not has no reference to time and place. The Birth and Infancy Narratives are an exception.

Sometimes Luke takes care to distinguish those addressed in teaching sections (C.) but in this he does not differ from Mark and Matthew. Within this category, however, there is one feature which is distinctive or almost so (Mt. 5–7 and Mk 8.34 are possible exceptions): that of addressing one group in the hearing of another group (6.17-19 and 7.1; 12.1, 13-16 and 22; 15.1-3; 16.1, 14; 20.45 R). It is notable that examples occur in R, QD and L material.

The evangelist's comment (D.) occurs quite often in Matthew, Mark and Luke, but it is not common in introductions, only in Matthew (11.20 QD), possibly in Mark (7.1-4) and in Luke at 18.1 and 19.11. This feature is not distinctive of Luke.

The phenomenon of foil questions, remarks and comments to introduce teaching (E.) is characteristic of Luke but it is not distinctive of his writing. Within the category, however, there are two features which are distinctive. First, there are two examples in Goulder's sub-category 'cloying piety' (11.27 L and 14.15 QD). Second, Luke sometimes has a question, request or comment from a speaker with Jesus responding to a wider audience, 11.1-2 QD; 12.13-15 L and 13.23-24 QD.

It is not distinctive of Luke, nor is it even characteristic of his Gospel, to set controversial teaching in a synagogue (F.). There are three examples of the feature in Mark, two in Matthew and four in Luke and not all of these, strictly speaking, introduce controversial teaching. On the other hand, settings at meals to which Jesus has been invited by a Pharisee are common. Again the occasions do not, strictly speaking, cover controversial teaching, but this sub-category is distinctive of Luke's Gospel and it is arguably distinctive of Luke as a writer in that it occurs in QD (11.37), L (14.1) and possibly R (7.36) material.

Re-introductions in mid-pericope (G.) is one of the most difficult categories to work with because of the arbitrariness of some of Goulder's divisions in Luke, so that in Goulder's scheme one could have a re-introduction where other scholars would have a fresh pericope. The feature is present in Luke on Goulder's division of the text but also in Mark on Goulder's division of the text. The feature would stand in both Gospels, and in Matthew too, on most natural divisions of the text. This feature is not, therefore, distinctive of Luke.

In closes to pericopae, it is characteristic though not distinctive of Luke to note the return home of characters (H.). There are examples of the feature in Mark and Matthew too. Sometimes the characters rejoice or praise God as they return home and this is almost distinctive of Luke. Notes of progress (in years) are distinctive of Luke's Birth and Infancy Narrative (I.). Inclusio is found in all the Gospels (J.).

Among Goulder's sub-categories, then, the following are distinctive or nearly distinctive of Luke's introductions and conclusions among the Gospels:

1.	When Jesus is addressing one audience it is often in the hearing of another audience.
2.	Twice, comments of a 'cloying piety' from an individual introduce Jesus' teaching.
3.	A question, request or comment from an individual sometimes leads to Jesus responding to a wider audience.
4.	Sometimes Luke sets the scene at a meal to which Jesus has been invited by a Pharisee.
5.	Sometimes characters rejoice as they return home at the end of pericopae.

Not only are these features found largely only in Luke but also to some degree they are distinctive of Luke as a writer, occurring in QD or R or both as well as in L.

Chapter 6

PROMPTITUDE AND ALACRITY (§3)

A. *Preliminary Comment*

Goulder lists fifteen examples of Luke's 'get-up-and-go attitude', 'his liking for promptitude and alacrity' (*LNP*, pp. 92-93), often seen in his use of ἀναστάς, -άντες (2/6/17+18).[1] I will look first at occurrences of the feature in Luke (B.) and then examples from Mark (C.) and Matthew (D.). Further, Goulder has two subsections, characters not being thoughtlessly hasty (§3.1) and lively and pejorative use of ἤρξατο (§3.2) which I will turn to afterwards (E. and F.).

B. *Luke*

There are many occasions on which Luke has his characters acting with promptitude or alacrity. Goulder draws attention to 4.39 R (*LNP*, p. 92), but it is often found elsewhere in his redaction of Mark (Lk. 6.8; 8.47; 22.45-46, cf. *LNP*, p. 677; 23.1 and 24.12). It occurs also in L material (1.39, cf. *LNP*, pp. 92 and 235; 4.29; 11.7-8; 15.18 and 20, cf. *LNP*, p. 614; and 24.33) though it is not found in QD. Goulder observes that the use of this participle is a Septuagintalism[2] but does not think that it is 'an irrelevance' (*LNP*, p. 92). It is worth noting in this regard that the participle is often used in contexts where Luke is depicting his characters acting with some kind of immediacy. In 4.39, for example, Luke combines παραχρῆμα with ἀναστᾶσα where Mark (1.31) has neither (cf. Lk. 5.25, below). In 1.39, Mary arises (ἀναστᾶσα) and goes to the hill country of Judah μετὰ σπουδῆς. Similarly, Peter gets

---

1. The occurrences of ἀναστάς, -άντες are listed by Hawkins, *Horae*, pp. 35-36.

2. It is described by Fitzmyer as 'pleonastic or redundant' which, when combined with a main verb 'connotes inception', *Luke I-IX*, pp. 114 and 362.

up and runs (ἀναστὰς ἔδραμεν) to the tomb (24.12) and the Prodigal Son gets up (ἀναστάς) and goes to his father who runs (δραμών) to meet him (15.20).

The depiction of suddenness is, in fact, quite characteristic of Luke, especially using the word παραχρῆμα (2/0/10+6), in redaction of Mark (4.39 and 8.47; cf. 5.25; 8.44, 55; 18.43 and 22.60 where Luke replaces Mark's εὐθύς with παραχρῆμα), in QD (19.11) and in L (1.64 and 13.13), usually expressing the immediacy with which one of Jesus's miracles takes effect.[3]

Luke uses other expressions too which may express suddenness, sometimes εὐθύς (6.49 QD, cf. *LNP*, pp. 92 and 374; it is never in L),[4] more often εὐθέως (12.36 QD, cf. *LNP*, pp. 92 and 544; 12.54 QD, cf. *LNP*, pp. 92 and 558; 14.5 QD, cf. *LNP*, p. 92; 17.7 L, cf. *LNP*, pp. 93 and 642), though he never adds εὐθύς or εὐθέως in his redaction of Mark. These are words which recede in Luke (together 18/41/7+10).[5]

Luke uses ἐξαίφνης twice (2.13; 9.39 R)[6] and on one occasion he has αἰφνίδιος (21.34). The use of ἐπεισέρχομαι in the same context (21.35) perhaps accentuates the mood of suddenness.[7]

Luke expresses haste by using ταχέως or ταχύς—the householder tells his servant to go out quickly (14.21 QD, cf. *LNP*, pp. 92 and 591), the servants are to bring the Prodigal his robe quickly (15.22, cf. *LNP*, pp. 92 and 614), the Dishonest Steward's debtor is to 'sit down quickly and write fifty' (16.6, cf. *LNP*, pp. 92 and 620) and vindication will

---

3. D. Daube, *Sudden*, has a good discussion of words for suddenness. See pp. 38-40 on παραχρῆμα. According to Daube, for Luke the meaning of παραχρῆμα 'is a question of immediate miraculous actualization of an order or prediction of Jesus, or one in Jesus' name, or some influence emanating from Jesus, or the impact of the spirit' (p. 39). He contrasts this with εὐθύς/εὐθέως which he says never describes immediate submission to an order by Jesus or the like (p. 65). Cf. C. Fabricius, 'Zu *parachrema*'.

4. Daube feels that the meaning of εὐθύς here (Lk. 6.49) is 'at once' or 'immediately' (*Sudden*, p. 63).

5. Hawkins's figures (*Horae*, p. 12). Hawkins adds that in narrative sections the figures are 12/34/1, Luke's one use being 5.13.

6. Daube gives figures of 0/1/2+2 for ἐξαίφνης. On 9.39, see *Sudden*, p. 31.

7. Daube thinks of occurrences of the verbs ἐπέρχομαι (0/0/3+4, Lk. 1.35, 11.22 R/QD and 21.26 R) and ἐπεισέρχομαι (here) as falling into this type of category—these words, especially ἐπεισέρχομαι, 'convey the threatening, desperate aspect of the happening' (*Sudden*, p. 35). Cf. BAGD, *ad loc*, defining ἐπεισέρχομαι as 'rush in suddenly and forcefully'.

come speedily (ἐν τάχει, 18.8, cf. *LNP*, p. 93).

Luke also likes σπεύδω—the shepherds hasten to see Jesus (2.16, cf. *LNP*, pp. 92 and 254) and Zacchaeus comes down quickly (19.5-6 × 2, cf. *LNP*, pp. 93 and 677). Goulder compares Luke's use of σπουδαίως in 7.4 (*LNP*, p. 380).

Further, Satan falls like lightning from heaven (10.18).

The variety of expressions for characters acting with promptitude and alacrity and the number of occasions on which these expressions are used indicate that this is indeed a marked feature of Luke's style, a feature which occurs in R, QD and L.

C. *Mark*

εὐθέως and εὐθύς, frequent and prominent features of Mark's style, often appear to have the meaning 'in due course' or 'forthwith' in Mark (for example Mk 1.21, 23, 29, 43; 8.10),[8] but on other occasions they may well be stronger in meaning, with some sort of immediacy being depicted. Sometimes this could be the immediacy of Jesus's healing (1.42, Leper; 2.12, Paralytic; 5.29, Woman with flux; 5.42, Jairus's daughter, εὐθὺς ἀνέστη; 10.52, Bartimaeus). It can be the immediacy of divine foreknowledge (2.8, Paralytic; 5.30, Woman). On one occasion it is the quick spreading of the report about Jesus (1.28) and several times the action in the Sower parable, and the Seed Growing Secretly, happens quickly (ch. 4).[9]

Goulder says that 'whereas in Mark Jesus tends to act εὐθύς, many characters in Luke are on their toes' (*LNP*, p. 92). This is undoubtedly true for Luke but, on the other hand, the same is also true of characters in Mark. Sometimes it is Jesus (1.10, 12, 20; 6.50 etc.) but at other times it is the disciples (6.45) or Judas (14.43, 45) or the crowd (9.15), the Gerasene Demoniac (5.2) or the father of the Epileptic (9.24). On a couple of occasions Jesus's opponents hold counsel εὐθύς (3.6 and 15.1). Most notably, Herodias's daughter goes in to the King εὐθὺς μετὰ σπουδῆς (6.25) and Herod responds εὐθύς (6.27). This is a good example because it is a character other than Jesus, in a story, only in Mark, with μετὰ σπουδῆς qualifying εὐθύς.

---

8.   Cf. Daube, *Sudden*, p. 60, though he probably underestimates the extent to which εὐθύς can convey immediacy in Mark.

9.   Cf. G.D. Kilpatrick in J.K. Elliott (ed.), *Language and Style*, p. 168 and E.J. Pryke, *Redactional Style*, pp. 87-96.

Further, it is arguable that Mark sometimes expresses promptitude or alacrity with words other than εὐθύς, again with other characters as well as Jesus. Although less frequently than Luke, Mark sometimes has a similar 'get-up-and-go' expressed by ἀναστάς: in 1.35; 7.24 and 10.1 concerning Jesus; 2.14, Levi following Jesus (cf. the witnesses at the trial in 14.57 and the High Priest in 14.60).

Mark has the *hapax* ἐξάπινα in his account of the Transfiguration (9.8, contrast Mt. 17.8 and Lk. 9.36) and the uncommon ἐξαίφνης in 13.36 (Householder), both of which may express suddenness.

Further, people often flee (φεύγω) in Mark—the herders of the Gerasene swine (5.14, cf. the pigs rushed, ὥρμησεν, over the precipice, 5.13); those in Judea (13.14); the disciples and the young man in the garden (14.50 and 52) and the women at the tomb (16.8).

Others run—the Gerasene Demoniac (5.6, ἔδραμεν), the crowd before the Feeding of the Five Thousand (6.33, συνέδραμον); the people in Gennesaret (6.55, περιέδραμον); the crowd before the healing of the Epileptic (9.15, προστρέχοντες); the Rich Man (10.17, προσδραμών) and a certain person at the crucifixion (15.36, δραμών).

It is interesting to note that in parallel material Luke often lacks Mark's references to characters acting with promptitude or alacrity. These six cases in Mark of characters running are absent from Luke. In Mk 5.6 // Lk. 8.28, Luke uses a different verb, as in Mk 6.33 // Lk. 9.11 (MA); 6.55 is part of the great omission; 9.15 is omitted in Luke's parallel (Lk. 9.37-38) as is Mk 15.36 (Lk. 23.44-49) and Luke omits the Rich Man's running (Mk 10.17 // Lk. 18.18).[10]

It is clear, then, that Mark too is fond of promptitude and alacrity and that Goulder's statement of the matter is oversimplified. Different characters act quickly or with immediacy and although εὐθύς is a favourite expression, often used with a weak meaning, Mark also has a variety of other ways of expressing suddenness, immediacy, haste, fleeing and running, evenly distributed in the Gospel, with several of the references missing in parallel sections in Luke.

D. *Matthew*

There are fewer occurrences of characters acting with promptitude and alacrity in Matthew. It is, nevertheless, a feature common in Matthew,

10. But cf. Cadbury, *Style*, p. 93, describing this phenomenon as 'strong words for the pursuit of Jesus, which Luke softens or omits'.

distributed evenly in the Gospel and in QC (Mt. 3.7 // Lk. 3.7;[11] and Mt. 24.27 // Lk. 17.24), QD (Mt. 25.15b-16), R (Mt. 14.31, contrast Mk 6.50-51; Mt. 21.19-20, contrast Mk 11.14 and 21; Mt. 24.29, contrast Mk 13.24 and Lk. 21.25; Mt. 28.7, contrast Mk 16.7; Mt. 28.8, though cf. Mk 16.8 and Lk. 24.12) and M material (Mt. 2.13; 10.23 and 23.33). Matthew is fonder of φεύγω than are Mark and Luke (7/5/3+2), but he has a diminished use of εὐθύς/εὐθέως and fewer other words for suddenness. In the examples listed, his vocabulary is φεύγω (2.13; 3.7; 10.23; 23.33), εὐθέως (14.31; 24.29; 25.15b-16), παραχρῆμα (21.19-20), ταχύς (28.7-8) and τρέχω (28.8).

E. *Sitting Down (§3.1)*

Goulder adds to his section a qualification: four examples of Lukan characters not being 'thoughtlessly hasty': in 10.39; 14.28, 31 and 16.6, they sit down (*LNP*, p. 93, cf. pp. 597-98 and 620). Here Goulder has given four examples, all from L material in the Travel Narrative, covering a parable (Unjust Steward, 16.6), sayings material (14.28, 31, Counting the Cost) and a story from Jesus's ministry (10.39, Mary and Martha).

There are plenty of other examples of people sitting down in the Gospel but there are no redactional examples. Some of Luke's references to sitting down are in Markan and Q material and one might say that the characters in Mark and Matthew are also not thoughtlessly hasty. Jesus himself sits down and calls the twelve to him in Mk 9.35 (contrast Lk. 9.46-48), some of the scribes are seated in Mk 2.6 (cf. Lk. 5.21), Levi is sitting at his tax office in Mk 2.14 (cf. Mt. 9.9 and Lk. 5.27), the crowd are seated about Jesus in Mk 3.32 (contrast Mt. 12.46-47 and Lk. 8.19-20), the Gerasene is sitting clothed and in his right mind in Mk 5.15 (cf. Lk. 8.35) and the young man is sitting on the right of the tomb in Mk 16.5 (cf. Mt. 28.2 but contrast Lk. 24). The children are sitting in the market-place in Mt. 11.16 QC (cf. Lk. 7.32) and the fishermen sit down to sort fish in Mt. 13.48 M.

11. Though here (Mt. 3.7), the fleeing from the coming wrath may envisage disordered and fearful movement rather than being necessarily speedy.

F. *Lively and Pejorative Use of* ἤρξατο *(§3.2)*

Goulder isolates eight examples of ἤρξατο used in what he calls a lively and somewhat pejorative sense (*LNP*, p. 93; cf. also pp. 274, 573 and 597-98).[12] Goulder's examples cover R (5.21), QC (12.45), QD (3.8 and 14.18) and L (7.49; 11.53; 13.25; 14.29; the first three of these could be designated QD). One might add also 13.26 QD (cf. *LNP*, p. 274); 14.9 L; 14.30 L and 23.2 R. Since the category spans different sorts of material in the Gospel, it may show that the feature is characteristic of Luke as a writer.

If characteristic of Luke, however, it is not quite distinctive of his Gospel. One of Goulder's examples is Lk. 12.45 which he shares with Matthew (Mt. 24.49). There are also some possible examples in Mark, at 8.11 (καὶ ἐξῆλθον οἱ Φαρισαῖοι καὶ ἤρξαντο συζητεῖν αὐτῷ, cf. Lk. 11.29), 14.65 (καὶ ἤρξαντό τινες ἐμπτύειν αὐτῷ, contrast Lk. 22.63) and 15.18 (καὶ ἤρξαντο ἀσπάζεσθαι αὐτόν, Χαῖρε, βασιλεῦ τῶν Ἰουδαίων). Mk 8.11 is similar to Lk. 5.21 which is on Goulder's list and Mk 14.65 is similar to Lk. 14.29, also on Goulder's list.

There are few examples of the feature in Mark and Matthew, however, and Goulder has certainly isolated a feature which is more marked in Luke than in either of his predecessors, a feature which is almost but not quite distinctive of his Gospel.

G. *Conclusion*

The expression of promptitude and alacrity is a prominent feature in Luke. It is in different strands of material, MK, R, QD and L. It is a feature which is, however, also prominent in Mark and present in Matthew. Sometimes Luke lacks the feature in parallel material.

Luke has several different ways of expressing promptitude and alacrity and a variety of characters act suddenly, immediately, with haste or at once. However, Mark has as many different expressions and as many different characters acting suddenly.

The feature is not, therefore, distinctive of Luke. Certain aspects of the feature are more characteristic than others, however. Luke's use of παραχρῆμα marks him out from Matthew and Mark and he usually

---

12. Contrasted with a pleonastic sense, on which see J.W. Hunkin, 'Pleonastic ἄρχομαι', and J.C. Doudna, *Greek*, pp. 111-17.

uses it of the immediate fulfilment of an order or a prediction by Jesus (19.11 is an exception).

Goulder is probably right to isolate Luke's use of ἀναστάς as expressing a mood of 'get-up-and-go'. It is certainly characteristic of the evangelist, but it is not distinctive in that it is found in Mark with a similar meaning on several occasions.

Of Goulder's two sub-categories, the first, that characters are not thoughtlessly hasty (§3.1), does not particularly distinguish Luke—Mark also has characters who sit down. On the second, ἤρξατο used in a lively and pejorative sense (§3.2), Luke's use is almost distinctive.

Chapter 7

HUMAN CHARACTERS (§4)

A. *Preliminary Comments*

Goulder's discussion of human characters in Luke is the longest section in his isolation of Lukan stylistic features in chapter three of *LNP*. He subdivides these into eight categories, and he refers to them regularly in the commentary. This is the category which more than any other shows, for Goulder, Lukan creativity of story material, particularly parables:

> It is this human three-dimensional quality which makes Luke the great story-teller of the New Testament (*LNP*, p. 93).

Both here and in *MLM*, Goulder contrasts Luke's human characters with Matthew's 'stock figures':

> People are either good or bad, wise or foolish, obedient or disobedient, merciful or merciless...In Luke on the other hand all is alive. His characters are many-sided: prudent despite being crooked, penitent although a publican, thoughtful for their brothers even in Hades (*MLM*, pp. 55-56).[1]

Goulder picks out three examples for special comment and these examples make up the bulk of his introductory presentation (on pp. 93-94). They are the Prodigal Son, along with his brother and his father (15.11-32); Joseph and Mary and characters in chs. 1–2 and the Unjust Steward (16.1-9). Goulder has selected these examples because they all have rough parallels in Matthew, the Prodigal Son in Matthew's Two Sons (Mt. 21.28-32), Luke 1–2 is paralleled in Matthew 1–2 and the Unjust Steward in Mt. 18.23-35. In all these cases, the parallels in Matthew are slight.

---

1.   Cf. Drury, *Parables*, p. 114, etc. Contrast B. Gerhardsson, 'If we do not cut': 'the narrative meshalim of the synoptic gospels never *psychologize*...emotion involves nothing but very general, elementary reactions, never anything which makes the character into an individual with contours of his own' (p. 331).

On the Two Sons, which Goulder speaks of as 'the most glaring example', 'Luke's characters are people' (*LNP*, p. 93), but in Matthew:

> The boys are stock figures, not human beings. Nine words apiece suffice to sketch in their characters (*MLM*, p. 56).

Arguably, though, the characters need to be stock ones to make the point required by the context (Mt. 21.31-32), where Jesus is putting in stark contrast the behaviour of some of the Jewish leaders and the behaviour of the tax-collectors and harlots, making them see how they stand ('Which one did the will of his father?', v. 31). The 'nine words apiece' simply show that Matthew's Two Sons is a short parable. Luke seems to use the same sort of parable, a short one with stock figures, when the context requires it. Lk. 7.41-43 is a short parable which makes a simple point in the presence of an adversary who is a Jewish leader. Here the creditors are stock figures, and only a few words suffice to sketch out their characters.[2] Here too the parable leads up to a question which convicts the one who answers it.[3]

The difficulty with the comparison between the Two Sons in Matthew and the Prodigal Son in Luke is that these two parables are quite different from each other. Verbal links between the two are minimal—Matthew talks about two τέκνα (Mt. 21.28) and Luke about two υἱούς (15.11) and the subject matter is different. Matthew's Two Sons illustrates the contrast between saying and doing (cf. Mt. 7.24-27), verbal refusal and actual compliance contrasted with verbal compliance and actual refusal. There is nothing like this in Luke's Prodigal.

Similarly, Goulder speaks about Mt. 18.23-35 and Lk. 16.1-9 as 'the two evangelists' parables on the Remission of Debt' (*LNP*, p. 94) but the links between these two parables are even more slight. Again, a comparison with Lk. 7.41-43 is instructive. It is another parable on the remission of debt, in Luke, with stock figures and not human characters,

---

2. Cf. J. Nolland, *Luke 1–9.20*, p. 356: 'The parable is reported in the barest of forms with an almost total lack of narrative colour'.

3. Cf. Goulder's comment on the Two Sons in Matthew, 'One boy declines to work and then changes his mind for no reason; the other says he will, and equally inexplicably does not' (*LNP*, p. 93) with his comment on the two debtors in Luke, 'Many commentators have commented on the "curious", "unheard of" behaviour of the money-lender...and no special explanation is offered for his generosity' (*LNP*, p. 401).

and if we were to compare this parable rather than Lk. 16.1-9 with Mt. 18.23-35, the conclusions would be quite different.[4]

Moreover, the problem of circularity rears its head. Goulder in chapter three of *LNP* is listing features, the distinctiveness of which is supposed to demonstrate that Luke created the L material in which they appear. An alternative view, and one which Goulder is attempting to combat, is that there are sources in the tradition for L material. Now, by comparing Matthew's Two Sons with Luke's Prodigal, and Matthew's Unforgiving Servant with Luke's Unjust Steward, Goulder is assuming his own thesis, namely that Luke does not have a source in tradition for his parables, but that he creates them from hints in Matthew. Goulder's thesis, that Luke is creating from hints in Matthew, needs to be demonstrated from the analysis of the distinctive features in the material before that thesis can be taken for granted in the analysis of the features.

At the end of Goulder's introductory section (on pp. 93-94), he says:

> Even where a Matthean character is real, like the Centurion, we learn
> from Luke that he was fond of his servant, friendly to the Jews, and the
> donator of a synagogue (*LNP*, p. 94).

There is, then, on Goulder's admission, at least one human character in Matthew and it might be added here that Matthew's scene, where the man comes forward and beseeches Jesus, is much easier to envisage than is Luke's more complex one with the sending of delegations in which the reader never actually meets the Centurion.

When Goulder then breaks down the category into sub-sections, similar exceptions to the rules appear. On Soliloquy (§4.1, B. below), Goulder gives examples from Mark, 12.6, 'They will reverence my son' and Matthew, 24.48, the Servant's 'My lord delays' (pp. 94-95) and on Conversation (§4.2, p. 95, C. below), 'the Tares is an exception' to the rule that long conversations only feature in Luke's parables. The question which naturally arises is whether or not these are just occasional exceptions to the rules or whether Goulder's 'Lukan' features are more pervasive in the other Gospels than he claims. Each of Goulder's sub-sections will be taken in turn.

---

4.   Goulder actually feels that 7.41-43 derives from Mt. 18.23-35 (*LNP*, pp. 400-402).

B. *Soliloquy (§4.1)*

1. *Luke*

Goulder (pp. 94-95) gives several examples of soliloquy in parables, 12.17-18 (Rich Fool), 15.17-19 (Prodigal Son), 16.3-4 (Unjust Steward), 18.4b-5 (Unjust Judge) and 18.9-14 (Pharisee and Publican).[5] The latter example only works if one can consider private prayer like this to be soliloquy (cf. p. 668).[6]

Goulder adds to these L examples one occasion on which Luke apparently enhances a soliloquy in Mark (Mk 12.6 // Mt. 21.37 // Lk. 20.13), adding τί ποιήσω; and transforming part of Mark's third person narration into direct speech, πέμψω τὸν υἱόν μοῦ τὸν ἀγαπητόν. Here, then, in Luke's redaction, there seems to be a sign of the evangelist's penchant for soliloquy.[7]

There is one example not in a parable which Goulder does not mention:

1.25:   Οὕτως μοι πεποίηκεν κύριος ἐν ἡμέραις αἷς ἐπεῖδεν ἀφελεῖν ὄνειδός μου ἐν ἀνθρώποις.[8]

While in this example Elizabeth reflects on circumstances, in all the other examples (with the exception of the prayers in 18.9-14), the characters are contemplating future action. Goulder points out the similarity between 12.17-18, 16.3-4 and 20.13 R. In all of these the characters ask τί ποιήω; and in 12.17 and 16.3, they also tell us the state of affairs ('I have nowhere to store my crops'; 'my master is taking the stewardship away from me'). Similarly in the other two examples, 15.17-19 and 18.4b-5, the characters reason out their position ('How many of my father's hired servants have bread enough to

---

5.   This feature of Luke's parables is often noticed, for example, Fitzmyer, *Luke X–XXIV*, p. 973, listing 12.45; 15.17; 16.3-4; 18.4-5 and 20.13 and comparing Sir. 11.19; Drury, *Parables*, p. 115 and *Tradition and Design*, p. 77; Bultmann, *History*, p. 191; Evans, *Saint Luke*, p. 601, drawing special attention to 20.13 R. Most comprehensive is Philip Sellew, 'Interior Monologue'.

6.   One probably should include it. The king's prayer in the chapel in *Hamlet* is usually called a soliloquy. Bultmann, *History*, p. 191, includes this as an example of soliloquy. See also p. 170 n. 10, below.

7.   In the commentary, Goulder compares 10.5, 'Peace to this house' with Luke's fondness for soliloquy (*LNP*, p. 474). The comparison is not an obvious one.

8.   Cf. Sellew, 'Interior Monologue', p. 243.

spare...?' and 'Though I neither fear God nor regard man...') In each soliloquy, the characters then work out what they will do, 'I will pull down my barns...' (12.18), 'I will arise and go to my father' (15.18) and so on (cf. *LNP*, p. 620).

With the exception, then, of 18.9-14, the L parable soliloquy has the form:

a.   The character reflects on circumstances (cf. 1.24-25), sometimes with τί ποιήσω;.

b.   The character states what he will do.

The form is present also in the soliloquy in 20.13 R.

2. *Mark and Matthew*

We have already seen that there is a soliloquy in a parable in Mark, shared with Luke (Lk. 20.13; also Mt. 21.37):

> Mk 12.6:   λέγων ὅτι 'Εντραπήσονται τὸν υἱόν μου.

There is also one in Matthew, again shared with Luke:

> Mt. 24.48:   Χρονίζει μου ὁ κύριος (cf. Lk. 12.45).

Matthew has another example in sayings material, again shared with Luke:

> Mt. 12.44:   τότε λέγει· Εἰς τὸν οἶκον μου ἐπιστρέψω ὅθεν ἐξῆλθον (cf. Lk. 11.24).[9]

There are two possible examples in Markan narrative material:

> Mk 5.28:   ἔλεγεν γὰρ ὅτι 'Εὰν ἅψωμαι κἂν τῶν ἱματίων αὐτοῦ σωθήσομαι (cf. Mt. 9.21 but contrast Lk. 8.44).
>
> Mk 6.16:   ἀκούσας δὲ ὁ 'Ηρῴδης ἔλεγεν, ''Ον ἐγὼ ἀπεκεφάλισα 'Ιωάννην, οὗτος ἠγέρθη (cf. Lk. 9.9 but contrast Mt. 14.2: καὶ εἶπεν τοῖς παισὶν αὐτοῦ...).[10]

3. *Conclusion*

It is almost distinctive of Luke to have soliloquy in parables (12.17; 15.17-19; 16.3-4; 18.4b-5 and possibly 18.9-14). There is only one example in Mark (12.6 // Mt. 21.37 // Lk. 20.13) and one in Matthew

---

9.   Cf. Drury, *Parables*, p. 115.

10.   Also possible is Jesus' prayer in Gethsemane (Mk 14.32-42): cf. Mary Ann Tolbert, 'a superb example of what is technically called "interior monologue"' (*Sowing*, p. 214).

QC (Mt. 24.48 // Lk. 12.45). There are no examples in Matthew QD or M. It would appear to be characteristic of Luke as a writer since he enhances the feature in R (Lk. 20.13) as well as having it in L.

Outside of parables, there are two possible occurrences in Mark (5.28 // Mt. 9.21 and 6.16 // Lk. 9.9), one clear one in Matthew QC (Mt. 12.44 // Lk. 11.24) and one in L (1.25).

The Lukan parable soliloquy has a distinctive form, reflection on circumstances followed by contemplation of future action. All the L soliloquies in parables, with the exception of 18.9-14, take this form, as does 20.13 R (i.e. 0/0/5) and in addition τί ποιήσω; comes three times (i.e. in parables 0/0/3, Lk. 20.13 R).

C. *Conversation (§4.2)*

1. *Preliminary Comments*

Goulder speaks only about conversation in parables:

> There is plenty of oratio recta in Matthew's parables, but it is almost all in the form of single exchanges, as between the Master and servants in the Talents (*LNP*, p. 95).[11]

Goulder, however, goes on to list Lk. 14.15-24 (Dinner; cf. also *LNP*, p. 591) and 15.11-32 (Prodigal) as two of his prime Lukan examples, saying of the Dinner that 'almost the whole parable is in oratio recta' with all the characters speaking. But neither this example nor the Prodigal feature much actual conversation. In 14.21-24 there is an exchange between the householder and his servant in which the householder speaks twice and the servant once (and also once without his actual words being recorded). This is three speeches, a little more than just a single exchange.

Much of 15.11-32 is, as Goulder says, in oratio recta and all the characters speak, but nowhere in the parable is there an exchange with more than two speeches, that is a single exchange, not really a conversation. In this respect the parable is not distinctive of Luke. As Goulder himself points out, plenty of oratio recta and single exchanges do not make a conversation. The Prodigal Son could be compared to

---

11. B. Gerhardsson, 'Illuminating', lists 'the utterances in the narrative meshalim' on pp. 277-78. He says 22 out of the 55 narrative parables lack speech altogether, four in Mark, nine in Matthew and nine in Luke. Twenty have one or two utterances, thirteen have three to eight.

Goulder's counter-example from Matthew, the Talents.

On the other hand, Goulder's third example is a genuinely impressive one: in Dives and Lazarus (16.19-31), the bulk of the parable is a conversation between Dives and Abraham, with six speeches between them.

2. *Luke*

In addition to Goulder's examples, one could also mention Lk. 10.25-37 (the Good Samaritan and its immediate context) which features eight speeches (four exchanges) between Jesus and the lawyer which contrasts with four speeches (two exchanges) in the near parallel Mk 12.28-34.[12] Other examples are 13.22-30 (Narrow Door, combining Q and L material) which has four speeches in two exchanges (vv. 25-27) and 16.1-9 L (Unjust Steward) which has two sets of three speeches. Also relevant is the conversation between Jesus and Simon the Pharisee in 7.39-47[13] which is quite similar to 10.25-37: Jesus is in discussion with an opponent and a parable forms part of the discussion.

There are also examples of conversation in non-parable material. In redaction of Mark, Luke apparently enhances a conversation on one occasion (Mt. 16.13-20 // Mk 8.27-33 // Lk. 9.18-22, Peter's confession). On one occasion in his editing of Q / Matthew, conversation is enhanced (Lk. 9.59-60, cf. Mt. 8.21-22, Would-be Followers). There are also conversations in L, when Zechariah is in the Temple (1.13-20 L), at the Annunciation (1.28-38 L) and on the road to Emmaus (24.17-26).[14]

Clearly, then, conversations occur regularly in Luke, both in parable and other material, and in L, QD and R.

3. *Mark and Matthew*

There are no examples of conversation in Mark's parables, and in Matthew's parables there are only three examples, all M, Mt. 13.27-30 (Tares, four speeches), Mt. 20.6-7 (Labourers in the Vineyard, three speeches) and Mt. 25.34-40 and 41-45 (Sheep and Goats, both times three speeches).

12. Cf. Drury, *Parables*, p. 133, on this example, 'Adding dialogue is an editorial habit of Luke's...'

13. On 7.36-50, see P. Cotterill and M. Turner, *Linguistics*, chapter eight, on conversation, specifically pp. 272-74.

14. Conversation is twice mentioned here, in 24.15 and 24.17; cf. Mk 9.33-34, with which cf. Lk. 9.46 and contrast Mt. 18.1.

If conversations are sparse in Mark's parable material,[15] they are common outside parables. Mk 8.14-21 (Bread), for example, has seven different speeches in exchanges between the disciples and Jesus; 10.35-45 (Sons of Zebedee) has six speeches in three exchanges. It is worth noting that in triple tradition material, conversations are regularly longer in Mark than they are in the Lukan parallel (cf. Mk 5.7-10 with Lk. 8.28-30; Mk 9.14-29 with Lk. 9.37-43; Mk 10.23-31 with Lk. 18.24-30 and Mk 14.26-31 with Lk. 22.31-34).[16]

Conversations are common outside parables in Matthew too. When commenting on Mt. 9.27-31 (Two Blind Men), Goulder says that 'The insertion of the brief conversation is also typical of Matthew' (*MLM*, p. 327). Occasionally, Matthew apparently enhances conversations in Mark (Mt. 15.10-20, contrast Mk 7.14-23; Mt. 17.9-13, contrast Mk 9.9-13; and Mt. 22.41-46, contrast Mk 12.35-37a). Conversations occur in QC (Mt. 4.1-11 // Lk. 4.1-13, six speeches in three exchanges), QD (Mt. 8.5-13, four speeches in two exchanges; contrast Lk. 7.1-10) and M (Mt. 17.24-27).

4. *Conclusion*

Goulder talks only about conversations in parable material. In Luke there are four clear examples, 13.22-30 QD; 14.15-24 QD; 16.1-9 L and 16.19-31 L, the latter instance particularly strong. There are no examples of conversations in parables in Mark. In Matthew there are three examples, all M, Mt. 13.27-30, Mt. 20.6-7 and Mt. 25.34-40, 41-45. This is a feature, then, which is characteristic of Luke's parable material, but which is not really distinctive of it.

Outside of the parables, conversation is not a special feature of Luke's writing. It is a regular feature in the stories of the triple tradition and is found in QC and in Matthew QD, R and M. Luke may enhance elements of conversation in Markan and Q material and there are plenty of conversations in L. On the other hand, though, the conversations in parallel Markan material are more often diminished than enhanced in Luke. Matthew has a longer conversation than Luke in Mt. 8.5-13 // Lk. 7.1-10.

Within the category, there are two examples of parables being told in

---

15. It is a simple but obvious point that one cannot have much conversation (unless one uses fable) in the nature world of Mark 4.

16. Other examples of conversation in Mark are 6.35-38; 7.27-29; 8.1-5; 8.27-30; 10.2-9; 10.17-22; 10.46-52; 11.27-33; 12.13-17; 12.28-34 and 14.17-21.

the context of conversation. In 7.36-50, the Parable of the Two Debtors
is told to illustrate a point to Simon the Pharisee and in 10.25-37, the
Parable of the Good Samaritan is told to illustrate a point for a certain
scribe. We might compare also 12.13-21; 12.41-48; 13.22-30; 14.15-24
and even ch. 15, in all of which the parable is led into by means of a
question or a comment (cf. §1.4, above, pp. 146-50). This is a specially
Lukan feature—the only possible example of this in Mark or Matthew
is Mt. 21.23-32.

D. *Work (§4.3)*

1. *Luke*
Goulder says that 'Luke is fascinated by work, and he includes details
(not always accurate) for the sake of it' (*LNP*, p. 95). He gives Lk. 6.48
as a QD example (cf. p. 373), in which Luke is more explicit about the
builder's building than is Matthew. Goulder also lists 14.15-24 in which
the dinner guests 'are explicit about inspecting purchases and testing
out new oxen' (*LNP*, p. 95), another QD example. One might add a
possible R example: there is more detail in Lk. 5.1-11 than there is in
Mk 1.16-20 and in particular:

> 5.5:   Ἐπιστάτα, δι' ὅλης νυκτὸς κοπιάσαντες οὐδὲν ἐλάβομεν.

This is mainly a feature of L and particularly the L parables. Goulder
gives as examples 10.34 in which the Good Samaritan pours oil and
wine on the man's wounds; 13.8 in which the worker asks if he can dig
about and put manure on the fig tree; 15.15-16 in which the Prodigal
Son works with the swine (cf. the brother also working in the field); and
17.7-10 in which the servant ploughs, keeps sheep and serves at table.

Other examples could be added: Martha is distracted with much serving (10.40); the Rich Fool plans to pull down his barns and build bigger
ones (12.18); there are sayings on building a tower and counting the
cost (14.28-30); the woman 'lights a lamp and sweeps the house and
seeks diligently' for the lost coin (15.8); and the Dishonest Steward
says: 'I am not strong enough to dig and I am too ashamed to beg'
(16.3).

2. *Matthew and Mark*
There is little concerning work in Mark. Simon and Andrew are 'in
their boat, mending their nets' in 1.19 // Mt. 4.21. In ch. 4, 'the Sower
sows the word' and the seed grows secretly, but the references have

allegorical counterparts, and there does not seem to be any interest in work for its own sake. An exception to this rule, though, is perhaps the Parable of the Tenants of the Vineyard:

Mk 12.1: Ἀμπελῶνα ἄνθρωπος ἐφύτευσεν καὶ περιέθηκεν φραγμὸν καὶ ὤρυξεν ὑπολήνιον καὶ ᾠκοδόμησεν πύργον καὶ ἐξέδετο αὐτὸν γεωργοῖς καὶ ἀπεδήμησεν.

Matthew too (21.33) has this echo of Isaiah 5.1-2 but Luke (20.9) lacks it, having only 'he planted a vineyard', thereby cutting the details about the man's work.

Matthew shows some interest in work. The birds of the air 'neither sow nor reap nor gather into barns' (Mt. 6.26 // Lk. 12.24 QC), a shepherd searches for his lost sheep (18.12-14 // Lk. 15.3-7 QC), 'two women will be grinding at the mill' (Mt. 24.41 // Lk. 17.35 QC) and three men trade with money in the Talents (25.14-30 // Lk. 19.11-27 QC).

It is arguable, however, that Goulder's point stands in spite of these references. In Matthew, the work involved usually bears some allegorical significance. In none of these references is there superfluous detail about the work, like Luke's oil and wine in the Good Samaritan or lighting the lamp and sweeping the house in the Lost Coin. A possible exception to this is Mt. 20.12, when some of the Labourers in the Vineyard complain that they have 'borne the burden of the day and the scorching heat', but for Goulder this is an allegorical representation of those who have borne the burden of the law (*MLM*, p. 410).

Among the Gospel writers, Matthew has the most references to workers (ἐργάτης, 6/0/4+1; of literal workers 6/0/3+1[17]) but if Matthew does refer to work in his Gospel, Luke seems to be more interested in the detail of the work they actually did.

3. *Conclusion*

There are regular references to work in L material, particularly the parables. The interest in work is also found in QD (6.48; 14.15-24) and possibly R (5.1-11) and so could be seen as characteristic of Luke as a writer. References to work are uncommon in Mark, but in Mk 12.1 there are details about the man's work in setting up the vineyard which Luke in his parallel omits (Lk. 20.9). Matthew has several references to work and workers but these references usually bear some allegorical

17. Mt. 9.37-38 // Lk. 10.2 × 2 QC; Mt. 10.10 // Lk. 10.7 QC; Mt. 20.1, 2, 8 M.

significance. With one or two small reservations, therefore, fascination with work is something distinctive of the third evangelist.

E. *Parties (§4.4)*

1. *Luke*

According to Goulder (*LNP*, p. 95-96), Luke's fascination by work is tempered by his fondness for parties.[18] He lists several examples: Elizabeth's neighbours and kinsfolk rejoice with her (1.58, cf. 1.62); there is a large party (δοχή μεγάλη) for Levi's conversion (5.29 R); three times Jesus eats with Pharisees, in 7.36; 11.37 and 14.1 (see above; on 14.1, see also *LNP*, p. 586); the last of these occasions is the context for the parable of the Great Dinner (14.15-24); and the shepherd (15.6) and the woman (15.9) invite friends and neighbours to celebrate when they find what was lost (also *LNP*, p. 606).[19] Goulder adds a qualification: that Luke dislikes selfish luxury, citing the Rich Fool (12.19), Dives (16.19) and even Martha (10.38-42) (*LNP*, p. 96).

To Goulder's list one might add an obvious example, the feasting when the Prodigal returns (15.22-24). A party may be envisaged also at the end of the Zacchaeus story (see 19.5-6). Further, Luke has instructions about who to invite to a dinner and how to behave when one is there (14.7-14).

Clearly this is a regular feature in Luke, with instances in both parable material and ordinary narrative material, with examples in Luke's redaction of Mark (5.29 and possibly 7.36) as well as his redaction of Q / Matthew (11.37; 14.15-24 and 15.6) and it is in L too (1.58; 15.9, 22-24; 19.5-6, cf. 12.19 and 16.19).

2. *Matthew and Mark*

There are fewer parties in Matthew and Mark. The tax-collectors and sinners eat with Jesus in Mk 2.15 (but see Lk. 5.29 above); Herod gives a banquet in 6.14-29 which leads to the death of John; and Jesus 'sits at table' with Simon the Leper in Mk 14.3 (but again see Lk. 7.36 above).

One saying in Matthew is relevant here:

---

18. There is abundant literature on this general theme, including D.E. Smith, 'Table Fellowship'; Cadbury, *Making*, pp. 251-53; J.R. Donahue, *Gospel*, pp. 140-46; J. Navone, *Themes*, pp. 11-37; B. Reicke, *Luke*, pp. 79-85.

19. Cf. also *EC*, pp. 1-2, quoted below, p. 294.

Mt. 11.19 // Lk. 7.24 QC: ἦλθεν ὁ υἱὸς τοῦ ἀνθρώπου ἐσθίων καὶ πίνων, καὶ λέγουσιν, Ἰδοὺ ἄνθρωπος φάγος καὶ οἰνοπότης...

Matthew does not have any stories of Jesus eating and drinking, however.[20] In parables, Matthew has a couple of marriage feasts: 22.1-14 and 25.1-13.[21] The feasting is sumptuous (Mt. 22.4, 10) but these big royal feasts contrast somewhat with Luke's smaller scale meals and parties.

3. *Conclusion*

Fondness for parties distinguishes Luke from Matthew and Mark. Mark implies a party (Mk 2.15) which Luke makes explicit (Lk. 5.29) and Herod's banquet (Mk 6.14-29) has dire consequences. Matthew has royal feasts (22.1-14; 25.1-13) but Luke's parties are more down to earth. Matthew (QC) represents Jesus coming 'eating and drinking' (11.19) in sayings material, but it is Luke who provides the concrete examples of this (7.36; 11.37; 14.1; 19.5-6) and not only does Jesus feast but so do the characters in his parables (14.15-24; 15.6, 9, 22-24; 16.19) and only Luke gives instructions about who to invite to a dinner and what to do when one is invited (14.7-14). Not only are the examples in both parable and non-parable material, but also they occur in R, QD and L.

F. *Excuses (§4.5)*

Goulder (*LNP*, p. 96) talks about Lk. 14.18 and 14.20, excuses in the Parable of the Great Dinner, and compares them with 11.7 ('The door is now shut... I cannot get up and give it to you', also *LNP*, pp. 498-99), 13.26 (excuses on judgment day, 'wonderfully transparent', *LNP*, p. 96), 16.3 (Unjust Steward's soliloquy) and Acts 23.27 (Claudias Lysias on the arrest of Paul).

The clearest of Goulder's examples are Lk. 11.7 and 14.18-20.[22] The weakest example is Acts 23.27. As Goulder says, Claudias Lysias gives

---

20. Though note that figures for 'eating and drinking' are 4/0/14+3.

21. Cf. γάμος 8/0/2: all Matthew's eight come in these two passages and Luke's two in parallel places, 12.36 and 14.8.

22. 14.19 should of course be listed. A good deal has been written on these excuses and often, too much is read into them, cf. P.H. Ballard, 'Reasons'; R.J. Karris, 'Poor and Rich'; J.D.M. Derrett, *Law*, pp. 126-55 and especially pp. 136-38; Jeremias, *Parables*, pp. 176-77; and Donahue, *Gospel*, pp. 141-42.

an account of the facts creditable to himself, but he is not really making excuses to Felix.

One other possible example would be Dives' speech to Abraham (16.27-28) on which Caird says: 'He is even disposed to make excuses for himself: if only someone had warned him in advance, he would have taken the necessary steps to avoid coming to this place of torment'.[23] This reading is different from Goulder's, however, which is more kindly towards Dives (*LNP*, p. 94, 'thoughtful of his brothers, even in torment').

Goulder's examples cover QD (14.18-20, cf. Mt. 22.5 where those invited do not offer excuses but merely 'make light of it'; 13.26) and L (11.7; 16.3).

There are no obvious examples of characters offering excuses in Matthew or Mark. John the Baptist anticipates excuses from Pharisees and Sadducees (Mt. 3.9 // Lk. 3.8, 'We have Abraham as our father') and in the Labourers in the Vineyard, those who are paid first protest at their treatment (Mt. 20.12). Neither of these examples really work, however. 20.12 is more of a complaint than an excuse and 3.9 is more of an argument and as they think, a genuine argument. Nearer to Goulder's examples from Luke is Mt. 11.16-19 // Lk. 7.31-35 in which 'this generation' is compared to children at the market place ('We piped to you and you would not dance... He has a demon... Behold, a glutton and a drunkard'). Even this example, however, is not the same as Goulder's clearest examples in which there is an element of insincerity or transparency. For Luke's interest in insincerity one might compare Lk. 20.20 R in which the spies who come to Jesus 'pretended to be sincere' (ὑποκρινομένους ἑαυτοὺς δικαίους εἶναι; cf. also the false charges in 23.2 R).

In summary, insincere, transparent excuses are a feature of Luke, found on several occasions (most clearly in 11.7 L and 14.18-20 QD but also 13.26 QD and 16.3 L). It is not a feature obvious in Mark or Matthew and might well be seen as distinctive of Luke.

G. *Guillotine Questions (§4.6)*

Goulder (*LNP*, pp. 96, 402, 485) lists three examples of 'guillotine questions' in two pericopae, the first to Simon the Pharisee after Jesus

---

23. G.B. Caird, *Saint Luke*, p. 192.

has told the parable of the Two Debtors, τίς οὖν αὐτῶν πλεῖον ἀγαπήσει αὐτόν; (7.42) and the other two in the conversation between Jesus and the Lawyer, Ἐν τῷ νόμῳ τί γέγραπται; πῶς ἀναγινώσκεις; (10.26) and τίς τούτων τῶν τριῶν πλησίον δοκεῖ σοι γεγονέναι τοῦ ἐμπεσόντος εἰς τοὺς λῃστάς; (10.36). Each time, the antagonist lays his head on the block with an answer which is inevitable, and Jesus concludes, 'You have judged rightly', 'You have answered right; do this, and you will live', 'Go and do likewise' and the opponent is left dumbfounded.[24] Perhaps, strictly speaking, 10.26 ought to be disallowed since if this is a guillotine question, the Lawyer lives through it and continues the conversation. The examples fall in L material, on both occasions with parables and on both occasions in pericopae which on Goulder's theory are built from a base in Mark (14.3-9 and 12.28-31 respectively).

There are no obvious examples of the same phenomenon in Mark but one pericope comes close, Mk 12.13-17 // Mt. 22.15-22 // Lk. 20.20-26:

Mk 12.16-17: καὶ λέγει αὐτοῖς, <u>Τίνος ἡ εἰκὼν αὕτη καὶ ἡ ἐπιγραφή</u>; οἱ δὲ εἶπαν αὐτῷ, Καίσαρος. ὁ δὲ Ἰησοῦς εἶπεν αὐτοῖς, Τὰ Καίσαρος ἀπόδοτε Καίσαρι καὶ τὰ τοῦ θεοῦ τῷ θεῷ. καὶ ἐξεθαύμαζον ἐπ᾽ αὐτῷ.

The Pharisees and the Herodians lay their heads on the block with the inevitable answer 'Caesar's'. The form of the pericope is similar to that of the Simon the Pharisee incident in Lk. 7.39-43 and the Lawyer's questions in Lk. 10.25-28 and 10.29-37. All of these have this form:

a. An opponent or opponents ask Jesus a question.
b. Jesus then poses them a question.
c. They provide the inevitable answer to the question.
d. Jesus concludes, leaving them either dumbfounded or shame-faced.

This same form occurs again in Mk 11.27-33 // Mt. 21.23-27 // Lk. 20.1-8 (Question About Authority) and similar is Mk 10.2-9 // Mt. 19.3-9 (Divorce).[25]

---

24. In the commentary, Goulder also appeals to the category for the question in 14.3 (*LNP*, p. 583), but this is quite different from the other examples—the opponents do not answer Jesus.

25. This form of controversy dialogue has long been recognized as a favourite rabbinic device, Bultmann, *History*, pp. 39-54, especially p. 41, and pp. 77-78; cf. E. Linnemann, *Parables*, p. 20, on its use with parables, 'There was no better means to reduce the view of an opponent *ad absurdum*, because with a parable he

It is noteworthy that in the Caesar pericope, Luke enhances the form by the addition of τοίνυν (Lk. 20.25), making it clear that Jesus' conclusion ('Then render to Caesar...') draws out the implication of their answer. Further, he enhances their dumbfoundedness (Lk. 20.26 R, καὶ οὐκ ἴσχυσαν ἐπιλαβέσθαι αὐτοῦ ῥήματος...).

More interesting still, though, are a couple of clear examples of guillotine questions, just like the ones Goulder adduces for Luke, in Matthew, one in M material and one in his redaction of Mark. First, in the parable of the Two Sons (Mt. 21.28-32):

Mt. 21.31: <u>τίς ἐκ τῶν δύο ἐποίησεν τὸ θέλημα τοῦ πατρός</u>; λέγουσιν, Ὁ πρῶτος. λέγει αὐτοῖς ὁ Ἰησοῦς, Ἀμὴν λέγω ὑμῖν ὅτι οἱ τελῶναι καὶ αἱ πόρναι προάγουσιν ὑμᾶς εἰς τὴν βασιλείαν τοῦ θεοῦ.

In the next pericope in Matthew, his version of the parable of the Tenants in the Vineyard (Mt. 21.33-46), Jesus concludes with:

Mt. 21.40-42: ὅταν οὖν ἔλθῃ ὁ κύριος τοῦ ἀμπελῶνος, <u>τί ποιήσει τοῖς γεωργοῖς ἐκείνοις</u>; λέγουσιν αὐτῷ, Κακοὺς κακῶς ἀπολέσει αὐτοὺς καὶ τὸν ἀμπελῶνα ἐκδώσεται ἄλλοις γεωργοῖς, οἵτινες ἀποδώσουσιν αὐτῷ τοὺς καρποὺς ἐν τοῖς καιροῖς αὐτῶν. λέγει αὐτοῖς ὁ Ἰησοῦς, Οὐδέποτε ἀνέγνωτε ἐν ταῖς γραφαῖς... (cf. v. 45).

As in the Lukan examples, here both times the question follows on from a parable, the antagonists themselves putting their heads on the block by supplying the moral of the parable, and Jesus then addressing them. Mt. 21.31, in particular, is remarkably similar to the Lukan examples, 'Which of them...?' (Lk. 7.42), 'Which of these three...?' (Lk. 10.36), 'Which of the two...?' (Mt. 21.31).

Also similar is Mt. 22.41-46 R. In the parallels Mk 12.35-37 // Lk. 20.41-44, the whole pericope is a monologue. In Matthew, however it is a conversation featuring a guillotine-type question,

Mt. 22.41: Συνηγμένων δὲ τῶν Φαρισαίων ἐπηρώτησεν αὐτοὺς ὁ Ἰησοῦς λέγων, <u>Τί ὑμῖν δοκεῖ περὶ τοῦ Χριστοῦ; τίνος υἱός ἐστιν</u>; λέγουσιν αὐτῷ, Τοῦ Δαυίδ. λέγει αὐτοῖς, Πῶς οὖν Δαυὶδ ἐν πνεύματι καλεῖ αὐτὸν κύριον...

could be convicted through his own verdict'; cf. also Charles E. Carlston, *Parables*, p. 43, including some useful bibliography. Also relevant is D. Daube, *New Testament*, pp. 141-57; and I am grateful to Dom. Henry Wansbrough for lending me his unpublished article, 'A Neglected Pattern in Jesus' Speech?' which deals with the same phenomenon.

After Jesus has spoken, they are dumbfounded (22.46).

It is evident that guillotine questions are not distinctive of Luke, with two clear examples with parables from Matthew, one of which is quite similar to the two Lukan examples. Examples of the general form are also found in Mark.

Luke's examples can be distinguished from Matthew's in one respect, however, in that Jesus on each occasion has just one opponent, Simon the Pharisee and the Lawyer, whereas in Matthew on both occasions there is a group. Luke then in the strictest sense has guillotine questions because the antagonist (singular) lays his head on the block.

H. *Lower-Class Heroes (§4.7)*

1. *Preliminary Comments*

Although in *LNP*, chapter three, Goulder calls this category 'Lower-Class Heroes', it has a variety of names in the commentary, 'heroes from the despised classes' (p. 487), 'dishonourable figures' (p. 499), 'suspicion of riches' (p. 537), 'dubious heroes' (p. 620), 'Lukan scandalous heroes' (p. 635-36) and 'disreputable heroes' (pp. 661 and 677). The terms 'despised', 'dishonourable', 'dubious', 'scandalous' and 'disreputable' qualify the 'lower-class' designation. Under the same heading, Goulder deals with not only lower-class people like beggars, lepers and prostitutes but also characters who, though middle-class enough, are 'unscrupulous', like the Unjust Judge (p. 661) or the Friend at Midnight (p. 499). Even the Rich Man of ch. 16 is called 'a horror figure' (p. 537). Goulder is contrasting these parable characters with the heroes in Matthew and Mark, 'only nice people' (p. 661).

The fluidity of Goulder's terminology here is a difficulty, however. The section begins to look rather like a hold-all category into which one can put most of the Lukan parable heroes. The Samaritan, the Unjust Judge and Lazarus are quite different from each other. One exemplifies kindness and is only disreputable because of his race, one is rightly dishonourable because he exemplifies injustice and the other is merely a very poor person about whom we know little else. Goulder also includes in this category examples of the *quanto potius* type, the Friend at Midnight (11.5-8) and the Unjust Judge (18.1-8). This category is by no means a narrow one, therefore, and some caution is required when dealing with it.

2. *Luke*

Goulder speaks about Luke's parable-heroes, 'a Samaritan, an unjust steward, Lazarus, a widow and a publican' (*LNP*, p. 97; also pp. 487, 620 and 662), and in the commentary he adds the examples of the Sinner of 7.36-50 (*LNP*, p. 400), the Rich Fool of 12.13-21 (*LNP*, p. 437) and Zacchaeus (19.1-10, *LNP*, p. 677). The Sinner and Zacchaeus are, of course, not parable-heroes but are heroes of L stories. The Rich Fool is listed as an example of Luke's 'suspicion of riches' (p. 537); he is clearly not 'lower-class', but he is certainly dishonourable or unscrupulous in his actions.[26] Also, the Unjust Judge and the Friend at Midnight ('too lazy to get up') are featured here, *'quanto potius* situations' (p. 97).[27]

To these examples one might add from Luke's parables 13.6-9 L (Fig Tree), where the vinedresser is the hero of the parable. This contrasts with the vine-keeper heroes of the Labourers in the Vineyard in Mt. 20.1-16 and the Tenants in the Vineyard parable in Mk 12.1-12 (and parallels). 17.7-10 L also has a servant as its hero, only doing what was his duty.

Outside the parables, passages like 1.51-53 L (Magnificat) and 6.20-21, 24-25 QD ('Blessed are the poor'; woe to the rich) might be taken as evidence for Luke's disdain for the rich and riches.[28] Further, 17.11-19 L, the Ten Lepers, again has a Samaritan hero and in 23.39-43 R/L, there is a penitent criminal (κακοῦργος).

Now most of these examples are from L material, so that it could be argued that lower-class/disreputable heroes are characteristic not so much of Luke as a writer as characteristic of his source material. However, one should not be too hasty in drawing this conclusion. If Luke had wanted to introduce disreputable or lower-class heroes into a story or a parable, he would have had to alter substantially the story or parable in his source. On a couple of occasions, on Goulder's theory, this is what Luke has done. 7.36-50 is based on Mk 14.3-9, and the story has been substantially altered by the introduction of a prostitute. In 23.39-43, Luke has made one of the criminals crucified with Jesus

---

26. Though cf. Derrett's popular theory, *Law*, pp. 48-77 and '"Take thy Bond"', of which Goulder does not approve (*LNP*, pp. 625-26).

27. C. Colpe uses the expression *a peiore ad melius* to describe the same way of reasoning in *TDNT*, VIII, p. 435 n. 265.

28. See on this topic Thomas E. Schmidt, *Hostility to Wealth*. Also useful is Luke Johnson, *Literary Function*.

into a hero when in Mark both criminals are villains (Mk 15.27 and 32).

One might note also that the material in this section, though predominantly in parables, is not limited to parables. Lower-class or disreputable heroes come in other stories (7.36-50; 19.1-10; 23.39-43), in a miracle story (17.11-19) and in sayings material (1.51-53; 6.20-21, 24-25 QD).

It should be added that there are a couple of possible counter examples. In 14.31 L, Luke has a 'king going to encounter another king in war', neither lower-class nor disreputable. In 19.11-27 QD, the Pounds, where Matthew (25.14-30) has a householder, Luke has a nobleman going to receive a kingdom. This is an unclear example, however, since Luke's hero in the Pounds is hated by his citizens whom he slays (19.14, 27). One could say, then, that even when Luke has someone from the upper-classes as a hero, he makes him a disreputable character. In 'Characteristics', Goulder says that Luke 'has kings, but not just for grandiloquence' (p. 55).

3. *Mark and Matthew*

Goulder (*LNP*, p. 97) says that although 'Mark and Matthew tell us that Jesus attracted lower-class people', they do not have lower-class heroes for their parables, with one exception, the Thief in the Night (Mt. 24.43 // Lk. 12.39) and Goulder says here that 'Matthew would never have introduced the suggestion that Christ was like a thief if Paul had not put it in his head' (*MLM*, p. 436).

However, even the lower-class or disreputable people attracted by Jesus might not be regarded as counter-examples of the phenomenon to which Goulder draws attention. They are not the heroes of the stories in which they feature. The tax-collectors and sinners are called by Jesus; and the leper, the sick and the lame, the woman with the flux and Bartimaeus (Mk 10.46, 'a blind beggar') are all healed by Jesus. These, then, are stories in which Jesus is the central figure, the hero. One exception to this rule is Mk 12.41-44 // Lk. 21.1-4, the Widow's Mite: she is not only very poor but also the heroine of the story, someone to whom Jesus draws attention.

Further, there is a handful of examples of lower-class, disreputable heroes in Mark's and Matthew's parables. As well as the Thief (Mt. 24.43 // Lk. 12.39), there is, in Mk 3.27 // Mt. 12.29 (cf. Lk. 11.21), a robber who binds the strong man and plunders his house. In addition, Mt. 24.45-51 // Lk. 12.41-46 features the Faithful and Wise Servant.

Here, attention is focused on the servant left behind by the master, who, in the second part of the parable (Mt. 24.48-51 // Lk. 12.45-46; cf. Lk. 12.47-48) is disreputable as well as lower-class, a 'wicked servant' who beats his fellow servants and eats and drinks with the drunken.

In the latter example, the servant provides an example of how not to behave. One might compare Mt. 18.23-35 which also features a disreputable, lower-class character (cf. v. 32, 'You wicked servant'). In this parable, on Goulder's interpretation, the King stands for God and the servant is the brother who does not forgive from the heart (v. 35), just as in Mt. 24.45-51 // Lk. 12.41-46, the Servant is the believer and the man going on the journey is God. Here there is some overlap with the L parables. The Unjust Steward (16.1-9), for example, stands for the believer and his master stands for God. Similarly, the Servant in 17.7-10 is the believer and his master God. Nevertheless, in these examples, Luke's characters provide examples of how the believer ought to behave rather than of how they ought not to behave.

There are no examples in Matthew's or Mark's parables in which God is compared in *quanto potius* manner to a disreputable character. In sayings material, however, there is an example:

Mt. 7.11 (// Lk. 11.13): εἰ οὖν ὑμεῖς πονηροὶ ὄντες οἴδατε δόματα ἀγαθὰ διδόναι τοῖς τέκνοις ὑμῶν, πόσῳ μᾶλλον ὁ πατὴρ ὑμῶν ὁ ἐν τοῖς οὐρανοῖς δώσει ἀγαθὰ τοῖς αἰτοῦσιν αὐτόν.

This is in the material which Goulder feels that Luke expanded to create one of his *quanto potius* parables, the Friend at Midnight (*LNP*, p. 499).

4. *Conclusion*

The difficulty with this category is the fluidity of Goulder's terminology. He combines 'lower-class' with 'disreputable' and assigns the creation of both types of hero to Luke's hand. However, Luke does have stories featuring both lower-class and disreputable heroes, and they occur particularly in parables but also in stories and sayings. The occurrences are almost always L but this need not be a great problem on Goulder's thesis since, as he says, 'a lower-class hero is hero of the whole parable' (*LNP*, p. 123). If, then, Luke were to introduce a lower-class or a disreputable hero into a Markan or a Matthean story, he could do nothing other than to change the story in the process. This could have happened in Lk. 7.36-50 which is possibly Luke's version of the

Anointing in Mk 14.3-9, transformed by the introduction of a sinning woman.

The parables in Matthew and Mark do not usually feature lower-class or disreputable characters as their heroes but there are exceptions, the Plunderer of Mk 3.27 // Mt. 12.29, the Thief in the Night of Mt. 24.43 // Lk. 12.39 and the Faithful and Wise Servant of Mt. 24.45-51 // Lk. 12.41-46. These are all both lower-class and disreputable. Likewise, Mt. 18.23-35 features a lower-class, disreputable character. Where Mark and Matthew have lower-class or disreputable characters in non-parable material, Jesus is usually the hero of the story. One exception is the Widow's Mite of Mk 12.41-44 // Lk. 21.1-4. This is a category, then, in which Luke's Gospel has a characteristic, almost distinctive stamp.

Some further distinctions could be made. The Plunderer, the only occurrence of a lower-class / disreputable hero in Mark, stands for Jesus, as does Matthew's (and Luke's) Thief. Outside these two examples, where lower-class or disreputable characters appear in Matthew, they represent the badly behaved believer whose end is condemnation (Mt. 18.23-35 and Mt. 24.45-51 // Lk. 12.41-46). Luke then stands out in two ways. First, his is the only Gospel which compares a disreputable character to God in a *quanto potius* situation (Friend; Unjust Judge). Second, with the exception of the Faithful and Wise Servant of Mt. 24.45-51 // Lk. 12.41-46, Luke is the only evangelist who has disreputable characters in parables who stand for the well-behaved believer (Samaritan, Unjust Steward, Servant who does his duty; Publican).

I. *Colourful Details (§4.8)*

1. *Preliminary Remarks*

Goulder uses the term 'colourful detail' to refer to two phenomena. First, it has reference to 'realistic details' in the parables which contrast with the details in Mark's and Matthew's parables which have 'allegorical counterparts' (*LNP*, p. 97). Second, in non-parable material he looks at the way in which Luke has lambs for Matthew's sheep (Lk. 10.3), egg and scorpion for bread and stone (Lk. 11.12) and ravens for birds (Lk. 12.24). Further, 'Mark's leper becomes 'a man full of leprosy' (Lk. 5.12), and Mark's 'fever' becomes a 'high fever' (Lk. 4.38; *LNP*, p. 97).

The latter examples from Mark probably arise from a want of redactional examples in this category. To say that the man is 'full of leprosy' rather than that he is a leper, or that Simon's mother-in-law has a high fever rather than a fever, is not to add colourful details to Mark's account; it is merely to make Mark's description of something which is fundamental to the story more precise.

Similarly, most of the examples given from Luke's supposed redaction of Matthew do not really make sense as Luke adding colourful details to Matthew. 'Lambs' is more precise than 'sheep' though it is also more appropriate because 'lambs in the midst of wolves' depicts the disciples' helplessness better than does 'sheep in the midst of wolves'. The ravens example is similar—Luke is being more specific; just as all lambs are sheep but not all sheep are lambs, so are all ravens birds and not all birds ravens.

In all of these examples, it is the presence of a parallel which enables Goulder to point to the 'colourful detail': they are places where Mark and Matthew have one thing and Luke apparently makes the reference more specific or colourful. This places Luke at an automatic advantage over Mark and Matthew since his Gospel is presumed to be the third. Goulder can compare Luke with two Gospels in the search for references which Luke makes more precise.

In relation to this, the 'ravens' rather than 'birds' example is interesting in that in the same pericope, Mt. 6.25-34 // Lk. 12.22-31, Matthew (as well as Luke) has 'lilies'. Now lilies are to flowers what ravens are to birds, a more limited, precise and colourful image. There is, however, no parallel which says 'flowers' so Matthew's colourful image goes by unnoticed. Indeed Matthew is rich with colourful images as a quick glance at *MLM* will show. Goulder says, for example:

> Matthew has rather more than three times [over Mark] the use of country images, and again we notice the detail of observation which has introduced so many of the most colourful countryside images—the wild plants, and the different types of ground (*MLM*, p. 102).

It is important to note, however, that Goulder's emphasis in this category, as in many of the other categories, is on Luke's parables. In 'Characteristics', Goulder says of Luke, 'The author is a painter and there is colour on his brush' (p. 57). Whereas many of the features in Mark's and Matthew's parables have allegorical counterparts, many of the features in Luke's do not. By 'colourful details', then, Goulder often means non-allegorical details, details which are in the story for the sake of the story. In *MLM*, p. 60, he speaks of 'Luke's love of colourful detail which cuts down the allegory content' and refers to 'colourful, non-allegoric touches' (*MLM*, p. 399). Goulder thinks of allegories as unimaginative and unrealistic and, therefore, Luke's stories show a 'vividness of imagination' and a 'realism' lacking in Mark and Matthew.

A look at Goulder's treatment of Luke's redaction of the parable of the Sower (*LNP*, p. 411) bears this out. On one hand, Goulder says that 'the main impact is to reduce the Markan detail' but on the other hand, he says that 'he elaborates the Markan story, so closely tied to its allegorical exposition, with colourful details without regard to their interpretation'. At first sight these two claims might appear to be contradictory, especially as some of the 'details' which Luke omits (and which Goulder himself lists) are colourful, like the sun rising and scorching (Mk 4.6). However, though colourful, the latter image has an allegorical counterpart (Mk 4.17, tribulation and persecution arises) and so, for Goulder, it is not like Luke's colourful, non-allegorical details.

Goulder probably includes the examples of colourful imagery and specificity in a category which is primarily about non-allegorical details in parables in order to show that Luke has a particular cast of mind. If the same cast of mind can be seen in Luke's redaction of Mark and Matthew in non-parable material, so the case for Lukan creativity in L parables is strengthened.

It is interesting to note that in this category, as in the previous one (Lower-Class Heroes), the terminology in Goulder's commentary again varies, from 'Luke's realism' (p. 292), to 'Luke's colourful specificity' (p. 501) to 'Lukan vividness of imagination' (p. 605).[29] These terms roughly correspond to the different types of material found under the general heading, 'Luke's realism' relating to the non-allegorical, realistic details which Goulder sees in the parables, 'Luke's colourful specificity' relating to Luke's redaction of Mark and Matthew where he makes references more specific, and 'vividness of imagination' relating to the cast of mind which is held to create both the specificity and the non-allegorical details.

The differing terminology does, nevertheless, create some problems. The overarching term 'vividness of imagination' involves a degree of

---

29. It is contrasted with 'Matthew's plain' (*LNP*, p. 540) or it is 'the colourful over the general' (p. 466); cf. also pp. 411, 488, 607, 612, 635, 678 and 681. The reference on p. 668 to '§4.8' is a misprint for §4.5, Excuses.

circularity in that it assumes what Goulder is attempting to prove, namely, that this feature comes not from tradition but from Luke's creative mind. Further, by varying the terminology, Goulder is able to bind together under the same general heading quite different material. Even within the non-allegorical sub-category, widely differing material is grouped together. The name Lazarus, for example, is the only name in the Gospel parable tradition[30] and elsewhere, Luke drops a name (18.35-43, Bartimaeus), but this is not regarded as a possible sign of a pre-Lukan source. Rather, it is included under the general heading, 'colourful details'. Similar to this is the mention of Jerusalem and Jericho, the only place names in the Gospel parable tradition.

2. *Luke*

The colourful details in the parables which Goulder lists (*LNP*, p. 97) are the names Lazarus (16.19-31 L)[31] and Jerusalem and Jericho (10.25-37 L; see comments above);[32] Luke's description of the House falling down because of the river flooding (6.47-49 QD); the ten-thousand and twenty-thousand soldiers (14.31 L); and details in the Friend at Midnight (11.5-8 L) as well as in the Prodigal Son (15.11-32 L).

In non-parable material, Goulder lists 10.3; 11.12 and 12.24, all QD, and 4.38 and 5.12, both R (see comments above). In the commentary Goulder adds 4.5 QD ('realism', omitting the devil's taking Jesus up the high mountain, p. 292); 8.4-8 R (added details in the Sower, p. 411); 10.25-37 L ('loving description of the details' of the Good Samaritan, p. 488); 15.5-6 QD (Lost Sheep, p. 605, cf. *MLM*, p. 60); 15.8-10 L (Lost Coin, 'Luke's imagination at work in the searching', *LNP*, p. 607); 16.19-31 L (Dives and Lazarus, 'full of colourful touches', p. 635); 19.1-10 L (Zacchaeus, 'sparkles with Lukan life', p. 678) and 19.11-27 QD (Pounds, v. 20, the napkin, p. 681). 4.5 should be omitted from this list since the 'realism' Goulder is speaking of is the absence of a detail from Matthew. Luke does not add a colourful or realistic detail of his own here.

Goulder's examples, then, cover R (8.4-8) and QD (6.47-49; 15.5-6; 19.20) as well as L. The examples come in parable material, in sayings

---

30. Cf. Gerhardsson, 'Illuminating', p. 277.

31. But Derrett gives the name significance in *Law*, pp. 86-99.

32. Though note the regular comment that this road is notorious for robbers, R. Funk, *Parables*, p. 32, 'Yes, that's the way it is on the Jericho road'; Linnemann, *Parables*, p. 53; Jeremias, *Parables*, p. 203.

(Ravens, Lambs etc.) and in stories (Zacchaeus). Other examples might be added to these, like the angel of the Lord standing on the right side of the altar of incense (1.11) or the cutting off of the right ear of the High Priest's servant (22.50 R). In 2.36, Anna's age is specified and in 13.11, the woman has had a spirit of infirmity for 18 years.

3. Mark and Matthew

Goulder does not mention any exceptions to the rules here. This is not surprising when one notes that Goulder confines 'colourful details' primarily to non-allegorical details in parables and specificity in Luke's redaction. It is quite commonplace, however, for scholars to point to the details in Mark's narratives.[33] Prominent among the features usually pointed out are Mk 4.38, Jesus ἐν τῇ τρύμνῃ ἐπὶ τὸ προσκεφάλαιον[34] and 6.39, sitting on the green grass, literally a colourful detail. There are also matters like the Aramaic loan words (5.41; 7.34) and the alabaster jar of ointment of pure nard (14.3 // Mt. 26.7 // Lk. 7.37-38).

Matthew has colourful imagery in poetry sections, especially in the Sermon on the Mount, the hairs of the head, the lilies of the field, the log and the speck.[35] There is colourful detail in the story material too, however, even when the pericopae are shorter than their parallels in Mark. There is the κράσπεδον τοῦ ἱματίου (Mt. 9.20 // Lk. 8.44 MA), for example, a detail not strictly necessary to the story (cf. Mk 6.56 // Mt. 14.36). Similarly in Mt. 9.23 R, Jesus sees τοὺς αὐλητάς (contrast Mk 5.38) at Jairus's house.

Perhaps most importantly, though, some of Matthew's parables do, arguably, contain non-allegorical detail. Goulder says that several of the details in 18.23-35 (Unmerciful Servant) are 'parabolic colour'

---

33. For example, see D.E. Nineham, 'Commentators often point to the presence of vivid, circumstantial details in Mark's narrative' ('Eye Witness Testimony', p. 21). Hawkins, *Horae* pp. 127-31 is a good check-list of such details. Luke is shown to suppress many of them.

34. Cf. Goulder's Review of Fuchs, pp. 198-99, '…the colour is taken out of the narrative, etc.: all tendencies which were to be emphasized in the post-Markan Church'.

35. Cadbury, *Style*, p. 116, makes a striking contrast to Goulder, 'The more picturesque and realistic terms in the first Gospel have in the third more general and vague equivalents, and no doubt this change is often due to Luke' (with examples, pp. 116-17); cf. p. 127, 'like Luke's tendency to generalization, so his tendency to omit numerals and proper names leads to loss of definite colour and realism' (with examples, pp. 127-31).

(*MLM*, p. 403) and so too are the third, sixth and the ninth hours, the idleness, the market place and the steward in 20.1-16 (*MLM*, p. 410) and the oxen and fatlings, field and merchandise in 22.1-14 (*MLM*, p 417, 'stock images'). Nevertheless, such 'colour' is not common in Matthew, as Goulder is keen to demonstrate (in *MLM*, pp. 47-69, for example).

4. Conclusion

Goulder's terminology for this category varies somewhat and this enables him to include differing phenomena under the same heading. Sometimes he is talking about a tendency to make a reference in a source more precise or specific and sometimes he is referring to non-allegorical, realistic detail in a parable. On the first of these, it is almost always the presence of a parallel in Mark or Matthew which enables Goulder to make the case and in none of the cases Goulder mentions does Luke actually add a detail; nor usually can one say that it is a detail in Mark and Matthew which Luke is making more colourful.

If one were able to think of these two factors as aspects of the same phenomenon, then there might be a persuasive case here for a Lukan trait which would feature in Luke's redaction of Mark and Matthew as well as in L. It would be in different types of material, parables, sayings, miracles. The matter is not this simple, however. Even if one can take these two aspects together, an additional problem is provided by the fact that Mark has several colourful, circumstantial details in miracle and other stories; Matthew too has some details as well as plenty of colourful imagery in sayings material.

On the non-allegorical, realistic details in parables, Goulder may be on firmer ground. Matthew occasionally has such details but when he does, they do not have the same degree of specificity or preciseness as do Luke's best examples, like the Good Samaritan and the Prodigal Son. Even here, though, there are uncertainties since widely differing data are collected together on the basis that they are 'non-allegorical'. I will return to the important issue of allegory below.

J. *Conclusion*

The three extended examples which Goulder gives of Luke's creation of human characters, the Birth Narratives, the Prodigal Son and the Unjust Steward all rely on parallels in Matthew to make their point.

This is problematic in that the parallels are slight and the argument partly circular. The Two Debtors in Luke is a counter-example.

Among the features within the category, there are varying degrees of distinctiveness. Soliloquy (§4.1) is characteristic of Luke in general and is distinctive of his parables. Luke has soliloquy nine times, six of these in parables. On one of these occasions the reference is shared with Matthew and Mark (Wicked Tenants) and here Luke enhances the soliloquy. On two occasions the references are shared with Matthew (Wise and Faithful Servant; House Swept Clean). Lukan soliloquy has a distinctive form: five times the reflection on circumstances plus the contemplation of future action, three times with τί ποιήσω;.

The Conversation category (§4.2) needs to be divided into two sections, parable and non-parable material. In parable material, the feature is characteristic though by no means distinctive of Luke, occurring on four clear occasions including one very good example (Dives and Lazarus). None of Mark's parables feature conversation but three of Matthew's do. Luke's examples span QD and L but not R material. Outside of parables, conversations are common in Luke but no more so than in the other Gospels.

Interest in Work (§4.3) may be distinctive of Luke. Useful references are found in L, QD and possibly R. Matthew does have references to work but shows no particular interest in the details of the work people do. The only text difficult here is Mk 12.1, omitted in the Lukan parallel.

Fondness for Parties (§4.4) is distinctive of Luke. Luke has Jesus at parties; characters in his parables have parties and examples occur in R, QD and L material. By contrast, Mark at best only implies one party and Matthew has royal feasts.

Excuses (§4.5) could be seen as being distinctive of Luke since there are no obvious examples in Mark or Matthew whereas in Luke there are several examples, from QD and L but not R.

Guillotine Questions (§4.6) are not distinctive of Luke. Although there are three good examples in Luke, there are also two clear examples in Matthew (one of them R) and a similar form is sometimes found elsewhere in Mark and Matthew. Luke's guillotine questions can be distinguished from Matthew's, however, in that he has only one opponent on each occasion and not a group.

The Lower-Class or Disreputable Hero category (§4.7) is a complex one, largely because it is wide ranging and Goulder's own terminology varies. There are a couple of examples of lower-class or disreputable heroes in parables in Matthew and Mark, the Plunderer in Mark (and parallels) and the Thief in Matthew (QC). Also, in his parables, Matthew does have disreputable characters who stand not for God or Jesus but for the believer who is heading for condemnation. Luke, on the other hand, is the only evangelist who has *quanto potius* comparisons in parables between a disreputable character and God (twice). His is the only Gospel in which there are parables which use disreputable characters to make a point about the well-behaved believer (four times). It is also characteristic but not quite distinctive of Luke to have disreputable heroes in non-parable material. The feature occurs almost entirely in L material. Possible exceptions could be seen in 7.36-50 and 23.39-43.

The feature Colourful Details (§4.8) is not straightforward. Goulder includes two aspects under the same heading, non-allegorical details in parables and specificity. That Luke has non-allegorical details in parables, in R, QD and L, is clear, though the designation 'non-allegorical detail' covers widely differing phenomena. Matthew and Mark have, by comparison, less non-allegorical details. Specificity, on the other hand, is not so distinctive of Luke, and colourful, circumstantial details are common in Matthew and Mark.

Of these eight features, then, at least four are distinctive or almost distinctive of Luke: soliloquy, parties, excuses and work. Guillotine Questions are characteristic without being distinctive. On the other three categories, extra qualifications need to be made. Conversation is characteristic but not distinctive in Luke's parables and not characteristic outside parables. Lower-class and disreputable heroes are characteristic of Luke in general and distinctive in certain respects. Colourful Details are in one respect characteristic, in another respect arguably distinctive.

Many would agree with Goulder that Luke is the 'great story-teller of the New Testament' (*LNP*, p. 94). Goulder's 'Human Characters' section attempts to go one stage beyond this, however, and give pointers that the very content, and not only the manner, style and form of the stories, is Luke's own creation. In our analysis, there are some encouraging signs for Goulder's thesis. Certain features, like soliloquy in parables, do indeed look as if they are Luke's own contributions to the stories in question. Others of Goulder's features, though, do not show sufficient signs of Luke's hand to demonstrate the case. This section, then, provides a partial corroboration of Goulder's thesis.

Chapter 8

MIDDLE-CLASS SETTING (§5)

A. *Preliminary Comments*

The reader might be surprised to see a section entitled 'Middle-Class Setting' (§5) so soon after a sub-category on 'Lower-Class Heroes' (§4.7). However, just as the terminology for that category varies, so here Goulder refers variously to 'the homely Lukan scale' (p. 562), 'the every day scale' (p. 613), 'middle-class standards of wealth' (p. 635) 'a middle-class level' (p. 499) and 'restricted wealth' (p. 642).[1]

These terms all refer to Luke's parables. Indeed, Goulder only discusses the parables under this heading, in spite of the fact that other material is conducive to the topic, like the interest in parties (§4.4, see above). Goulder's primary concern here is with the economic setting of the parables, what Goulder often calls a parable's 'scale'. The same theme is prominent in both 'Characteristics' (pp. 54-55) and *MLM*, where he says:

> Every parable in Luke shows the same trend, to a realistic, credible, country-gentleman type of scale...Matthew's parables are on the grand scale, and are different from Mark's village scale and Luke's middle-class, realistic scale (*MLM*, p. 62).

B. *Luke*

Goulder (*LNP*, pp. 98-99) gives several examples of middle-class setting in Luke's parables. These examples fall, one might say, into three sub-categories, the first on the background or setting of the

---

1.   Other references to this category are found in *LNP*, pp. 401, 589-90, 594, 619, 657 and 681. Note also that in the introduction Goulder describes Luke's characters as having a 'realistic middle-class' background (p. 102) and the parables have 'familiar economic settings' (p. 122). Cf. Drury, *Parables*, p. 142.

parables. Lk. 14.15-24, the Great Dinner, is compared with the parallel Wedding Feast in Mt. 22.1-14, Luke's story reflecting 'the middle-class world of Luke's own experience' (p. 98). Goulder particularly comments on the one servant in Luke; Matthew, by contrast, has 'droves of servants'. Likewise in L, the masters in the Fig Tree (13.6-9) and the Servant of all Work (17.7-10) have only one servant to work for them. Goulder feels that the Prodigal Son (15.11-32 L) is on the same sort of scale. Further, for Luke, to build a Tower (14.28-30 L) involves investment requiring careful thought.

A second sub-category would be Luke's treatment of the rich. Goulder says that Luke 'does not care for them' and that they are 'not very rich even so', thinking of the Rich Fool (12.13-21) and Dives (16.19-31). They contrast with rich men in Matthew's parables who might well be symbols for God.[2]

Third, Goulder also attempts to show that Luke's amounts of money are 'more believable'. If a denarius is a labourer's wage for a day (Mt. 20.1-16), then one talent, equivalent to about six-thousand denarii, would be twenty years' pay. Thus the ten-thousand talents owed by the Unmerciful Servant (Mt. 18.23-35) would be an absolutely colossal amount. Goulder contrasts this with Luke's Pounds (19.11-27) in which the servants are given one *mna* each, equivalent to about a hundred denarii and so about three months pay. Other sums 'on the level of everyday life' are the five-hundred denarii and fifty in the Two Debtors (7.41-43), the debts in the Unjust Steward (16.1-9) and the sums mentioned in the Good Samaritan (10.25-37) and the Lost Coin (15.8-10). In *MLM* (p. 62), Goulder calculates that 'The largest sum of money owed in Luke is a quarter of Matthew's smallest investment'.

One of the examples in the first of these sub-categories, the Fig Tree (13.6-9), may not be a strong example. Only one servant, 'the vine-dresser', is mentioned, but he need not be thought of as the man's only servant.[3] One example from the third sub-category, the Pounds (19.11-27), is not so clear either. The amounts of money are indeed smaller than those mentioned in the Matthean Talents (Mt. 25.14-30) but at the

2. On economics in Luke, see Karris, 'Poor and Rich'; Johnson, *Literary Function*; W.E. Pilgrim, *Good News*; D.P. Seccombe, *Possessions* and W. Stegemann, *Gospel*.

3. Similarly, no wife is mentioned in the Prodigal Son but this does not necessarily mean that the father is to be imagined as unmarried; cf. Bultmann, *History*, pp. 189-90.

same time, Luke, on Goulder's paradigm, must have made the setting less middle-class and more aristocratic: Matthew's hero is a 'master' with 'servants' who goes on a 'journey' whereas Luke's is a 'nobleman' who goes away into a 'far country to receive a kingdom' (v. 11). He is able to give cities as rewards to his servants. This might well be regarded as a counter-example.

Almost all of Goulder's examples are in L material. In *LNP* he gives no R examples but there is one possibility: in Mk 12.1-12 (Tenants in the Vineyard), the man sends three servants and then 'many others' whereas in the parallel Lk. 20.9-19, just the three are sent. 14.15-24 provides a QD example, a case in which Luke has, on Goulder's hypothesis, changed the grand scale of Matthew's royal wedding feast to make it more every-day.

One L parable probably ought to be added to Goulder's list, 11.5-8, the Friend at Midnight, in which there is no sign of servants. The man himself has to get up.[4] One might also notice a couple of noble professions in the parables, a judge as well as the widow in 18.1-8 and a physician in Jesus' saying at Nazareth (4.23).

In non-parable material, one might refer to the dinners in 7.36; 11.37 QD and 14.1 (§1.6, see above) and also the parties in Goulder's §4.4 (see above). In addition to 19.11-27, a nobleman receiving a kingdom, a possible counter-example would be 14.31-32, a king going to war.[5]

C. *Mark*

Goulder does not refer to Mark in this section of *LNP* but elsewhere he points to 'farmers' in two of the ch. 4 parables, the Sower and the Seed Growing Secretly. On both occasions, they 'sow the seed unaccompanied' (and in the second of these, he harvests himself too) for this is 'Mark's village scale' (*MLM*, p. 62). The hero of the Vineyard parable, however, owns the vineyard which he lets out to tenants and he has many servants (Mk 12.1-12). This would seem to be a man of a higher class than the ch. 4 farmers. Goulder explains the difference by saying

4. Actually, in Jeremias's view, this parable reflects a poor Palestinian village setting (*Parables*, pp. 157-58), but Goulder (*LNP*, p. 499) says 'there is no evidence for any of this!' and cross-references to §5.

5. Cf. that in Lk. 11.14-23 (Beelzebub), the fully-armed man guards the αὐλή which might be read as 'palace' in contrast to the οἰκία of Mt. 12.29 // Mk 3.27. This would then be a QD or even an R example.

that this man is the absentee landlord familiar in Galilean life (*MLM*, p. 61). The fact is, nevertheless, that God is being compared to the owner of a vineyard, the sort of parable scale which Goulder associates more with Matthew.

The farmers in Mark 4 who work without any servants would be poorer than the heroes of some of the L parables, but, on the other hand, the Vineyard owner with his droves of servants would be richer than the heroes of some of the L parables. One other parable in Mark, 13.32-37, features a householder with servants who are left in charge while he goes away. The exact setting envisaged here cannot be determined, but the (plural) servants show that the householder is richer than some of Luke's parable heroes.

If the class-settings of the parables vary, the same is true, to some extent, outside parables in Mark: as well as the lower-class characters mentioned above, the first disciples are fishermen with hired servants (1.16-20); Jesus heals the ruler of a synagogue (5.21-43); there is the story from the court of Herod (6.14-29); there is a rich man unable to give up his possessions in 10.17-31; and 'those who are supposed to rule over the Gentiles lord it over them' (Mk 10.42).

D. *Matthew*

Goulder describes Matthew as 'the lover of the grand scale' (*MLM*, p. 61). Three parables are particularly notable, Mt. 18.23-35 (M, the Unmerciful Servant) in which it is a king settling account with servants, one of whom owes ten-thousand talents; 22.1-14 (Q, Marriage Feast) in which a king gives a banquet and he has many guests and many servants; and 25.14-30 (Q, Talents) in which five, two and one talents are given for investment.

In *MLM* (p. 61), Goulder points to redactional examples: Mark's mustard bush becomes a δένδρον (Mk 4.30-32 // Mt. 13.31-32, but in Luke too it is a δένδρον, 13.18-19); he adds more servants to the Tenants in the Vineyard (Mk 12.1-12 // Mt. 21.33-46) and Goulder surmises that the householders go away for longer in Matthew than in Mark (comparing Mk 13.32-37 with Mt. 24.45-51 in which the servants know neither the 'day' nor the 'hour'). Further, Goulder points out that in the Tares (Mt. 13.24-30), in contrast with the Seed Growing Secretly (Mk 4.26-29), there are servants to do the work.

Of these examples, Mt. 13.31-32 is not clear: even if Matthew's tree is bigger than Mark's shrub, still one man sows it in his own field — he does not have a gardener. This is, moreover, a case of Mark-Q overlap rather than pure R.

Goulder also suggests that Mt. 25.1-13 reflects the grand scale since 'ten bridesmaids…are retinue for a rich man's daughter' (*MLM*, p. 61). This example is unclear, however, because we do not have clear information about Jewish wedding customs from this period,[6] and the virgins may simply be the village girls. There are no other clear examples of the grand scale in the parables, but there may be signs of it in other material. In Mt. 2.1-12, the Magi are rich and Herod the Great's royal court appears in the same story. Kings and palaces also appear in two sayings in Matthew (11.8 // Lk. 7.25 and 17.25 M).

On the other hand, however, the scale in Matthew is not always so grand and is often akin to the varying settings in Mark and Luke. In Mt. 7.24-27 (// Lk. 6.47-49), each man builds his own house, apparently without the aid of servants. Just as the Mustard Seed might be regarded as small scale, so its pair, the Leaven, is a household parable (Mt. 13.33 // Lk. 13.21). The parable of the Treasure and the parable of the Pearl (Mt. 13.44-46) are both on the level of restricted wealth: the man had to sell everything he had to buy the field and the merchant had to sell everything he had to buy the pearl. These men, therefore, were neither very well off nor poor.

Mt. 18.10-14 // Lk. 15.3-7 provides another possible example: the man himself goes in search of the lost sheep. He leaves the ninety-nine: there are no spare shepherds here (cf. Lk. 2.8-20, shepherds plural). Further, in Mt. 21.28-32, the Two Sons, the setting is not grand scale. The father requires the two sons to work in the vineyard — presumably he cannot afford them to be idle. This example is important because Goulder feels that Luke derives the setting of his Prodigal Son from the Two Sons in Matthew. In Mt. 20.1-16, again there is no grand scale, here the Labourers all work in the Vineyard for only a denarius a day.

Goulder does not regard any of these as counter-examples; often he finds something in these parables which illustrates the grand scale. 'The very fall of the house on the sand is great', he says (*MLM*, p. 61), and 'his housewife puts leaven into the meal enough for 162 people'. It is often a question of perspective: Goulder counts the treasure and the pearl as examples not in spite of but because of the fact that they

---

6.   Cf. Jeremias, *Parables*, pp. 172-73; Linnemann, *Parables*, pp. 189-90.

'exceed in value all that their discoverers possess'. On the Lost Sheep, Goulder draws attention not to the one shepherd but rather to his one-hundred sheep.

If, then, it is true that there are parables on the grand scale in Matthew, it is clear that they are not the only kind. In M, Q and Markan material, it is not always the case that 'Matthew moves among the millionaires' (*MLM*, p. 61).[7]

E. *Conclusion*

Goulder focuses in this category on the setting or scale of the parables, a theme prominent in some of his earlier work. He gives several examples of middle-class or every-day settings in Luke's parables (14.15-24; 15.11-32) and draws attention to the presence of only one servant in 13.6-9, 14.15-24 and 17.7-10. Amounts of money are on a homely scale (particularly 10.25-37 and 15.8-10; also 7.41-43 and 16.1-9) and Luke does not like rich people (12.13-21 and 16.19-31).

Support for Goulder's thesis is found in the fact that examples span both QD and L. One possible R example is the decrease in the number of servants in Luke's version of the Tenants in the Vineyard (20.9-19). Further, there are a few examples of middle-class type settings outside the parables though Goulder does not use this in his argument.

The evidence is not, however, quite as straightforward as Goulder suggests. There are counter-examples in Luke, a king in 14.31-32 L and a nobleman going to receive a Kingdom in 19.11-27 QD. Further, more importantly, Mark and Matthew do not each fit easily into their respective moulds 'village scale' and 'grand scale'. There is a range of settings in Mark's parables and although Matthew does have royal settings and massive amounts of money (Mt. 18.23-35; 22.1-14; 25.14-30), elsewhere, in Markan, Q and M material, the scale varies and sometimes he has the middle-class setting which Goulder says is the preserve of Luke (7.24-27 Q; 13.31-33 Q; 13.44-46 M; 18.10-14 Q; 21.28-32 M). 20.1-16 M shows that amounts of money are not always colossal in Matthew.[8]

---

7. Goulder's comment refers to Matthew's parables. Goulder thinks that Matthew's church was middle-class (*MLM*, p. 9), in agreement with Kilpatrick, *Origins*, pp. 125-26.

8. Cf. Craig Blomberg's criticism of Goulder, though it is overstated: 'For almost every example of a parable set in a village, town or city in the particular

It is an obvious point, but one worth making, that context can be important. Goulder says that the debt in Mt. 18.23-35 is 'astronomical' (*MLM*, p. 62),[9] but for the parable to work, the debt has to be colossal since, if one reads it as allegory (as Goulder does), the King represents God and the debt the believer's sin which God forgives. A smaller, 'down-to-earth' amount would not make the required point and, in fact, there is a more realistic amount in this parable, that owed to the Unmerciful Servant by one of his fellow-servants, a hundred denarii. God has forgiven a huge debt (many sins); the believer should not think twice in forgiving comparatively meagre debts (sins against him).

The point is an important one. Goulder prefers his view to the alternatives because:

> If Jesus told a span of parables, some with millionaires and some with middle-income farmers, it would be unlikely that the doctrinal interest, for which an evangelist might choose his parables, would exactly correspond with the tricky details of income level (*LNP*, p. 123).

In Mt. 18.23-35, however, the doctrine, forgiving others as God has forgiven us, a Matthean doctrine (cf. Mt. 6.12, 14-15), may well have conditioned the scale of the parable; the amounts are not arbitrary. Where the contrast in this parable is between amounts remitted by God and amounts remitted by the believer, the contrast in Luke's parable in 7.41-43, the Two Debtors, is between different amounts remitted by God, represented by five-hundred denarii and fifty denarii respectively, so that one loves the master more than the other. Here the doctrine of the parable does not require the massive contrast in amounts of Mt. 18.23-35.

This is probably not always the case, though. The doctrine behind Matthew's Wedding Feast (22.1-14) and of Luke's Great Dinner (14.15-24) is similar but the scales of the two parables are different. Goulder's theory is that Luke has altered Matthew's scale to make it 'less flamboyant' (*LNP*, p. 98). Likewise Luke has turned Matthew's talents into pounds (*LNP*, p. 98).

Gospel which supposedly emphasises these locations and their corresponding scales of simplicity or grandeur, an exception can be found elsewhere in that Gospel to counter Goulder's perceived patterns' (*Interpreting*, p. 120).

9.   For discussion on the hugeness of the debt, see Linnemann, *Parables*, pp. 108-109, and more recently, T. Naegele, 'Translation'.

This, however, shows Goulder's theory to be in something of a no-win situation. On one hand it is always in Goulder's interest to provide, where possible, R and QD examples of a feature in order to explain its presence in L. Here a tendency towards middle-class settings is seen to be present in QD, apparently confirming Goulder's thesis. On the other hand, though, if one is going to say that Luke has altered the scale in Matthew's parables to produce parables of his own on a more everyday, homely scale, it becomes quite possible to imagine Luke altering the scale of parables he received from oral traditions to produce L parables with middle-class settings. Perhaps, then, the evidence here points towards a degree of Lukan creativity in the L material, but not on the kind of scale which Goulder is imagining.[10]

10. Cf. Gerhardsson, 'Illuminating', p. 297, 'It would certainly be an unreasonable simplification to regard all narrative meshalim peculiar to one evangelist as secondary' but Luke's parables in particular are likely to have been reworked: 'We notice in Luke that professions from the milieu around early Christian communities are reflected in a way that has few equivalents in Mark and Matthew. The theory of a Lucan *Sonderquelle* can hardly provide a sufficient explanation of that.'

Chapter 9

ALLEGORY AND ILLUSTRATION-STORIES (§6 AND §7)

A. *Allegory (§6)*

1. *Preliminary Comments*
In four of the seventeen sections which make up the discussion of 'the Lukan story', Goulder deals specifically with the parables, concentrating more on form than on content. His section 6 is about Allegory, 7 is on Illustration-Stories, 8 is on Hortatory/Ethical Parables and 10 is on the Parable as Lead-in. In this chapter, I will look at the first two of these. First, I will look at allegory.

The treatment of allegory in *LNP* is different from Goulder's treatment of previous sections. It is not a feature which Goulder is isolating and specifying as specially Lukan. He is here looking instead at the way in which Luke uses allegory, especially in comparison with Mark and Matthew. In this way he specifies distinctively Lukan traits within the general category.

Goulder has also written influentially about allegory in 'Characteristics' and *MLM*, and it will be rewarding to look at his general argument.

2. *The Sliding Scale of Allegory Content*
The keynote of Goulder's work on the parables is the emphasis that there should be no 'black and white distinction' between parable and allegory. 'Few distinctions have been more ill-starred for the criticism of the Gospels', he says (*MLM*, p. 56) and adds:

> Parables are on a continuum, with greater or lesser allegory-content: with Matthew it is regularly greater, and with Luke regularly less (*LNP*, p. 100).

In speaking of a 'continuum', Goulder is actually in good company. Dan O. Via, writing at about the same time that Goulder was writing

'Characteristics', says:

> The rigid distinction between parable and allegory on the basis of whether there is one or many points of comparison is arbitrary because a careful consideration of Jesus's stories shows that intermediate or mixed forms do occur.[1]

'The difference', says Via, 'is one of degree, not of kind'.[2]

Goulder is not in such good company, though, in attempting to quantify the continuum, trying to show exactly how allegorical each evangelist is. In 'Characteristics' (p. 59), he speaks of 'a sliding scale of allegory-content which it is possible to represent mathematically' (p. 59).[3] Goulder counts up the 'features' or 'points' in a parable, asking how many of these correspond in the meaning of the parable:

> If all the points correspond, we say the parable has an allegory-content of 1: if, say, three points out of ten correspond, we say the parable has an allegory-content of 0.3 ('Characteristics', p. 59).

The overall figure for Mark is 75 per cent, for Matthew 82 per cent and Luke 60 per cent. The experiment is repeated in *MLM* (pp. 56-60) and summarised in *LNP* (pp. 99-100).[4] The difficulty is that it is not always easy to isolate which aspects of a parable are allegorical and which are not. On only three occasions do the evangelists append an interpretation

---

1. Dan O. Via, *Parables*, p. 13. But Via adds that 'the criterion of difference is not the quantitative one of how may points of comparison there are between the parable and its referent' (p. 15).

2. Via, *Parables*, p. 14. Cf., among others, Matthew Black, 'Parables'; R.E. Brown, 'Parables'; C.F.D. Moule, Review of Jeremias; and other literature cited below. A good recent summary of this and other issues in parable research is C.L. Blomberg, *Interpreting*, particularly pp. 20-21 and 29-69, including a good bibliography, but Blomberg does not give Goulder any credit for criticising the parable-allegory distinction.

3. For the term 'sliding scale' in reference to allegory, cf. Northrop Frye, *Anatomy*, p. 91.

4. Blomberg comments in a footnote: 'his figures concerning the percentage of allegorical details in the various parables also seem inflated' (*Interpreting*, p. 121), but it is not clear what Blomberg means by this. He says that Goulder's 'Characteristics' article has been 'highly influential' (p. 121) and he is quite critical of it (pp. 121-22), but it is unlikely that he has read it carefully: he represents Goulder as saying that there is 'slightly less allegorizing' in Matthew than in Mark (p. 121) and he confuses Goulder's distinction between application and interpretation (p. 122).

to a parable, and even here counting is difficult. On the Dragnet (Mt. 13.47-50), for example, Goulder notes that Matthew 'gives us the interpretation himself' and this leads, he says, to 'a minimum of subjectiveness' (*MLM*, p. 57). 'The parable', Goulder continues, 'has ten points, all of which have meanings to Matthew' (*MLM*, p. 57) and Goulder lists the points. However, the interpretation which Matthew gives (Mt. 13.49-50) only has a few of these points; indeed it only deals with the second half of the parable, so there is some subjectivity about Goulder's interpretation even here.

In his discussion in *LNP* (pp. 99-100), Goulder draws special attention to the Friend at Midnight (11.5-8), with 'an allegory-content of five points out of thirteen, or just under 40%'. Goulder has not chosen a special example to suit his case here; several other L parables have a similarly low figure in 'Characteristics' and *MLM*. Nevertheless, the isolation of the thirteen features illustrates further the difficulty with the counting. On v. 6, for example, Goulder lists 'three loaves' and 'the visiting friend' as two of the eight non-allegorical points or 'colour'; the last clause, 'I have nothing to set before him', Goulder does not mention. The 'three loaves', however, could be seen as corresponding to whatever the Christian is praying for; the friend on a journey could be the necessity ('whatever he needs') and 'nothing to set before him' could be the Christian's lack.

3. *Allegory and Realism*
There is a related issue here and it is something which comes through strongly in *MLM*, and more strongly still in *LNP*, that Luke is seen as the great story-teller of the New Testament largely because he is happy to cut down on elements of allegory in order to improve a parable—the story is told for its own sake. Goulder says:

> It is just that he cannot have both a detailed allegory and a realistic story, and he prefers the latter (*LNP*, p. 100).

Luke, with his 'vividness of imagination' has human characters and colourful details and such things are contrasted with allegory. On the Two Sons, for example:

> The characterlessness of the Matthean family, and the unpersuasiveness of the too-allegorical plot, are an offence to him: he drops the allegory, as so often (§6) and turns the characters into real people (§4) (*LNP*, p. 610).

The 'continuum' from greater to lesser allegory content is, then, correlated with another continuum, from lesser to greater realism. Goulder says:

> A corollary of Luke's interest in the story, of his many-sided characterization, of the colourfulness of his incidents and the realism of his settings, is a much lower allegory-content (*LNP*, p. 99).

This assumption, that the greater the allegory-content, the less realistic is the parable, is shared with others who have written on the parables; indeed it is basic to most who put parable and allegory in opposition to each other.

Many would agree with Goulder that Luke's parables are, in general, more realistic than Matthew's and that they are often, in general, less allegorical. The important question is, however, whether they are more realistic because they are less allegorical.[5] Goulder here has an important insight in 'Characteristics' which he does not carry forward into *MLM* or *LNP*:

> The narrator may have his eye more closely on the open story or more closely on the hidden meaning. If he has his eye more closely upon the open story it is likely, but not certain, that a fair number of points in the story will not have corresponding detailed meanings. It is not certain because, despite his interest in the life of the story, he may have picked a very good parallel, where there are a number of accidental correspondences (p. 58).

Goulder does not go far enough even here, however. Some of the most effective parables are those which cohere well at both the story level and the meaning level. The fact that one might recognise God's welcoming of sinners in the father's running to kiss and embrace the Prodigal, for example, adds to the resonance of the story.[6] This may mean that the correspondence between story and meaning is intentional rather than 'accidental'. A good parable may have detailed allegorical

---

5.   This involves, of course, the question of how one defines allegory and in general, New Testament scholars probably assume too narrow a definition. Contrast, for example, Drury's definition of allegory, 'a concatenation of symbolic persons, places, things and happenings, which signifies a parallel concatenation in the actual world' (*Parables*, p. 5), with the Concise Oxford English Dictionary (Seventh edition, 1982), 'narrative description of a subject under guise of another having similarities to it'. Goulder's use of the word is, thankfully, quite clear because he uses it relatively, attempting to quantify the degree of allegory in a parable.

6.   Cf. Drury, *Parables*, p. 117.

correspondences as well as being, on the story level, natural or believable.

The issue is perhaps clearest when one looks at what Goulder calls 'colourful details' (§4.8) which often translates into 'non-allegorical details' (see above, pp. 185-90) and involves an element of circularity. The possibility of a detailed allegory which features colourful details is excluded by Goulder's own definition.

The counting up of correspondences between story and meaning then becomes more difficult as the relationship between 'colourful' and 'non-allegorical' breaks down. In Mt. 20.12, for example, those who were paid last complain about 'the burden of the day and the scorching heat'. This detail could be mentioned in order to stress how unfairly treated they feel, adding to the story by striking a sad note. On the other hand, it could be that, as Goulder feels, 'the burden and heat is the Law' (*MLM*, p. 410). Or both may be right, in which case one has an allegorical correspondence which is also a colourful detail.

Similarly, in Lk. 15.5-6, the shepherd puts the lost sheep on his shoulders and has a party to celebrate. Goulder says that this is a 'colourful detail which cuts down the allegory content' (*MLM*, p. 60, cf. *LNP*, p. 605).[7] It could, however, be described as an image of God (or Christ) drawing the sinner back to Himself, like the father's running to kiss and embrace the Prodigal (15.20); and the party is the angels rejoicing. Again, allegory and realism do not need to be opposed and again, the counting of correspondences is problematic.[8]

Furthermore, Goulder's counting of correspondences concentrates the reader's attention on content; one can miss the form which para bles take. Matthew, for example, like Luke, has conversations in his parable material (see above, pp. 172-73). On one occasion, the Tares (Mt. 13.24-30), there are two exchanges between the man and his servants—their speech makes up the bulk of the parable. There is nothing in the interpretation, however, which corresponds to this conversation: it is simply a device which adds vividness to the narrative

7.   Cf. Linnemann, *Parables*, p. 67: 'For the shepherd in Lk. 15.5 to lay the sheep on his shoulders is a decorative accretion in comparison with Matthew's version, and so another sign that the latter is more original.'

8.   Cf. Blomberg, *Interpreting*, p. 51, 'Many would argue that the best allegories are quite realistic as pieces of fiction in their own right, and that part of their artistry is leaving their audiences in doubt about just what details are supposed to have a double meaning.'

and, though it does not reduce the allegory content of the parable, certainly it adds to its realism.

Indeed, all sorts of features can enliven a parable without compromising the allegorical content. In Matthew's parables, for example, characters' postures are often mentioned: in the Dragnet, the men sit down to sort out the fish (Mt. 13.48); the Unmerciful Servant falls on his knees (18.26) and his fellow-servant falls down (18.29); the Labourers in the Vineyard 'stand idle' (20.3, 6); the Ten Virgins nod off (25.5) and rise again (25.7). None of these features has an allegorical correspondence; they are merely part of good story telling.[9]

The problem is that it is easier, when dealing with allegory, to isolate and give meanings for characters, objects and tangible things like a king, a servant, an account, a debt, a field or a seed, than it is to do the same with less tangible things. In the Labourers in the Vineyard (Mt. 20.1-16), Goulder lists eleven out of seventeen points which have allegorical significance (*MLM*, p. 410)[10] but most of these seventeen points are characters, places, objects, time of day and so on. Goulder does not pick out the workers 'agreeing' for a denarius a day, mentioned at the beginning and at the end of the parable (20.2 and 13). It is a detail which is easy to miss, especially if one is busy looking for allegorical correspondences, but it has a key function in the story, in showing that the householder is fair to those he employed first: he keeps his word to them so that they have no ground for complaint.[11] There is a similar feature in the Tares, Mt. 13.28-30a:

> The servants said to him, 'Then do you want us to go and gather them?' But he said, 'No, lest in gathering the weeds you root up the wheat along with them. Let both grow together until the harvest...'

---

9.   Note, once again, a slight difference in emphasis between 'Characteristics' and Goulder's later work. In 'Characteristics', p. 60, Goulder says, 'St Matthew is an artist with his parables, despite his interest in allegory...He is not a thoroughgoing allegorist consciously devoting himself to the meaning, or he would not have been so successful a storyteller.' Goulder is less inclined to praise Matthew's storytelling in *MLM* and *LNP*—the nearest he comes is *LNP*, p. 22, 'a fine parabolist'.

10.   An oddity here is that Goulder gives the figure, 11 out of 17, as 0.65, which is right, but on p. 59 it is 0.59. Similarly, on 22.1-14, the figure is 0.95 on p. 59 but 1.0 on p. 417.

11.   Cf. Linnemann, *Parables*, p. 82.

Bultmann sees this exhortation to patience as the key to the parable[12] but when Goulder counts up the features, he does not mention it,[13] no doubt because it is missing from the interpretation in 13.36-43.

4. *The Meaning Spoiling the Story*
Goulder attempts to illustrate Matthew's greater propensity for allegory by the theory of 'intrusions' into the story:

> Matthew in particular is liable to allow elements from the 'meaning' to seep into his parable and spoil the story, as when the rude wedding guests all live in the same city, which is burnt, or returning masters have a private hell under the stairs. Luke never does this (*LNP*, p. 100; cf. p. 550 and *MLM*, p. 59).[14]

The first example is from Mt. 22.1-14, the Wedding Feast, and the second is from Mt. 25.14-30, the Talents, in which 'the worthless servant' is cast into 'the outer darkness'. Actually, the conclusion of the Talents is very similar to the conclusion of the Wedding Feast:

> Bind him hand and foot, and cast him into the outer darkness; there men will weep and gnash their teeth (Mt. 22.13; cf. 25.30).[15]

Certainly the thought changes quickly from the world of the story to comment on it, but this is not very different from what is sometimes found in Luke. The conclusion to the parable of the Faithful and Unfaithful Servant in both Gospels ends with thoughts on punishment and hell in which one is half still in the world of the parable and half in comment upon it (cf. Mt. 24.51 and Lk. 12.46b-48).[16] In Lk. 12.47, the reader cannot be sure whether to take ὁ κύριος αὐτοῦ as referring to Jesus or to the master in the parable or both. Similarly, it is a famous

---

12. *History*, p. 187, followed by Jeremias, *Parables*, p. 81.

13. But Goulder does list as one allegorical feature 'growth' which 'is the advance of time' ('Characteristics', p. 59).

14. But contrast 'Characteristics' (p. 60) where Goulder understates such 'intrusions': 'In twenty parables he can be convicted only once with certainty of spoiling the story for the meaning—the incident of the king's armies and the burning of the town in the Marriage-Feast. Perhaps we should add some slightly unreal references to hell.'

15. Goulder refers to this as 'a private hell for offensive wedding-guests' in 'Characteristics', p. 54 (= *MLM*, p. 61) when he is talking about scale.

16. This is given as another example of meaning spilling over into the story in *LNP*, p. 550 and *MLM*, p. 59.

difficulty to know where in the Unjust Steward (Lk. 16.1-13) the parable ends and the application begins.[17]

Further, Goulder's own discussion of Luke's Pounds (19.11-27) comes close to describing the same phenomenon. 'The allegory has ruined the parable', he says (*LNP*, p. 100), and 'Although the bystanders are speaking, Luke goes steaming on, "I tell you . . ."' (*LNP*, p. 681).

5. Aspects of Luke's Redaction

In Goulder's discussion of the category (*LNP*, pp. 99-100), he recognises the importance of looking at the tendencies present in R and QD in order to help establish whether or not the L material is Luke's own composition.

Goulder mentions three allegorical details which Luke drops from Mark's Sower (Mk 4.1-9 // Lk. 8.4-8): the seed springs up quickly because there is no depth of earth (Mk 4.5, not in Lk. 8.6); the plant withers in Mk 4.6 'because it had no root' and in Lk. 8.6 'for lack of moisture'; and in Mk 4.6 the sun scorches, missing in Lk. 8.6. Goulder notes that 'the missing Markan allegorical points are all taken up by mistake in the Interpretation' ('Characteristics', p. 61, Mk 4.13-20 // Lk. 8.11-15). It might be, then, that Luke was attempting to improve the story for its own sake in spite of points he wanted to make in the Interpretation, like the coming of temptation (Lk. 8.13) which would have corresponded to the sun rising and scorching.

Goulder also suggests that the allegorical content of the Wicked Husbandmen (Mt. 21.33-46 // Mk 12.1-12 // Lk. 20.9-19) is reduced by Luke who has no parallel to Mk 12.5 in which a third servant is killed and many others are beaten and killed. These represent the prophets:

> He knew that some of the prophets had been killed (e.g. Zechariah); it is just that he is prepared to lose two points from Mark's allegory (the prophets and their killing) for the sake of improving the story (*LNP*, p. 99; cf. 'Characteristics', p. 61).[18]

The issue is not clear, however, as a quick glance at *MLM* will show:

> In the Wicked Husbandmen, Luke also a). omits the non-allegorical hedge and winepress and tower, and b). follows the Matthean

---

17. Cf., for example, C.H. Dodd, *Parables*, pp. 17-18, and Creed, *St Luke*, pp. 202-203.

18. Cf. Charles E. Carlston, *Parables*, p. 78.

allegorized[19] order, 'they cast him out of the vineyard and killed him' (*MLM*, p. 60).

Here Goulder says that Luke ends up with a greater allegory count (0.85) than Matthew (0.76) and Mark (0.65). A complicating factor, though, is that in *LNP*, Goulder follows Marshall in disputing that being cast out of the vineyard before the death is allegorical:

> There is no sign of such thinking behind Luke and it is natural to take the vineyard as a symbol for Israel, not Jerusalem (*LNP*, p. 693).

Marshall, and Goulder in *LNP*, may be right, but equally, everything does not need to cohere in a detailed way between story and meaning; the image of the son cast out may be enough to evoke the idea of Jesus being cast out of the city.[20] Either way, the different opinions which Goulder himself holds on this further illustrate the difficulty of the counting up of correspondences.[21]

Even if one does not allow the death outside the gate as allegorical, Luke has still omitted the hedge, winepress and tower, as well as retaining several other allegorical features, and we would have a parable which at the same time has a good story and high allegory content. Much the same is true of one of the Q parables, the Banquet (Mt. 22.1-14 // Lk. 14.15-24). Although Goulder's allegory figures for this parable are 0.95 for Matthew and 0.64 for Luke, he also says that Luke's secondariness 'is made certain by the added allegory of the Gentile mission' (*MLM*, p. 418). If on Goulder's theory, then, Luke is adding allegory, it is questionable whether one can also speak of his having 'a marked aversion from allegory' (*MLM*, p. 59). Drury picks up on this and says:

＊

19. Goulder uses the verb 'allegorize' (cf. *MLM*, p. 57, 'I am concerned merely to show that Matthew allegorizes...') to refer to the intentional writing of an allegory or making an existing one more allegorical (cf. also 'de-allegorize'). This usage is different from that urged by Caird in *Language*, p. 165, 'To allegorize is to impose on a story hidden meanings which the original author neither intended nor envisaged; it is to treat as allegory that which was not intended as allegory'.

20. Cf. Caird, *Language*, p. 166, takes the allegorical explanation here for granted.

21. It is not surprising to find a different stress in the two books. In *MLM* (cf. p. 58), Goulder is attempting to show how Matthew has enhanced elements of allegory in Mark; in *LNP*, Goulder is attempting to show the opposite to be true for Luke. This case presents a conundrum because it is a MA.

Such confusion can be avoided by simply dropping the *a priori* assumption that Luke is unallegorical. His text shows that he can handle both the simply realistic and the allegorical. This parable in comparison with Matthew's version shows him combining both well...It is not that Luke eschews allegory but that he has other ways of telling parables as well: realistic ways which can happily include and bear allegorical significance.[22]

Goulder in turn responds to the criticism[23] and says that Luke is not averse 'from allegorical correspondences as such' (*LNP*, p. 100), adding:

But he is never content with a colourless allegory, and at every point adds life and humanity to his *Vorlage* (*LNP*, p. 591).

This is just the point, that allegory need not be colourless.

In another Q parable, the Lost Sheep (Mt. 18.12-14 // Lk. 15.3-7), much the same is true. Goulder gives allegory figures of 0.86 for Matthew and 0.6 for Luke (*MLM*, p. 59) but it is not necessary to regard all the colour in the Lukan account as non-allegorical (see above, p. 206).[24]

On the parable of the Pounds (Lk. 19.11-27), Goulder says: 'the allegory has ruined the parable... Even Lukan parables are not always successful' (*LNP*, p. 100). At first sight this is a little odd because Goulder's allegory figure for the Talents (Mt. 25.14-30) is higher in *MLM*, 0.72, than it is for the Pounds, 0.59 (p. 59). Likewise on the Great Supper/Banquet parables, the figures are 0.64 for Luke and 0.95 for Matthew in spite of the fact that in *LNP*, Goulder says 'Luke has the fuller allegory' (p. 100). Here some extra clarity is required. Goulder specifies the added allegory in the Pounds as the 'nobleman receiving a kingdom' (*LNP*, p. 100) and this corresponds to Jesus ascending to receive a kingdom (cf. p. 680).[25] As with the Great Supper, then, 'the fuller allegory' is not a question of all the individual features but,

22. *Parables*, p. 124; cf. p. 117. This is one of few disagreements between Goulder and Drury.

23. Cf. Goulder's Review of Drury's *Parables*, 'I find much that is valuable, including the allegorical element in Luke, which I had disputed' (p. 174).

24. Cf. Drury, *Parables*, p. 140: 'Luke shows himself able to combine allegory with natural vividness'.

25. Goulder does not in *LNP* specify the added allegory in any detail, perhaps because he assumes it is obvious to the reader. It is made clear, however, in *TTM*, p. 44; cf. 'Already?', p. 32 and Dodd, *Parables*, p. 120.

rather, it refers to one important allegorical plot change. There it is the added mission to the Gentiles and here it is Jesus departing and returning as King.

The only L parable to which Goulder draws attention in his introductory section is the Friend at Midnight (see above, p. 204). Also relevant, though, is Goulder's §7 on 'Illustration-Stories' and we will look at this below.

In the commentary, Goulder rarely refers to this section (only *LNP*, pp. 336,[26] 550-51, 588-91 and 610). Perhaps this is because allegory is not one of Goulder's positive, distinctive Lukan features like 'guillotine questions' or 'soliloquy' to which the reader can quickly and easily be referred.

6. *Conclusion*

Goulder has made an important contribution to scholarship of the parables by criticising the often perceived opposition between parable and allegory and suggesting instead that parables are on a continuum, from greater to lesser allegory-content.

Goulder's views on allegory in Luke have changed a little, partly no doubt because of Drury's corrective that one should not assume that Luke is necessarily unallegorical. Nevertheless, the assumption that allegory is necessarily unrealistic still pervades much of *LNP*. The assumption is not correct because there are parables which can be seen as both allegorical and realistic, like the Lost Sheep or the Banquet. Goulder's statement that 'he cannot have both a detailed allegory and a realistic story' (*LNP*, p. 100) can be challenged.

Where we are able to compare Luke with Mark, the evidence goes both ways. Luke's Sower is less allegorical than Mark's; his Wicked Husbandmen is more allegorical (and more realistic). Similarly, in Luke's treatment of Q parables, one often finds colourful, non-allegorical details but equally, there are often colourful, allegorical features. In both the Banquet and the Pounds the added allegory is a major plot development.

---

26. Here Goulder mentions Drury's view (*Parables*, pp. 126-27) that Luke has added an allegory to Mark's Patch (Luke 5.36-37): cf. his Review of Drury, p. 173. When Goulder talks about parables he is dealing almost always with what Gerhardsson calls 'the narrative meshalim' as opposed to 'aphoristic meshalim' like this (see 'Narrative Meshalim', particularly pp. 339-42 on nomenclature).

It is not possible, then, to identify a clear tendency away from allegory in Luke's Mark and Q parables. Luke does not have 'a marked aversion from allegory' (*MLM*, p. 59). Nevertheless, Goulder is probably right that the L parables have a markedly lower allegory-content.

It is difficult, however, to quantify the allegory-content in Luke's parables, as indeed it is in Matthew's and Mark's. Goulder's counting of features is subjective, sometimes omitting features which could be allegorical in Luke and features which might not be allegorical in Matthew. Further, the correlation between high allegory-content and low realism can ignore the parable's form including matters like the use of dialogue.

Goulder points to a couple of occasions on which Matthew apparently spoils a parable by allowing the meaning to seep into the story (Wedding Feast; Talents) but the same could be claimed on at least one occasion for Luke (Pounds; cf. Unfaithful Servant and Unjust Steward).

However, even if one did find a clear anti-allegorical tendency in Luke, this would only place Goulder in the same sort of no-win situation which one sees in §5, Middle-class Setting. If Luke demonstrably reduced allegory in Mark and Q parables, so also might he have reduced it in sources for L parables. If he apparently did so more in L (Goulder's figures are 60 per cent for Luke overall but 40 per cent for L), his taking these parables solely from oral traditions might itself be an adequate explanation for the heightened tendency. We will return to this issue below (pp. 284-86).

B. *Illustration-Stories (§7)*

1. *Isolation and Definition*
Goulder's paragraph on 'illustration-stories' or *Beispielerzählungen* is relatively uncontroversial. The classification *Beispielerzählungen* goes back to Adolf Jülicher[27] and it is followed by, among others, Bultmann[28] and Linnemann.[29] In English, they are usually called either 'exemplary stories', 'example stories' or 'illustration-stories'. Gerhardsson calls

---

27. A. Jülicher, *Gleichnisreden*. The preliminary discussion of *Beispielerzählungen* is in Vol. 1, pp. 112-5 and the discussion of the four *Beispielerzählungen* in Vol. 2, pp. 585-641.
28. R. Bultmann, *History*, pp. 177-79.
29. E. Linnemann, *Parables*, pp. 4-5.

them 'narrative meshalim of an example type'.[30] Creed approves of the designation and provides a succinct definition:

> They are stories which, by giving examples of types of character, convey directly their own moral.[31]

Jülicher identified four illustration-stories, the four Goulder lists, the Good Samaritan (Lk. 10.25-37), the Rich Fool (12.13-21), Dives and Lazarus (16.19-31) and the Pharisee and the Publican (18.9-14). Almost all scholars who accept the designation agree on these four. Sometimes others are added: Bultmann suggests that Lk. 14.7-11 (The Wedding Guest) and 14.12-14 (The Proper Guests) might be 'the first part of an exemplary story'[32] and Creed suggests that the Prodigal Son 'almost falls into the same category'.[33] Gerhardsson claims that the parts of parables in which human behaviour is elucidated are, strictly speaking, example stories, for instance the Ten Virgins who 'have prepared themselves badly or well for the arrival of the bridegroom'.[34]

2. *Challenges to the Consensus*

Even if there are other possible examples and partial examples, it is commonly accepted that there are four clear, full illustration-stories. The view is not unanimous, however. Norman Perrin is sceptical on the basis that 'the distinction is not being made on grounds of language or literary form' but rather on the basis of 'their supposed function on the

---

30. B. Gerhardsson, 'Illuminating', p. 272.

31. J.M. Creed, *St Luke*, p. lxix. Creed is cited by Drury as his source for the distinction in *Parables*, pp. 134 and 154. But also Creed does not acknowledge the debt to Jülicher. Actually Drury does not follow through the idea that these are distinctive illustration-stories and agrees with J.T. Sanders (*Jews*, p. 61) in following Loisy on Dives (*Les evangiles synoptiques*, vol. 2, p. 177). On definition, see also B.B. Scott, *Hear Then*: 'An example story has no figurative element but offers an example of correct behaviour or of negative behaviour to avoid' (p. 29); cf. Fitzmyer, *Luke X-XXIV*, p. 883.

32. R. Bultmann, *History*, p. 179.

33. J.M. Creed, *St Luke*, p. lxix.

34. B. Gerhardsson, 'If We Do Not Cut', p. 332. C.F. Evans talks about 'parables of the "tale" type' which 'teach by narration of a particular incident rather than by analogy' (*Saint Luke*, p. 467), including not only the Good Samaritan (p. 467), Rich Fool (p. 522), Dives (p. 611) and the Pharisee and the Publican (p. 641), but also the Unjust Steward (p. 595), Prodigal Son (p. 588) and Unjust Judge (p. 635).

lips of Jesus'.[35] However, it is not necessarily true that the distinction between parable and example rests on a supposition about their function in Jesus' ministry. Goulder thinks that these are illustration-stories and that Jesus did not speak any of them. It is clear, after all, that the Good Samaritan is framed in Luke as an illustration of the right sort of behaviour, 'Go and do likewise' (10.37).

The most important challenge to the consensus is provided by John Dominic Crossan in his article 'Parable and Example in the Teaching of Jesus'[36] which spawned a debate which dominated the first two volumes of *Semeia*.[37] This is not a debate into which I have liberty to enter here, but it is worth noting that Crossan's objection to these parables as exemplary stories is on the level of the historical Jesus. His analysis of the Good Samaritan in particular is dependent on his own historical-critical work which separates the parable from most of its context in Luke.[38] Crossan actually takes it for granted that as they stand in Luke they read as exemplary stories.

3. *Goulder's Argument*
Goulder's perspective and methodology is markedly different from Crossan's. Not only does Crossan assume the correctness of the 2ST which Goulder is attacking[39] but also, for Crossan, recovering Jesus' original parables is the beginning of exegesis[40] whereas for Goulder, it is speculation in which he is not prepared to indulge until first he has considered the option of taking the parables as products of the minds of the evangelists.[41]

---

35. Norman Perrin, *Jesus*, p. 100.

36. Pp. below are cited from *NTS* 18. Note also Ernst Baasland, 'Zum Beispiel'.

37. Crossan is followed enthusiastically by Perrin, *Jesus*, pp. 162-65, against his own earlier opinion in *Rediscovering*; also John Donahue, *Gospel*, pp. 129-34; and, more cautiously, R. Funk, 'Good Samaritan', particularly p. 76; cf. his *Parables*, p. 31. Crossan's major critic is Dan O. Via, 'Parable and Example Story'; cf. his *Parables*, pp. 11-13. Crossan responds to Via in 'Structuralist Analysis'. Via responds in 'Response to Crossan'.

38. Crossan, 'Parable and Example', p. 291; cf. Via, 'Parable and Example Story', p. 112.

39. See particularly 'Parable and Example', pp. 287-91: Crossan thinks that the Good Samaritan originally stood in Q.

40. Cf., for example, the title of his book which states his presupposition, *In Parables: The Challenge of the Historical Jesus*.

41. It should be added that Goulder does not refer to Crossan's article.

Further, where Crossan only 'notes in passing that all are from Luke',[42] Goulder makes this his key point. 'This is a new type of parable not found outside Luke', he says ('Characteristics', p. 61; cf. *MLM*, p. 60). Likewise, 'All four instances come in Luke, none in the other Gospels'; it is 'a type not found outside Luke'; they are 'all in Luke'; there is 'no instance of the genre elsewhere' (*LNP*, pp. 101, 489, 537, 635; cf. p. 668).

Here one sees a clear example, in small frame, of Goulder's basic, underlying argument for Lukan creativity. The fact that illustration-stories are unique to Luke suggests, for Goulder, that such stories were not known to Matthew or to Mark and consequently that Luke probably created them. There are, however, other logical possibilities. The exemplary stories could be Jesus' own, in which case only Luke had access to them, or only Luke chose to include them, what Goulder calls 'the selection hypothesis'. Alternatively, Luke could have transformed original parables of Jesus into exemplary stories (Crossan's view). Alternatively again, one could take a middle position which incorporates elements of all of these views: Luke could have creatively reworked stories which he received from oral traditions, traditions which may have had some (now impossible to discern) origin in Jesus' ministry.

It is difficult to know, however, how one can choose between the options. In other categories, help comes from looking at Luke's treatment of Matthew and Mark—then one can see whether the same tendencies are apparent in R and QD as well as L, and so whether the features in question are characteristic of Luke as a writer. This is, no doubt, one of the reasons that Goulder suggests a relationship between this category and those which he discusses either side of it in *LNP*, Allegory and Hortatory Parables (*LNP*, p. 101).[43]

Goulder does warn the reader in advance that 'in time', the help which one gets from looking at R and QD 'will give out' (*LNP*, pp. 86-87). Under such circumstances, one needs to ask whether Goulder's overall solution is more plausible than any of the available alternatives. We will return to this question below (pp. 287-90).

---

42. P. 285. Cf. B.B. Scott, *Hear Then*, p. 29: 'That all four occur *only* in Luke should arouse suspicions about the proposed genre'.

43. Cf. 'Characteristics' and *MLM* (p. 60) in which the illustration-stories are covered in the discussion of allegory: 'St Luke was no lover of allegory. Indeed four of the 'L' parables are not parables at all in the sense of offering some *tertium comparationis* ...' ('Characteristics', pp. 60-61).

Chapter 10

HORTATORY PARABLES (§8)

A. *Preliminary Comments*

Another important keynote of Goulder's work on the parables is the distinction between 'indicative' and 'imperative' parables. Mark's and Matthew's parables are primarily indicative and Luke's are primarily imperative:

> Luke introduces an almost unbroken element of imperative parables into an almost unbroken tradition of indicative parables (*MLM*, p. 50; cf. 'Characteristics', p. 64).

By 'indicative' parables, Goulder means those which 'describe the action of God or Christ' (*LNP*, p. 101); 'they point to the situation as it is' (*MLM*, p. 48). By 'imperative' parables, he means those which 'point the Christian's duty' (*MLM*, p. 48); they are parables 'carrying a direct suggestion of what the Christian should do' (*MLM*, p. 50).

Gerhardsson, one of the few scholars who has commented on this, approves of Goulder's 'fruitful distinction'.[1] He says that indicative parables 'show how something *is*' whereas imperative parables 'inculcate what the listeners *shall do*'.[2]

For Goulder, the imperative parable involves two distinct though related facets: first, the nature of the narrative of the parable and second, the function and application of the parable. On the first of these one might note, for example, Goulder's statement that:

> Mark and Matthew are laying the stress on the action of God, Luke on the human *response* (*LNP*, p. 401).

---

1. B. Gerhardsson, 'Narrative Meshalim', p. 353.
2. B. Gerhardsson, 'Narrative Meshalim', p. 353. The parables Gerhardsson lists as imperative are mainly but not all in Luke. They are not all the same as the ones Goulder lists.

On the second of these facets, an example is provided by Goulder's statement that:

> The Lukan parables are told to encourage the Christian to pray, to be faithful, and to count the cost, and to warn him of the perils of money (*MLM*, p. 50).

Here the function, and the application, of the parable is stressed: it is told in order to exhort the Christian to action.

An example of the first facet, whereby the narrative is imperative in nature, is Goulder's discussion of the Tower Builder:

> It is not, of course, an exposition of God's action, like the Markan, and most of the Matthean parables, but an *imperative*, hortatory parable, challenging the would-be Christian to commitment (*LNP*, p. 597).

An example of the second facet, in which the parable functions in Luke as exhortation because of its application, is seen in Goulder's comment on Lk. 16.9, appended to the Unjust Steward:

> It is an *imperative*, hortatory conclusion as with so many other Lukan parables (*LNP*, p. 622).

It is, nevertheless, important to see that the two facets are not separated by Goulder, and the distinction is to some extent an artificial one. For Goulder, the hortatory application of the parable arises from the imperative nature of its narrative. Luke has, in Goulder's view, composed the parable himself with the hortatory application in mind.

Goulder differs here from standard form-critical opinion. Dibelius, in his section on 'Exhortations', attempts to show that parables often received secondary, 'hortatory' applications. The Unjust Steward, for example, 'contains no exhortation for common life' but it was provided with such an exhortation in Lk. 16.9. The basic thesis is that:

> The tendency of the Churches to derive as much exhortation as possible from the words of Jesus must have affected the handing down of the parables.[3]

He states further:

> The effort to provide the Churches with as many exhortations as possible sometimes occasioned complete misunderstandings of parables.[4]

---

3. M. Dibelius, *From Tradition*, p. 257; quotation on the Unjust Steward, p. 248; the relevant pp. are 248-58.

4. M. Dibelius, *From Tradition*, p. 248.

Examples of this are seen in Lk. 12.57-59 (Settling with Accuser) and 14.7-11 (Wedding Guests).

Dodd too saw the parables as having been corrupted in the church by a hortatory motivation[5] and Jeremias says:

> Standing thus between the Cross and the Parousia, the Church, looking for the guidance of Jesus, found itself forced by the altered conditions to interpret those parables of Jesus which were intended to arouse the crowd to a sense of the gravity of the moment, as directions for the conduct of the Christian community, thus shifting the emphasis from the eschatological to the hortatory interpretation.[6]

For these scholars, there is a descent into hortatory application which takes place in the early church. For Goulder, on the other hand, the difference is at the level of the evangelists, between Matthew and Mark on the one hand and Luke on the other.

Goulder is similar to these scholars, however, in his use of the term 'hortatory'. He says that there would be little point telling a parable if it did not have some impact on the listener's attitudes and in indicative parables, a general response like 'Repent' is often expected.[7] This is in contrast to the specific responses which arise from Luke's imperative parables, like counting the cost and avoiding the dangers of materialism. Likewise, Dibelius uses 'hortatory' in the sense of 'exhortation for common life' and for Jeremias, 'hortatory' apparently refers to giving 'directions for the conduct of the Christian community' (see quotations above). Thus the 'imperative' can even be called the 'ethical'.[8] In practice, then, the distinction Goulder is making is one between the general and the specific or between the ethical and the eschatological.

Just as Goulder has modified his views on allegory, so too his opinion has changed a little on hortatory parables. In 'Characteristics', Goulder speaks about 'the development of *Response*-parables' ('Characteristics', p. 62), primarily a characteristic of Luke. For Mark and Matthew, 'a parable is something which adumbrates the action of

---

5. Dodd talks about the 'homiletic' or the 'paraenetic' motive (*Parables*, p. 101).

6. J. Jeremias, *Parables*, p. 44; pp. 42-48 are on 'The Hortatory Use of the Parables by the Church'.

7. Cf. Goulder's letter quoted by Gerhardsson, 'Narrative Meshalim', p. 353.

8. The term 'ethical' is used in Goulder's title to this section in *LNP* (p. 101), but it is used afterwards only once (p. 102).

God' ('Characteristics', p. 63), but in two Matthean parables, the Lost Sheep and the Unmerciful Servant, 'We see the beginning of the slide into hortatory parables, so often deplored' ('Characteristics', p. 63). In *MLM*, by contrast, there is 'a sharp cleavage' between Mark and Matthew on one side and Luke on the other (*MLM*, p. 49). Now in Matthew, 'the only parable with an imperative sense is the Lost Sheep' (*MLM*, p. 50) and:

> The contrast with Luke is very striking: his parables are almost all imperative parables (*MLM*, p. 50).

Goulder's position in *LNP* is the same with regard to Matthew: 'almost all' are indicative parables (*LNP*, p. 101); but his position with regard to Luke is modified: 'others of Luke's parables are indicative, like Matthew's' (*LNP*, p. 101). The key point in *LNP* is, therefore, that there are several imperative parables in Luke's Gospel and that this distinguishes it from Mark and almost distinguishes it from Matthew.

B. *Luke*

1. *Redaction*

In his discussion of this category in *LNP*, Goulder hardly comments on Luke's treatment of Mark. In 'Characteristics' and *MLM*, however, he discusses the Interpretation to the Sower (Mk 4.13-20 // Lk. 8.11-15), saying: 'five small additions emphasize the moral of faithful endurance by the Christian' ('Characteristics', p. 63)[9] so that 'even the Sower becomes a sermon' (p. 64). Goulder does not make the same point in *LNP*, perhaps because he is no longer convinced of its persuasiveness. After all, as soon as it has been admitted that the added details in Luke have a paraenetic function, one might see the details already present in Mark as serving a paraenetic purpose. This is Dodd's view[10] and Goulder is aware of it ('Characteristics', p. 63).[11]

It is possible to see Luke enhancing the paraenetic in Mark on one other occasion, the Lamp (Mk 4.21-25 // Lk. 8.16-18). In Luke, the

---

9. *MLM*, p. 50: 'four small changes'.
10. C.H. Dodd, *Parables*, p. 135, 'The interpretation is indeed a moving sermon upon the parable as text'.
11. Cf. Dibelius, *From Tradition*, pp. 257-58, and Carlston, *Parables*, p. 76, 'now the individualistic, ethical and paraenetic emphases predominate'.

exhortation more clearly flows from the simile: there is no break in Jesus' speech and an οὖν is apparently added.

Goulder comments only in passing on Luke's treatment of Matthew. The Great Dinner (Lk. 14.15-24 // Mt. 22.1-10), he says, is an indicative parable, but he adds:

> Even here an ethical interest is not far away: when the Christian gives a dinner, he is to invite the poor, like the man in the parable (*LNP*, p. 102).

'The poor, the maimed, the blind and the lame' do occur in both the parable (Lk. 14.21) and in the exhortation which immediately precedes it (14.14) but in the parable this is at best only a subsidiary theme.[12] The point is not a strong one and Goulder does not lay much emphasis on it.[13]

In 'Characteristics' and *MLM* Goulder also mentions the Pounds (Lk. 19.11-27) as an example of the phenomenon:

> The Pounds drops Q/Matthew's 'Be ready' for a Lukan appeal for πίστις: they thought the kingdom of God was about to appear at once, which was not so—the message is now 'Labour on' as with the Servant's Reward, 'Be faithful with God's money' as with the Unjust Steward ('Characteristics', p. 64; cf. *MLM*, p. 50).

This is not very convincing, however, and in *LNP*, Goulder describes both the Faithful and Wise Servant (Mt. 24.45-51 // Lk. 12.41-48) and the Pounds as indicative: they 'still' warn of Christ's coming in judgment (*LNP*, p. 101).[14]

Also in 'Characteristics', Goulder discusses the Two Builders (Mt. 7.24-27 // Lk. 6.47-49):

> The greater emphasis on the activity of the man in the Lukan version turns the point more towards the Christian's responsibility to lay a strong foundation (p. 64).

This idea is also dropped in *MLM* (p. 56) and *LNP* (p. 97) in favour of the 'colourful detail' explanation of the extra features in Luke.

---

12. And according to Dibelius, *From Tradition*, p. 248, Matthew has appended 22.11-14 (Wedding Garment) in order to bring out a hortatory application.

13. There is no reference to hortatory interpretation of this parable in the commentary, *LNP*, pp. 588-94.

14. Cf. Bultmann, *History*, p. 191 on the 'law of End-stress'—'the servant who has not used the money entrusted to him is presented last, so as to accord with the hortatory nature of the story'.

Lk. 12.35-40 (Watchful Servants; Thief) might also be mentioned. This pericope combines, on Goulder's theory, aspects of Mk 13.32-37 (Watchful Servants), Mt. 24.43-44 (Thief) and Mt. 25.1-13 (Ten Virgins). The message seems to be an imperative one:

> Let your loins be girded and your lamps burning, and be like men who are waiting for their master to come home from the marriage feast... You also must be ready; for the Son of Man is coming at an unexpected hour (Lk. 12.35, 36 and 40).[15]

This does not, however, clearly illustrate a tendency towards hortatory parables in Luke. First, the exhortation is substantially that of Mk 13.35-37 and the passages in Matthew 24–25 with the message to stay awake or to be ready.[16] Second, the imperative is not a specific, ethical one but a general, eschatological one. Nevertheless, the following verse, 12.41 QD, 'Lord, are you telling this parable for us or for all?', might illustrate that for Luke, parables can be told with specific audiences and specific purposes in mind.

Gerhardsson[17] lists The Defendant (Lk. 12.57-59) as a narrative mashal with an imperative element. Since the parable has a parallel in Mt. 5.25-26, it could be seen as a QD example of the phenomenon. This is not clear, though, because for Gerhardsson, Mt. 5.25-26 is not a narrative mashal.[18] Further, Matthew 5.25-26 is clearly imperative and so this example might be exhibiting the opposite tendency from the one we are looking for. Bultmann saw the Lukan similitude as original, transformed into an exhortation by Matthew.[19] Jeremias says:

> There can be no doubt that Luke is right: the parable is an eschatological one, a parable of crisis... The divergence between the two Evangelists reveals a characteristic shift of emphasis, namely, a movement from the eschatological to the hortatory point of view. Luke emphasizes God's eschatological action, Matthew, the disciples' conduct.[20]

---

15. Bultmann, *History*, pp. 184-85, deals with imperative applications like Luke 12.40.

16. Cf. Carlston, *Parables*, p. 85, 'As in Mark the stress is paraenetic'.

17. B. Gerhardsson, 'Narrative Meshalim', p. 354.

18. B. Gerhardsson, 'Narrative Meshalim', p. 344.

19. Bultmann, *History*, p. 96.

20. *Parables*, p. 44. But this is the faulty logic whereby Jeremias apparently assumes that Luke's setting is authentic because Matthew's is not (cf. Sanders and Davies, *Studying*, pp. 174-75).

A similar example is the Closed Door (Lk. 13.23-30), also listed by Gerhardsson as a narrative mashal with an imperative element,[21] and also with a non-parabolic parallel in the Sermon on the Mount (Mt. 7.13-14 and 21-23). Again the example is not clear. Although Lk. 13.23 gives the pericope an imperative thrust, it is not easy to decide whether or not one should, with Gerhardsson, describe the teaching as narrative parable. Certainly the language is more blatantly metaphorical in Luke than in Matthew, with a householder, a door and knocking, but much of the language is prophetic rather than parabolic ('Then you will begin to say...you will say...').

At best, then, it would seem that Luke's treatment of Mark and Matthew in this category helps Goulder's thesis only a little. Furthermore, some evidence goes directly against Goulder's thesis. Goulder regards Matthew's version of the parable of the Lost Sheep (Mt. 18.10-14) as 'the only parable [in Matthew] with an imperative sense': 'the moral is plain, and for the apostles, *Pascite agnos meos*' (*MLM*, p. 50). The difficulty is that Luke's version of the parable (Lk. 15.3-7) lacks this clear hortatory application. Sanders, for example, comments on Lk. 15.7 and 15.10:

> Without these applications the implication of the sayings might be hortatory: 'You too seek the lost'. Matthew gives an application of the similitude of the Lost Sheep which points in this direction: 'So it is not the will of my Father who is in heaven that one of these little ones should perish' (Mt. 18.14).[22]

If Luke read Matthew, then, and if Sanders's (and others') reading is correct, then Luke has on one occasion given an imperative parable an indicative interpretation.

2. *L*

Goulder lists several L parables which are imperative (*LNP*, p. 101). He begins with the four illustration-stories and continues with the Friend at Midnight (11.5-8), the Tower and Embassy (14.28-32), the Unjust Steward (16.1-9), the Servant of all Work (17.7-10) and the Unjust

---

21. B. Gerhardsson, 'Narrative Meshalim', p. 354.

22. Sanders and Davies, *Studying*, p. 184, referring to Bultmann, *History*, p. 184; cf. also Bultmann, p. 171. Sanders thinks that the application in Matthew too must be queried. Cf. Jeremias, *Parables*, p. 40, for the view that Luke's setting is primary.

Judge (18.1-9). The messages these parables impress on the hearer are: 'loving our neighbour' (Good Samaritan); disposing of wealth (Rich Fool; Dives); humble prayer (Pharisee and the Publican); 'that they should always pray and not faint' (Unjust Judge, Friend at Midnight); 'to increase the disciple's faithfulness' (Servant of all Work); to be faithful with money (Unjust Steward)[23] and to count the cost (Tower and Embassy).

In the commentary, as well as in 'Characteristics', Goulder also counts the Two Debtors (7.41-42) as imperative. This example is less clear than the others. When discussing the Two Debtors, Goulder says:

> Mark and Matthew are laying stress on the action of God, Luke on the human *response*. Just as he is concerned that we should beware of covetousness, go and do likewise, always pray, etc., so here the stress lies on love as a response to forgiveness (*LNP*, p. 401; cf. 'Characteristics', p. 64).

Clearly, Goulder is here discussing the application of the parable, the first facet of the discussion of hortatory parables mentioned above. Certainly in applying the parable to Simon, Jesus addresses him directly, 'You...you...you' (Lk. 7.40, 43, 44, 45, 46). The parable itself, however, is not imperative in the other sense in which Goulder uses the term: it is not imperative in nature in the same way as is, say, the Friend at Midnight. Rather, the parable is indicative in that it 'describes the action of God or Christ'. The creditor (God) forgives debts of contrasting amounts—the parable does not go on to describe the debtors' reactions to this except in so far as Simon provides their likely reactions when asked. But even given this application, the parable does not have an obvious exhortation for the reader. Goulder says that it 'teaches us to be grateful for our redemption' ('Characteristics', p. 64) but at best this is only the point of the whole pericope, 7.36-50; it is not a message easily drawn from the parable alone.

The Prodigal Son (Lk. 15.11-32) is similar. Goulder says:

> The three parables in ch. 15 speak of God's joy in sinners' penitence, but the unspoken moral is rather insistent, that more virtuous Christians should welcome them too (*LNP*, p. 102).

---

23. Contrast *MLM*, p. 50, where the Unjust Steward is likened to the Rich Fool and Dives which all 'warn of the perils of money'; but cf. 'Characteristics', p. 64.

In other words, this is an indicative parable with at least a hint in the direction of hortatory application. Goulder is a good deal more forthright in the commentary, however:

> It is hard to resist the conclusion that the parable has a double message, for the listener is made to feel first the relief and happiness of repentance and then the propriety (ἔδει) of rejoicing in the turning of sinners. Both messages are *hortatory*; they are not indicative, descriptive of the actions of God, but imperative, urging a proper line of conduct on the Christian, like so many of the other Lukan parables (*LNP*, p. 614).

The second message, urging the proper rejoicing when sinners repent, is indeed hortatory. The first is less clearly so. The only imperative which can result from the listener being 'made to feel first the relief and the happiness of repentance' is 'Repent!' but this cannot be seen as one of Goulder's specific, ethical imperatives.[24] This point is rather, as Goulder first recognized, an indicative one, speaking of 'God's joy in sinners' penitence'. This is, after all, the general message of the ch. 15 parables, spoken in response to charges made by Pharisees and Scribes in 15.1-2.

There are, however, other indications of Luke's interest in hortatory parables in L material. If one allows 'aphoristic meshalim' (Gerhardsson's term) as well as the narrative parables, one might notice the following example:

Lk. 4.23: καὶ εἶπεν πρὸς αὐτούς, Πάντως ἐρεῖτέ μοι τὴν παραβολὴν ταύτην· Ἰατρέ, θεράπευσον σεαυτόν.[25]

Lk. 14.8-11 (Wedding Guests) is also described as 'a parable' (14.7)[26] and clearly it is imperative, 'When you are invited...do not...'.

As Goulder says in *LNP*, 'others of Luke's parables are indicative, like Matthew's' (p. 101). He lists mainly Q parables, the Mustard Seed,

---

24. Cf. 'Characteristics', p. 64, where Goulder attempts to distinguish between repentance as a 'general challenge arising from a kingdom-of-heaven parable' and a 'practical demand to the Pharisee in the presence of the Publican'.

25. This would contrast with similar 'parables' in Mark, like 3.23-27 'How can Satan cast out Satan?...' which are clearly indicative. But see also below, p. 226, on Mk 7.14-23.

26. Gerhardsson lists it as a narrative mashal with an imperative element, 'Narrative Meshalim', p. 354. The others in Luke he lists are the Good Samaritan, Friend at Midnight, Watchful Servants, Burglar, Defendant, Closed Door, Unjust Steward and Servant's Reward. There are some odd omissions here, Rich Fool, Tower Builder and the Embassy, Unjust Judge and Pharisee and Publican.

the Leaven, the Great Supper and the Pounds, but also the ch. 15 parables which include the Lost Coin and the Prodigal Son, both L. One could add to these the Barren Fig Tree (13.6-9) which in 'Characteristics' (p. 64), Goulder lists as imperative with the message 'Repent!' (but see above, p. 219).

C. *Mark and Matthew*

For Goulder there are no imperative parables in Mark:

> The most that can be taken in expected Response is some such generality as 'Watch!' 'Be ready!' 'Believe the Gospel!'. They are parables of existential challenge and eschatological crisis in the approved manner ('Characteristics', p. 63).

For Gerhardsson, who does not use the ethical/eschatological, specific/general distinctions, Mark has one imperative parable, 13.32-37, the Watchful Servants.[27] This parable is actually a good example of an indicative parable with an imperative message. It begins, 'It is like...' (v. 34) and concludes with 'Watch, therefore'.[28]

If one allows 'aphoristic meshalim' into the discussion, there is one other example of an imperative parable in Mark, in 7.14-23, the meaning of which is that one should be morally upright and that one can eat non-kosher food.

Even in *MLM*, Goulder allows that Matthew's version of the Lost Sheep (Mt. 18.12-14) is imperative and this fact is difficult for Goulder's thesis. As we saw above, Luke's version is, if anything, less clearly imperative than is Matthew's, a difficulty for the thesis of *LNP*. But in addition, the fact does not sit easily with the thesis of *MLM* that the non-Markan sections of Matthew are Matthew's own creation. Goulder says:

> It is not even uncharacteristic in being an imperative parable, for the imperative is masked under, 'So it is not God's will...', and remains formally indicative, like every other parable in Matthew (*MLM*, p. 399).

Expressions like 'masked under' and 'remains formally indicative' are

---

27. B. Gerhardsson, 'Narrative Meshalim', p. 354.

28. If Goulder's lectionary theory is correct, then the message here has an added specificity, cf. *EC*, p. 294: 'The church must take heed and watch—watch literally, sitting up through the Paschal vigil, watch figuratively with a life of obedience ready for the End'.

not appropriate to the thesis that Matthew himself has composed the parable. Such language is more appropriate to the theory that Matthew has written up into characteristically indicative form a parable which came to him as imperative. When Goulder comments on the parable in his general discussion in *MLM* (p. 50), he says that though it has an 'imperative sense', 'Matthew still sees the parable in indicatives'. Goulder here comes close to the form-critical consensus he is attempting to challenge.

Goulder's comments on the Unmerciful Servant (Mt. 18.23-35) are similarly problematic. This parable is regarded as imperative in 'Characteristics' (p. 63) but in *MLM*:

> The Unmerciful Servant in 18 also begins, 'The kingdom of heaven may be compared....', and concludes, rather to our surprise, 'So also my heavenly Father will do to everyone of you, if you do not forgive your brother from your heart'; the parable is about God's judgment on the unmerciful, and only secondarily suggests an imperative about our own behaviour (p. 50; cf. p. 402).

The introduction and conclusion to the parable demonstrate how Matthew has framed the parable; they do not necessarily establish the parable to be indicative through and through, especially if the conclusion comes 'to our surprise'. Again, Goulder's own language sits uncomfortably with his thesis that Matthew has composed the parable. The possibility is that Matthew has overwritten a parable which came to him in imperative form. But even as it stands in Matthew, it may be too weak to say that the imperative is only secondary. The parable depicts the 'response' of the sinner to God's forgiveness, teaching the necessity of forgiving the brother from the heart (vv. 22 and 35), a hortatory message.[29]

Others of Matthew's parables have, Goulder says, 'only a general moral'. One of these is the Two Builders (Mt. 7.24-27) which, Goulder says, is an indicative, judgment parable (*MLM*, p. 50), 'to show that it is doers and not sayers who will enter the kingdom of heaven' (p. 309). It is arguable that here, too, Goulder understates the case for the hortatory motivation in Matthew. The message to 'hear and do' Jesus' words seems to be stressed in the parable: one man hears Jesus' words and does them (7.24) and the other hears them and does not do them

---

29. See further *LNP*, pp. 400-401, where Goulder sees the Unmerciful Servant as the source for Luke's 'response' parable, the Two Debtors.

(7.26). There is no mention of 'saying' in contrast to 'doing'. This might well be seen as a 'response' parable, depicting the right way to respond to Jesus' teaching.

For Goulder, the parables of Matthew 24–25 (Thief, Faithful and Wise Servant, Ten Virgins, Talents, Last Judgment) 'carry no more than the general moral, Watch' (*MLM*, p. 50).[30] This is largely true: like Mark's Watchful Servants (Mk 13.32-37), the Ten Virgins has the form indicative parable, 'The kingdom of heaven shall be compared...' (Mt. 25.1) with exhortation at the end, 'Watch therefore' (Mt. 25.13). Nevertheless, it is noticeable that these parables do not clearly 'describe the action of God or Christ'. Rather, there is an extent to which these too are response parables. The believer can be faithful and wise (Mt. 24.45-47) or wicked (24.48-51), wise or foolish like the Ten Virgins (25.1-13) and either prudent with what one has been given or not like the men in the Talents (25.14-30).

D. *Conclusion*

Goulder's view is that Luke introduced some imperative parables into his Gospel in distinction from Mark and Matthew whose parables are almost all indicative. An indicative parable is one which describes the action of God or Christ; an imperative parable either a) depicts the believer's response to God's action or b) can be interpreted as providing a specific or ethical exhortation to the believer, or often both.

Luke does not exhibit a clear tendency towards interpreting or overwriting Mark's and Matthew's parables so as to make them hortatory. The tendency could be seen in Luke's treatment of Mark's Sower and Matthew's Banquet but it is not obvious. The evidence of the Lost Sheep may go in the opposite direction.

There is a good number of imperative parables in L material. The fact that there are several indicative ones as well means that Goulder's modified position in *LNP* is justified. Even here, though, Goulder overstates the case for imperative parables, especially with regard to the Prodigal Son.

Mark does not have any imperative parables on Goulder's definition but the Watchful Servants in Mk 13.32-37 with the message 'Watch!' would qualify on a less strict definition. The same is true of the

---

30. Gerhardsson's three imperative parables in Matthew are the Thief, Faithful and Wise Servant and the Ten Virgins, 'Narrative Meshalim', p. 354.

parables in Matthew 24–25, especially the Thief, the Faithful and Wise Servant and the Ten Virgins. Two parables in Matthew are also imperative in the specific or ethical sense, the Lost Sheep and the Unmerciful Servant.

Goulder is clearly correct that Luke favours imperative parables. On Goulder's definition, there are more imperative parables in Luke than there are indicative ones, particularly in L, and Luke has many more imperative parables than Matthew or Mark. It is not, however, a distinctive feature of Luke's writing.

The language of a 'slide' ('Characteristics', p. 63) from Mark and Matthew to Luke is more appropriate than that of a 'sharp cleavage' (*MLM*, p. 49) between them. One could see the slide as running from purely indicative parables, like the Mustard Seed, to indicative parables with an imperative twist, like the Watchful Servants, to more imperative parables, like the Friend at Midnight. Gerhardsson's view is judicious:

> It is obviously wrong to regard the indicative and the imperative functions as alternatives. The basic function of a narrative mashal is to illuminate something, and this function is by nature indicative... When a mashal has an explicitly imperative character, it is still indicative but something has been added, an imperative element.[31]

As Gerhardsson recognizes, Goulder's distinction between the indicative and the imperative is a helpful contribution to parable scholarship. Further, our study partly bears out Goulder's conclusion on the topic since the hortatory motivation is characteristic, though not distinctive, of the L parables. However, a troubling factor has arisen in the course of the discussion. Goulder's theory that Matthew composed all the Q and M parables looks less likely in the light of cases like the Lost Sheep (Mt. 18.10-14) which looks like an indicative parable pressed into service to make an imperative point. Similarly, the notion that Luke composed all the L parables looks less likely in the light of cases like the Two Debtors (Lk. 7.41-42) or the Prodigal Son (Lk. 15.11-32), indicative parables apparently used, in the first case entirely and in the second partially, to make imperative points.

Such tension between content and context in Lukan parables may tell against aspects of Goulder's thesis and requires further examination. This topic will form a substantial part of the subsequent chapter.

31. B. Gerhardsson, 'Narrative Meshalim', pp. 353-54.

Chapter 11

MUDDLE (§9)

Goulder's section 9, on Muddle, falls into a second general category of Lukan stylistic features. It is like several that follow, all of which are used by Goulder in order to explain the text on the basis of his thesis, 'Inference of Setting' (§13), 'Combination of Sources' (§15), 'Splitting of Sources' (§16) and 'Transfer of Elements' (§17). Also relevant in this connection are 'Similar Words with a Changed Meaning' (§20), 'Price of Improvements' (§19), 'Poetic Clumsiness' (§21) and 'Tautological Duplication' (§22).

In this category there is a greater degree of subjectivity. Few would argue with Goulder's isolation of examples of soliloquy in the Gospel parables. Many would agree with Goulder that there is a general tendency in Luke towards more realistic parables. Here, however, Goulder is more often alone, and his work is more imaginative, more hypothetical, and at the same time, less easy to test. Further, several of the same features in this category are used by Goulder to explain Matthew's compositional procedure too.

Muddle is an important feature for Goulder: he refers to it nearly twenty times in the commentary. A pressing reason for this suggests itself. Goulder's thesis gives Luke a highly creative role and needs to deal with the problem of inconsistencies, incongruities and mismatches between content and context, parable and application. Goulder needs to give some account of data which are the starting-point of form-critical and source-critical consensus, matters which lie at the heart of the 'standard paradigm' which Goulder is attempting to replace.

This impression is confirmed by the fact that the feature has its counterpart in Goulder's explanation of Matthew's 'midrashic method'.[1] In

---

1. It is also a feature of Mark—see Goulder's, 'Those Outside (Mark 4.10-12)', especially p. 300; cf. also 'St Luke's Genesis', p. 16.

MLM (p. 35), Goulder discusses 'inconsistencies' which result from Matthew's work 'abbreviating' Mark. On the Leper, he says:

> Large crowds attend Jesus down from the mountain, and apparently witness the healing of the leper; who is told, however, following Mark, to tell no one (8.1, 4) (p. 35).[2]

Goulder adds that 'there are perhaps thirty minor muddles of this kind'.[3] The feature is being used cleverly here in order, largely, to demonstrate the thesis that Matthew used Mark and no other major source. Contradictions are not signs of Matthew combining sources, Mark and Q, Mark and M or M and Q, nor are they proof that stories change during transmission in oral tradition. Rather, they are actually elements of Matthew's own midrashic method in expanding Mark.

The importance of this feature in Goulder's thesis on Matthew can be seen clearly from his discussion of Matthew's attitude to the Law (*MLM*, pp. 15-21). For some scholars, the apparently diverse views of the Law are signs of the use of different sources or traditions.[4] Goulder, then, needs to explain how the same phenomena make better sense on the basis of his own thesis. He says that Matthew has modified Mark's radical stance on the Law, working in his own conservative viewpoint, but some contradictions remain:

> Matthew's inconsistency is that he dare not apply his principle in a thoroughgoing way. When it comes to washing, dietary laws, or divorce, he wants to have the best of both worlds, and compromises. (*MLM*, p. 20).

Goulder is conscious of the alternative view and he criticizes it:

> It is, of course, a naïve mistake to suppose that wherever we have inconsistency we have a different source. Matthew is inconsistent in lots of ways, and on an issue as large as this inconsistency is exactly what we should expect with the confrontation of two irreconcilable principles (*MLM*, p. 21).

---

2. Cf. Goulder's Review of Kingsbury, p. 165.

3. Outside of the introduction, Goulder rarely alludes to the feature in *MLM*, cf. pp. 319, 339 and 376-77. Appeal to muddle also forms part of Goulder's argument on the MA at Mt. 22.68—see above, pp. 103-104.

4. For a good summary of approaches to Matthew on the Law (including Goulder), see G. Stanton, 'Origin and Purpose', pp. 1936-37.

This is a strong move.[5] By making inconsistency a characteristic of
Matthew the redactor, a problem for the thesis becomes a solution
provided by it. Nevertheless, Goulder is probably a little too forthright
to talk about the opposing view as being founded on 'a naïve mistake'.
It would only be a mistake to assume that inconsistency is always and
inevitably a sign of a different source. It needs to be recognised, and
Goulder himself often does recognise it, that inconsistency may well be
the result of the use of sources.

Just as in *MLM* muddle can arise from Matthew's use of Mark, so in
LNP muddle sometimes results from Luke's use of Mark. Luke sets the
Feeding of the Five-Thousand in Bethsaida (Lk. 9.10), rendering the
statement 'We are in a lonely place here' (Mk 6.35 // Lk. 9.12) an
incongruity (*LNP*, p. 433). If, though, this is like Goulder's treatment of
Matthew, unlike it is the proposal that Luke also muddles when he
combines sources. On the Temptations (Mk 1.12-13 // Mt. 4.1-11 // Lk.
4.1-13), for example:

> The combination of Mark's πειραζόμενος with Matthew's hungering
> *after* the forty days leaves the reader in a Lukan muddle (*LNP*, p. 297).

On the other hand, Luke can be muddled when using just Matthew.
After the command to 'Follow me' in Lk. 9.59, the man is told to 'go
and proclaim the kingdom of God'. The latter is 'glossed from Matt.
10.7':

> But the reader is then left wondering how the man can at the same time
> follow Jesus and also go and preach. We have a characteristic minor
> Lukan muddle, as indeed we also did in vv. 52f., where Jesus sends his
> disciples ahead to prepare for him, and is then there himself (*LNP*,
> p. 461).

Goulder, therefore, uses the theory of Matthew's and Luke's
propensity for muddle as a means of explaining the text on the basis of
his thesis that Luke read Matthew (which for Goulder entails Markan
priority and no Q). This is in partial agreement with standard source-
criticism: first, in using it, on occasions, as a sign of Luke's or
Matthew's dependence on Mark and second, in using it as a sign, on
occasions, of the combination of two sources. It is only partial
agreement, however, since first, it is not necessarily a sign of the
combination of two sources and second, when it is two sources, it is

5.　　Contrast Morton Smith's opinion, Review of *MLM*, p. 606.

Luke using Mark and Matthew or two different texts from Matthew.

The most important and controversial aspect to Goulder's discussion is his proposal that Luke has a tendency to muddle even when he is not working directly with source materials:

> The slight ambiguity over the point of some of the parables is part of a more general Lukan unclarity. Who is my neighbour?, asks the lawyer, i.e. the man I am to care for: Who was neighbour, replies Jesus, to him who fell among the thieves?, i.e. the man who cared for him. Simon correctly answers Jesus' parable that he who is forgiven most loves most; after a few lines Jesus concurs, 'Therefore, I say to you, her sins which are many are forgiven, because she loved much' (*LNP*, p. 102).

These are instances of what John Muddiman calls 'mismatch between content and context'.[6] They are cases where most interpreters would see the application not quite fitting the parable, showing that Luke has taken the parable over from another source, whether oral or written.[7] Muddiman, in his review of *LNP*, comments:

> But when this sort of thing happens in Mark- and Q-sections of Luke, it is, according to Goulder, his sources that have muddled him, whereas in L material, it seems to be Luke's unaided proclivity toward muddled-ness! Simpler by far, surely, is to admit that the illustrative parables in these sections had some earlier existence and slightly different meaning in oral tradition, before Luke pressed them into the service of his narrative.[8]

This is, however, the very conclusion that Goulder is keen to avoid. It is characteristic of Goulder's writing for potential weaknesses like this to become constituent parts, even strengths, of the thesis. In general, this need not be a problem, since Goulder's explanation is competing with other explanations of the data for plausibility.

The difficulty which arises, however, is that there is at least a hint of circularity. Goulder says that 'Luke is quite capable of making a muddle on his own' (*LNP*, p. 103), 'and does not require a second

---

6. Review of *LNP*, p. 178.

7. See, for example, Crossan, 'Parable and Example', p. 268: his source-critical work is done on the basis that Lk. 10.29 does not match 10.37 which 'indicates the possibility of some sort of literary combination of divergent sources'; cf. Scott, *Hear Then*, p. 192.

8. Review of *LNP*, p. 178; cf. Harvey, Review of *MLM*, p. 191. Often in L material, Goulder speaks about Luke combining different models (e.g. *LNP*, p. 402) or different texts from Matthew or Mark (e.g. *LNP*, pp. 622-23).

source to get his wires crossed' (*LNP*, p. 709; cf. p. 796) but one might ask how Goulder can know this. The logic is that Luke makes muddles not only in triple tradition and double tradition material but also in L material, and since it is Goulder's thesis that Luke composed the L material, it follows that Luke must have been capable of making a muddle on his own. This is a case of Goulder assuming rather than proving his thesis and, having assumed it, using the assumption as part of the proof.

Further, Goulder probably has the arguing too easy. There is an element of arbitrariness in the way in which each example of 'muddle' is explained on the basis of his thesis and it means that the phenomenon is difficult to specify or to define. Many and various features are covered under the general heading 'Muddle'.

There are cases, for example, of changes of setting leading to contradiction, as in the resetting of the Feeding of the Five Thousand in Bethsaida (*LNP*, p. 433) or bringing the Nazareth sermon forward (p. 303). There are, second, examples of 'the crossing of wires', especially between parable and application (Two Debtors, p. 402; Good Samaritan, p. 490; Friend at Midnight, p. 498; Unjust Steward, pp. 622-23). Third, there are occasions on which sayings are not appropriate to the settings which Luke provides for them. Examples of this are Lk. 9.57-60 and 10.1-2 (*LNP*, p. 461, quoted above, p. 232; *LNP*, p. 466).[9] Other examples do not fit into any of these categories (Zechariah's deafness, *LNP*, p. 244; the Temptation, p. 297, quoted above, p. 232; the Centurion's embassies, *LNP*, p. 378; tombs for the prophets, pp. 522-23, cf. p. 526; 'not a hair of your head', p. 709; 'those in authority', p. 731; 'twelve thrones', p. 732; also cf. pp. 265-66).

The examples given, and their explanations, range from plausible to strained. Some muddle over the Five Thousand in Bethsaida is highly plausible: explanations are not forthcoming in the commentaries.[10] Similarly, Luke's version of the story of the Centurion's Servant has

---

9.   A possible explanation for this is the tension between the implied audience, the reader of the book who is being told to pray for labourers and to go and preach the gospel, and the audience in the narrative. The artificiality of this fictional audience may be creating the 'muddle'.

10.   Marshall, *Gospel of Luke* attempts an explanation: 'The indications are that they were further round the E side of the lake than Bethsaida, possibly in gentile territory (the Decapolis) where Jews might not be sure of a welcome' (p. 360).

often been seen as secondary because of the sending of embassies.[11] On some occasions, alternative explanations are more plausible, particularly in the case of apparent mismatch between context and content.

Most difficult, however, are those cases which make up the bulk of Goulder's examples, where muddle is one among several possible explanations. In 1.62, for example, Luke may have intended κωφός from the outset to mean both deaf and dumb or, on the other hand, the deafness may have crept in by mistake.[12] On 11.47-48, the building of the prophets' tombs, Luke may have misunderstood the saying he has taken over from Matthew or, on the other hand, the point could be that these lawyers are building heavy tombs for the prophets so that they 'never return to trouble the living'.[13]

The difficulty for the interpreter is one of methodology. There are no obvious criteria for deciding between the options on offer. Should appeal to 'muddle' compete on a par with explanations which make sense of the text as it stands? For Goulder, there are so many clear examples of the phenomenon that the benefit of the doubt on other occasions is declined. Perhaps, though, in unclear cases, it would actually be safer to prefer explanations which see Luke's writing as coherent and intelligent. Under these circumstances, one would only appeal to muddle when such explanations are lacking.[14]

Whether or not one agrees with Goulder on this example or on that, however, it is clear that very different phenomena are being included under the same heading. When an isolated stylistic feature becomes as elastic as this, the reader might begin to have doubts about whether it is really there at all. We have encountered this before, especially in the 'Lower-Class Heroes' grouping (§4.7). No doubt the defence could be made that Goulder is describing here not so much a stylistic feature as a

11. See, for example, Fitzmyer, *Luke X-XXIV*, pp. 648-49.

12. Sometimes it is just assumed that by κωφός Luke meant deaf and dumb, e.g., Fitzmyer, *Luke I-IX*, p. 328; cf. Creed, *Saint Luke*, p. 25.

13. So Caird, *Language*, p. 208, cf. *Saint Luke*, p. 159 and Fitzmyer, *Luke X-XXIV*, pp. 946 and 949, the point being that as lawyers, they want no prophetic voice to add to the Torah. But Evans says: 'The version is without logic as it stands' (*Saint Luke*, p. 508); cf. Knox, *Sources*, Vol. 1, pp. 94-102.

14. Cf. James Dunn's criticism of Räisänen's contradictory Paul: a reading which emphasises tortured thinking or contradiction should not be ruled out but it is a hypothesis of 'the last resort': 'basic to good exegesis is respect for the integrity of the text and, in the case of someone like Paul, respect for his intellectual calibre and theological competence' ('Works of the Law', p. 523).

cast of mind - this is often the tenor of his remarks on Lukan muddle:

> We shall find many such minor incongruencies: it is best to concede that
> Luke's mind is not exact (*LNP*, p. 103).

The feature can even be described as 'Lukan indecision' (p. 303) and Goulder feels that: 'Luke, like other men, has difficulty making up his mind' (p. 466). Even here there are problems, however. Muddle cannot be a distinctive Lukan cast of mind because Matthew too, as we have seen, is depicted as having similar difficulties and in *MLM*, 'inconsistency' is characteristic of 'midrash' in general.[15]

In short, therefore, there are several problems with the isolation of this feature. There is at least a hint of circularity as well as of subjectivity; varying phenomena are included under the same heading and the feature is almost as Matthean as it is Lukan.

Perhaps one further problem should be mentioned. Goulder says,

> Luke's genius is in the telling of stories. He lacks a clear head to satisfy
> our pedantries (*LNP*, p. 490).

The reader has to ask how plausible this picture of Luke is, how likely it is that a 'genius' of story-telling would regularly trip himself up. Further, Goulder often appeals to an extraordinarily precise Luke, especially in 'inference of setting' (see below, Chapter 13). The problem is one of coherence: Goulder requires two theses to be true, Luke is in some ways muddle-headed, in others clear-headed.[16]

Finally, however, in defence of Goulder, it needs to be noticed that what he has done is to project onto the evangelist's mind a tension which has often been observed in the Gospel, between the artistic and the discordant, leading Evans to suggest that if Luke had been a painter, he would have been an impressionist:

> For in too many cases for it to be accidental his word-pictures, which are
> so impressive and winning when viewed at a distance, tend on closer
> inspection to become blurred and confused.[17]

15. Goulder does not give examples of the phenomenon from other 'midrashic' writings.

16. The same combination is also a feature of John, especially in 'An Old Friend Incognito', p. 324, 'the familiar Johannine mixture of skill and muddle'; cf. *LNP*, p. 323.

17. *Saint Luke*, p. 42; cf. the excellent summary in Cadbury, *Making*, p. 334, 'Luke's narratives often suggest just such a failure to think the situation through. This natural and almost inevitable defect only the most rigid self-criticism can

Goulder's explanation of extensive Lukan muddle has, then, high-
lighted an interesting problem in the interpretation of Luke and his
solution is, if sometimes implausible, not impossible.

avoid. Imagination rarely is aware of minor inconsistencies, and we need not be
surprised if a writer like Luke sometimes makes such slips, though we may distrust
our own power of detecting them. Often we are only sure that he has failed to make
his stories perfectly clear to us.'

Chapter 12

ORATIO RECTA REPETITIONS (§11)

A. *Preliminary Comments*

Goulder explains that

> Many a preacher tells his story and underlines its point by a homiletic
> 'So then, brethren' conclusion. Luke, with more skill, contrives to put
> the repeated moral in the mouth of his characters (*LNP*, p. 103).[1]

Goulder gives seven examples of this phenomenon, all from Lukan
parables, almost all of these in L (p. 104). In the commentary a couple
of non-parabolic examples are added (see below, pp. 310-11).

In the examples given by Goulder, it is not always clear that it is a
moral which is being repeated. In most of the examples, in fact, it is an
important aspect of the plot which is being given emphasis. Goulder
himself recognizes this in so far as his description of the feature varies
a little. It can be 'the moral' which is repeated in direct speech (p. 598),
or 'his point' (p. 606), 'key messages' (p. 613) or 'key words' (p. 662).
A good compromise is the statement that 'Luke likes to stress his point
by repeating in oratio recta' (p. 561). Further, on one occasion Goulder
speaks not of repetition but of 'oratio recta expansion' (p. 470).[2]

This variation is not important, however. A general definition is
clear: Goulder is talking about the repetition of a point within a
pericope in the direct speech of one of the characters. Sometimes the

---

1. Cf. Haenchen: 'This technique of repetition is one to which Luke always
resorts when he wants to impress something particularly on the reader' (*Acts*,
p. 357).
2. The feature is already noticed in *MLM*; cf. pp. 399-400 on the Lost Sheep,
'the shepherd's words to the company...repeat and drive home the point in the
customary Lukan way'; Goulder compares the Prodigal Son (p. 400 n. 52; cf.
p. 403; cf. also comments on Matthean repetition below, pp. 240-42).

original point is made in third person narration, sometimes in the mouth of a character.

This stylistic feature, like soliloquy or conversation with which it overlaps, lends itself straightforwardly to analysis. Does the feature occur in R and QD sections as well as in L? Is it found predominantly in the parables? Does it feature at all in Mark or Matthew?

B. *Luke*[3]

1. *R and QD*

Goulder does not give any R examples of this feature but he may have overlooked two possible examples, Lk. 8.24-25 (Storm-Stilling; contrast Mk 4.39, 41, a different form of the question, without the statement that Jesus 'commands wind and water'; cf. Mt. 8.26-27) and:

Lk. 19.31, 33-34: καὶ ἐάν τις ὑμᾶς ἐρωτᾷ, Διὰ τί λύετε; οὕτως ἐρεῖτε ὅτι Ὁ κύριος αὐτοῦ χρείαν ἔχει...Τί λύετε τὸν πῶλον; οἱ δὲ εἶπαν ὅτι Ὁ κύριος αὐτοῦ χρείαν ἔχει (contrast Mk 11.1-10).

Goulder gives several QD examples, 15.4-6[4] (Lost Sheep; pp. 104 and 606; contrast Mt. 18.12-14), and in the commentary, 7.19-20 (Messengers from John; pp. 388-89; contrast Mt. 11.3) and 10.9, 11 (Mission Discourse; p. 470; contrast Mt. 10.7 and 11). 7.19-20 is a particularly clear example since the wording of the repetition is identical.[5] Further, the verses which follow on immediately, Lk. 7.21-22, give another possible example of the feature: Jesus is said to cure many and he then announces this to John's disciples. Mt. 11.4-5 has only the oratio recta and not the preceding description.

3. On repetition in Luke, see Cadbury, 'Four Features', of which pp. 88-97 are on 'Repetition and Variation'; cf. his *Making*, chapter 16; R. Morgenthaler, *Die lukanische Geschichtsschreibung*. Luke's 'fondness for repetition' was already noticed by J.H. Ropes in 1901, 'Observation'.

4. In *LNP*, p. 104, Goulder quotes vv. 4 and 6 but there is also a close parallel between vv. 5 and 6.

5. Goulder is a little misleading, however, when he says that this is like the Centurion who 'told his embassy what to say and they said it in 7.3-5' (*LNP*, p. 389). In 7.3-5, the direct speech adds to but does not repeat the (assumed) Centurion's charge.

2. *L*

All the remaining examples Goulder gives are from L parables, all in the Travel Narrative (all p. 104), Lk. 13.6-7 (Fig Tree; also p. 561); 14.29-30 (Tower Builder; also p. 598); 15.8-9 (Lost Coin; also p. 607); 15.18, 21, 24 and 32 (Prodigal; also pp. 613-14); 18.2, 4 (Unjust Judge; also p. 662). These examples are all clear.

A good example not mentioned by Goulder is the following:

1.41, 44: καὶ ἐγένετο ὡς ἤκουσεν τὸν ἀσπασμὸν τῆς Μαρίας ἡ Ἐλισάβετ, ἐσκίρτησεν τὸ βρέφος ἐν τῇ κοιλίᾳ αὐτῆς...ἰδοὺ γὰρ ὡς ἐγένετο ἡ φωνὴ τοῦ ἀσπασμοῦ σου εἰς τὰ ὦτά μου, ἐσκίρτησεν ἐν ἀγαλλιάσει τὸ βρέφος ἐν τῇ κοιλίᾳ μου.

Other possible examples are 7.38, 44-46 (The Sinner), 10.40-41 (Mary and Martha) and perhaps also 16.24-25 (Dives).

There is, then, no doubt that this is a recurring feature in Luke's special material.[6]

C. *Mark and Matthew*

On the other hand, though, the feature is also common in the other Gospels.[7] In Mark, there are many instances, for example:

Mk 2.16: καὶ οἱ γραμματεῖς τῶν Φαρισαίων ἰδόντες ὅτι ἐσθίει μετὰ τῶν ἁμαρτωλῶν καὶ τελωνῶν ἔλεγον τοῖς μαθηταῖς αὐτοῦ, "Ότι μετὰ τῶν τελωνῶν καὶ ἁμαρτωλῶν ἐσθίει;

Here one might contrast the parallels Mt. 9.11-12 and Lk. 5.30, both of which omit Mark's notice in v. 16a. Another clear example is:

Mk 10.32-33: ἦσαν δὲ ἐν τῇ ὁδῷ ἀναβαίνοντες εἰς Ἱεροσόλυμα...Ἰδοὺ ἀναβαίνομεν εἰς Ἱεροσόλυμα...

Here, Mt. 20.17-18 is similar but Lk. 18.31 has only Jesus' statement.

Other examples are found at Mk 1.22, 27 (Capernaum Synagogue; cf. Lk. 4.32, 36);[8] Mk 2.8 (Paralytic; cf. Mt. 9.4 and Lk. 5.22);

---

6. There is also an outstanding example of the feature in Acts 10–11, Peter and Cornelius.

7. The classic study on Markan repetition is F. Neirynck's *Duality in Mark*.

8. This example is affected both by one's reading of the MSS and by one's punctuation of the verse. However it is read, though, the links between 'teaching' and 'authority' remain. There is, further, an obvious link between the teaching being 'new' and 'not as the scribes'.

Mk 3.31-32 (Mother and Brothers; cf. Mt. 12.46-47;[9] contrast Lk. 8.19-20 which omits the 'standing outside'); Mk 5.27-28 (Woman with Flux; cf. Mt. 9.20-21; contrast Lk. 8.44); Mk 5.38-39 (Jairus; contrast Mt. 9.23-24 and Lk. 8.52 which omits the 'tumult' element); Mk 7.2-3, 5 (Traditions; contrast Mt. 15.2); Mk 8.1-2 (Four Thousand; contrast Mt. 15.32); Mk 8.11-12 (Sign; cf. Mt. 16.1-4; contrast Mt. 12.38-42 // Lk. 11.16, 29-32); Mk 11.20-21 (Fig Tree; cf. Mt. 21.19-20); Mk 11.28-29, 33 (Authority; cf. Mt. 21.23-27; contrast Lk. 20.1-8 which has parallels to the first and third but not the second of Mark's 'by what authority...' question/statements); Mk 12.29-32 (Commandment; contrast Mt. 22.34-40 and Lk. 10.25-28); Mk 14.35-36 (Gethsemane; contrast Mt. 26.39 and Lk. 22.41-42);[10] Mk 15.46 and 16.3 (Stone; contrast Mt. 27.57–28.10 and Lk. 23.50–24.11).[11]

Oratio recta repetition, although it never occurs in a parable, is a common feature in Mark's Gospel. Further, although there are a couple of examples of Luke enhancing the feature in R material (see above, p. 239), the feature is more often diminished in the Lukan parallel (see the parallels to Mk 2.16; 3.31-32; 5.27-28; 5.38-39; 10.32-33; 11.28-29 and 33; 14.35-36; and 15.41 and 16.3).

In Matthew's parallels to Mark, the feature is also often diminished (see the parallels to Mk 2.16; 5.27-28; 7.2-3 and 5; 8.1-2; 12.29-32; 14.35-36; 15.46 and 16.3) but also, like Mark and Luke, he has his own examples of the feature, found in M (13.24-28; 25.31-46), QC (7.3-5), QD (11.20-21 and 25.14-30) and R (28.7, 10) material. Most relevant to Goulder's thesis is the occurrence of the feature several times in Matthean parables, for example the Unmerciful Servant (Mt. 18.21-35):

Mt. 18.26, 29: πεσὼν οὖν ὁ δοῦλος προσεκύνει αὐτῷ λέγων, <u>Μακροθύμησον ἐπ' ἐμοί, καὶ πάντα ἀποδώσω σοι</u>...πεσὼν οὖν ὁ σύνδουλος αὐτοῦ παρεκάλει αὐτὸν λέγων, <u>Μακροθύμησον ἐπ' ἐμοί, καὶ ἀποδώσω σοι</u>.

---

9. The oratio recta repetition is only there in Matthew if one reads 12.47 with Greeven; N-A[26] places the verse in square brackets. If one does read the verse, the parallel is stronger in Matthew than in Mark, εἱστήκεισαν ἔξω / ἔξω ἑστήκασιν.

10. Cf. also Mk 14.33-34 // Mt. 26.37-38 and Mk 14.37 // Lk. 22.45-46 for other possible examples of oratio recta repetition in the same pericope, the first not present in Lk. 22.39-40 and the second not present in Mt. 26.40.

11. Other possible but less impressive examples include Mk 13.1-2, contrast Mt. 24.1-2 and Lk. 21.5-6; Mk 14.43, 48 // Mt. 26.47, 55, the repetition not present in Lk. 22.47-53; Mk 15.3-4 // Mt. 27.12-13, not in Lk. 23.1-5.

It occurs also in 13.24-30, the Tares; 25.14-30, the Talents and 25.31-46, Sheep and Goats and possibly 22.11-12, Wedding Garment.[12] On one of these occasions, the parable of the Talents, Luke has a parallel (Lk. 19.11-27) in which the degree of oratio recta repetition is substantially reduced.

Goulder is aware of this element in Matthew and, indeed, some of the above examples are used in *MLM* to show that Matthew too is fond of repetition (Unmerciful Servant, pp. 402-403; Talents, p. 403, contrasting Luke's Pounds; Sheep and Goats, p. 444).[13] Goulder makes a distinction, however, between the evangelists' use of repetition: in Matthew it is 'to give higher relief to a contrast' whereas in Luke it is 'to drive home a teaching' (*MLM*, p. 403, n. 64). This probably needs modifying in two ways. First, we have seen in Luke that it is not always a 'teaching' or a 'moral' which is being repeated, and, second, the repetition in, say, the Wheat and the Tares in Matthew is clearly not 'to give higher relief to a contrast'. But further, whatever the motivation for and function of the feature, 'oratio recta repetition' is undoubtedly present, and is common, in all the Synoptics.

D. *Conclusion*

Oratio recta repetition is a common feature in Luke. It occurs in R and QD material, but it is primarily a characteristic feature of the L material, in which it occurs mainly in parables. The feature is by no means distinctive of Luke, however. It is common in Mark, and Luke often reduces elements of it in parallel passages. The feature is also common in Matthew. It is not as common in his parables as it is in Luke's, but the Parable of the Talents (Mt. 25.31-46) provides an

---

12. Cf. Bultmann, *History*, p. 191, on 'the law of repetition' in parables—'typical of popular story telling', including the Talents and the Unmerciful Servant among examples.

13. Goulder is partly dealing here with the potential difficulty for his thesis that doublets might show different sources: 'doublets constitute no argument for the use by Matthew of two different sources' (*MLM*, p. 38). His answer is to stress that doublets, and repetition in general, are characteristic of Matthew, and 'repetitiveness is too common a rabbinic trait to need illustration' (p. 37). Cf. also Goulder's regular point in *MLM* that Matthew is fond of turning third person narration into oratio recta, pp. 242, 287, 298-99, 334, 339, 347 and 418.

outstanding example of oratio recta repetition not present in its parallel in Luke (19.11-27).

This feature is, then, characteristic but not distinctive of Luke. Goulder's overall case is a cumulative one, and the more stylistic features like this prove not to be distinctive, the less cumulative weight his thesis will have. However, even if the feature had proved distinctive of Luke, on its own it could only have provided evidence for a limited degree of Lukan creativity: this is the kind of stylistic trait which an author might easily work in to his sources. The synoptic parallels often provide us with a version of the story which does not have oratio recta repetition, therefore it is in the nature of the feature that one can imagine the story being told without it.

Chapter 13

INFERENCE OF SETTING (§13)

A. *Preliminary Comments*

'Inference of Setting' (p. 105) is like 'Muddle' before it and several
other sections after it, one of Goulder's proposed means of understanding how Luke's mind worked and how he proceeded when he
wrote his Gospel.[1] Although the feature forms a vital part of the thesis
that Luke knew Matthew and Mark and no other substantial sources, it
is not, even for Goulder, distinctively Lukan. Just as Goulder has
proposed on various occasions that Matthew, Mark and John were all
involved in 'Muddle', so too he has proposed that the other evangelists
used inference. It is, in fact, at the heart of the argument of *MLM*.
'Midrash' is defined from its root *darash*, 'to probe or examine' (*MLM*,
p. 28) and Jewish writers from the Chronicler to the rabbis had a
doctrine of inspiration whereby they would think 'Things must have
been so (in view of the light cast by passage x): therefore they were so'
(*MLM*, p. 31). Goulder explains:

> The process of elaborating such new stories is a controlled religious
> exercise, which the Jews called 'discovery' (*midrash*), *the discovering of
> what must have happened*: it does not mean, as has sometimes been
> thought, the making up of fairy stories ('The Empty Tomb', p. 206;
> Goulder's italics).

In *LNP* the term 'midrash' is dropped (pp. 127-28) though Goulder
retains the essential idea. Goulder now uses several different words to
describe the creative process and one of these is 'inference'. Just as in
MLM the Chronicler's work was midrashic, so now he works by
inference.[2]

---

1.   Cadbury's 'Indication of Setting' (*Style*, pp. 119-26) discusses the same
essential phenomenon.
2.   John too used his considerable 'powers of inference' in order to add

Some of the difficulties encountered elsewhere are here too. There is an element of circularity and to this we will return. Further, the description of the feature is not exact. Goulder gives examples of Luke's 'inference of setting' in his introduction, but in the commentary the feature is usually simply called 'inference' and it can be connected with characters or plot developments.

In order to understand and analyse this feature properly, it will be best to look at each of Goulder's examples in turn. He says that 'A number of such inferences will be suggested in the commentary' (*LNP*, p. 105), and it is in the nature of the feature that inferences have to be 'suggested' rather than pointed out. Goulder does not assert but argues each case of inference, however, and the reader needs to decide whether or not the arguments explain the evidence convincingly.

B. *Goulder's Examples*

1. *The Catch of Fish (Luke 5.1-11)*

Luke is held to have discovered what actually happened when the first disciples were called in Mk 1.16-20 // Mt. 4.18-22. Goulder's explanation is detailed (pp. 316-22) — he accounts for each element of the story, most of it in terms of Luke's powers of inference. The key element is that Luke inferred the disciples' motivation in following Jesus:

> For in Luke's belief fishing was done with the aid of lights by night (5.5); and his predecessors describe Peter and Andrew as casting their nets in what is plainly daytime. It seems clear to him therefore that they are desperate: *they have toiled all the night and taken nothing* (p. 318; Goulder's italics).

Mark and Matthew say that James and John were mending their nets (καταρτίζοντας τὰ δίκτυα, Mk 1.19 // Mt. 4.21):

> Now how can one take nothing all night and find holes in the nets in the morning? Plainly (runs the evangelist's logic), something has happened...Jesus will have told Simon to launch out into the deep and let down for a catch... It is this huge catch which will have convinced Simon of the Lord's divine power' (pp. 318-19).

Beloved Disciple material to his Gospel, 'An Old Friend Incognito', p. 502. For the same phrase of Luke, see *LNP*, pp. 319 and 747.

Goulder has worked out Luke's inference by drawing together three threads: the idea that Luke envisaged fishing at night,[3] the assumption that the disciples were fishing in the daytime in Matthew and Mark and the fact that James and John were putting their nets in order in Matthew and Mark. However, we only know that Luke thought fishing could take place at night by 5.5, 'we have toiled all night', but Luke is supposed to have done his inferring from Mark and Matthew. This is a new element which Luke has introduced, and to use the verse as part of the proof of Luke's creation of the incident draws one into a circle. In any case, though, the opposition between day and night is artificial: the Markan and Matthean accounts say nothing about when the event occurred.

Further, καταρτίζοντας could just as well mean 'washing' the nets as 'mending' holes in them, and it is James and John and not Simon and Andrew who are doing it. By the time the reader is introduced to James and John in Mk 1.19 // Mt. 4.21, Simon and Andrew have already left their nets to follow Jesus (Mk 1.18 // Mt. 4.20). The reader would correctly infer from the Markan/Matthean account that Simon and Andrew were called first and responded immediately and that James and John were found putting their nets in order subsequently.

Luke cannot, therefore, have made the inference which Goulder suggests because the supposed basis of the inference is absent. On Goulder's theory, Luke has disregarded very important elements of the Markan/Matthean account, and if Luke is distorting elements of the text from which he is supposed to be making his discoveries, there is something wanting in both the coherence and the plausibility of the theory.

2. *The Widow of Nain's Son (Luke 7.11-17)*

Luke is at this stage looking at Matthew rather than Mark. At 6.20-49 he has written his own version of the Sermon and then, following Mt. 8.5-13, he has reproduced the story of the Centurion's Servant (Lk. 7.1-10). When writing the Widow at Nain, Luke has an eye on Matthew 9 (pp. 381-85); details are drawn from Mt. 9.18-26 (Jairus's daughter) and the outline comes from Mt. 9.1-8 (Paralytic) and so, too, does the setting of the story, 'inferred by Luke from his *Vorlage* in Matthew 9' (p. 384). Mt. 9.1 speaks of Jesus coming to 'his own city'. Luke infers (wrongly) that this means Nazareth, and since the previous story was

---

3.   For Luke's interest in the night, see Cadbury, *Making*, pp. 249-51.

set in Capernaum (Centurion, Lk. 7.1), and since he thinks of Jesus going round (περιῆγεν, Mt. 9.35) cities and villages in Galilee, 'Luke', Goulder suggests, 'may reasonably have concluded that the place where his raising story belongs is the town next in circuit after Nazareth' which is Nain (p. 385). The direction of the tour is anti-clockwise since Jesus next goes to the Sea of Galilee (8.22) and Bethsaida (9.10).

The first and most obvious problem with this theory is the notion that Luke would have mistaken Matthew's 'his own town' for Nazareth. Goulder explains:

> By τὴν ἰδίαν πόλιν Matthew intends Capernaum, as may be seen from comparison with Mk 2.1; but any ordinary reader would be virtually certain to understand the words to mean Nazareth (p. 385; cf. also p. 119).

Luke has momentarily become, then, like 'the ordinary reader' and this is in spite of the fact that Luke is simultaneously held to be a sophisticated reconciler who has a detailed knowledge of both Mark and Matthew. One can reasonably assume that Luke had read both Mk 2.1 which sets the story in Capernaum and Matthew's and Mark's description of Nazareth as τὴν πατρίδα αὐτοῦ (Mk 6.6 // Mt. 13.54) rather than as τὴν ἰδίαν πόλιν.

Luke is, then, held to be both ingenious and obtuse at the same time, and the question the reader needs to ask is whether it is plausible that Luke could have made such an obvious mistake. In any case, though, Mt. 9.1 would seem to refute the theory since Jesus 'gets into a boat and crosses over' to come to his own city. If Goulder is right that Luke's Palestinian geography is good (*LNP*, pp. 117-19), an inference that Matthew means Nazareth would be out of the question. Here, then, Luke either wrongly infers the setting or his geography is good—one cannot have both.

Further, the argument is circular. To establish Goulder's anti-clockwise circuit, one requires the proposition that Luke thinks Jesus went to Nazareth before he went to Nain. The five points which make up the circuit are Capernaum (Lk. 7.1), Nazareth, Nain (Lk. 7.11), the Sea of Galilee (Lk. 8.22) and Bethsaida (Lk. 9.10). If one takes away Nazareth, the clear anti-clockwise circuit disappears. An aspect of what is being argued is assumed as part of what is being proved.

Finally, it is by no means certain that Luke is looking at Mt. 9.1 here, and I will return to this problem in the next chapter (pp. 258-60).

3. *The Sinner (Luke 7.36-50)*

Goulder proposes that Luke draws forward Mk 14.3-9 and uses his 'skill in inferring unmentioned details' to expand the story (p. 399). Luke makes several calculations. First, the woman must be disreputable—'unaccompanied women roaming the streets at night are not likely to be respectable' and she has ointment worth three hundred denarii—'where is Luke to think a virtuous woman would have got such a sum?' She must then have spent 'the wages of her sin' on the myrrh as an act of penitence. Second, Mark's Simon must have been a healed leper 'since lepers did not entertain normal society but lived apart (17.12)'; he is well off because he can invite lots of guests, and these guests must have been Pharisees because 'they fall to criticizing the poor girl' and Luke tends to stereotype self-righteous Pharisees (all p. 399).[4]

Some of this may strike the reader as problematic. Mark says that Simon was a leper, not that he was healed: to refer to Lk. 17.12 may just beg the question. Mark does not site the action in the evening[5] and Luke need not have assumed that this was an evening meal: Goulder himself lays some stress on the lunchtime setting of the meal with the Pharisee in 11.37 (see below, p. 251).

On the other hand, though, much of Goulder's argument is quite plausible. Scholars have long troubled over the relationship between this story and Mk 14.3-9 (as well as John 12),[6] and Goulder's solution makes sense of Luke's omission of the Anointing at Bethany from his Passion narrative. The procedure supposed, of bringing forward a Markan story and elaborating it, is not unparalleled: the same thing may well have happened over the Rejection at Nazareth in Lk. 4.16-30.[7] The links between the stories are difficult to play down. It is particularly noticeable that they have a similar shape or plot: reclining in Simon's house, a woman anointing, criticism of the woman, commendation of the woman by Jesus.

Perhaps what most would find difficult here is the degree of detail which, on Goulder's theory, is added to the Markan account. Inference

---

4.   See also Lk. 16.14 where the Pharisees are φιλάργυροι (cf. *LNP*, p. 628).

5.   But Jn 12.2, δεῖπνον.

6.   Goulder discusses different interpretations on pp. 403-405.

7.   Goulder believes inference to be at work here too, though he does not refer to the section (see pp. 299-310), probably because the 'setting' is not being inferred—it comes from Matthew; cf. the summary in 'Knowledge', pp. 144-45.

alone does not explain it, and Goulder brings forward two further theories on this passage. First, Luke brings the story of the Anointing forward 'because Atonement is a sufficiently important Holy Day to justify the transfer' (p. 399) and second, Luke is still looking at Matthew 9, on which he draws for details, using also Mt. 18.23-35 for the parable of the Two Debtors. Judgment here, then, depends partly on how one assesses Goulder's 'Combination of Sources' (Chapter 14, below) and the lectionary theory (Part Three, below).

4. *Ministering Women (Luke 8.2-3)*

Goulder comments on the women in Lk. 8.2-3, comparing Mk 15.40-41:

> Mark had 'who ministered to him'; Luke has 'who ministered to them out of their substance'. This looks like an inference, for διακονεῖν might imply provision (Matt. 25.44; Rom. 15.25). Luke, forever in quest of explanations (§13), wonders where the money came from to support the Lord's company in a prolonged tour, and Mark's comment on the women's 'ministering' seems to supply the answer (p. 409).

This appears quite plausible.[8] Goulder adds, though, a rare note here that the names of Joanna and Susanna 'must be from the *Sondergut*'.[9] If so, it would seem likely that Luke would know not just their names but also their functions and, indeed, Goulder is for once 'in two minds' about whether or not this is the case.[10]

5. *Withdrawal to Bethsaida (Luke 9.10)*

When commenting on the Five Thousand, Goulder says:

> Herod is after Jesus at 9.9, and at 9.10 Jesus withdraws apart to a town called Bethsaida, which is not in the Markan parallel: but is mentioned

---

8.   Cf. Evans, *Saint Luke*, pp. 366-67: the suggestion is 'implicit' in Mk 15.40-41 (assuming that 14.50-51 is a printing error). Also on p. 365, 'It could reflect independent historical research on his part'.

9.   In striking contrast to Goulder's claim in 'The Empty Tomb', pp. 211-13 that the names of the women in Mk 15–16 were 'discovered' by means of midrash.

10.   Contrast also 'Order of A Crank', pp. 115-16, where Goulder sees Lk. 8.1-3 as based on Mt. 8.14-17, the healing of Peter's mother-in-law who 'ministered' to them, and the 'healing' of many δαιμονιζομένους. This is the kind of 'moment that hypotheses like ours can be put to the test', but contrast *LNP* in which Luke is looking at Mt. 9.35 and Mk 15.40-41, not Mt. 8.14-17.

soon after at Mk 6.45—it looks as if Luke knew that Bethsaida was outside Herod's dominion and in Philip's (p. 105).[11]

This suggestion is quite plausible, especially as Luke involves himself in incongruities by relocating the Feeding here (see above, p. 234).

6. *Rejection at Samaria (Luke 9.51-56)*

Goulder proposes that Luke wanted to know why Jesus, in Mk 10.1, went to Judea via Transjordan and says:

> The reason is suggested by Mt. 10.5; there will have been a preliminary incident in which Jesus sent the disciples ahead into one of the Samaritan villages...and they will have been refused. This would then account for both the exclusion of Samaria at Mt. 10.5 and the turn eastwards (p. 459).[12]

On the assumption that Luke knew Matthew as well as Mark, this suggestion is quite plausible. It has the virtue of explaining two oddities. First, this pericope goes against the grain for Luke in so far as the other two references to the Samaritans in the Gospel are positive (10.25-37 and 17.11-19; cf. Acts 8); an inference from Mt. 10.5 would help to explain this. Second, it sheds light on the vexed question of Luke's geography. This pericope and the inferences Luke is making form an important part of Goulder's argument that 'the geographical implications of Luke's writings are in fact astonishingly accurate' (p. 117). An inferred rejection at Samaria would indeed be a reason to see Jesus travelling to Jerusalem at first going eastwards. On the other hand, however, Luke does not here, or anywhere in the central section, make it clear that Jesus journeyed eastwards through Galilee.[13]

---

11. There is no reference to this in the commentary, p. 433, where other reasons are given. Cf. Nolland, *Luke 1–9.20*, p. 440, 'No really satisfactory explanation has yet been offered for Luke's relocation of the feeding to Bethsaida'. Streeter's explanation (*Four Gospels*, p. 176) is similar to Goulder's: Luke has made a deduction from Mk 6.45 that Bethsaida was near where the feeding took place. For a good discussion of the geography, see J.A.T. Robinson, *Priority*, pp. 62-63.

12. Goulder does not designate this as an example of 'Inference' with a reference to §13, but it is clearly envisaged as an example of the phenomenon. Goulder (p. 462) attributes the tentative suggestion of a link between Mt. 10.5 and Lk. 9.51-56 to M. Miyoshi, *Der Anfang*, p. 11.

13. Another possible example of inference here is that the incident gives an explanation of the surname in Mk 3.17, βοανηργές, ὅ ἐστιν Υἱοὶ Βροντῆς (cf.

7. *A Pharisee Invites Jesus to Lunch (Luke 11.37-38)*

As Goulder points out, the scene set in Lk. 11.37-38, where Jesus does not wash before his meal, recalls Mk 7.1-23 // Mt. 15.1-20. 'It looks as if Luke has made two inferences', Goulder says:

> First, they will hardly have known to make such a criticism if they were not at the same meal; second, the meal will have been given by one of their own party, as elsewhere in Luke (§1.6). But then what meal will it have been? In the preceding verses Jesus has walked on the water in the fourth watch of the night (Mt. 14.25)...clearly (to the inferring evangelist) he will have been ready for his lunch (p. 105; cf. also more fully on pp. 517-18).

This is not so straightforward or plausible. The inferring which Luke is supposed to have done concerns the setting of the Markan/Matthean incident: Luke supposes that the controversy which they relate took place at lunch time. If Luke did infer that setting, it is odd that he should have removed the story from the context in which they place it. Goulder would claim that Luke is following Matthew's time scale here, and that the story is in the Matthean order, but even on this logic there is a big jump from Matthew 12 (Beelzebub; Unclean Spirit; Sign of Jonah), directly paralleled in Lk. 11.14-32, to Matthew 15, indirectly paralleled in Lk. 11.37-38.[14] Goulder's Luke feels that Jesus, at this stage in the story, was 'ready for his lunch' but since Luke omits Matthew's and Mark's preceding pericopae (Walking on Water; Healings), his Gospel lacks the motivation for Jesus being ready for a meal.

8. *Myriads Treading on One Another (Luke 12.1)*

After the denunciation of the Pharisees and the Lawyers in 11.37-54, Luke resets the scene in 12.1 before the warning about 'the leaven of the Pharisees', ἐν οἷς ἐπισυναχθεισῶν τῶν μυριάδων τοῦ ὄχλου, ὥστε καταπατεῖν ἀλλήλους. Goulder proposes that 'Luke has again been at work inferring' (p. 529). There are myriads because in 'the previous story in Matthew' (p. 528), Jesus feeds four thousand men plus women and children, that is ten or twenty thousand people, μυριάδες,

Creed, *Saint Luke*, p. 141): Luke could have specified James and John with this in mind.

14. There is an even bigger jump to Mt. 23 which Luke turns to for the rest of the chapter.

> But how could nearly twenty thousand people get close enough to hear
> the Lord? Plainly they must have been treading on one another (p. 529).

Again, this is problematic: the theory is that Luke has inferred a setting
for material he found in Matthew and Mark and then he has removed it
from the context which they provide. Just as in the previous example
Luke loses the reason for Jesus' need for a meal, so here Luke has, on
Goulder's theory, lost the reason for the many thousands by omitting
Matthew's and Mark's previous pericope (the Four Thousand, Mk 8.1-
10 // Mt. 15.32-39).

In any case, on Goulder's theory Luke is inferring a setting in 12.1
for just the one saying from Matthew (and Mark), on the leaven of the
Pharisees (Mt. 16.6 // Mk 8.15). After this, the substance of Lk. 12.1-12
is mainly from Matthew 10 for which, of course, Matthew has another
setting.

Further, Goulder's premise that the thousands must have been
treading on one another in order to hear Jesus is dubious. Luke often
depicts crowds hearing Jesus, presumably without trouble, and on the
one occasion when he numbers the crowd, the Five Thousand (Lk.
9.10-17), he has Jesus 'speaking to them of the kingdom of God' (v.
11).[15]

9 *'About a Stone's Throw' (Luke 22.41)*
Mk 14.35 // Mt. 26.39 has Jesus 'going on a little' from the disciples in
Gethsemane. Goulder says:

> Luke infers (§13) that the distance was 'about a stone's throw', because
> that explains how the disciples could observe what was to follow
> (p. 740).

The suggestion is plausible. This is also treated as an element of Luke's
'concreteness', Goulder's §18—'Luke has been much more specific'
(p. 108).

10. *Kindling a Fire in the Courtyard (Luke 22.55)*
Goulder says:

> Mark...brings Peter into the courtyard, and has him sit with the servants
> warming himself 'by the blaze' (πρὸς τὸ φῶς). Luke infers how this

---

15. Crowds press or throng round Jesus on other occasions: Lk. 5.1; Mk 3.9;
Mk 5.31 // Lk. 8.45.

came to be (§13): 'when they had lit a fire in the middle of the courtyard...' (p. 747).

This sounds quite plausible and is, in fact, an excellent redactional example of the phenomenon.[16]

11. *The Hearing before Herod (Luke 23.6-12)*

The Hearing before Herod is unique to Luke in the Gospel tradition, but Goulder proposes that Luke has 'discovered' it in Matthew's regular designation of Pilate as ὁ ἡγεμών. Goulder gives examples of princes (Exod. 15.15 and Job 42.17) and a king (Mt. 2.6) being given the title ὁ ἡγεμών and says:

> So, since both Matthew's trial scene and his mockery scene begin with reference to ὁ ἡγεμών, it is open to Luke to understand this prince as Herod; and the indications are that he accepted this possibility (p. 58).

Goulder then gives evidence (pp. 758-59) of links between Luke's trial before Herod and Matthew's trial before Pilate. In both, Jesus is questioned, he does not answer and there are accusations from chief priests and others; afterwards Jesus is scourged. Goulder suggests further that Luke inferred good relations between Pilate and Herod (23.12) from Pilate's presence with 'the governor' in Matthew 27.

This is an ingenious proposition, but it is unlikely to win any adherents. In supposing that Luke separated and then distinguished between 'Pilate' and 'the governor' in Matthew, the theory presupposes a degree of pedantry in Luke which the account itself contradicts.

While it is true that Luke does not call Pilate ὁ ἡγεμών, it is also the case that he does not call Herod ὁ ἡγεμών and elsewhere in the Gospel, Herod is a tetrarch (3.1, 19; 9.7-9; Acts 13.1, cf. Acts 12 'King' Agrippa) and the related verb ἡγεμονεύω is connected with Pilate in 3.1 (ἡγεμονεύοντος Ποντίου Πιλάτου τῆς Ἰουδαίος).[17]

Further, it is quite clear that the terms 'Pilate' and 'the governor' are used interchangeably in Matthew 27. Verses 15 and 17, for example, clearly demonstrate the link:

16. Cf. Donald Senior, *Passion*, p. 96.
17. Cf. Lk. 20.20 where ὁ ἡγεμών most naturally refers not to Herod but to Pilate. The word ἡ ἡγεμονία is connected with Tiberius in 3.1.

Mt. 27.15, 17: κατὰ δὲ ἑορτὴν εἰώθει <u>ὁ ἡγεμὼν</u> <u>ἀπολύειν</u> ἕνα τῷ ὄχλῳ δέσμιον ὃν <u>ἤθελον</u>...συνηγμένων οὖν αὐτῶν εἶπεν αὐτοῖς <u>ὁ Πιλᾶτος</u>, Τίνα <u>θέλετε</u> <u>ἀπολύσω</u> ὑμῖν...[18]

C. Conclusion

Some of Goulder's suggestions of Lukan inference are plausible. In particular, the suggestions that Luke has made redactional additions to Mark at 22.41, 'about a stone's throw', and 22.55, the fire being kindled, are strong. The suggestion about Bethsaida (9.10) is likely and the suggestion about the Ministering Women (8.2-3) is quite possible. The extensive inference supposed in Lk. 7.36-50 (Sinner) is quite plausible but does not explain the whole pericope. Luke 9.51-56 (Rejection in Samaria) is similar.

Less plausible are the theses on the Catch of Fish (5.1-11), the Pharisee inviting Jesus to lunch (11.37-38) and the Myriads (12.1). For the first of these to work, Luke will have to have distorted the text (Mk 1.16-20 // Mt. 4.18-22) from which he was supposed to be making inferences. On both 11.37-38 and 12.1, Goulder is proposing that Luke behaved quite oddly: he inferred settings for Matthean/Markan events; he then removed these events from their original context and, by doing so, lost the reason behind settings he had inferred. This touches on the wider issue of Luke's order in the Travel Narrative and it does not lend support to Goulder's thesis that Luke was working systematically through Matthew.

Least plausible, though most ingenious, are the theses about Nain (7.11) and the hearing before Herod (23.6-12). On both occasions Luke is supposed to have been quick in his inferences but slow in realizing that they were wrong. By 'his own town' Matthew does not mean Nazareth and by 'the governor' Matthew does not mean Herod.

It is in these last two cases that Goulder can be seen to be looking most eagerly for some justification for Luke's having created L stories.

---

18. There is one further apparent reference to the feature on p. 742 concerning 22.43-46 but §13 is probably a misprint for §18. See also p. 774: Luke 'uses his powers of inference (§13) to fill in some of the details' of the Resurrection story, on which, see below, p. 258. The explanation of the Resurrection by means of inference is a recurring feature: cf. 'The Empty Tomb' which sees Mark 'discovering... what must have happened' (p. 206) and *MLM*, pp. 447-49, for example p. 449, 'Mark implies a Galilean appearance, which Matthew supplies'.

In the case of Herod, Goulder makes this explicit: before he introduces his theory he says that Luke 'cannot simply have manufactured a hearing before Herod from nothing' (p. 758). This touches on a point which is stressed in *LNP*. Goulder says:

> I cannot emphasise too strongly...that I do not think he ever created anything *ex nihilo*' (p. 123).

The technique of 'inference', sometimes called 'discovering' (pp. 319 and 774), is one of the key ways in which Goulder sees Luke doing his creative work.[19] It is a clever means of letting Luke off the hook: Goulder is attempting to demonstrate the lack of historicity in the L material at the same time as placing Luke in the Biblical tradition of, say, the Chronicler (see particularly pp. 123-28).

Even if wrong about some of the examples he gives, however, Goulder has established a good case for 'inference' as a Lukan procedure since some of his examples, and especially those in redactional matter, appear quite plausible. The question the reader is left with is one of the extent of the procedure, whether it will do as an all-embracing explanation for the creation of whole pericopae, or whether it makes more sense to see Luke inferring only the odd element or detail in a story. The truth probably lies somewhere between the two.

---

19. There are other occasions where Goulder appeals more generally to the feature without expounding clearly how he sees Luke doing the inference or discovering. On p. 319, he lists 13.10ff, 14.1ff and 17.11ff.

Chapter 14

COMBINING SOURCES, SPLITTING SOURCES AND
TRANSFERRING ELEMENTS (§15, §16, §17)

A. *Preliminary Comments*

Combination of Sources (§15), Splitting of Sources (§16) and Transfer
of Elements (§17) are like Inference of Setting (§13): they are proposals concerning Luke's method of composition designed to undermine belief in a special Lukan source. In a section on 'Luke's Special
Material' which is attempting to demonstrate that Luke had no special
source, L, the reader might at first wonder how one can talk about
splitting and combining sources. This is a key point in Goulder's thesis,
however. The L material is not spun out of Luke's head but on close
examination is seen to feature aspects of Mark and Matthew which are
combined, divided up or transferred to different contexts.

As with Inference of Setting, Goulder is arguing a case and the
reader is asked to judge its plausibility. The three features will be taken
in turn.

B. *Combination of Sources (§15)*

This is another feature which is not limited to Luke. Goulder appeals
to a similar phenomenon in *MLM* (pp. 44-46) as an explanation
of Matthew's midrashic procedure under the general heading
'Composition Miracles'. The Chronicler, as often, provides the model—
he 'fuses two stories from Kings into one' (*MLM*, p. 44) in both 2
Chronicles 21 and 2 Chronicles 28 and 'in a similar way, Matthew
combines elements from different Markan miracles' (*MLM*, p. 45). Mt.
9.27-31 (Two Blind Men) combines Bartimaeus (Mk 10.46-52) with

the Bethsaidan Blind Man (Mk 8.22-26) and the Leper (Mk 1.40-45).[1] Matthew 12.22-32 is 'an omnibus healing controversy' and Matthew combines again at 8.28-34 (Gadarene Demoniacs), 20.29-34 (Two Blind Men, for a second time) and combines most ambitiously in 8.5-13 (Centurion, combining the Paralytic and the Syro-Phoenician Woman).

On Luke, Goulder draws attention particularly to the narratives of the Passion and the Resurrection. Luke combines the two Markan meetings of the Sanhedrin into one (Lk. 22.66–23.1, *LNP*, pp. 106 and 752-55); he combines the drugged wine with the sharp wine at the Crucifixion (Lk. 23.36, pp. 106 and 766); and at the Resurrection, his two angels are a combination of Mark's young man inside and Matthew's angel outside (Lk. 24.4, pp. 106 and 774).

Other examples overlap with the 'Muddle' category and are cases in which Luke creates inconsistencies by combining sources or working with several different 'models' (on which, see above, Chapter Eleven). The clearest example of this is 7.36-50 (Sinner; p. 106, cf. p. 402), but Goulder also draws attention to the Temptation (4.1-13, p. 297), the Centurion (7.1-10, p. 106) and 22.30 (Twelve Thrones, p. 732). Luke combines without creating a muddle in the Widow at Nain (7.11-17, p. 106).

Goulder aims here, as often, to take a feature which one can observe in Luke's treatment of Mark and to show that it is present elsewhere too. In this way, Goulder is beginning with the common ground between himself and his opponents and attempting to take them one stage further. The idea of conflation of sources is, after all, presupposed by most who accept the 2ST, especially for Matthew. The fresh element which Goulder is adding is the notion that the combination of sources might explain not only triple tradition passages in Matthew and Luke but also Q and M passages in Matthew, and Q and L passages in Luke. 'The extent of the technique is', Goulder says, 'much greater than is often supposed' (*LNP*, p. 106).

For many of the examples Goulder has made a strong case: Luke's version of the Centurion's Servant differs from Matthew's account at some of the very points which it shares with the Cornelius story in Acts 10. Likewise, it is quite plausible that in 7.11-17 (Widow of Nain),

---

1. Schweizer has (independently) the identical view, 'Matthew is trying to fill what he felt to be a gap... He uses the Markan account of the healing at Jericho but transfers it to the vicinity of Capernaum, drawing on motifs from that account as well as on the verses he omits from the healing of the leper.' (*Matthew*, pp. 230-31).

Luke has drawn on the raising of the widow of Zarephath's son in 1 Kings 17, especially as we know from Lk. 4.27 that he was aware of the story.

If one assumes Lukan knowledge of Matthew as well as of Mark, combination of the two sometimes appears plausible, for example in Lk. 24.4,

> Mark speaks of a young man sitting on the right inside the tomb, wearing a white robe; while Matthew describes the angel of the Lord as sitting on the stone, with his face like lightning and his clothing white as snow. Luke sees these as two separate angels, then, and combines the description of their apparel (*LNP*, p. 774).

Although Luke also has two angels at the Ascension where there is no justification in Matthew and Mark (Acts 1.10),[2] Goulder's explanation has strength over against alternative explanations of dealing with a contradiction between Mark's and Luke's accounts of the resurrection while maintaining Luke's knowledge of Mark.

If, however, it is sometimes plausible to see Luke drawing together, into one pericope, elements from different sources, it is not clear that the phenomenon will bear all the weight which Goulder puts on it. In particular, the phenomenon simultaneously supports and is supported by Goulder's theories of the reconciliation of Matthew's order with Mark's. This is particularly evident in the discussion of Luke 7.

With the Centurion (Lk. 7.1-10), Luke has reached Matthew 8.5-13 and after this, he finds stories paralleled in Mark. Goulder explains:

> Luke has told the stories of Mk 1.21–3.19 on the understanding that they were a detailed account of what was told in outline in Mt. 4.13b-25. But now here are some of the same stories again in Mt. 8-9, told in a different order (pp. 381-82).

These stories, Goulder feels, 'are not to be so lightly put aside':

> Such deeds are the substance of the Gospel to Luke and he is not minded to omit them. But how can he include them when their virtual duplicates are found in his next chapter in their fuller, Markan form? (p. 382).

So Luke combines details from these stories with 1 Kings 17 for the Widow of Nain (Lk. 7.11-17, pp. 381-87), and with Mk 14.3-9

---

2.   Cf. 'Mark 16.1-8 and Parallels', p. 236: the doubling of angels is a Lukan characteristic so a sign that he has read Mark; the description of the clothes is a sign he has read Matthew.

(Anointing at Bethany) and Mt. 18.23-35 (Unmerciful Servant) for the Sinner (7.36-50, pp. 397-406).

There are, however, a couple of difficulties here. First, by ignoring the stories in Matthew 9, Luke would not be omitting them. Rather, he would merely be telling them in their Markan sequence. On Goulder's thesis, Luke is not always so careful to observe every detail of the Matthean order. When Luke has reached Matthew 13, for example, he comes to 'the continuous Markan story which he has already handled' and: 'The pressure of a sequential following of Matthew is lifted, and he can attend to other matter' (p. 516).

Second, there is a slight tension in Goulder's argument. On the one hand Luke is supposed to be working through Matthew and Mark, meeting each obstacle as he comes to it ('But now here are some of the same stories') but on the other hand he clearly has a plan of what he is going to do ('their virtual duplicates are found in his next chapter').

These criticisms are not decisive, however. Goulder could be wrong about the motivation for Luke's drawing from Matthew 9 in Luke 7[3] but at the same time right that Luke has drawn from Matthew 9. Perhaps the most decisive point in his favour is that the relevant stories stand together in Matthew 9, the Paralytic followed by the Call of Matthew followed by the Jairus complex whereas in Mark they are separate (Mk 2 and 5).

Perhaps the greatest difficulty with Goulder's theory is the connection he makes between the combination of sources and the evangelists' creativity. The degree of Goulder's boldness may here undermine some of the credibility of the thesis. To return to the Centurion's Boy, for example, Goulder says, on Matthew:

> A second version of the paralytic at Capernaum, and of the Gentile woman's daughter, are run together, with other matter, to give the Centurion's Boy, the only healing in the new material (*MLM*, p. 46; full exposition on pp. 319-21).

Then 'by assimilating it to the episode of Cornelius', Luke 'carries the process a stage further' (*MLM*, p. 321) and adds details from Jairus too (also *LNP*, pp 106 and 376-81). Thus, by the time the story has reached its final stage in Luke, it is a mosaic of aspects of the Syro-Phoenician

---

3. Luke shares some language with Mt. 9 here which is not in the Markan parallels; see pp. 383-84 and 398; but Luke has 'Go in peace' in 7.50 in common with Mark 5.34 and not Matthew.

woman, the Paralytic at Capernaum and Jairus's daughter from Mark, Cornelius from Acts and of course the parallel story in Matthew.

When viewed in this way, there is an excess of explanations which detracts from the coherence and plausibility of Goulder's thesis. The Centurion's Boy is an extreme example but it is not very different from, say, Luke 7.36-50 which utilizes parts of five separate pericopae in Matthew and Mark. Under such circumstances, Goulder's supposedly simple solution to the Synoptic Problem begins to look quite complex, and the reduction in the number of sources results in a multiplication of the number of aspects which are utilized from the sources which Goulder does postulate.

C. *Splitting of Sources (§16)*

The converse process Goulder does not, apparently, regard as being quite so widespread. He refers to it only once explicitly in the commentary (p. 207) and in the introduction (pp. 106-107), three examples are given. The first is the denunciation of the Pharisees and Scribes in Matthew 23 which in Lk. 11.37-54 is divided into three woes on the Pharisees and three on the lawyers. If one accepts Lukan knowledge of Matthew, Goulder's argument is quite plausible, especially since there is an analogy in the supposed treatment of Matthew's Beatitudes, eight divided into four beatitudes and four woes.[4] Indeed one might say that belief in Luke's use of Matthew necessarily entails the view that Luke has 'split' his source here, unless, of course, Luke had independent access to other sources for this material.

Goulder's second example is less straightforward:

> In Matthew 1 Jesus is the descendant of David and Abraham, and the angel of the Lord tells Joseph that his wife to be will bear a son, and what name he is to give the child. In Luke 1 Zechariah and his wife are modelled on Abraham and Sarah and the angel of the Lord tells him that his wife will bear a son, and what name he is to give the child: the annunciation of Jesus' birth is made to his mother, and is in terms of the prophecies to David, though with similar naming specification (p. 106; cf. p. 207).

As often, Goulder has moved from a more easily observable example to one which requires more argument and imagination. Luke has divided

---

4. Lk. 6.20-26 and 11.37-54 are compared by Goulder on pp. 519-20.

up two elements of his source, Matthew's genealogy which features David and Abraham, and the annunciation to Joseph; Luke has then superimposed developments of the David and Abraham motifs onto the annunciation stories. There are difficulties here. First, Luke has not simply divided his source (Matthew) but has used it so creatively that it is no longer easily discernible in his Birth Narratives.[5] When the division of a source is so difficult to spot, the reader might wonder whether it is there at all. Second, the Abraham motifs are not concentrated in the Zechariah story: Lk. 1.37, 'For with God nothing will be impossible', part of the annunciation to Mary, clearly echoes Gen. 18.14.

Goulder's third example is similar though less Lukan creativity is involved:

> In Mark Jesus maintains a silence through his trial by Pilate, and after his condemnation is mocked by the soldiers with a 'royal' robe. In Luke Jesus is still tried and condemned by Pilate, but his silence, and the soldiers' mockery with a splendid robe, are transferred to a subsidiary trial before Herod (pp. 106-107).

This is a second explanation for the hearing before Herod, the first being that Luke 'inferred' the hearing from Matthew's use of the term ὁ ἡγεμών in the trial before Pilate. The two explanations are not incompatible and might almost be said to support each other: Matthew's ὁ ἡγεμών would provide the motivation for Luke's division of material in his main source, Mark. While the inference argument is not convincing (see above, pp. 253-54), this one on the division of sources is more plausible, especially as Goulder suggests Luke's political motivation:

> Offensive suggestions both about Jesus' respect to governors and about Roman discipline are thus transferred to a more acceptable target (p. 107).

An important question arises from this, however, on the designation of the category. Twice Goulder has used the term 'transfer' and, indeed, the phenomenon he is here describing is more the 'transfer of elements' than the 'splitting of sources'. If this had been used as an example for the subsequent section which I will look at below, only two examples would have remained, Luke 1 and Lk. 11.37-54, and one

---

5. Others, like Drury (*Tradition and Design*), who see Luke working from hints in Matthew for the Birth Narratives, have not spotted this. The chief authority on the Birth Narratives is R.E. Brown, *Birth of the Messiah*.

of these (Luke 1) is far from being a clear example. Goulder is probably right, therefore, not to lay any great emphasis on this feature which at best is found only 'occasionally' (p. 106).

D. *Transfer of Elements (§17)*

This is another feature on which Goulder does not lay any great stress, referring to it only twice in the commentary (pp. 371 and 742) and giving just a handful of examples in the introduction (p. 107). It is not actually at all controversial to claim that Luke has transferred elements from one pericope in his sources to a context other than that pericope's parallel in his Gospel. It is a widespread feature, already observed by Hawkins who devoted a whole section of his *Horae Synopticae* to 'Words Differently Applied', explaining the phenomenon as the result of oral transmission of material during which 'the round of the words adhered to the speaker's mind more distinctly than the recollection of their original position and significance'.[6]

Cadbury too notices the phenomenon and lists 'Phrases of Mark Misunderstood or Transferred by Luke'[7] and he adds:

> The process of transferring phrases is still more amply exemplified in Matthew's use of his sources. To it are due many of the doublets in Matthew.[8]

Indeed when one turns to *MLM*, Goulder discusses 'Doublets' (pp. 36-38) as an aspect of Matthew's 'Midrashic Method', and several of the examples involve Matthew in bringing forward elements from Mark. Since the Markan source is then also reproduced later, to create the doublet, strictly speaking this is not 'transfer' of elements, but one could easily think of other examples of Matthew drawing forward Markan matter which he does not reproduce later, like the saying on Salt (Mt. 5.13-14) which is paralleled in Mk 4.21 but omitted by Matthew in his parallel to Mark 4 (Mt. 13). Or Mk 11.25, on Goulder's theory, Matthew brings forward to use in the Lord's Prayer (Mt. 6.9-13). As with the combination of sources, this is not, then, a distinctively Lukan procedure.

---

6.   Hawkins, *Horae*, pp. 67-77; this quotation, p. 77.
7.   Cadbury, *Style*, pp. 96ff.
8.   Cadbury, *Style*, p. 103.

Most of the examples Goulder gives are, not surprisingly, from Luke's use of Mark rather than his use of Matthew. Matthean or 'Q' elements are, after all, transferred to many different contexts in Luke, especially in the Central Section. Goulder first cites Jesus' teaching in a boat, moved by Luke from later in Mark (3.9; 4.1) to the Call of the Disciples (Lk. 5.2-3) where there is the additional explanation of the inference of setting (see above, pp. 245-46)—as often, Goulder's features overlap. Second, Luke brings forward 'You are the son of God' (Mk 3.11) to 4.41 (// Mk 1.34) and the feature 'is missing in the "true" parallel, Luke 6.18' (p. 107).

The one example from Luke's use of Matthew is the angels' ministering to Jesus in the Temptation in Mt. 4.11, held over to the angel ministering when Jesus sweats drops of blood in 22.43-44 (p. 742). For Goulder, the apparent 'transfer' provides evidence (among other evidence) that one should read 22.43-44 in Luke, but there is a degree of circularity in this type of argument.

Goulder also discusses, under this heading, the transfer of elements from Mark and Matthew to Acts, in particular elements from Jesus' trial in Mark 14 transferred to the trial of Stephen in Acts 7. Goulder confesses to finding the feature 'puzzling' (p. 107), suggesting that Luke viewed the Church as the body of Christ, freely interpreting the life of the apostles from that of their Lord. Since this is largely the thesis of *Type and History in Acts*, it is surprising that Goulder makes no reference to this book in *LNP*. The thesis of Luke working creatively in Acts could, after all, add weight to Goulder's thesis on the Gospel.

E. *Conclusion*

All three of these features function in Goulder's thesis to add weight to the notion that Luke never created anything from nothing: he was always working from the sources he had available and because the sources were Mark and Matthew, Luke allows us to see his workings.

There is considerable overlap between these three features. Both the splitting of sources and the combination of sources involve transferring elements and some of the examples Goulder gives of 'combining' and 'splitting' might happily sit in the 'transferring' category, elements of Matthew 9 in Lk. 7.36-50, for example, or elements of Mark's Trial before Pilate in Luke's Hearing before Herod. There is overlap too with other categories like 'Inference' (again, Herod) and 'Muddle' (again, 7.36-50; also, 7.1-10 and others).

Neither combination of sources nor transfer of elements are limited to Luke. *MLM* proposes a good deal of combination for Matthew, particularly in 'composition miracles'. Transfer of elements creates some of Matthew's doublets, and other material.

The basic ideas involved in the three features are not particularly controversial: combination of sources, the most important of the three, is presupposed by many synoptic theorists and the transfer of elements has been comprehensively treated by Cadbury. The processes Goulder imagines, however, extend beyond just 'combining' and 'splitting' sources: Luke works creatively as he combines and divides, especially in the Birth Narratives and in ch. 7.

As a result, Goulder's theories here vary between uncontroversial and highly speculative. Although the speculative aspects are sometimes believable, they are also open to the charge of making Goulder's supposedly simple solution to the Synoptic Problem appear quite complex, especially as Goulder deprives himself of reference to the flexibility and fluidity which appeal to oral tradition could give. This is particularly the case in the proposed theories about the Centurion's Boy and the Sinner, both in Luke 7. An additional problem in Luke 7 is the issue of order: although it is possible that Luke has utilized elements from Matthew 9 here, Goulder's proposals on Luke's motivation for doing so are implausible.

Chapter 15

OTHER LUKAN FEATURES

A. *The Parable as Lead-in (§10)*

Three of Goulder's special Lukan features under his general heading 'The Lukan Story' remain. The first of these is 'the parable as lead-in' (§10, p. 103). Goulder gives four instances of this feature, three in his introduction and one more in the commentary. Three of the examples given are of L parables occurring before double or triple tradition material, 11.5-13, the Friend at Midnight before 'Ask and you shall receive...' (pp. 103 and 498); 12.13-31, the Rich Fool before 'Do not be anxious...' (pp. 103 and 537) and 18.9-17, the Pharisee and the Publican before 'Let the children come to me' (p. 667). Goulder says that in the first two cases, 'The parables look as if they were Luke's creation out of the logia material in Matthew' (p. 103), and in 18.9-17, Luke is prefacing Markan material with 'a newly wrought parable of his own' (p. 667).

With Goulder's fourth example, a problem presents itself. He says:

> We have a similar feature at 6.39, where Luke prefaces the Q logia on beams and motes with, 'And he also told them a parable, Can the blind lead the blind?...': this time the 'parable' is from Matthew also (p. 103; cf. p. 369).

The material in Lk. 6.39-42 is all Q, Mt. 15.14 ('And if a blind man leads a blind man....'), Mt. 10.24 ('A disciple is not above his teacher...') and Mt. 7.3-5 (beams and motes). If then Luke has here drawn a short 'parable' from the sources available to him in order to lead into Matthean logia, it is at least possible that on the other three occasions, Luke has not created the parables but has drawn them from different sources. Goulder is attempting here to draw an analogy between Luke's procedure when using Q material with his procedure in L passages. Sometimes this methodology is helpful; here it casts doubt on the basic argument.

A further difficulty is the designation of the feature as 'parable as lead-in'. It is by no means clear that the parables of 11.5-8; 12.13-21 and 18.9-14 mark the introductions of the sections in which they appear. The Friend at Midnight (11.5-8) has an obvious relationship not just with 11.9-13 but also with 11.1-4, the Lord's Prayer.[1] Likewise, the Pharisee and the Publican (18.9-14), also on prayer, has as clear a relationship with 18.1-8 (the Unjust Judge) as it has with 18.15-17, and it is, in any case, twice as long as the passage from Mark to which it is supposed to be a preface. Moreover, both here and with the Rich Fool, Goulder makes his pericope divisions in between the parable and the teaching into which it is supposed to be leading[2]—Goulder does regard 12.13-21 and 12.22-31 and 18.9-14 and 18.15-17 as distinct pericopae. His claim, then, that 'lead-in parables are an extension of the Lukan introductions' (p. 103) does not stand up to scrutiny.

Indeed there are few if any clear examples in the Gospels where a parable does act as a lead-in to non-parabolic speech. Gerhardsson claims:

> There is not one single place where a narrative mashal appears as a kind of proem in a speech, a fanfare drawing the interest to a message which is then developed in general, discursive language.[3]

Gerhardsson feels that the only two examples which come near are the Sower in Mk 4.3-9 (and parallels) and the Lost Sheep in Lk. 15.3-7 and, by contrast, there are many occasions on which a parable 'is placed as a powerful final element'.[4]

In addition, it is worth noting that Goulder appeals to a similar compositional procedure in Matthew too. In *MLM* (pp. 322-23), Goulder expounds the Two Claimants to Discipleship (Mt. 8.19-22) as

---

1. Cf. Bultmann, *History*, p. 324: 'Luke has composed a section on the theme of prayer: 11.1-4 the Lord's Prayer, 11.5-8 the parable of the importunate friend, 11.9-13 exhortation to intercession. He has also brought together the sayings about inheritance, the story of the rich fool and the sayings about Anxiety in 12.13-34.'

2. Contrast Fitzmyer, *Luke X-XXIV*, p. 971: the Rich Fool 'is meant as a commentary on Jesus' saying about greed (12.15)' but contrast Marshall, *Gospel of Luke*, pp. 521-22, 'It could be argued that Luke composed it (and the introduction) as a suitable preface to the Q material in vs. 22ff' but Marshall does not want to argue this. Further, the pericope begins with one of Goulder's foil questions (12.13, see above, pp. 183-88).

3. 'Narrative Meshalim', p. 349.

4. 'Narrative Meshalim', p. 349.

'a midrash on Mark's Storm' which follows on from this (Mt. 8.23-27): the other boats (Mk 4.36) become the two followers in Matthew and the προσκεφάλαιον in Mk 4.38 becomes 'the Son of Man has nowhere to lay his head' (Mt. 8.20). In other words, Matthew composes a story to lead into traditional material. Like Luke, Matthew does this with parables also: he 'composes the Two Sons in the Vineyard out of the immediately following vineyard parable (21.28ff, 33ff)' (*MLM*, p. 322).[5] Again this is a new creation prefacing traditional material. It is not exactly the same as the feature in Luke since in Matthew the parable leads into another parable, but the similarity is clear.[6]

Goulder's section on 'the parable as lead-in' is one of his less impressive Lukan stylistic features. He gives four examples but one partly undermines the argument in being from Q and not L and there are difficulties with the designation of the feature, and especially with the claim that it is related to the Lukan introductions. One might add that there is a degree of circularity in the argument. Goulder says that two of the parables in question 'look as if they are Luke's creation out of the logia material in Matthew' (*LNP*, p. 103), and this is apparently because they are 'extraordinarily apt' (*LNP*, p. 103). The conclusion of the argument, that Luke has composed some parables to lead in to traditional material, is also to some extent the premise of the argument.

B. *Fives and Tens (§12)*

1. *Preliminary Comments*
Goulder says (pp. 104-105) that Luke, unlike Mark and Matthew, likes fives and tens. He counts on his fingers and often has the ratio 10:1 (pp. 104-105). The aim of this section is to see whether or not the evidence from the Gospels bear this out.[7]

---

5.   In Matthew, on both occasions, it is partly because of a lection in hand (*MLM*, pp. 322 and 415).

6.   The opposite is also supposed by Goulder to be happening in *LNP*, p. 564, where the Bent Woman (Lk. 13.10-17) 'provides an introductory story' to make the meaning of the Mustard Seed 'plain'.

7.   F.W. Danker says that Goulder has 'conflicting statements concerning Luke's numerical preferences' (Review of *LNP*, p. 164). But Goulder is dealing with differing phenomena, 'fourfold parallelism' (*LNP*, pp. 113-14) and 'pairs rather than threes' (pp. 114-15) are aspects of Luke's poetry. Fives and tens are mentioned by Luke in parables or sayings; cf. also 'doubled visions' (p. 105).

2. *Luke: Redaction*

Goulder does not give any examples from Luke's redaction of Mark, nor are there many. In Lk. 9.14 R, Jesus has the Five Thousand sit down in groups of 'fifty or so' (but cf. Mk 6.40). In Lk. 8.8, Mark's 'thirtyfold and sixtyfold and a hundred fold' (Mk 4.8; cf. 4.20) becomes simply 'a hundredfold' but on the other hand, at Lk. 18.30, Mark's 'hundredfold' (Mk 10.30) becomes 'manifold' (πολλαπλασίονα).

There are a good number of QD examples of the feature. Goulder draws attention to four (pp. 104-105; also pp. 530, 554, 591 and 681), five sparrows sold for two dinars (12.6), five in one house divided (12.52), the dinner guest who has bought five yoke of oxen (14.19) and numbers in the parable of the Pounds (19.11-27). The strength of these examples is that they occur in both parable and non-parable material and that they involve Luke both in introducing numbers (12.52; 14.19) and in changing Matthew's numbers (12.6, cf. Mt. 10.29). On the other hand, however, the verses in which these numbers occur do not always contain only these numbers. Five sparrows occurs with two dinars; the five in one house are divided two against three and three against two; and the man who has five yoke of oxen is one of three guests.

The Pounds is a strong example—ten servants, one unprofitable; the first servant's pound makes ten, the second servant's makes five; there are rewards of five cities and ten cities; and one pound is given to the man with ten.

3. *L*

There are plenty of examples of fives, tens and the proportion 10:1 in L material. Goulder draws attention to 7.41-42 (500 denarii and 50 denarii, pp. 104 and 401-402); 15.8-10 (ten coins, one lost, pp. 104 and 607); 16.5-7 (a hundred measures of oil to fifty measures, p. 104); 16.28 (five brothers, pp. 104 and 636) and 17.11-19 (ten lepers, one thankful, pp. 104 and 646). Again Goulder's case is strong because the examples given are in both parable and non-parable material. A small qualification is necessary on 16.5-7 which, Goulder says, 'works on the same principle' as the debts in 7.41-42 (p. 104), but the ratio 100:50 is quite different from 500:50 and Goulder does not mention the 100:80 measures of wheat in the same parable.

Further, there are other numbers in Luke. In 2.36-37, for example, Anna has seven years and then eighty-four years. Seventy or seventy-two are sent out in 10.1, two by two. The Samaritan gives the innkeeper two denarii (10.35); the Friend asks for three loaves (11.5); the Fig Tree is given three years plus one (13.7); a woman has a spirit of infirmity for eighteen years (13.11, 16); there are ten thousand soldiers against twenty thousand (14.31) and Zacchaeus will restore fourfold (19.8).[8] There is among these numbers, though, hardly any uniformity or common theme. Goulder seems to be right that Luke favours fives, tens and the proportion 10:1.

4. *Mark and Matthew*

There are lots of different numbers in Mark.[9] The Paralytic is carried by four men (Mk 2.3, dropped in // Lk. 5.18 and Mt. 9.2); the herd of swine numbers two thousand (Mk 5.13, dropped in // Lk. 8.32-33 and Mt. 8.32); Jairus's daughter was twelve and the woman had a flow of blood for twelve years (Mk 5.25, 42 // Lk. 8.43, 42); four thousand are fed with seven loaves and seven baskets are picked up (Mk 8.1-10); and there are seven brothers in the Sadducees' question (Mk 12.18-27). This gives just a few examples.

Goulder says that fives and tens are 'rare' in Mark, especially in 'parables and sayings matter' (p. 104). This is quite right. In Mk 10.30 (// Mt. 19.29, contrast Lk. 18.30, above, p. 268), they receive a hundred-fold now in this time. Other than this, there is the Feeding of the Five Thousand in which there are five loaves and the people sit down in hundreds and fifties (Mk 6.40).

There are different numbers in Matthew too: in the Genealogy, fourteen three times (Mt. 1.1-17); one Lost Sheep among a hundred (Mt. 18.10-14 // Lk. 15.3-7); and forgiveness seven and seventy times (Mt. 18.21-22 // Lk. 17.4) among others.[10]

Matthew does, however, have fives and tens, and in parable material too. Goulder recognizes (pp. 104-105) both the Ten Virgins (Mt. 25.1-13) and the Talents (Mt. 25.14-30) and treats them as exceptions to the

---

8. Some numbers were not open for Luke to change, circumcision on the eighth day (1.59 and 2.21), for example.

9. Numbers in the Gospels, especially Mark, were a favourite concern of Farrer, for example *St Matthew and St Mark*, p. 113: 'One can scarcely put one's finger on an inexplicable number in St Mark'.

10. Cf. Davies and Allison, *Matthew*, pp. 85-87 for numbers in Matthew: the evangelist likes the number three, but also two and seven. See also Hawkins, *Horae*, pp. 163-67 and M.-J. Lagrange, *Saint Matthieu*, pp. lxxxiv-lxxxvi.

rule. Both parables have tens and fives and the Talents even has the 10:1 ratio (Mt. 25.28). Further, although the scale is different, tens occur also in Mt. 18.23-35 (Unmerciful Servant), ten thousand talents and a hundred denarii. This is, perhaps, rather too many examples of fives and tens for one to be entirely comfortable with the notion that they are distinctive of Luke.[11]

5. *Conclusion*

Goulder's claims that 'Luke likes fives' (p. 530), that he 'has tens a number of times' (p. 104) and that he 'is fond of the one-in-ten proportion' (p. 646) are justified. Although other numbers occur in the Gospel, none are as common as five or ten, especially in the parable material. Fives and tens occur not only in L but also in QD; there are hardly any occurrences in R.

Fives and tens are rare in Mark but not in Matthew. Both fives and tens occur in two adjacent Matthean parables, the Ten Virgins and the Talents (though Luke adds extra tens to his parallel parable of the Pounds). One should perhaps add the Unmerciful Servant to the list (Mt. 18.23-35).

The evidence shows that it is possible but not probative that fives and tens in L are an aspect of Luke's own creation. It is possible because, if one assumes that he used Matthew, Luke can often be seen to be adding fives and tens to his source. It is not probative because the feature is not distinctive of Luke: since fives and tens appear in Matthew, they may also have been present in other traditions which came to Luke.

C. *Doubled Visions (§14)*

Goulder explains that

> A feature of Luke's story-telling is the repeated way in which the divine will is made plain by communication to two people, or groups of people, independently (p. 105).

Several examples are given from both the Gospel and Acts and the

---

11. Goulder's figures for δέκα are 3/1/11+1 and πέντε, 12/3/9. Hawkins gives 3/1/10+1 for δέκα, his Lukan figure presumably made up of 14.31; 15.8; 17.12, 17; 19.13 × 2; 19.16, 17, 24, 25. Six of the occurrences of δέκα are in Luke's Pounds. I am unsure how one can arrive at an eleven figure. Of Matthew's twelve uses of πέντε, seven are in the Talents.

feature is, Goulder says, 'not present in any other Gospel'. If Goulder is right, then, it satisfies both the conditions set out in *LNP*, p. 87, of occurring regularly and in marked contrast to Mark and Matthew.

On both aspects, though, qualification is required. First, Goulder gives three examples from the Gospel and two examples from Acts. This is not a large number and further, it becomes clear on examining them that 'doubled visions' is too specific a description of the feature. The first example (p. 105) is indeed a doubled vision, the announcement of the conception of John to both Zechariah and Mary (Lk. 1.13 and 1.36). The second example (pp. 105, 222 and 257) is more a series of repeated visions or revelations, of the birth of the Christ to Mary (1.26-38), to Elizabeth with John in the womb (1.39-45), to the Shepherds (2.8-20) and to Simeon (2.25-35).

The third example from the Gospel (p. 105) is the appearance of the risen Christ to Cleopas and his companion and also to Simon (24.13-35). One might add to this the subsequent appearance of Christ in 24.36-53, but it emerges from this pericope that Luke did not think of the resurrection appearances as 'visions' in the same way that, say, the appearances of angels in Luke 1–2 are 'visions': Luke stresses Jesus' 'flesh and bones' (v. 39).

The two examples from Acts are the appearance of Jesus to Paul and Ananias's subsequent vision (Acts 9.1-16) and then the visions to Peter and Cornelius (Acts 10.1-23; cf. 10.30-33 and 11.4-10).[12] These are the strongest examples of the phenomenon, successive doubled visions, perhaps serving to impress the message on the reader.[13]

The feature is, then, not common but it is present on important occasions, at the births of John and Jesus, at the resurrection and at the beginning of the mission to the Gentiles. This leads to the second qualification of Goulder's position: doubled visions are distinctive of Luke largely because there are few parallels to this material. There is no account of the birth of John in the other Gospels, and there are no resurrection appearances in Mark; of course there are no parallels in Matthew and Mark to the Cornelius story and the Paul and Ananias

12. On repetition in the Cornelius complex, see Ronald D. Witherup, 'Cornelius'.

13. It is probably no coincidence that both of these episodes are repeated in other ways—twice more we hear of Paul's conversion (Acts 22.6-16; 26.12-18) and Acts 11.4-18 repeats the substance of Acts 10. On this, see S.G. Wilson, *Gentiles*, pp. 161, 176-77 etc.

story. It might be added that multiple resurrection appearances are in
the tradition (1 Cor. 15), and in Matthew, Jesus appears first to the
women (Mt. 28.9-10) and then to the disciples (28.16-20). In summary,
Goulder is probably right to point to doubled visions as a distinctive
Lukan feature but one might have some reservations: it is not common
and occurs in material which is largely unparalleled in Matthew and
Mark.

Chapter 16

CONCLUSION TO PART II

A. *The General Argument*

Goulder argues that Luke's Special Material is packed with features which occur 'regularly' and 'in marked contrast with the earlier Gospels' (*LNP*, p. 87). His explanation for this is that the material must be Luke's own creation: his only sources are Mark and Matthew; there is hardly any *Sondergut*.

The questions which naturally arise concern how regularly the features occur and how distinctive they are of Luke. Having looked at each feature listed under Goulder's main heading 'The Lukan Story', I am now in a position to summarize results and review the general argument.

Although Goulder does not make the distinction himself, his features fall broadly into two groups. The first covers Introductions and Conclusions to Pericopae (§1 and §2), Promptitude and Alacrity (§3), Human Characters (§4), Middle-Class Setting (§5), Illustration-Stories (§7), Hortatory Parables (§8), Oratio Recta Repetitions (§11), Fives and Tens (§12), Doubled Visions (§14) and perhaps Allegory (§6) and The Parable as Lead-in (§10). These features are in the strict sense proper to Goulder's argument: he attempts to demonstrate that they are distinctive of Luke or that tendencies within the category (introductions, conclusions, allegory) are distinctive of Luke.

The second group covers Muddle (§9), Inference of Setting (§13), Combination of Sources (§15), Splitting of Sources (§16) and Transfer of Elements (§17). Here Goulder is making proposals concerning Luke's compositional procedure. Although these proposals are used to support the general claim of Lukan creativity, they do not function in the argument in the same way as do the features in the other group. Where one can point to features like fives and tens or oratio recta repetitions in the text, one cannot so clearly point to, for example, inference of setting.

Comparison with *MLM* illustrates this point. Features in the first group mostly contrast with features characteristic of Matthew. Luke has human characters, Matthew has stock characters; Luke's settings are middle-class, Matthew's are aristocratic; Luke has hortatory parables, Matthew indicative ones; Luke has low allegory-content, Matthew high allegory-content. Most of these oppositions are already clear in Goulder's 'Characteristics' article.

On the other hand, Luke shares with Matthew most of the features in the second group. Just as Luke muddles, so too Matthew is involved in inconsistencies (and so are Mark and John). Luke 'infers' and Matthew 'discovers' (and so do Mark and John). Luke combines sources and Matthew combines miracle stories; both transfer elements from one story to another.

It is in this second group that Goulder is more speculative and ambitious. He has to devote more time to these features in the commentary than he does to those in the first group. His argument here is a general one: Luke's hand can be seen in inferring, muddling and transferring, therefore, such matters, when added to the other features, make the case for Lukan creativity stronger.

In what follows, first I will recapitulate the most important points from each chapter above. Then I will summarize these points and comment on them and finally I will draw out the implications for Goulder's thesis, with further comment. For ease of reference I will use Goulder's own numbering of the features (§1, §2 etc.)

B. *Recapitulation*

1. *Introductions and Conclusions to Pericopae (§1 and §2)*
An initial difficulty with Goulder's first two categories, Introductions and Conclusions to Pericopae, is that Goulder makes his own divisions between pericopae and not all of them are straightforward. A particular oddity is 12.41 ('Are you telling this parable for us or for all?') which stands at the beginning of one of Goulder's triads in spite of the fact that it would more naturally be described as a 're-introduction in mid-pericope' (§1.7). Appeals to standard 'Lukan rubrics' are not clear.

'Elaborate Introductions' (§1.1) are not distinctive of Luke, nor does he even have an obvious tendency towards them. Luke's redaction of Mark shows him sometimes making Markan introductions more elaborate, sometimes less. It is characteristic of Luke to have reference to time and place in the Birth and Infancy Narrative but elsewhere it is not common.

Distinguishing 'those addressed' in teaching sections (§1.2) does not mark out Luke from Matthew and Mark but sometimes he is more specific than they. One distinctive feature within the category is the addressing of a particular audience in the hearing of a secondary audience, especially clear in 20.45 R.

The 'evangelist's comment' (§1.3) is not distinctive—all the evangelists have such comments. In introductions it is neither common (only 18.1 and 19.11) nor distinctive (cf. Mt. 11.20 QD and Mk 7.1-4).

'Foil questions, requests and comments' (§1.4) are common in all three synoptics but are particularly characteristic of Luke. The two examples of 'cloying piety' (11.27 and 14.15, §1.5) are distinctive. Also distinctive is the question by a specific person or specific people with a response by Jesus to a wider audience. Controversial teaching set in a synagogue is not distinctive or even characteristic of Luke, but there are three examples of controversial teaching set at meals with Pharisees in the Gospels, all in Luke (§1.6).

Re-introduction in mid-pericope (§1.7) is not a straightforward sub-category because it involves the question of Goulder's own divisions of pericopae—there is an element of circularity. On almost any division of the text, however, the feature is characteristic of Luke, though not distinctive.

In closes to pericopae (§2), the returning home of characters (§2.1) is characteristic but not distinctive of Luke. Characters rejoicing as they return home is almost distinctive of Luke. Notes of progress are distinctive of Luke's Birth and Infancy Narrative (§2.2). Inclusio comes in all the Gospels (§2.3).

2. *Promptitude and Alacrity (§3)*

Some aspects of Promptitude and Alacrity mark out Luke from Matthew and Mark: the use of παραχρῆμα, particularly concerning the fulfilment of an order, and the lively and pejorative use of ἤρξατο (§3.2). The use of ἀναστάς to denote 'get-up-and-go' is characteristic of Luke. Sitting down (§3.1) comes in Mark too.

3. *Human Characters (§4)*

This section is the most important to the thesis on the L material. Goulder's contrast between Matthew's Two Sons and Luke's Prodigal

Son is problematic. It is not clear that the two parables are parallel to one another and Luke too, when the occasion requires it, has a short parable with stock characters, the Two Debtors. Further, Goulder gives an exception to the general rule: Matthew's Centurion (at 8.5-13) is quite human.

The general category has eight subsections. Soliloquy (§4.1) is distinctive of Luke and especially his parables—there is just one example in Mark (12.6 which Luke enhances, 20.13) and one further one in Matthew (12.44 QC), but there are several examples in Luke, mainly in the form: reflection on circumstances with τί ποιήσω; plus statement of future action.

Conversation (§4.2) is not so distinctive of Luke, though it is characteristic of his parables. There are no conversations in Mark's parables, but there are three in Matthew's. Outside parables, conversation is not a special feature in Luke.

Interest in the details of Work (§4.3) is, with some reservations, distinctive of Luke. The main reservation is the omission of the details of the work from Mark's Wicked Husbandmen.

Parties (§4.4) are clearly distinctive of Luke. They occur in parable and non-parable material and in R, QD and L material.

Excuses (§4.5) are distinctive of Luke. There are at least four of them in Luke (11.7 L; 13.26 QD; 14.18-20 L; 16.3 L) and none in Matthew or Mark.

Guillotine Questions (§4.6) are characteristic of Luke but not distinctive. There are good examples in Mark and Matthew, especially Mt. 21.31. The guillotine question with the single opponent is distinctive of Luke.

In §4.7, one needs to distinguish between 'lower-class' and 'disreputable' heroes. Neither aspect is distinctive of Luke, but his is the only Gospel to contain *quanto potius* comparisons in parables (twice) and parables which use disreputable characters to make a point about the well-behaved believer (four times). It is also characteristic but not quite distinctive of Luke to have disreputable heroes in non-parable material. It is mainly a feature of L.

Colourful Details (§4.8) involves two phenomena, occasions on which Luke is more specific than Mark or Matthew (ravens/birds, lambs/sheep) and non-allegorical details in parables. On the first of these, Luke has the advantage in Goulder's scheme of being the third evangelist and there are plenty of colourful details in Matthew and

Mark. On the second, extra comment is required (§6, below).

4. *Middle-class Setting (§5)*

Goulder deals here with the 'scale' of Luke's parables. He is right that there is plenty of middle-class setting: the Great Dinner (Lk. 14.15-24), the Prodigal Son (15.11-32) and the Servant of all Work (17.7-10) in particular. Amounts of money are on a comparatively homely scale and Luke is not positive towards the rich. The feature pervades QD and L and possibly R too and it occurs in non-parabolic as well as parabolic material. There are, however, counter-examples from Luke as well as a range of different settings in Matthew and Mark. This is a characteristic, not a distinctive feature in Luke.

5. *Allegory (§6)*

Goulder is probably right that the L parables have a markedly lower allegory content than the other Gospel parables, but one cannot identify a clear tendency away from allegory in Luke's versions of Mark and Q parables. Goulder's criticism of the parable-allegory dichotomy is valuable, but he tends to oppose allegory and realism unnecessarily, equating 'colourful detail' with 'non-allegorical detail'. The attempt to quantify the allegorical content of the Gospel parables is problematic.

6. *Illustration-Stories (§7)*

Beispielerzählungen, if one accepts the designation, occur only in Luke. The question of Lukan composition turns largely on one's opinion of Goulder's §6 and §8, with which Goulder aligns this feature.

7. *Hortatory Parables (§8)*

Hortatory Parables are characteristic of L material but are less clearly characteristic of Luke's redaction of Mark and Matthew. Just as Luke has some indicative parables, so too Matthew has some imperative parables, the Lost Sheep (Mt. 18.10-14) and the Unmerciful Servant (Mt. 18.23-35), both problematic for Goulder's thesis. To speak of a 'slide' from Mark and Matthew to Luke is more appropriate than to speak of a 'sharp cleavage' between them.

8. *Muddle (§9)*

For Goulder, an aptitude to muddle is shared by all the evangelists, though Luke particularly muddles when attempting to apply parables.

There are some difficulties. First, it is subjective: what Goulder sees as muddle, others might see as profundity. Second, there is a marked element of circularity in the manner of arguing. Third, there is a question of coherence: this category does not sit easily with that on 'Inference'. Fourth, most seriously, there is an element of arbitrariness in the way in which each example of muddle is explained in terms of his own thesis: in Mark and Q sections Luke muddles his sources whereas in L sections Luke muddles without sources. Nevertheless, Goulder has made a strong general case for some Lukan muddle; several of his examples are plausible.

9. *Oratio Recta Repetitions (§11)*
Oratio recta repetitions are characteristic but not distinctive of Luke. Examples are mainly in the L parables but there are some in QD and R. There are several good examples in Mark and Matthew. It is easy to imagine Luke adding oratio recta repetition to whatever sources he possessed.

10. *Inference of Setting (§13)*
Inference corresponds largely with 'midrash' in Matthew. The evangelists do not create from nothing; Luke is cleared from any charges of intentionally writing fiction. Goulder's suggestions vary between plausible, possible and unlikely. It is probable that there is some inference in Luke, but it is not on the scale Goulder proposes.

11. *Combining Sources, Splitting Sources, Transferring Elements (§15, §16, §17)*
The basic ideas behind these categories are uncontroversial but Goulder uses them in unique ways to argue for Lukan creativity. Goulder's Matthew uses the same procedures. A difficulty in the case of combining sources is that the thesis becomes more complex.

12. *Other Features (§10, §12, §14)*
The parable as lead-in (§10) is not common and it is dubious to regard it as an 'extension of the Lukan introductions'. One of the examples given is from Q which may undermine the thesis from within. A similar procedure is used by Matthew in *MLM*. There may be an element of circularity.

Fives and tens (§12) are characteristic of Luke; they come in QD and L material but not R. They are rare in Mark but not in Matthew (Ten Virgins, Talents) so they are not clearly distinctive of Luke.

Doubled visions (§14) are, with some reservations, distinctive of Luke. There are not many of them and they occur in material which has few parallels. 'Doubled Visions' may be too specific a description.

C. *Summary and Comment*

1. *Distinctive Features*

Often, both of the conditions, that a feature should occur regularly and in marked contrast to Matthew and Mark, are satisfied. Distinctive features are: notes of progress in the Birth and Infancy Narrative (§2.2); ἤρξατο used in a lively and pejorative sense (§3.2); Soliloquy in parables (§4.1); interest in the details of Work (§4.3); Parties (§4.4); Excuses (§4.5); Illustration-stories (§7) and Doubled Visions (§14).

2. *Characteristic Features*

Also, often, both conditions are not satisfied: features can be characteristic of Luke without being distinctive: Foil Questions and Comments (§1.4); Re-introduction in mid-pericope (§1.7); Return Home of characters at the end of pericopae (§2.1); Promptitude and Alacrity (§3); Conversation in parables (§4.2); Guillotine Questions (§4.6); Lower-class Heroes (§4.7); Middle-class Setting (§5); Hortatory Parables (§8); Oratio Recta Repetitions (§11) and Fives and Tens (§12).

3. *Problematic Features*

On a few occasions, the features, or aspects of them, are not clearly characteristic: there are difficulties over the Evangelist's Comment (§1.3); Controversial Teaching Set in the Synagogue (part of §1.6); Inclusio (§2.3); Colourful Details (§4.8, specificity aspect) and the Parable as Lead-in (§10).

4. *Distinctive Aspects*

It is often the case that certain aspects in a particular category are distinctive. Sometimes Goulder will have made the extra distinction; sometimes it becomes obvious as one looks at the feature. These are the occasions: a particular audience addressed in the hearing of a wider audience (Those Addressed, §1.2); a question asked by a specific speaker with Jesus' response to a wider audience (Foil Questions and Comments, §1.4) and twice, foil questions of a 'cloying piety' (§1.5); controversial teaching set at a meal with a Pharisee (§1.6); characters rejoicing as they return home (§2.1); παραχρῆμα used of the fulfilment of a command of Jesus (Promptitude and Alacrity, §3); a parable told as the result of a foil question or comment (§4.2, Conversation); guillotine questions with single opponents (§4.6); aspects of disreputable heroes (§4.7); and a master with one servant (§5, Middle-class Setting).

5. *Designation*

A difficulty throughout has been the question of designation. Some of Goulder's categories are all-embracing, allowing one to count a variety of features under one simple heading. This is especially the case in the Lower-class Heroes category (§4.7) where Goulder's own designation of the feature in the commentary varies considerably. The same criticism is pertinent in the case of Middle-class Setting (§5) which is really a question of the scale of the parables. Differing phenomena are included under the 'Muddle' heading (§9); the parable as lead-in (§10) is not carefully defined; Doubled Visions (§14) is too specific a term and Goulder discusses a good deal more than just 'Inference of Setting' under that heading (§13).

The variation in terminology and application often occurs between the introduction and the commentary. This creates a problem: in the commentary Goulder will refer somewhat casually to a certain feature which he has discussed in the introduction, leading perhaps to a false sense of security in the conclusions reached.

The difficulty with this phenomenon is most clearly illustrated from the subsection 'Colourful Details' (§4.8). Among the examples Goulder lists are the specification of Jerusalem and Jericho in the parable of the Good Samaritan and the naming of Lazarus in the Dives parable, but this is a question of one's perspective on the evidence. It might be said that since place names are never mentioned in any of Luke's other parables, Jerusalem and Jericho are a sign of un-Lukan, pre-Lukan tradition. Likewise, Lazarus is the only named person in the Gospel parables and elsewhere Luke drops a name (Bartimaeus).

The point in such cases will be, then, that one may be looking not so much at a Lukan habit of mind as at a clever means of classifying disparate material.

6. *Circularity*

Another problem which has been encountered throughout is the question of circularity. Re-introductions in mid-pericope (§1.7) issue largely from Goulder's own, sometimes unusual, pericope divisions. Some of the examples of 're-introduction in mid-pericope' then serve to reinforce those divisions rather than to bring them into question. Likewise, some of the examples of Inclusio (§2.3) only work with Goulder's pericope divisions. In both cases, potential difficulties are solved by other aspects of the thesis which, in turn, bolster the overall thesis.

Similarly circular is Goulder's use of his own comparison between Matthew's Two Sons and Luke's Prodigal Son, 'the most glaring instance' of the 'contrast' between Luke's human characters and Matthew's stock figures (§4, p. 93). The contrast only works, however, if one assumes Goulder's thesis that Luke has created his parable of the Prodigal Son from Matthew's parable of the Two Sons. The thesis that Luke's characters are human, based partly on this comparison, then serves to reinforce the assumption that Luke's Prodigal Son is based on Matthew's Two Sons. This is a particularly important point since Goulder places a good deal of emphasis on the Two Sons/Prodigal Son comparison; it is a focal point not only of *LNP* but also of 'Characteristics' and *MLM* (see further, below).

The underlying argument in the 'Muddle' section (§9) may also be circular. In Luke's Mark and Q material, inconsistencies result from the use of sources. In L material, the same sorts of inconsistencies are due to Luke's muddled mind. Since it is Goulder's thesis that Luke has created the L material, it follows that Luke must have been capable of muddling without sources. Here it is arguable that Goulder assumes his thesis and then uses the assumption as part of the proof.

D. *Conclusions*

1. *Lukan Creativity*

In spite of several difficulties, at the conclusion of this study there is a partial corroboration of Goulder's thesis on the L material. Since so many of the features which Goulder isolates are distinctive, with many of the remaining ones characteristic, it is clear that Luke has left his stamp on the L material. Much of L is, as Goulder says, 'the substantial handiwork of the evangelist' (*LNP*, p. 122).

The presence of any given Lukan feature in L material is not necessarily an indication of Lukan creativity. After all, one of the more distinctive features, soliloquy in parables, occurs once in Mark (12.6, Tenants in the Vineyard); fives and tens occur in adjacent parables in Matthew (Virgins, Talents, Matthew 25) and the paralytic returns home in Mt. 9.7 MA. On any given occasion, though, the presence of a Lukan feature is likely to be a sign of Lukan creativity. To assign pervasive characteristics of an author's style and interests to pre-Lukan tradition would be unlikely to be persuasive, especially as so often the features are found not only in L, but also in Luke's redaction of Q/Matthew.

2. *The Question of Sources*

If, however, Goulder has demonstrated that Luke wrote creatively in his special material, it does not follow from this that Luke had no substantial sources for it. Let us recall some key passages from the *LNP* commentary section. First, on the Good Samaritan (10.25-37) Goulder says:

> Not only is the language substantially Luke's own: the stylistic features which I have just listed make up the very stuff of the parable. If we took them away there would be nothing left (*LNP*, p. 491).

Second, on the Rich Fool (12.13-21):

> Some of the...details could, of course, have been merely added in by Luke: but others concern the whole mode of the parable—the illustrative story, imperative point, the rich man as horror figure, the animus against wealth, death rather than parousia, the run-up to 12.22-34, and even the soliloquy. What sort of parable is left if we take all these elements away? (pp. 537-38)

These quotations are interesting not least because of Goulder's claim that Luke never created anything *ex nihilo* (p. 123 etc.), a striking contrast to 'If we took them away there would be nothing left'. More importantly, though, there may be flaws in the conception of the argument. Goulder's question, 'What sort of parable is left if we take all these elements away?', is supposed to be rhetorical but there may actually be a reasonable answer to it: if one took all the features away, key aspects of the plot would still be left. In the case of the Rich Fool, much of the essential framework of the story would remain: a farmer's land brings forth plentifully and he builds bigger barns to store his grain and his goods for years to come.

It is at least possible that Luke shared such aspects of the plot of the parable with traditions which he inherited. Comparison with Luke's proposed treatment of Matthew is instructive. In his parable of the Pounds (Lk. 19.11-27), Luke is, on Goulder's thesis, overwriting Matthew's parable of the Talents (Mt. 25.14-30). One of the special Lukan features added to the Matthean account is the ten servants, one of whom is unprofitable, with which one might compare ten lepers, one of whom is thankful, or the woman who had ten coins and lost one (§12). Yet the underlying Matthean plot with the three servants is still evident in Luke in that one never hears about the other seven servants and the third becomes 'the other' (as Goulder theorises, *LNP*, p. 681).

Here, then, on Goulder's thesis, Luke shares important aspects of the plot of the parable with his source, Matthew, but he also develops the story with characteristically Lukan features. It is not difficult to spot the underlying plot in Luke's Pounds because we have Matthew's Talents in front of us and this is the key point, that it is in the nature of the L material as special material that it would not be so easy, if possible at all, to descry precise plots of earlier versions of the stories: this does not mean that earlier versions did not exist.

Comparison between Goulder's proposals on L material and his discussion of Q material is, therefore, helpful. The parable of the Great Supper (Mt. 22.1-14 // Lk. 14.15-24) is more illuminating still. Here, Goulder lists several special Lukan features: human characters, excuses, middle-class setting, conversation, fives, promptitude and allegory (pp. 588-92). Here, though, Goulder does not ask 'what is left of this parable if one removes these points?' because, of course, there is a Matthean parallel. Instead it is noticeable that Goulder says that 'at every point Luke adds life and humanity to his *Vorlage*' (i.e. Matthew; p. 591) and simultaneously, 'For all Luke's alterations, the parable retains Matthew's structure' (p. 589).

Again one can see, on Goulder's thesis, the plot which underlies a Lukan parable. As with the Pounds, on Goulder's assumptions, Luke has developed that plot in characteristic ways. In the Pounds, Luke has added extra servants (and the allegorical political element). In the Great Supper, he has the additional allegory of the Gentile mission.

Further, the existence of a very Matthean parallel to this very Lukan parable alerts us to the possibility that just as Luke was capable of transforming characteristically Matthean parables, so too in L material he might have transformed parables which were quite characteristic of his sources, a point which can again be illustrated from Goulder's discussion of the Great Supper. Goulder argues against attempts to find an original Q version of the parable and says:

> To standard theorists, the existence of common structure and language in the two parables shows that both took over a Q parable; and (on Jülicher's principle, that Jesus' parables had a single point) this can be recovered by stripping away both the Matthean allegory in the body of the story and the Lukan allegory at the end. Polag (pp. 70f) is thus left with the featureless rump to which the Q hypothesis inevitably tends (*LNP*, p. 592).

Now, as Goulder has shown, it is possible to see the parable as Luke's transformation of Matthew 22.1-14 and the Matthean version, which for Goulder is composed by the evangelist, is far from being a 'featureless rump' (cf. *MLM*, pp. 415-18). On Goulder's theory, Luke has recast Matthew's own story, altering the scale and adding characteristic features, with his own message at the end.

Surely it is possible, then, on the basis of Goulder's own arguments on Q passages, that in L material Luke is transforming traditional stories and sayings which had their own peculiar features which are now impossible to recover, just as one could not recover a parable like Mt. 22.1-14 from a study of Lk. 14.15-24 alone. If one had only Luke, one might be successful in recovering some of the features which Luke has in common with Matthew but one would have little idea of the characteristically Matthean features which Luke lacks. On this comparison between Q and L material, the 'featureless rump' would be in the one case the matter which Luke shares with Matthew and in the other case the matter Luke shares with L. The difference between the material would be that in the one case we can recover the original with all its colour (Matthew) and in the other case we cannot.

3. *Oral Traditions*

An important question arises from this. Luke does not, apparently, always overwrite Q material with the same markedly Lukan features as we see in the L material. On the Two Builders, for example, Goulder finds only two of his Lukan features in the redaction, work (§4.3) and promptitude (§3) (*LNP*, pp. 373-74). This touches on the difficulty which many scholars have faced in the study of Luke: why is the evangelist sometimes so conservative in his redaction and at other times apparently so free? John Muddiman suggests in his review of *LNP*:

> If...the L material came to Luke in still fluid oral form, that would itself both explain the higher incidence of Lukan stylistic features, and also—a major problem for Goulder's theory—explain how and why Luke should have decided to treat his source sometimes very conservatively (Mark and the verbatim Q sections) and at other times with such freedom and imagination.[1]

Goulder does not take the question of oral traditions seriously; indeed the theoretical possibility of their existence is hardly considered by Goulder. This is perhaps the greatest single lack in Goulder's thesis, especially since he spends so much time dispensing with theoretical lost written sources.

The theory of oral sources for some of the L material does not simply explain the data as well as Goulder's theory of no substantial sources; sometimes it explains the data better. His 'Muddle' phenomenon (§9), for example, remains a problem. There is an element of arbitrariness (and circularity) in the way in which the feature reinforces the thesis that Luke used Mark and Matthew as well as providing evidence that Luke had no sources in L material.

Goulder's examples of 'Muddle' are better explained consistently. Thus, in agreement with Goulder, Luke will be muddling Mark and Matthew/Q in double and triple tradition material. Against Goulder, Luke will be muddling oral traditions in his special material. In cases like the Two Debtors (Lk. 7.41-43), the Good Samaritan (10.25-37) and most famously the Unjust Steward (16.1-13), Luke will be creating a mismatch between content and context by reapplying parables which originally had different points.

Similarly suggestive for the thesis of oral sources behind some of the L material is the data to which Goulder draws attention in his 'Hortatory Parables' section (§8). Against Goulder, the Two Debtors (Lk. 7.41-43) is best viewed as an indicative parable, depicting the action of God. In agreement with Goulder, the application in 7.36-50 is imperative, stressing love as the appropriate response to forgiveness. Since, as Goulder has demonstrated, Luke has a preference for imperative parables, this situation is best accounted for on the theory that Luke

---

1.   J. Muddiman, Review of *LNP*, p. 178.

adopted an indicative parable from the tradition in order to make an imperative point in his story.

Likewise, the Prodigal Son (Lk. 15.11-32) is clearly an indicative parable, depicting God's joy in sinners' penitence, as on one occasion Goulder admits (see above, pp. 224-25). Again there is at least a hint in the direction of hortatory application, urging the Christian to welcome repentant sinners, as Goulder stresses. This, once more, is a state of affairs better explained by the thesis of Luke's use of oral traditions than by the thesis of no substantial sources. Stronger examples still are found in Matthew: twice it looks likely that Matthew has changed to indicative form parables with essentially hortatory messages (Mt. 18.10-14, Lost Sheep; 18.23-35, Unmerciful Servant).

When Goulder speaks about 'the philosophical priority of consideration for the simple before the complex', he draws attention to the fact that he expounds Luke 'without any elastic hypothetical lost documents at all' (*LNP*, p. 24). Goulder's work is a refreshing, and often justified, challenge to theories of lost documents, but it is doubtful whether one should extend this 'priority of consideration' to cover also the theory of oral traditions which are going to be, by their very nature, lost.

4. *Creative Rewriting of Traditions*

If, then, it seems likely that Luke has been particularly creative in L sections and that he has used some oral traditions, it is worth noting that many of Goulder's own special features lend themselves to such a thesis. One could imagine, for example, Luke altering the scale of parables ('Middle-class Setting', §5) which he received from oral tradition, especially since, on Goulder's thesis, one can see him changing the scale in Matthew's parables (Great Supper, Pounds).

Similarly, if Luke demonstrably reduced the number of allegorical elements in Mark and Q parables (§6), so also could he have reduced them in L parables and if, with Goulder, one agreed that Luke's L parables are less allegorical than Luke's Mark and Q parables, his taking them solely from oral tradition might itself be adequate explanation for the heightened tendency.

Similar arguments would be possible on Hortatory Parables (§8) but also relevant are many of the other features. Just as Luke enhances the soliloquy in Mk 12.6 (Lk. 20.13), so too he could have written soliloquys into parables he received from oral tradition. Likewise, conversation, excuses, colourful details and oratio recta repetitions might all be aspects of the manner in which Luke writes up the traditions he receives.

It should be added, however, that this kind of explanation, though it is persuasive for much of the material, will not do for all of it. The possibility that Luke has, on occasion, created a story himself without any substantial sources should not be ruled out and it is one of Goulder's most important contributions to Gospel studies that he keeps asking us to take the possibility seriously. The difficulty with the thesis is here, as often elsewhere, what Evans calls its 'all or nothing character'[2]—Goulder requires Luke in L material always to be writing with the same degree of creativity, always with the same lack of substantial sources.

5. *Goulder's Alternatives*
Goulder reaches his overarching view of the L material by characterizing and then dispensing with two alternatives. As usual, Goulder is concerned mainly with the parables. The first view is 'the selection hypothesis', the idea 'that certain communities selected from the pool according to their needs' (*LNP*, p. 87). The second is 'the standard view' which originated with Dodd and Jeremias: the parables are essentially Jesus' own, 'but the evangelists have *transformed* them from eschatological, crisis-parables to hortatory, church-oriented teaching, often in allegories' (*LNP*, p. 57; Goulder's italics). Goulder comments:

> The standard view is in difficulties, from failing to see how distinctive are the parables which we find in each of our Gospel traditions. The Lukan community has not only oriented the Lukan parables to the doctrinal needs of its members; it has also put its parables into a middle-class-scale, highly characterized, soliloquizing mode, with disreputable heroes, etc. If the selection hypothesis is rejected, we have nothing left but to ascribe these features to the activity of the Lukan community (*LNP*, p. 57).[3]

What Goulder describes as 'the standard view' is, however, quite old-fashioned and by caricaturing his opponents a little, Goulder is gaining

2. C.F. Evans, 'Goulder and the Gospels', p. 432.
3. Cf. 'Characteristics', pp. 65-67 and *MLM*, pp. 63-64. Goulder is referring at this stage to 'the Lukan community' but he goes on to 'save one further unevidenced hypothesis' and 'say "Luke" for short throughout' (*LNP*, p. 87).

an unfair advantage over them. Dodd and Jeremias pre-date the advent of redaction-criticism and much contemporary scholarship actually stands somewhere between the Dodd-Jeremias school and the general view represented by Goulder (and also Drury). A 'standard view' might be described in this way: many of the parables may well go back to Jesus but oral transmission has exercised its influence and just as importantly, so has each evangelist-redactor.[4] Thus many of Goulder's insights could be accepted at the redaction-critical level without compromising belief in sources for L material.

Goulder deals with 'the selection hypothesis' by saying:

> This is implausible, not only because it is hard to specify these [the communities'] needs, but also because most of the features of difference are not doctrinal. Why should any community prefer Matthew's Two Sons to Luke's Two Sons? (*LNP*, p. 57)

The argument is by no means so clear-cut, however. First, to take Goulder's comparison between Matthew's Two Sons and Luke's Prodigal Son, one might spot differences between the 'doctrine' of each. Matthew's Two Sons is concerned with saying and doing, verbal refusal and actual compliance contrasted with verbal compliance and actual refusal, but there is nothing like this in Luke's Prodigal Son which seems rather to be concerned to stress the correct response to repentance. Each of these themes is quite genial to the respective evangelists, preaching and practice in Matthew (e.g. Mt. 7.24-27, Two Builders; 23.3; cf. hypocrisy) and welcoming sinners in Luke (e.g. Lk. 7.36-50, Sinner; 19.1-10, Zacchaeus).

It is possible to imagine, then, Matthew and Luke each 'selecting' these parables from tradition. In addition, the 'needs' to which Goulder refers do not have to have been purely 'doctrinal'. The art of constructing a narrative produces its own demands—the evangelists might have chosen to use a particular parable because it was appropriate at a given point in the Gospel. This is true even on Goulder's thesis: in his category 'the parable as lead-in' (§10), Goulder draws attention to Lk. 6.39 where the evangelist apparently uses an appropriate Q logion

---

4.   A good recent example of this balanced view is Sanders and Davies, *Studying*, especially p. 176. The view which Goulder caricatures a little in *MLM*, p. 64 is actually quite similar to this, 'We do not possess a gallery of parables, all of which are substantially the parables of Jesus, but which the handling of the churches or the tendency of the evangelists has distorted and spoiled'.

('Can the blind lead the blind?') to introduce other Q material (beams and motes) taken from elsewhere in Matthew (*LNP*, p. 103). It is only a small extension of the principle to imagine Luke drawing other appropriate parables from sources unknown to us.

Further, when dealing with 'the selection hypothesis', Goulder seems to be imagining one 'pool' which contained all of the pre-Gospel parables. The picture is apparently of one huge mass to which all the evangelists had equal access. On this model, it will always be necessary to ask why an evangelist prefers one parable to another, the Two Sons, say, to the Prodigal Son. If, however, one were to imagine a live oral tradition with which the evangelists themselves interacted, the evangelists' non-selection of certain parables ceases to be a problem.

It is necessary to discuss 'the selection hypothesis' at this length because, although Goulder describes it as 'pre-modern', implying that it is disreputable, actually it is often this and not 'the standard view' which is the opponent in the underlying argument. When Goulder is making his conclusions on the Lukan features, for example, he says:

> It is much more likely that repeated features will be from Luke than that repeated words will. For words may be indicative of interest: Luke might, for example, deliberately select stories about rich people which the others did not, and so have more instances of πλούσιος...But features are much more subtle and so less liable to being selected. If Jesus told a span of parables, some with millionaires and some with middle-income farmers, it would be unlikely that the doctrinal interest, for which an evangelist might choose his parables, would exactly correspond with the tricky details of income level (*LNP*, p. 122).

Here, quite clearly, Goulder has 'the selection hypothesis' in mind and the argument has a further flaw: Goulder drives too strong a wedge between 'the doctrinal interest' and 'the tricky details of income level'. The best illustration of this is the comparison between Mt. 18.23-35 (Unmerciful Servant) and Lk. 7.41-43 (Two Debtors). Goulder says:

> He [Luke] feels, as so often (§5) ill at ease with Matthew's millions, and brings the figures down to the kind of debt all too familiar to his own congregation (*LNP*, p. 401).

This is to ignore the meaning, or 'the doctrinal interest' of the respective parables. If one reads the Unmerciful Servant as an allegory, as Goulder does, the first debt, ten thousand talents, is colossal because the king represents God and the debt is the believer's sin which God forgives. There is a more 'down-to-earth' debt in the parable, the one hundred denarii owed by a fellow-servant, representing sins committed against a believer by his fellow-believer. The Matthean doctrine of forgiving our debtors as God has forgiven us (cf. Mt. 6.12, 14-15; 18.15-22) is made not in spite of but by means of the contrasting debt amounts—they are not 'tricky details'.

In Luke's Two Debtors a colossal debt is not required by the doctrine of the parable, that one who is forgiven more will love more; two contrasting, more down-to-earth amounts will suffice.

It will not, of course, always be the case that doctrine and setting will be related in this way, but even when there is no clear correlation, one can imagine Luke altering the scale of parables which came to him from oral tradition. On Goulder's thesis itself, one can see Luke altering the scale of Matthean parables (Great Supper; Talents/Pounds). This casts further doubt on Goulder's criticism of 'the selection hypothesis'—an evangelist might 'select' a certain parable for its 'doctrinal interest' and then change its scale.

Through all of these matters, it becomes clear that a hypothesis which imagines the evangelists selecting certain materials from the traditions they received may not be as outdated and disreputable as Goulder suggests. The evangelists are all involved with making choices about what material to include and what to omit. Goulder's Luke does this with Matthew and Mark; it is only a small extension of the principle to imagine him doing the same with oral traditions. The word 'selection', however, is not a helpful one. Just as Luke, on Goulder's thesis, interacts with the traditions he finds in Matthew in Mark, to some extent making them his own, so too one can imagine the evangelist interacting creatively with oral traditions, making them to a large extent his own.

The difficulty, in short, with Goulder's thesis on the L material is the logic of the argument: either the whole of any given parable comes from Luke or the whole of it comes from the tradition; since there are so many Lukan features in the parables, the parables must come from Luke and not from the tradition. The argument does not work because it assumes as its opponent not so much a standard redaction-critical viewpoint as an outmoded 'selection hypothesis'. If one were, on the contrary, to accept a redactional-critical approach and to combine it with aspects of what Goulder calls 'the selection hypothesis', many of Goulder's insights could be accepted: Lukan creativity but not at the expense of no substantial sources in L.

6. *Summary and Final Comment*

Goulder concludes his discussion of Luke's special material by saying:

> A lower-class hero is hero of the whole parable, and a succession of human, non-allegorical features, with soliloquies, etc., can only be removed from the canvas at the cost of leaving not much paint on the picture. So the practical result of isolating the Lukan features is constantly to increase the element of Lukan creativity, and to make more difficult the hypothesis of the Lost Source (*LNP*, p. 123).

Goulder has successfully isolated several Lukan features, the pervasiveness of which suggests that in L material Luke is particularly creative. This is Lukan creativity on the kind of scale which would necessitate the abandonment of any theory on which the evangelist draws conservatively on a written L text. Goulder has not, however, given adequate attention to the possibility that Luke has creatively written up stories which he received from oral traditions; much of the data he presents makes best sense on such a view.

In his special material Luke is not merely drawing inspiration from hints in Matthew. Rather, to extend Goulder's metaphor, Luke is painting his own versions of earlier pictures. He uses his own shades, his own favourite colours, making his characters lively and human. Some of the features in the earlier pictures are genial to his taste; other features he adds himself. At times Luke's genius creates imaginative settings for his paintings; at other times his ambition is greater than his capability. Goulder's important contribution to the study of L material is, however, the demonstration that these paintings are indeed Luke's own handiwork.

Part III

THE LECTIONARY THEORY

Chapter 17

INTRODUCTION TO PART III: THE LECTIONARY THEORY

A. *Preliminary Comments*

At the beginning of *The Evangelists' Calendar*, Michael Goulder questions 'the calling of the various biblical units by the term *sepher*, βιβλίον, a book: for we handle books daily, and we think we know what the word means'. Goulder attempts to imagine the situation in the first century and asks:

> Did one walk down the Argiletum and say to a bookseller, 'Good morning. A copy of Horace's *Satires* please. Oh, and have you *The Acts of the Apostles*? By Dr Lucas, of Corinth'? How were ancient books advertised? It was often the practice for an author to become known by giving readings in public or at private dinner-parties. Did Luke perhaps give readings at dinner-parties? If so, to judge by the general tenor of the Gospel at least...they will have been Christian dinner-parties; and Christian dinner-parties sound like church services (*EC*, p. 1).

He goes on to argue that the gospels are 'too long and too rich' to be read 'all at one sitting', that later use shows subdivision for lectionary purposes, and:

> The use suggests the intention: perhaps the Gospel was first meant for church reading (*EC*, pp. 2-3).

It would be difficult to underestimate the importance of the lectionary theory in Goulder's work. Of his first two books on the Gospels, *MLM* was 'partly given to calendrical claims' and *EC* was 'wholly' given to the lectionary theory (*LNP*, p. 147). Goulder has also written an article expounding 'The Liturgical Origin of St John's Gospel',[1] and he revised his lectionary theory on the synoptics

1.   Goulder revised the paper in 'The Paschal Liturgy in the Johannine

in *LNP*, chapter five.[2] One might see in this preoccupation with the theory, especially in the 1970s, an earlier attempt at 'a single unitary hypothesis, one overarching theory' which explains how the Bible came to be.[3] Goulder says, for example:

> The lectionary theory which I am inviting my readers to consider is not a frail attempt to undergird a corner of biblical literature. It is an attempt to interpret the whole of Scripture as liturgical, in origin and in use (*EC*, p. 131).

B. *The Passion as Liturgy*

Aspects of Goulder's theory have, at first sight, quite a compelling nature. Strongest of all is what might be described as the starting point of the hypothesis, the Passion narrative in all four Gospels. The theory is little known[4] and it is worth rehearsing (see *MLM*, pp. 191-92 and 195; *EC*, pp. viii-ix and 293-304; 'Liturgical Origin', pp. 206 and 215-16; *LNP*, pp. 148-56 and 177). 'It cannot escape the simplest hearer of the Passion story', Goulder says, 'that it is divided into three-hourly units: they are marked almost continuously in the text', and where there are differences between the Gospels—as on the time of the Crucifixion, between John (19.14) and the others, or on the time of the Sanhedrin trial, between Luke (22.66) and the others—the events are still timed to fall every three hours (*EC*, p. 297; cf. *LNP*, p. 149).

The Last Supper takes place 'when it was evening' (Mk 14.17), that is 6 p.m. Jesus then goes to Gethsemane and says, 'Simon, are you asleep? Could you not watch one hour?' (14.37). He comes a second and then a third time when he says 'the hour has come' (v. 41). If Gethsemane is set at 9 p.m., after the Last Supper, this would place the arrest at midnight. Peter then denies Jesus, while the

---

Church' (unpublished, read to the St John Seminar of S.N.T.S. at Göttingen on 27 August 1987). I am grateful to Professor Goulder for lending me this paper. I do not have space to deal with the John theory in detail.

2.   Also relevant are 'The Empty Tomb', 'The Apocalypse as an Annual Cycle of Prophecies' and references in 'The Order of a Crank' (pp. 114-15).

3.   The later attempt being the thesis of *TTM*. I quote here from the Inaugural Lecture of the same name.

4.   This might be surmised from the lack of reference to it in the relevant literature.

trial takes place, at cockcrow, 3 a.m., and Luke may even imply that
the three denials took place at hourly intervals (Lk. 22.59). The trial
before Pilate takes place πρωΐ, at dawn, 6 a.m. (Mk 15.1) and the
most famous of the time indications occurs in the crucifixion
narrative: 'it was the third hour, when they crucified him' (15.25),
'And when the sixth hour had come, there was darkness over the
land until the ninth hour...' (15.33). The burial takes place 'when
evening had come' (15.42), 6 p.m. and a full twenty-four hours have
elapsed since the Last Supper.

Goulder says that Jews 'did not just make do through life with
three-hour watches' (*LNP*, p. 148) and he suggests that Mk 13.35-37
sheds light on the situation:

> Watch therefore—for you do not know when the master of the house
> will come, in the evening, or at midnight, or at cockcrow, or in the
> morning—lest he come suddenly and find you asleep. And what I say
> to you I say to all: Watch.

There are some obvious links with with the Passion narrative.[5] The
Last Supper took place 'in the evening', Peter denied Jesus 'at
cockcrow', Jesus was brought before Pilate 'in the morning' and
Jesus in Gethsemane finds Peter and the others 'asleep' and
commands them to 'watch'.

Goulder deduces from these data that the matrix within which the
Passion narrative was developed was a liturgical one. 'The Gospel
was born from the womb of the liturgy' (*EC*, p. 297). The earliest
church will have held a twenty-four hour vigil from 6 p.m. to 6 p.m.
on 14/15 Nisan, while Jews (or other, non-Christian Jews) were
celebrating Passover. At each watch the appropriate story would
have been read and Jesus' return might have been expected. Such a
vigil was observed not only in the 30s (*EC*, pp. viii. and 297; *LNP*,
pp. 254-55), but it continued into the communities which produced
the Gospels.

The theory for the Passion narrative in the Synoptics might be
represented in a table:

---

5.   Contrast Trocmé, *Passion*, p. 12: 'Mark 13.37 is an excellent ending for
the Gospel of Mark, since no part of chs. 1–13 points to the presence of a
Passion narrative in the same book', possibly the greatest weakness of Trocmé's
book. Contrast R.H. Lightfoot, *Gospel Message*, pp. 48-69, to which Goulder
refers in *LNP*, p. 149.

Table I: *The Liturgical Arrangement of the Synoptic Passion Narrative*[6]

	Mark	Matthew	Luke
6 p.m.	14.12-25 Last Supper	26.17-29 Last Supper	22.1-23 Last Supper
9 p.m.	14.26-42 Agony	26.30-46 Agony	22.24-38 Supper Conversation
Midnight	14.43-52 Arrest	26.47-56 Arrest	22.39-53 Agony; Arrest
3 a.m.	14.53-72 Trial, Denial	26.57-75 Trial, Denial	22.54-65 Peter's Denial
6 a.m.	15.1-15 Pilate	27.1-26 Judas, Pilate	22.66–23.12 Trials
9 a.m.	15.16-26 Crucifixion	27.27-37 Crucifixion	23.13-32 Pilate; Via Dolorosa
Noon	15.27-33 On the Cross	27.38-45 On the Cross	23.33-43 On the Cross
3 p.m.	15.34-47 Death, Burial	27.46-66 Death, Burial	23.44-56a Death, Burial

C. *The Rest of the Year*

Goulder's theory on the Passion Narrative was anticipated by Philip Carrington who wrote two books, *The Primitive Christian Calendar* and *According to Mark*, in which a liturgical function for Mark's Passion forms part of an argument for the lectionary origin of Mark's Gospel. The similarity between Goulder and Carrington ends here, however, in that Carrington assigns Mark 14–16 to Passover-Easter but the rest of the Gospel, Mark 1–13, comprises readings for a year beginning at the end of Tishri. Goulder describes both this and Etienne Trocmé's *The Passion as Liturgy* as 'broken-backed

---

6.   Table I is based on Goulder's Table VIII, following *EC*, p. 306, bottom right-hand corner, but updates it with the breakdown of the sections in *LNP*, pp. 155-56. Cf. the table on p. 177 for Mark and Luke. Cf. also the table in 'Liturgical Origin', p. 206 and *MLM*, p. 195, for Matthew. In both the latter table and in *EC*, parts of some of the sections are allotted differently, e.g., in *EC*, the section for 6 p.m. is Mark 14.12-21, whereas in *LNP* it is 14.12-25.

approaches' and suggests that they can be avoided (*LNP*, p. 156).[7]

Goulder proposes that not only the Passion narratives but also the whole of Matthew, Mark and Luke are designed to be read as lectionary books, fulfilling, in order, the relevant feasts and fasts in a Jewish-Christian year. Once the Passion stories are pegged to Passover-Easter, the correspondences with the festal calendar begin to establish themselves. First, *MLM* develops a scheme for Matthew. Goulder takes the sixty-nine numbered divisions of Codex Alexandrinus (A) as a guide for the Matthean lections and then sections of the Gospel are shown to correspond with the appropriate Jewish festivals and fasts as follows:

Table II: *The Lectionary Scheme for Matthew*[8]

Mt. 5(–7)	Sermon on the Mount	Pentecost
Mt. 11	Messengers from John etc.	New Year
Mt. 12.22-45	Beelzebub, Jonah	Atonement
Mt. 13.1-52	Harvest Parables	Tabernacles
Mt. 17–19	Transfiguration, Church Law	Dedication
Mt. 23; 24–25	Pharisees, Ready for Parousia	Passover

Goulder's scheme also provides for both 9th Ab and Purim, Mt. 9.9-14 (Question on Fasting) for the former and 22.1-14 (the Marriage Feast) for the latter.

Goulder suggests that there is sufficient space for readings for ordinary sabbaths intervening between these festivals and fasts. Chs. 14–16, for example, would provide enough readings for the three months between Tabernacles (ch. 13) and and Dedication (chs. 17–19).

MLM was written up from the Speaker's Lectures in Oxford of 1969–71. The lectures of 1972 then formed *EC* (1978) which develops in detail a lectionary theory for Luke which had already been presented briefly in an appendix to *MLM* (pp. 452-73). Whereas the more Jewish Matthew had festivals like Tabernacles spread over eight days with readings for each day, Luke is said to have had just weekly readings, and not on the sabbath but on the first day of the

7.   Trocmé follows Carrington on the Passion, but he is ignorant of Goulder.

8.   Table II is adapted from the one in *EC*, p. 214. For details on how each section fits with each of the liturgical occasions, see Chapter 21, below.

week. Many of these readings provide the fulfilments of weekly OT lections (*sidrôt*, Torah readings; *haphtarôt*, readings from the Prophets) in an annual cycle, and much of *EC* is given over to reconstructing such a cycle.

Luke, then, is read in a cycle in which 20.1–24.53 is followed by 1.1–4.13, and in which these sections run parallel with the *sidrôt* from Genesis.[9] Lk. 4.14–6.19 then runs parallel to Exodus, Lk. 6.20–8.25 to Leviticus, Lk. 8.26–9.50 Numbers and Lk. 9.51–20.18 Deuteronomy (see *EC*, chapter three; the readings are set out clearly in a chart on pp. 103-104). A good deal of Luke, the whole of the central section, corresponds to Deuteronomy since three sections of Luke are taken together with each *sidrā* from Deuteronomy.[10] These triads, Goulder explains, are used by Luke each week in the instruction of catechumens leading up to their baptism at Easter (*EC*, pp. 90-95).

After discussing 'Luke and the Annual Torah Cycle', Goulder says that: 'What we need now is a further test' (*EC*, p. 102). Goulder, therefore, reconstructs a first century cycle of readings from the Histories and 1 Maccabees (*EC*, chapter four; see the tables on pp. 139-40) and shows correspondences with the already fixed lections in Luke (*EC*, chapter five; table on p. 156). Further correspondences are adduced with Isaiah, with comments also on the Minor Prophets (*EC*, chapter six; table on pp. 181-82) and, finally, Goulder turns to the Writings and notices correspondences with Ecclesiasticus in particular (*EC*, chapter seven). Goulder proposes that in addition to the correspondences with the weekly sabbath cycle, Luke also, in the appropriate places, has readings for important Jewish feasts (see Table III, below).

EC also develops the theory for Matthew (chapter eight). Correspondences with the weekly OT readings, according to an annual cycle, are clarified, and Goulder makes a case for the serial reading of Paul's epistles in Matthew's church.

---

9.   The first *sidrā*, Genesis 1.1–6.8 falls opposite Luke 20.1–21.4. This is because of the necessity of reading the Passion story at Passover–Easter time, in the middle of Nisan. Therefore the Gospel begins with *sidrā* 5, Gen. 23.18–25.18. See further on this point below, p. 311.

10.   Goulder draws inspiration from C.F. Evans's famous article, 'Central Section' (restated in *Saint Luke*, pp. 34-37) but also cf. Farrer, 'Dispensing', pp. 77-79.

The book concludes (chapter nine) with the theory that Mark is a six-and-a-half-month lectionary book, running from New Year to Passover, echoing weekly OT readings as well as the major festal themes (anticipated in *MLM*, pp. 199-201). Table III shows where the festivals and fasts fall in Mark and Luke:

Table III: *The Lectionary Scheme for Mark and Luke*[11]

Pentecost		Lk. 3.1-20 John the Baptist
New Year	Mk 1.1-20 John, Baptism, Kingdom	Lk. 7.18-35 John and Jesus
Atonement	Mk 2.1-22 Paralytic, Levi, Fast	Lk. 7.36-50 The Sinner
Tabernacles	Mk 3.7–4.34 Multitudes etc., Harvest	Lk. 8.1-21 Harvest
Dedication	Mk 7.1–9.29[12] Corban, Transfiguration etc.	
Passover	Mark 14–15 Passion	Luke 22–23 Passion
Easter	Mark 16 Resurrection	Luke 24 Resurrection

D. *Goulder's Restatement in Luke—A New Paradigm*

Goulder notes in *LNP* that his lectionary theory was 'generally greeted with scepticism' and this scepticism, he says, has forced him to re-examine it. He now makes a distinction which, he says, was unclear to him at the time, between the theory of festal lessons at appropriate intervals in the Gospels and the theory of week-by-week sabbath readings in the Gospels, echoing the synagogue OT readings (*LNP*, p. 147). The latter thesis 'needs to be shelved, though it does not need to be abandoned', Goulder says, and no further reference is made to it in the book. The correspondences which are regarded as

11. Table III is based on the ones in *EC*, following p. 306, and *LNP*, pp. 175-77. For further details, see Chapter 21, below.

12. Goulder does not give Luke a Dedication reading in the two charts of *EC*, pp. 103 and 347; cf. p. 90.

clinching the case are those concerning the themes of particular festivals and fasts.

At the same time, only 'the major Jewish festivals' and fasts are discussed: New Year, Atonement, Tabernacles, Passover and Pentecost. It is notable in particular that Dedication, an important part of the earlier case for Matthew and Mark, finds reference only in a footnote (*LNP*, p. 194 n. 27) and likewise, Purim (*LNP*, p. 194 n. 28).[13] Also, Goulder is less sure of the division of Matthew, 'preferring now a common sense criterion to the obedient following of the Alexandrinus kephalaia' (*LNP*, p. 170).

Goulder has, then, modified his lectionary theory in important ways. The most immediately striking difference, however, between *MLM* and *EC* on the one hand and *LNP* on the other is the major change in emphasis. The lectionary theory dominates Goulder's work in the 1970s[14] but by the late 1980s it has receded in importance.[15] The shift can be illustrated most clearly from Goulder's changing views on how Luke ordered his Gospel. In *EC*, Goulder presses the point that the lectionary theory provides a plausible milieu for the growth of the Gospel and adds:

> But it is not merely a plausible suggestion: *it is what Luke himself says that he is doing in his Prologue*...Luke uses καθεξῆς five times, always meaning 'in series'... If Luke meant that he had taken trouble to provide a chronological order, then he has promised goods which he cannot deliver...Why should καθεξῆς not mean 'in *liturgical* order'? Such an exegesis would have two immediate merits: it safeguards the 'order' meaning of the word, and it makes sense of Luke's emphasis (*EC*, pp. 8-16; these quotations pp. 8, 10 and 12-13, Goulder's italics).[16]

One might contrast this with Goulder's comments in *LNP* (pp. 198-204):

---

13. Cf. also *LNP*, p. 194 n. 26, 'There is no need to posit an eight-day festal use in the Marcan church' and contrast *EC*, pp. 256-62.

14. The lectionary theory also appears in the article 'The Fourth Book of the Psalter' and even 'On Putting Q to the Test', p. 234.

15. When F.W. Danker reviews *LNP*, he does not even mention the lectionary theory.

16. It is worth noting that it was Goulder's original intention to call *EC* *Kathexes*—see 'The Empty Tomb', p. 208 n. 2.

> Our first instinct is to suppose that he means a chronological order;
> and we are encouraged in this by the fragments Eusebius has
> preserved for us from Papias...Luke is writing a reconciliation of
> Mark and Matthew to reassure Theophilus that the apparently
> dissonant Gospel tradition is trustworthy (*LNP*, pp. 199 and 200).

Here, there is no mention of the lectionary theory: it has withdrawn
into the background in Goulder's interest to push his major thesis
that Luke has read Matthew as well as Mark.

The question which will be addressed in this section is whether
Goulder's lectionary theory, particularly as it is restated in *LNP*,
stands up to scrutiny. In Chapter 18, I will look at how the lectionary
theory has been received and whether it remains plausible or not.
Two particular criticisms of the theory are common, first that it is
not consonant with what we know of early Christian worship and
second that there is little or no evidence for Jewish lectionary
practice as early as Goulder proposes. I will deal with these points in
Chapters 19 and 20.

It will be worth remembering that Goulder is not the first person to
have claimed that Jewish lectionaries lies behind the Gospels. We
have already noted Philip Carrington's contention that Mark was
written as a lectionary book. Before him, three others had made
similar claims, A. Wright on Luke in 1900,[17] P. P. Levertoff on
Matthew in 1928[18] and in a more thoroughgoing way, R. G. Finch on
all the Gospels in 1939.[19] After Carrington, and perhaps best known,
came Aileen Guilding who, in *The Fourth Gospel and Jewish
Worship*, in 1960, expounded the thesis that John is 'a commentary
on the OT lectionary readings as they were arranged for the synagogue in a three year cycle'.[20]

Goulder is aware of those who have gone before him, and he
warns:

> Dr Carrington, in a moment of unhappy confidence, spoke of
> mathematical calculation, and I sense a similar note, *Heureka*, behind
> the work of Dr Guilding: yet neither does Guilding agree with

17. A. Wright, *St Luke*.
18. H.L. Goudge and P.P. Levertoff, 'St Matthew'. The relevant 'Special
Introduction' by Levertoff is on pp. 128-29.
19. R.G. Finch, *Synagogue Lectionary*.
20. A. Guilding, *Fourth Gospel*, p. 3. Much of Guilding's book is devoted to
reconstructing a triennial cycle.

Carrington, nor I with either, nor, I think, does any established scholar. Let the reader beware (*EC*, pp. 101-102).

Goulder, however, can be as confident as those he criticizes. Just as Carrington says of one piece of evidence, 'It fits our theory like a glove, and I do not see how it can be accidental',[21] so too Goulder says, 'Forty-nine landfalls cannot be accidental: the lectionary theory is correct' (*EC*, p. 155).[22] Likewise, Guilding on one occasion lists a series of parallels and comments:

> The chances against their occurrence twice in the same order by accident are enormous.[23]

This is hardly different from Goulder's statement that:

> The chances against this pattern occurring by accident are very large (*MLM*, pp. 192-93).

The argument from the unlikeliness of correspondences occurring by accident is still Goulder's key argument for the plausibility of the lectionary theory in *LNP*. A great deal turns on how one evaluates this kind of argument, and in Chapter 21 I will attempt to test it.

21. P. Carrington, *Primitive Christian Calendar*, p. 26.
22. These forty-nine landfalls are 'lections [in Luke] which either fit or presuppose a reference to the *sidra* or Histories reading for the day' (*EC*, p. 155).
23. A. Guilding, *Fourth Gospel*, pp. 49-50.

Chapter 18

REACTIONS TO THE LECTIONARY THEORY

A. *Preliminary Comments*

When commenting on the lectionary theory, scholars are usually, not surprisingly, impressed with Goulder's boldness. Stephen Farris says that *EC* is 'spectacularly audacious'[1] and Leon Morris says that Goulder has 'an awe inspiring capacity for sweeping hypotheses'[2] and Drury notes:

> He has a big case to prove, involving virtually the entire Bible in much more than passing reference.[3]

Michael Prior, who calls *EC* 'the most exciting contribution to biblical scholarship in many decades',[4] says that:

> At times Goulder is driven more by the momentum of his enthusiasm than by the power of the evidence—he seems at times to be afflicted with Midas' gift that everything he touches becomes liturgical gold.[5]

Nevertheless, Prior is convinced that 'Goulder's basic instinct is right'[6] and Drury sounds a similarly cautious but optimistic note in his review of *EC*, speaking of 'a new discipline of biblical criticism, fully serious and possessed of considerable historical plausibility'.[7] Only J. Duncan M. Derrett is unequivocally positive about the lectionary theory,

1.   S. Farris, *Hymns*, p. 36.
2.   L. Morris, 'The Gospels', p. 137.
3.   J. Drury, Review of *EC*, p. 71.
4.   M. Prior, 'Revisiting Luke', p. 3.
5.   M. Prior, 'Revisiting Luke', p. 3.
6.   M. Prior, 'Revisiting Luke', p. 3.
7.   J. Drury, Review of *EC*, p. 71; cf. *Tradition and Design*, p. 141, which accepts Goulder's festal scheme for Matthew.

however, when he says that Goulder's case for Matthew 'is very well sustained'.[8]

These scholars are in the minority.[9] Goulder notes that *MLM* 'received some considerable and friendly reviews' but adds that 'all were restrained on the lectionary side' (*LNP*, p. 192 n. 1). Reviews and critiques of *EC* went on to greet Goulder's theory 'with scepticism' (*LNP*, p. 147). Morna Hooker, for example, gives twelve reasons for saying that it 'lacks not simply evidence, but plausibility'.[10] The most critical is Leon Morris who, having written a short book on the subject of lectionaries and the New Testament in 1964,[11] followed this up with an article dealing mainly with Goulder, 'The Gospels and the Jewish Lectionaries' in 1983. Morris's major criticism of all lectionary theories is an insistent demand for evidence, for example:

> Evidence of conformity to Judaism is largely a matter of worshipping in Jewish synagogues from time to time. It is, of course, not improbable that Jewish Christians conformed more closely to Jewish liturgical practice than did Gentile Christians. But we have little evidence for this and we must go on the evidence we have. There is more evidence that Christians distanced themselves from Judaism.[12]

If Morris overuses the word 'evidence' a little, his comments about early Christian worship and Jewish synagogue liturgy are, nevertheless, of key interest and these issues will be taken up in detail in Chapters 19 and 20 below. Here 'evidence' is clearly of some import: Goulder's theory to remain plausible should be consonant with what we know about both Jewish and Christian worship.

At the same time it needs to be noticed that it is in the nature of a theory like Goulder's that it is speculative: it is unlikely that we will ever 'know' the truth of the matter. Probative evidence of the kind

8.   J. Duncan M. Derrett, 'Midrash in Matthew', p. 55. His hope that 'a Guilding rediviva will rehabilate while reforming a Johannine lectionary hypothesis' (p. 56) is an oddity in that Goulder hardly agrees with Guilding at all (e.g. *EC*, p. 102).

9.   There was some enthusiasm in the 1950s and 1960s for Carrington and Guilding: N.H. Snaith, Review of Guilding; H.A. Blair, 'Gospel'; S.E. Johnson, 'New Theory'. Guilding enjoys a brief rediviva in A.N. Wilson, *Jesus*, pp. 50-52.

10.   M. Hooker, Review of *EC*, pp. 92-93.

11.   L. Morris, *New Testament*.

12.   L. Morris, 'The Gospels', p. 140.

Morris wants will inevitably, to a large extent, be lacking.[13] Goulder himself says:

> We must be clear from the start that there will never be enough evidence to 'prove' the case. I can never hope to achieve more than a plausible reconstruction, and to reject this as 'speculative' is to miss the point; when we have no adequate evidence, our alternatives are to speculate or to go ignorant (*EC*, p. x).[14]

It will be worth looking, then, at how far reactions to Goulder's lectionary hypothesis damage the plausibility which Goulder claims for it. I will group together and enumerate the criticisms.

B. *Specific Objections*

1. *The Place of the Lectionary Theory in Goulder's Paradigm*
Several scholars, as we saw above, want to express unease with the lectionary theory while at the same time approving of much of the rest of Goulder's thesis. Henry Wansbrough, for example, says that *MLM* 'is certainly one of the most important books on Matthew's method of composition and working to be published in recent years', but he expresses his 'hesitation about the lectionary theory', wondering whether it will stand the test of time.[15] The difficulty which criticisms of this kind pose for Goulder is that in his earlier work, the lectionary theory is intertwined with the theory of the evangelists' creativity. Goulder concludes *MLM* by saying of Matthew:

> He was the Church's liturgist and the Church's poet, adapting Mark by midrash and through lection (*MLM*, p. 475).

Likewise, when Goulder discusses Mark 16 in his article 'The Empty Tomb' (1976), it is natural to him to expound Mark's creativity in terms of the lectionary theory. The Passover *haphtarah* would have been, he says, Josh. 7–10, featuring the story of the five kings coming forth from the cave at Makkedah and subsequently being hanged on trees (Josh. 10). Goulder says:

---

13. Cf. J. Alex Sherlock, Review of *MLM*, p. 340; cf. L. Sabourin, Review of *MLM*.

14. Cf. N.H. Snaith's review of Morris's *New Testament*, p. 130: 'Mr Morris certainly accepts negative evidence too easily'.

15. H. Wansbrough, Review of *MLM*, p. 49.

To a church that believed all of scripture had been fulfilled in Christ, and especially that he rose again according to the scriptures, the repeated recital of these words on Easter day could hardly fail to excite attention ('The Empty Tomb', p. 209).[16]

Now the fact that 'midrash' and 'lection' go side by side like this is regarded by Goulder (in *MLM* and *EC*) as a strength of his overall thesis. The lectionary theory provides a control for the midrashic theory: the latter is not a thesis without limits. For others, however, the linking of the two has been seen as a weakness. One of Drury's few criticisms of *EC* is that there is 'a certain totalinarianism with resulting strain'.[17]

A further point is relevant here. Evans asks:

Are any literary and theological structures in the Gospels an accidental by-product of the provision of lections?[18]

Mary Ann Beavis echoes this when she says:

Internally, the way in which Mark has arranged his material, especially his use of such devices as *inclusio* (intercalation), makes the lectionary theory implausible.[19]

Likewise, Drury comments on Goulder's claim that καθεξῆς in Luke means 'lectionary order':

This fails to abolish the competition of the view that it is historiographical—the connections of prophecy and fulfilment. There are grounds here for a plea for co-existence and wariness of the intentionalist fallacy.[20]

It is worth noting, however, that Goulder does not claim that the lectionary theory will cure every ill. 'The lectionary is not to be expected', Goulder says, 'to solve every problem unaided' (*EC*, p. 18).

Further, this issue is largely addressed by Goulder in his restatement of the calendrical theory in *LNP*. The lectionary theory has receded in

16. Cf. John Thurmer, Letter.

17. J. Drury, Review of *EC*, p. 73.

18. C.F. Evans, 'Goulder and the Gospels', p. 432; cf. Drury, Review of *EC*, p. 72.

19. M.A. Beavis, *Mark's Audience*, p. 46. She specifies that 'Goulder's fragmentation of the "parable chapter" ruptures the thematic links among the narrative units' (pp. 47-48) but Goulder in *EC*, on which Beavis is commenting, is dividing up Mark 4 (together with Mark 3) to create readings for an eight-day Tabernacles celebration.

20. J. Drury, Review of *EC*, p. 72.

importance and since it no longer occupies the centre of the stage, the 'midrashic' theory can be expounded with freedom. In Goulder's earlier work, the lectionary theory acts as a control to the 'midrashic' theory. Now it has more of the nature of an optional, if useful extra. The shift in emphasis is most clearly seen when Goulder comes to expound Mark 16 in *TTM* (chapter twenty-four): Mark is still held to have created the story of the Empty Tomb but there is no reference at all to his finding help from Joshua 10.

2. *The Division of the Text*

It is a key part of Goulder's case in *MLM* that the divisions in Codex Alexandrinus have lectionary significance (*MLM*, pp. 180-83). The claim has been received with little sympathy. J. Alex Sherlock says that 'To argue from textual divisions three or four centuries removed from the autograph is tenuous'.[21] Perhaps the greatest difficulty, though, is the issue of the length of the sections which the manuscript divisions produce. Mitton says:

> If one were writing a book to serve as a lectionary, one would aim to make the readings roughly of a similar length. But in the scheme suggested some are as short as two verses and others longer than two chapters.[22]

One might ask, for example, how plausible it is that Matthew himself would have divided into two lections the story of the Woman with the Flux and the Synagogue Ruler's Daughter (Mt. 9.18-26, *MLM*, pp. 325-26).[23]

Goulder amends this aspect of the theory, however, in *LNP*, saying that he prefers now 'a common-sense criterion' to the Alexandrinus divisions (*LNP*, p. 170). Nevertheless, difficulties over dividing Matthew remain and I will discuss a particularly serious case below in Chapter 21.

Goulder does not rely on manuscript divisions for Luke, and he feels that the issue of dividing the text is straightforward 'thanks to his liking

---

21. J.A. Sherlock, Review of *MLM*, p. 340.

22. C.L. Mitton, Review of *MLM*, p. 98. But Mitton wrongly attributes this to 'the need to establish links with the corresponding OT passage'. It is rather a question of the rigidity of manuscript divisions. Murphy O'Connor compares the length of the Sermon on the Mount with Peter's Mother-in-Law, Review of *MLM*, p. 305.

23. See further on this issue below, pp. 354-55.

for ornate openings and closures' (*LNP*, p. 170; cf. *MLM*, pp. 455-56 and *EC*, pp. 73-76). Goulder himself observes, however, that it is not always easy to see where Luke is marking the introduction to a new pericope and the case in *LNP* is, in fact, still hampered by the constraint of having to divide up the text for lectionary purposes. Luke's central section is divided into triads each with a governing theme, the suggestion being that Luke took three sections a week from 9.51 onwards for the instruction of converts leading up to Easter baptism, but Goulder's own view about where to make the divisions has changed substantially (contrast *EC*, Table VIII, following p. 306 with *LNP*, pp. 176-77)[24] and this inevitably casts some doubt on the supposed clarity of Luke's divisions. Further, one has to ask how plausible it is that Luke would have decided to end one of the triads half-way through the material about Watchful Servants (Lk. 12.35-48) so that the following week's triad begins with Peter's question in 12.41, 'Lord, are you telling this parable for us or for all?'[25]

3. *Correspondences*
One of the strongest criticisms of Aileen Guilding's theory was that she compared such a massive range of Old Testament texts with each section of John that it was not at all surprising that she was able to draw attention to correspondences.[26] Goulder is conscious of this and says:

> My own freedom has been severely limited...I do not have three years of readings to choose between, nor two simultaneous points of departure, nor elasticity of readings of up to a month either side, nor variant *haphtarah* traditions, like Guilding (*EC*, p. 305).

However, Goulder has certainly not avoided the same kind of criticism. Hooker notes that 'Luke is linked with no less than six sets of Old Testament readings',[27] therefore, there is plenty of material to draw on. This is not too serious a criticism: Goulder claims that the lectionary

24. The divisions from the beginning to the end of a triad are the same in *EC* and *LNP* up to 12.1 but then they diverge greatly, coming together again at 14.25, diverging again at 17.20. The difficulty is largely that in *LNP*, Goulder is spreading Luke 9.51–21.38 over fourteen weeks whereas in *EC*, he is spreading the same material over thirteen weeks. In the table in *EC*, 14.22 is a misprint for 14.24.

25. See further on this above, pp. 136-38.

26. Cf. Morris, 'The Gospels', p. 130; M.E. Boismard, Review of Guilding, and R.E. Brown, Review of Guilding.

27. M. Hooker, Review of *EC*, p. 93.

theory would stand without Isaiah, the Twelve and the Psalms (*EC*, p. 306). Hooker, however, also says:

> The readings suggested from the Torah are fairly long—often several chapters in length. It is frequently a simple matter to find *some* kind of correspondence between some section of it and the alleged gospel parallel.[28]

She adds that 'Goulder tends to skate over the significance of important Old Testament passages which are used out of sequence in the Gospels'.[29] Further, the correspondences do not all come in the right places for Goulder's theory which for Hooker suggests that 'though the suggested parallels may be correct, the straitjacket of a lectionary theory is wrong'.[30]

Harvey says:

> It is in the nature of allusions (and of midrash) that the influence of one text upon another is not always clear.[31]

Similarly, Mitton claims:

> Sometimes the parallels claimed are very forced and verses have to be treated in an unnatural way to make them fit into the desired patterns.[32]

These are important points. Goulder's case in *EC* primarily depends on the matter of correspondences and these scholars are pointing to a degree of flexibility which undermines the plausibility of the thesis. Once more, though, the restatement in *LNP* avoids most of the difficulties. Here, the correspondences adduced are all with the themes of particular feasts or fasts. Morris is one of the only scholars to comment directly on this aspect of the thesis when he refers to Goulder's statement that we need a 'fairly striking correlation between the Jewish holy days and the passages in the Gospels which correspond with them' (*EC*, p. ix) and he comments:

---

28. M. Hooker, Review of *EC*, p. 92; cf. C.F. Evans, 'Goulder and the Gospels', p. 431, 'The OT is a large and repetitive book...'

29. M. Hooker, Review of *EC*, p. 93. Cf. E.P. Sanders, Review of *MLM*, p. 454 on the weekly *sidrôt*; also L. Sabourin, Review of *MLM*, p. 92.

30. M. Hooker, Review of *EC*, p. 93.

31. A.E. Harvey, Review of *MLM*, p. 192.

32. C.L. Mitton, Review of *MLM*, p. 98.

> We must assume the lectionary hypothesis before there is any such correspondence.[33]

This contention is a little odd, however, since the relevant question is surely not one of whether the correspondences exist, but rather of whether they are good enough to make the thesis likely. This issue, the question of the strength of the correspondences with the themes of the relevant feasts, will be taken up below, in Chapter 21.

4. *The Kind of Lectionary Envisaged*

Goulder proposes that both Matthew and Luke are designed to be read beginning after Passover, from the end of Nisan.[34] Hooker feels that this is problematic and says:

> For all three synoptic gospels, Goulder's scheme links the first reading for the Jewish New Year—from Genesis—with the events immediately before the Passion; the *beginning* of each gospel is linked with the *fifth* reading from the Torah. This is a serious weakness. If Christian worship was so closely linked with Jewish, why did not the gospels begin at the same point?[35]

Hooker is partly wrong here. Although Matthew and Luke begin their Gospels in parallel to the fifth *sidrā*, Mark begins his at New Year and the twenty-sixth *sidrā* would be read on the sabbath near to it (*EC*, pp. 245-48; Table VIII, following p. 306).

More importantly, Hooker's criticism here is not strong. One might ask which, for Goulder, is the dominant force, the emerging Christian year or the Jewish year on which it was based? In light of the centrality of Jesus' death and resurrection in the gospel message, it is difficult to imagine the evangelists not making that the climax of their story and so, if Goulder is right that the Gospels are lectionary books, one would expect them to have concluded at Passover time, and then Matthew and Luke would be required to begin their Gospels at the end of Nisan.

A related but more serious point concerns the length of the cycle for Mark which runs from New Year to Easter, for six and a half months. Evans asks in passing:

33. L. Morris, 'The Gospels', p. 145.
34. *LNP*, pp. 174-75: Lk. 1.5-25 is assigned to Nisan IV; cf. *EC*, Table VIII, following p. 306: Lk. 1.5-25 is assigned to Iyyar I.
35. M. Hooker, Review of *EC*, p. 92.

Is a lectionary for half a year plausible or a monstrosity?[36]

Goulder, apparently, thinks that it is plausible and it is instructive to notice how he argues the point. He says that Jewish New Year would be 'the most natural option' (*LNP*, p. 157; cf. *EC*, p. 243) for the beginning of Mark's Gospel and adds:

> A New Year beginning for Mark explains in a convincing way the growth of the Gospel as a genre... The Gospels grew backwards from Passovertide, backwards from the Passion. Inevitably, with time, the urge was felt to make something of a continuous story of Jesus' ministry, extending back from the last journey to its opening with John Baptist. The step was taken by Mark in Rome, in virtue of his familiarity with the Petrine traditions. He began at New Year, and it is for this reason that his Gospel looks like a Passion story with an extended introduction (*EC*, pp. 244-45).

Goulder is suggesting here that his thesis becomes more plausible because of its explanatory power. 'A Markan beginning at New Year would not only be natural', Goulder says, 'it would also explain a lot' (*EC*, p. 245). The difficulty with such an appeal in this context is that the 'extended introduction' would more naturally stretch back as far as the previous Nisan, rather than stopping short in Tishri. One might ask what the church read from Nisan to Tishri each year. Further, if Mark has found it desirable to provide readings for New Year, Atonement and Tabernacles, it is surprising that he did not choose to provide a reading also for Pentecost.

Goulder is aware of the difficulty here, and he comments with his usual wit:

> Six and a half months' readings are not satisfactory: well, Mark only promised to give us 'the beginning of the Gospel' (*MLM*, p. 201).

He adds that 'there is no sale for six-and-a-half-month lectionaries' and continues, 'Churches wanted a cycle that ran round the whole year and this is exactly what Matthew and Luke were designed to supply' (*EC*, p. 245). This is actually an outstanding example of a feature which we have seen several times in Goulder's work: the transformation of a potential weakness for his thesis into a constituent part, even a strength, of it. The thesis for Mark, Goulder is admitting, is unsatisfactory, but 'Mark's unsatisfactoriness is Matthew's invitation' (*MLM*, p. 201). The

36. C.F. Evans, 'Goulder and the Gospels', p. 430.

half-year Mark becomes the cornerstone of his argument about the development of the Gospel genre. In *LNP*, he goes on to ask whether one can test the hypothesis and suggests, among other things, that one would expect Matthew to look like 'Mark prefixed by a new first half', a strong point since the sequential following of Mark by Matthew really begins from Chapter 12—'the general shape of the Gospel fits the requirement well' (*LNP*, p. 159).

The difficulty with this kind of argument is to know how one can assess it. Certainly, the successful explanation of the structure of Matthew adds credibility to the thesis. On the other hand, though, one should probably not allow this to obscure the fact that a truncated lectionary of this kind lacks not only plausibility but also any historical precedent. Further, the best way to judge the idea will be examine it on its own terms and to look at how strong the correspondences are between the themes of the festivals adduced by Goulder and the passages to which he assigns them in Mark and this I will attempt below, in Chapter 21.

5. *Acts and Luke*

One of the difficulties with Goulder's theory on Luke is that it makes Acts stand out in a curious way. If, as Goulder says in a slightly different context in *EC*, 'sauce for the goose is sauce for the gander' (p. 241), one should probably expect Acts, like Luke, to be a lectionary book. Although in *EC* Goulder does suggest that Acts is a liturgical book (p. 17), he has never produced a lectionary theory for Acts and it is difficult to see how it could be done. There is hardly enough material in Acts 1 to cover the six or seven weeks between Easter, in Luke 24, and Pentecost, in Acts 2. There are greater difficulties still as one reads through Acts. In 20.16, Pentecost has come round again and Atonement is mentioned in 27.9. If one were to take serious note of these markers in the text, it would be hard work to make Acts a series of readings for a year.

The evidence from Acts is troubling in another way also. Since Acts, unlike the Synoptics, actually mentions Pentecost and Atonement, it draws attention to the relative freedom which Goulder inevitably has in his theories for the Synoptics. They only specifically mention Passover (and by implication Easter) and so, although Goulder 'pegs' the Passion to Passover-Easter and claims that the other festivals and fasts fall into place, he does not have the additional constraint of having to peg any other section to any other festival.

6. *Conclusion*

There are some important difficulties for Goulder's theory. Mark is supposed to be a lectionary book for half a year which, in spite of Goulder's attempt to make it the basis of the development of the Gospel genre, lacks both plausibility and historical precedent. Also problematic is the lack of provision for Acts on the lectionary theory.

Another difficulty is the question of how the lectionary theory relates to the rest of Goulder's thesis: some have been unhappy about the way in which the 'midrashic' theory is intertwined with the lectionary theory.

Some have felt that the inevitable rigidity of Goulder's hypothesis fails to account for all the data; a particular difficulty is the division of the text. Related to this is the question of correspondences: doubts have been expressed both about the number of Old Testament texts to which appeal is made in *EC* and about the quality of the resulting correspondences.

The latter three points are all in some measure dealt with in Goulder's restatement of the theory in *LNP*. Here a rigorous following of manuscript divisions is abandoned, the correspondences with the Old Testament lections are shelved and the lectionary theory overall recedes in importance. Nevertheless, the division of the text remains a difficulty and the question of correspondences is still relevant to the festivals and fasts and is treated below.

Evans comments:

> The argument is vulnerable at various stages but hardly open to knock-down objections.[37]

This is a sound judgment: no one of these points is decisive. Goulder says, however, that 'The claim to be plausible rests on the cumulative nature of the argument' (*EC*, p. 304), and a handful of difficulties might be seen cumulatively to diminish the impressiveness of Goulder's argument.

---

37. C.F. Evans, 'Goulder and the Gospels', p. 430.

C. *The Passion as Liturgy: Strengths and Weaknesses*

Perhaps the most surprising feature of the literature written in response to Goulder is the scarcity of any comment on Goulder's theory on the Passion narrative.[38] There are, nevertheless, difficulties with the theory. Most importantly, Goulder does not distinguish as clearly as he might between arguments for a liturgical origin for the Passion narrative and arguments for the continuing liturgical function of the texts. Symptomatic of this approach is the fact that Goulder speaks of Etienne Trocmé's *The Passion as Liturgy* in the same breath as mentioning Philip Carrington's work (*LNP*, pp. 148 and 156), but there is a fundamental difference between Carrington and Goulder on the one hand and Trocmé on the other. Carrington, in anticipation of Goulder, claims that Mark 14–16 was written to be read at Passover-Easter whereas Trocmé's theory is that:

> The original form of those narratives was a liturgical text used as the basis of a solemn commemoration of the sufferings and death of Jesus by the Jerusalem church within a few years of the actual events.[39]

Like Trocmé, Goulder thinks that the Passion narrative was developed liturgically from early on. Unlike Trocmé, he thinks that the Passion narratives as they stand in the Gospels were designed by the evangelists with the liturgy specifically in mind.

This observation is important particularly in relation to Goulder's internal evidence. It is possible, after all, that the three-hour divisions which are marked in the text are hangovers from earlier liturgical practice now defunct.[40] The fact that some units of text do not have time indications could be telling. In Goulder's scheme, two important time indications are missing: nothing marks 9 p.m. in Mk 14.26-42, and there is no marker for midnight in Mk 14.43-52.[41] Likewise, neither Matthew, Luke nor John have markers for 9 p.m. and midnight, and

---

38. Only Morris remarks on it, 'The Gospels', p. 143: 'But when we ask for evidence we are given nothing but a brilliant hypothesis'.

39. E. Trocmé, *Passion*, p. 91.

40. Cf. E. Trocmé, *Passion*, p. 79: 'The timetable was part of the original story and was progressively eliminated when its meaning was not perceived any longer, that is, when the Passion narrative became a mere record of events'.

41. Cf. E. Trocmé, *Passion*, pp. 78-79, thinks of a twelve-hour timetable, from 6 a.m. to 6 p.m.

neither Matthew nor Luke say when Jesus was crucified, unlike Mark in 15.25. If the evangelists were writing their accounts with the liturgy in mind, one might have expected them to be meticulous about making clear when the appropriate section was to be read.

Other aspects of the internal evidence, however, might tell in favour of the view that the evangelists constructed their Passion narratives on the basis of a Paschal liturgy. One of Goulder's key texts, the exhortation in Mk 13.35-37, strikes an insistent note and, if its relevance is at least partly that of preparing the congregation for a vigil, it is noteworthy that it is spoken not just to the disciples but also 'to all'.[42] Further, in Matthew 24–25 there is greater emphasis still on 'keeping watch' and not slumbering in view of the delay of the master (particularly Mt. 25.1-13), and the householder does not know 'in what part of the night the thief was coming' (Mt. 24.43). In Mt. 24.6, 'At midnight there was a cry, "Behold, the bridegroom!"'[43]

Goulder's theory is, of course, speculative and the difficulty which one constantly faces with the lectionary theory is the element of conjecture. The question which arises is: how can one assess Goulder's theory? What criteria can one use? Goulder suggests that the key question is one of plausibility and one way of looking at this is to ask whether Goulder's theory of the origin and function of the Passion narrative in the four Gospels is more or less plausible than any of the alternatives.

Here, in fact, is one of the strengths of Goulder's hypothesis: there are so few viable alternative explanations for the occurrence of the three-hour feature. Jeremias,[44] like many others,[45] notes that the temporal references in Mark's Passion narrative are more precise than anything else in the Gospel but he does not offer a clear explanation. Some[46] suggest for Mk 15.33-34 // Mt. 27.45-46 // Lk. 23.44 (darkness

---

42. Goulder's liturgical theory here is not easy to reconcile with his more recent theory on Mk 13: see his 'The Phasing of the Future' and *TTM*, chapter 12. I am grateful to Professor Goulder himself for this observation.

43. In Luke, there is no such insistent note in the build-up to the Passion Narrative; the command to watch comes earlier on (Lk. 12.35-40).

44. J. Jeremias, *Eucharistic Words*, pp. 61-62.

45. For example C.F. Evans, *Saint Luke*, pp. 875-76; for Bultmann, *History*, pp. 273-74, the time references are Mark's own editorial work.

46. For example Schweizer, *Matthew*, p. 514: and this is why Matthew omitted the time note in Mk 15.25.

comes over the earth at the sixth hour) a fulfilment of Amos 8.9 but this explanation will only do for this one reference in the Synoptics. It does not help with any of the other time references, nor with Jn 19.14 where one has the same time reference, the sixth hour, but a different event, Jesus' crucifixion.

The liturgical theory gains some ground, then, from the lack of convincing alternative explanations of something which is a prominent feature in the Passion narratives. It becomes more plausible in that it explains many of the problems commonly seen in the Passion narratives. Pretty well every commentary notes the impossible time span and Trocmé remarks on 'how unlikely it is from the historian's point of view, because it crams too many events into much too short a time'.[47] Trocmé's theory, like Goulder's, has the advantage of explaining the historical difficulty both of a night trial and a trial on a festal day.[48]

Further, the liturgical theory is able to explain the difference in dating between the Synoptics and John. The suggestion that the Johannine Passion narrative was recited on 14 Nisan, for which second century Quarto-deciman practice offers some support, would, Goulder says, release us from 'the intolerable dilemma hitherto posed by the dating of the Johannine Passion':

> Either we have had to suppose that John was right; and that all three Synoptics were therefore wrong...it is incredible in every way. Otherwise we have to suppose that John was playing ducks and drakes with a chronology which was known to all Christians for the sake of his symbolism of Christ the lamb: a picture which defenders of Johannine historicity have correctly laughed out of court. But we know that churches come to believe that history is according to their established liturgical observance ('Liturgical Origin', pp. 216-17).[49]

This is a strong point and adds plausibility to the hypothesis by means of its explanatory power.

---

47. E. Trocmé, *Passion*, p. 79.

48. See, among others, J. Jeremias, *Eucharistic Words*, p. 52; Nineham, *Saint Mark*, pp. 398-405; P. Winter, *Trial* and D.R. Catchpole, *Trial*.

49. Goulder goes further in his unpublished 'The Paschal Liturgy in the Johannine Church': 'the Johannine dating of the Passion is primitive and correct' (p. 22 n. 31).

D. *Conclusion*

Goulder's theory has impressed many by its boldness but few by its plausibility. Evans says that it is not vulnerable to 'knock-down objections' but, nevertheless, several criticisms undermine its credibility. The fact that the lectionary theory is so closely bound up with the 'midrashic' theory in Goulder's earlier work does cause a certain strain in its demand for 'all or nothing'. Further, the theory is at times inevitably rather too rigid and the need to divide the text evenly causes problems. There are doubts over both the quantity and the quality of the correspondences Goulder adduces.

These points are all, to some extent, dealt with by Goulder in his restatement of the theory in *LNP*. More serious are two further points. First, the proposal that Mark is a six-and-a-half month lectionary is a difficulty in spite of the fact that Goulder attempts to make it the cornerstone of the theory of the development of the Gospel genre. Second, Goulder's theory does not make adequate provision for the Acts of the Apostles.

If, however, there are weaknesses in Goulder's thesis, his theory on the Passion narrative is relatively strong, accounting for famous difficulties like the night trial, the implausible twenty-four hour time-span and the difference in date between John and the Synoptics. One important difficulty with the theory, however, is that the data could be held to support a liturgical origin rather than a continuing liturgical function for the Passion narrative.

This touches on the issue of how much we know about early Christian worship, one of the points most commonly made in comments on Goulder's theory. This will be the subject of the next chapter.

Chapter 19

EARLY CHRISTIAN WORSHIP

A. *Preliminary Comments*

Many of those who have commented on lectionary theories have maintained that they go against the grain of what evidence we have about Christian worship in the first century. It is one of Morris's most insistent points and the subject requires serious examination. The following specific criticisms have been made:

1) The charismatic nature of early Christian worship excludes the likelihood of a lectionary, and Christians are unlikely to have been influenced so strongly by Judaism.

2) Goulder's picture of Easter baptism and a trained catechumenate is anachronistic.

3) There is too little evidence for Christians celebrating festivals or observing fasts.

These points will be taken in turn and then I will return to the question of Passover and Passion.

B. *Charismatic Worship*

Leon Morris suggests that 'The charismatic nature of New Testament Christianity as a whole is difficult to fit in' with Goulder's theory.[1] He points specifically to 1 Corinthians 14 and says that Paul's picture of Christian worship does not mention the reading of set passages, and it is 'scarcely consistent' with the use of a lectionary.[2] Mitton says:

> On the question of the use of liturgy in the early Church, one man's guess is almost as good as another's. We really know nothing about it. Such knowledge as we have is little more than speculation based on

---

1.   L. Morris, 'The Gospels', p. 141.
2.   L. Morris, 'The Gospels', p. 141.

ambiguous hints within the New Testament...Our own judgement would
incline towards that of Conzelmann on this point: 'The primitive Church
had other concerns than the construction of a liturgy. It concealed within
itself tremendous energies that could not be fettered to fixed forms'.[3]

Similarly, Beavis comments on 'the almost complete absence of New
Testament references to anything resembling a "liturgy of the Word" in
early Christian worship'. She adds that 'the only New Testament
passage which refers to scripture reading in a public setting is 1 Tim.
4.13' which speaks of 'the public reading (ἀνάγνωσις) of scripture'.
This reference, she says, is late and 'there is no specifically liturgical
element' in the verse.[4]

Beavis goes on to emphasise, along with several of Goulder's critics,[5]
a quotation from Justin Martyr, *1 Apol.* 67:

> The memoirs of the apostles or the writings of the prophets are read *as
> long as time permits* (μέχρις ἐγχωρεῖ); then, when the reader has ceased,
> the president verbally instructs and exhorts to the imitation of these good
> things.[6]

Bock feels that this text is decisive:

> Does not Justin's language bring into question altogether the fixed
> reading schedule? Is not the impression one of informality with no set
> schedule of serial reading?[7]

In connection with this, Morris claims that:

> We cannot assume that people who made Christ so central in their
> worship happily accepted a way of worship from those who rejected
> Christ.[8]

These points vary in strength. Morris's claim about the unlikelihood

---

3. C.L. Mitton, Review of *MLM*, p. 99.
4. M.A. Beavis, *Mark's Audience*, pp. 48-49. But against this see *EC*, p. 3.
5. Other than those cited below, see J.D.G. Dunn, *Unity and Diversity*, p. 147.
6. Cf. W.O.E. Oesterley, *Jewish Background*, p. 117.
7. D.L. Bock, *Proclamation*, p. 25. Cf. W.D. Davies, 'Reflections', p. 130:
'Had Justin Martyr had a fixed lectionary in mind, he would have used some such
phrase as κατὰ τάξιν'. Cf. L. Morris, *New Testament*, p. 25: the passage 'makes it
quite clear no lectionary was in use'.
8. L. Morris, 'The Gospels', p. 143. Cf. W.D. Davies, 'Reflections', p. 130:
'There was little that Christianity took over neat from Judaism, and particularly in
its worship is this the case'. Cf. R.P. Casey, 'St Mark's Gospel', p. 367 and James
S. Stewart, Review of Carrington, p. 429.

of the imitation of Jewish ways is not persuasive since Goulder roots his lectionary hypothesis in a development beginning in the 30s in Jerusalem, among Jewish Christians. Moreover, the comment is really not applicable to Matthew whom most would see as willing 'to draw from his store both new and old' (Mt. 13.52).

Further, Goulder makes a relevant general point:

> Although Christianity often saw itself as a radical movement away from Judaism doctrinally, it is noticeable that breakaway religious movements, such as Anglicanism, Lutheranism, or Methodism, tend to be rather conservative in matters of worship (*EC*, p. 4).[9]

In addition, there is some second century evidence of Christians, and especially Jewish Christians, observing Jewish festivals and fasts (see below, p. 325).

The passage from Justin does, on the other hand, pose problems for Goulder's thesis. Typically, Goulder attempts to use the text in his own favour. He quotes it alongside 1 Tim 4.13 as evidence that the scriptures were read in Church, 'followed by exhortation and exposition in the liturgy' (*EC*, p. 15). Goulder explains that:

> Our concern is the tell-tale clause which has been added to the OT reading 'as long as time permits'. We can hear the president saying, 'As time presses this morning, brethren, I propose that the lector limits our OT reading to Lev. 1, rather than the whole of Lev. 1-5' (*EC*, p. 53).

Where most would regard the important clause as referring to the readings in general, Goulder takes it as referring specifically to the Old Testament reading. Evans's judgment here is sound: Goulder's solution is neat 'though not very plausible'.[10]

The evidence from Justin is not decisive since it could be the case that the evangelists' communities in the first century used a lectionary and that Justin's church in the second century did not. Nevertheless, one should not underestimate the importance of the quotation. The passage is one of the clearest pieces of evidence on early Christian worship and it does not tell in favour of Goulder's lectionary hypothesis.[11]

---

9. Morris responds by asking why the church eventually abandoned the Jewish lectionary ('The Gospels', p. 147).

10. C.F. Evans, 'Goulder and the Gospels', p. 431.

11. But cf. C.F. Evans, 'Goulder and the Gospels', p. 431: the passage 'does not amount to a denial of fixed lessons'.

C. *Celebration of Festivals*

It is essential for Goulder's thesis that the observation of Jewish festivals and fasts was widespread in the first century. Morris, however, claims that:

> There is not much evidence concerning the Christians and the Jewish festivals and what there is is against.[12]

The evidence he quotes is all from the Pauline corpus. There are three important texts:

> Gal. 4.10-11: You observe days, and months, and seasons, and years! I am afraid I have laboured over you in vain.

> Rom. 14.5-6: One person esteems one day as better than another, while another esteems all days alike. Let every one be fully convinced in his own mind. He who observes the day observes it in honour of the Lord.

> Col. 2.16: Therefore let no one pass judgment on you in questions of food or drink or with regard to a festival or a new moon or a sabbath.

In his earlier book on the topic Morris quotes the same texts and remarks:

> It is difficult to see what this means if it is not a vigorous repudiation of the whole idea of the liturgical year.[13]

The evidence is certainly not this conclusive, however. Evans, as usual, is a little more sympathetic to Goulder and says:

> We simply do not know from external evidence whether first century Christians observed Jewish feasts or not. Gal. 4.10 and Col. 2.16 (which Goulder quotes) would seem to imply that they did not, but that need only go for Gentile Christians in the Pauline area, and even there Passover/Easter might be an exception.[14]

---

12. L. Morris, 'The Gospels', p. 145.

13. L. Morris, *New Testament*, p. 38; cf. 'The Gospels', p. 141.

14. C.F. Evans, 'Goulder and the Gospels', p. 431. Morris himself quotes 1 Cor. 9.20 and says that Paul was prepared to act as a Jew among Jews ('The Gospels', p. 139).

Even this, however, is probably not as fair to Goulder as the evidence allows since these very passages from Paul show that at least some Christians, and not only Jewish Christians, were inclined to observe special occasions: 'You observe days...', 'he who observes the day...'[15] Moreover, it could be argued that the issue in Gal. 4.10 is what the Galatians' observance implies to Paul: it is a sign of dependence on the law for salvation.[16] This is tantamount to denying Paul's work with them—'I am afraid I have laboured over you in vain!'—and it is seen as a return to bondage: 'how can you turn back again to the weak and beggarly elemental spirits, whose slaves you want to be once more?' (v. 9). In Romans, where the issue is different, Paul's view is less impassioned, and he is happy for the weaker brethren to observe days if their conscience demands it ('Let every one be fully convinced in his own mind').

Further, Paul's letters are not the only evidence. One particularly interesting text is *1 Clem.* 40.2, 4:

> He commanded us to celebrate sacrifices and services, and that it should not be thoughtlessly and disorderly, but at fixed times and hours... So then those who offer their oblations at the appointed seasons are acceptable and blessed, for they follow the laws of their master and do not sin.[17]

The mention of disorder might remind one of 1 Corinthians 14. It is possible that *1 Clem.* 40.2, 4 represents a development of Paul's teaching in 1 Corinthians 14 in terms of 'fixed times and hours'. It is notable also that the celebration of appointed seasons is given as a command of the Lord. This contrasts with the notion in Rom. 14.5 that it is optional and, since *1 Clement* comes chronologically between Paul and Justin, it is at least possible that it reflects more closely than either the practice of the evangelists.

Morris draws attention to the other relevant texts, 1 Cor. 16.18, Acts 20.16 and Acts 27.9 but he says that they appear to be 'no more than

---

15. Contrary to Morris: 'there is no NT evidence that the first Christians remembered any of these [festivals] liturgically, not even the Passover' ('The Gospels', p. 144).

16. Cf. E.P. Sanders, *Paul*, especially pp. 17-20, and *LNP*, p. 131 for Goulder's view.

17. This passage is not quoted by Goulder but cf. P. Carrington, *Primitive Christian Calendar*, p. 41; J. Van Goudoever, *Biblical Calendars*, p. 151 and W.D. Davies, 'Reflections', p. 134.

notes of time and do not form evidence that the Christians observed these days'.[18] Morris, however, probably underestimates the importance of this evidence. Both 1 Cor. 16.8, 'I will stay in Ephesus until Pentecost' and Acts 27.9, 'the fast had already gone by', do not so much give mere notes of time as the kind of accidental or incidental information which hints that liturgical occasions like these were observed as a matter of course, even by Paul. Moreover in Acts 20.16, there is another element: '...for he was hastening to be at Jerusalem, if possible, on the day of Pentecost'. Luke thinks that Paul wanted to be in Jerusalem by Pentecost, and, in portraying Paul as eager to observe a Jewish festival, he may be showing that he found no objection to the idea of festal worship.

Although this evidence is limited and does not prove that Luke is likely to have observed Jewish festivals and fasts, these scattered references do clearly add some strength to Goulder's claim that festal worship was widespread among Christians in the first century. It is worth adding, of course, that Luke makes a great deal of Pentecost in Acts 2 and this, too, is in Goulder's favour.

For the Gospels themselves, there is no conclusive direct evidence. Goulder appeals to Mt. 23.3:

> Matthean Christians had to do all that the scribes and Pharisees ordained on Moses' seat, and that certainly included festal worship (*LNP*, p. 150).[19]

The best evidence, though, is probably John since his Gospel constantly comes back to Jewish Festivals, Passover in chs. 2 and 6 and 13–20, another festival in ch. 5, Tabernacles in chs. 7 and 8 and reference to Dedication in 10.22. It is standard in the commentaries to expound the relevant sections against the background of the festivals at which they are set,[20] but there is no agreement as to whether John's constant references demonstrate any continuing observance of the Jewish festal year in the community. Goulder himself lays little stress on the evidence from John, no doubt because the scattering of festivals across the Gospel, with three Passovers, makes it impossible that John is a

---

18. L. Morris, 'The Gospels', p. 141.

19. On Mt. 23, see most importantly Kenneth Newport, *Sources*.

20. Cf. for example R.E. Brown, *John*, on Guilding's 'impressive' list of parallels to John 6. He refers to Guilding's theory again in comments on John 7, 10, 18 and 19.

lectionary book which has readings for each of the festivals in order, like the Synoptics.

Festal worship continued to be practised in several branches of the church. While Origen mentions the day of the lord, the Sabbath, Passover and Pentecost (cf. *C. Cels.* viii.22), John Chrysostom says, as New Year and Tabernacles are approaching:

> Others will join the Jews in keeping their feasts and observing their fasts. I wish to drive this perverse custom from the Church right now.[21]

D. *The Problem of Baptism*

One of Hooker's criticisms of Goulder's thesis is that his picture of 'a settled community with lections for Sunday use and a catechumenate trained week by week in preparation for the baptismal service at Easter' is 'anachronistic'.[22] Here Hooker is going to the heart of Goulder's theory. Easter baptism is practised, according to Goulder, by the communities behind all four Gospels. Mark 7–13, comprising readings from Dedication to Passover, makes up the catechesis for Marcan Christians and explains some of the basic features of Mark's Gospel, the famous point that it is a 'Passion narrative with an extended introduction' and the fact that most of the teaching matter is contained in Chapters 7–13 (*EC*, pp. 275-78).

More importantly, on Luke, 'the liturgical setting, with Easter and Baptism ahead' helps to explain the structure of Luke 'with its long Journey that never seems to advance':

> This is the means of instructing the new converts, and of reminding the old, of the nature of their calling... He has filled out the Journey section with triple measures of catechesis, pressed down, shaken together and sometimes running over (*LNP*, pp. 171-72; cf. also *EC*, pp. 90-95).

Further, the theory explains Mt. 28.16-20:

> This is Easter day and the catechumens are waiting to be baptised: what could be more suitable than that the authority of the risen Jesus should be cited for the occasion? (*MLM*, p. 449).

It is also the basis for Goulder's theory on John. Johannine Christians

---

21. *Discourses Against Judaizing Christians*, I.5; cf. Van Goudoever, *Biblical Calendars*, pp. 151-63, for a survey of relevant material.
22. M. Hooker, Review of *EC*, p. 92.

gathered on the evening of the 13th/14th Nisan, and John 13 provides the backdrop for the baptism ('Liturgical Origin', pp. 206-207, 215). Here we find one of Goulder's brilliant suggestions:

> There is no break between Jn. 13 and 14, and it would be natural to think that the two chapters were delivered together, at the Baptism. At the end of 14, however, comes the surprising break of the Marcan text, 'Arise, let us go hence': perhaps the Johannine churches had two rooms, a baptistery and an assembly room, and this was the signal to proceed from the one to the other ('Liturgical Origin', p. 215).

Therefore, if Hooker is right that this picture is anachronistic, much of Goulder's lectionary theory falls with it. The earliest evidence to which Goulder appeals for Easter baptism is Matthew itself (*EC*, p. 91), but this can be, of course, somewhat circular. Goulder refers also to Hippolytus, *Apostolic Tradition* 20–21 which assumes baptism at Easter and Tertullian, *de Baptismo* 19 which says that the Pasch provides the day of greatest solemnity for baptism (*EC*, p. 91).[23] There are other references too, but Goulder stresses that the church probably took over a Paschal initiation rite from Judaism, citing Exod. 12.48 and Joshua 5 which associate Passover with circumcision and *b. Pes.* 91b–92a (Hillel and Shammai on proselyte baptism) and *y. Pes.* 8.8 (R. Eleazar b. Jacob on baptism and the Pasch).

Even if this evidence does suggest an early origin for the practice of Easter baptism, however, the idea of a pre-Easter catechism is less easy to establish. Goulder puts forward the *Didache* (*EC*, pp. 276-77) but at best this provides only indirect evidence. He suggests also Hippolytus, *Ap. Trad.* 16–18 and notes that we actually possess the Catecheses of Cyril of Jerusalem, given in about 348 CE (*EC*, p. 91). Again, one has to judge whether this is early enough to make Goulder's case likely.

There is a greater difficulty still, however, with the thesis of pre-Easter catechism in that Luke does, apparently, give some indication of baptismal practice in Acts. Morris observes that Luke repeatedly mentions people getting baptized spontaneously, without any period of instruction.[24] Luke could, of course, in Acts, be harking back to an earlier golden period of the church in which people quickly repented, believed and were baptized. Now the church had settled down, feverish expectation of the eschaton had diminished a little, Christians no longer

---

23. On the general question, a useful study is G.R. Beasley-Murray, *Baptism*.
24. L. Morris, 'The Gospels', pp. 132-33.

pooled all their money and they had to sit a three-month course before they could be baptized. This may be true and so, once again, Hooker's criticism, echoed by Morris, does not amount to a 'knock-down objection'. The criticism does, however, diminish the plausibility of Goulder's theory since Luke, the one for whom Goulder most stresses pre-Easter catechism, is the same one who, in Acts, give us some indication of what baptism was like in the earliest times.

E. *Passover and the Passion: The External Evidence*

Above, we noticed that Goulder's theory about the origin of the Passion narratives in the Gospels was one of the stronger parts of his lectionary theory. The question now relevant is whether or not there is any useful external evidence for the kind of paschal vigil which Goulder is proposing.

Goulder appeals to Egeria and 'all the earliest lectionaries from both the Jerusalem and the Byzantine traditions' (*EC*, p. 297; cf. *LNP*, pp. 151-52) and he refers also to *Mekilta ad Exod.* 12.42, quoting the first century R. Joshua b. Hananiah, for a Jewish tradition that the Messiah would come on Passover night:

> On that night they were redeemed and on that night they will be redeemed (*EC*, p. 293; *LNP*, p. 153).[25]

Also relevant is the *Didascalia Apostolorum*, chapter 21:

> You must thus fast when they (the Jews) celebrate Passover, and be zealous to fulfil your vigil in the midst of their Massoth (quoted in *EC*, p. 297, 'Liturgical Origin', p. 208 and *LNP*, p. 152).[26]

Further, both the *Epistula Apostolorum* 15 and Melito's Paschal Sermon witness to an all-night Passover vigil (*EC*, p. 294; *LNP*, p. 152).

This evidence varies in strength. Clearly, these references do show that the kind of vigil which Goulder is proposing has reasonably early parallels. The reference from the *Didascalia* is, at first sight, quite impressive, and dates from the third century; Melito's sermon and the *Epistula Apostolorum* are second century. There is a difficulty, however,

---

25. With references also (on *EC*, p. 293 and *LNP*, p. 153) to *Exod. R.* 15.1 and 18.12; an old Passover poem, 'The Four Nights' in *Frag. Targ. Exod.* 15.18 and Jerome, *Comm. Matt. ad* 25.6. Goulder has collected these references from Jeremias, *Eucharistic Words*.

26. See R.H. Connolly for an ET and commentary, *The Didascalia Apostolorum*.

with much of this evidence which is easy to miss. The vigil Goulder is suggesting for the Synoptists is on 14th/15th Nisan, or, for the Asians and John, on 13th/14th Nisan. In the year of the Passion, and so on one year in seven, this is Maundy Thursday/Good Friday. Most of the early evidence, though, does not clearly witness to a Maundy Thursday/Good Friday vigil but rather hints at an Easter eve fast, or even a two-day fast from Good Friday to Saturday.[27] Here the *Testamentum Domini*, dating form the second half of the fourth century, is explicit:

> Let the end of the Pascha be after the Saturday, at midnight (2.12).[28]

Not only is the vigil on the Saturday night rather than the Thursday night, but also it finishes much too early for Goulder's theory, at midnight.

It could be argued, and in some measure this is how Goulder does argue, that the evidence from the second century and beyond only demonstrates the general parallel with a proposed first century paschal vigil. If there was such a vigil in the first century, it is likely, after all, that it will have been connected with the Jewish Passover which is moveable. In this scenario, the vigil will have become fixed to Easter eve as Holy Week began to be established. It needs to be noticed, nevertheless, that the evidence which Goulder adduces is not conclusive, and that it does not point as specifically as Goulder suggests to exactly the kind of vigil he is proposing.

F. *Conclusion*

There is little clear information on worship in the New Testament period relevant to Goulder's theory. Some have claimed that Goulder's theory is unlikely in the light of passages like 1 Corinthians 14 and that worship in the first century was rather too charismatic to have allowed use of a lectionary. Such general criticism of the theory is not strong, especially if Goulder is right that breakaway religious movements are often conservative in matters of worship. More serious is the

27. For a useful recent introduction to the issues, see Peter G. Cobb, 'History'. Cobb takes it for granted that the *Didascalia*, chapter 21, is referring to Holy Saturday (p. 462).

28. Quoted from J. Cooper and A.J. Maclean, *Testament of the Lord*. Similar is Jerome, *Comm. Matt.*, *ad* 25.6, quoted by Goulder, *EC*, p. 293, though without the explicit reference to the Saturday.

comment in Justin Martyr that the memoirs of the apostles or the writings of the prophets were read 'as long as time permits' which seems to reflect a church in which a lectionary was not being used.

Gal. 4.10, Rom. 14.5 and Col. 2.16 have been used by some as evidence that the first century church did not observe Jewish festivals and fasts. However, in some respects these passages point to the contrary: they show that there was a desire, at least among Jewish Christians and Jewish Christian sympathisers, to keep the festal occasions. Gal. 4.10 is not directed against the observance of days as such; rather, Paul sees such observance as a sign that the Galatians are now depending on the law for salvation. Moreover, *1 Clement* 40 provides direct evidence, and Matthew, John and Acts may provide indirect evidence, of a tendency towards conservatism in matters of worship.

The evidence which Goulder adduces for Easter baptism is quite early, and the practice seems to have been widespread. The training of catechumens before Easter, which supposedly lies behind Mark and Luke, is less early. The great difficulty, though, especially for Luke, is that converts in Acts are baptised quite spontaneously.

Evidence for a Paschal vigil is also quite widespread and early. Goulder's theory does not pay sufficient attention to the fact that at least from the second century, Christians were keeping the Paschal fast on the Saturday night, the evening before Easter.

Most damaging of all these points is the quotation from Justin Martyr. Some of the other criticisms simply cast a little doubt on Goulder's theory. The point about celebration of festivals for which there is good first century evidence is the least problematic. This is an interesting conclusion in that Goulder's restatement in *LNP* stresses the parallels in the Gospels with the festal year.

If it is possible, then, that the evangelists' communities were 'observing days, and months, and seasons, and years', one will want to know if one can go a stage further and say that they might have designed their Gospels with the festal occasions (other than Passover-Easter) in view. Two things will help in this enquiry. First, one will want to know how valid are Goulder's claims for a Jewish lectionary cycle already being established by the first century. This will be the subject of Chapter 20. Second, one will want to know just how impressive are Goulder's correspondences between the themes of the festivals and fasts and relevant sections of the Gospels. This will be the subject of Chapter 21.

Chapter 20

JEWISH LECTIONARIES

A. *Preliminary Comments*

Many have criticized Goulder on the question of Jewish use of lectionaries in the first century. It is one of Morris's main points:

> It is not at all clear whether any lectionary in fact existed in New Testament times, and if one did we are far from having established what lections were read on particular days.[1]

This is echoed by Dunn,[2] Hooker,[3] D.R. Catchpole[4] and L. Sabourin who says that theories based on reconstructed Jewish lectionaries are 'doomed to failure'.[5] The Jewish expert J. Heinemann is also quite decided about the issue. He says that one can reach 'quite definite conclusions that there was no single, generally accepted Sabbath lectionary in use in the first century, and that all assertions regarding the reading of any particular weekly portion at fixed times of the year are entirely unfounded speculation'.[6]

There are actually three aspects to the question and it is important to distinguish between them:

1) What is the evidence for the reading of Scripture in the synagogues of the first century?

2) How early were the Scriptures read according to a set order?

3) When established, did the order follow an annual cycle beginning

---

1. L. Morris, *New Testament*, p. 10. The issue is discussed both here (pp. 10-24) and in 'The Gospels' (pp. 134-39).
2. J.D.G. Dunn, *Unity and Diversity*, p. 147: 'no evidence'.
3. M. Hooker, Review of *EC*, p. 92.
4. D.R. Catchpole, Review of *MLM*.
5. L. Sabourin, Review of *MLM*, p. 92. Cf. Harvey, Review of *MLM*, p. 188 and Sanders, Review of *MLM*, p. 454.
6. J. Heinemann, 'Triennial Lectionary Cycle', p. 41.

in Nisan, as Goulder proposes? In connection with this point, it is necessary to ask whether lectionaries can be reconstructed with any degree of confidence.

These points will be taken in turn.

B. *The Synagogue and the Reading of Scripture*

Scholars are almost unanimous on this point: at least some first century synagogues read the Law and the Prophets on a regular basis. Several texts witness to this:

Philo, *Fragment* 630-31: 'He commanded all the people to assemble together in the same place and to sit down with one another, to listen to the Law with order and reverence, in order that no one should be ignorant of anything it contains.'

Josephus, *Contra Apionem* II.175: Moses ordained: 'that every week people should desert their occupations and assemble to listen to the law and to obtain a thorough and accurate knowledge of it.'

Acts 15.21: 'For from early generations Moses has had in every city those who preach him, for he is read every sabbath in the synagogues.'

Acts 13.27: 'They did not...understand the utterances of the prophets which are read every sabbath.'

Only Morris raises a question here. He says that those proposing lectionary theories need to demonstrate that the synagogue itself is old enough to meet the case.[7]

C. *Reading according to a Set Order*

Mishnah tractate *Megillah* 3.4 speaks of the readings for the four 'special' sabbaths in Adar, then says:

On the fifth they revert to the set order (*likh^e sidrān*). At all these times they break off (from the set order in the reading of the Law): on the first

---

7. L. Morris, 'The Gospels', p. 134-35; cf. *New Testament*, pp. 12-13; but see J.W. Bowker, 'Speeches in Acts', p. 98. For recent studies on the synagogue, see, among others, S. Safrai, 'The Synagogue' and Lester L. Grabbe, 'Synagogues', who notes that if the synagogue in Palestine is a post-Maccabean phenomenon, it allows little time for the development of lectionary cycles (p. 409).

days of the months, at the (Feast of the) Dedication, at Purim, on days of
fasting, and at Maamads and on the Day of Atonement.[8]

Goulder takes it for granted that 'set order' means 'lectionary order'
(*EC*, pp. 61-62).[9] An objection to this might seem to be *t. Meg.* 4.10
(also *b. Meg.* 31b), where R. Meir (mid-second century) says:

> At the place where they leave off at the Sabbath morning service, they
> begin at the afternoon service; where they leave off at that service, they
> begin on Monday; where they leave off on Monday they begin on
> Thursday; and where they leave off on Thursday, they begin on the
> following Sabbath.

Meir's contemporary, R. Judah ben Ila'i, holds that the proper order is
to begin at each Sabbath morning service where the reading of the
previous Sabbath ended. Both rabbis are referring to continuous
reading, R. Meir between all services and R. Judah between Sabbath
services. G. F. Moore comments:

> It is clear from this that the authorities recognised no division of the
> Pentateuch into lessons of fixed length, or a cycle of lessons to be
> finished within a fixed time.[10]

Goulder, not surprisingly, interprets the same passage as giving support
to his own theory. He says that Meir is referring to a breaking up of the
large weekly *sidrā* so that Leviticus 1–5, for example, would be taken
in parts, Leviticus 1 on the Sabbath, Leviticus 2 on the Monday and so
on (*EC*, p. 57). This solution is like Goulder's reading of the passage
from Justin, cited above (p. 418), and it may be another instance of
Goulder reading a potential weakness for his thesis as a strength. It is a
possible but less natural reading of the text and one might compare
Heinemann's judgement on the same passage:

> The very existence of the above ruling in the second half of the second
> century makes nonsense of the assumption that one single, fixed
> lectionary was in use at the time.[11]

Even if Goulder is right, though, the material is not early enough to
establish the use of a fixed cycle in the first century. Indeed, nothing

---

8.   Quoted from H. Danby, *The Mishnah*.
9.   Cf. L. Crockett, 'Luke 4.16-30', p. 20: the expression *hesidran* 'seems to
suggest an ordering of Pentateuchal reading for the sabbaths of the year'.
10.   G.F. Moore, *Judaism* vol. 1, p. 299.
11.   J. Heinemann, 'Triennial Lectionary Cycle', p. 45.

from the first century or earlier witnesses directly to the use of any sort of lectionary. This is probably the most common and the most justified criticism of the lectionary theory. Nevertheless, the fact that there was no authoritatively established, universally accepted lectionary does not rule out the possibility of some provincially used lectionaries. It is difficult, after all, to imagine who would authorise a lectionary and how, if authorised, a lectionary could be practically enforced.[12]

Goulder also offers a general point in favour of serial reading of the Law:

> Only consider Josiah's dismay (2 Kings 22.11ff) when he heard of the discovery of the roll of the Law in the Temple: *ignoratio Legis neminem excusat.* Now, there is no surer way of leaving some parts of the Law unread than to pick and choose each sabbath: if all is vital, all must be read, and the only methodical way to read is to read in series (*EC*, p. 5).

This point has some force. Philo (*Fragment* 630-31, quoted above) equates public reading of the Law with public knowledge of the whole of the Law, 'in order that no one should be ignorant of anything it contains'. Further, one might remember warnings like Deut. 28.58-59: 'If you are not careful to do all the words of the Law which are written in this book...then the LORD will bring on you and your offspring extraordinary afflictions'. Although this general point tells in favour of continuous reading in order, so that nothing is missed out, it does not, however, necessarily tell in favour of a set, lectionary order. There is a fine line between continuous reading from service to service and continous reading according to an already fixed order. The natural reading of the dispute between R. Meir and R. Judah b. Il'ai would suggest that there was a desire to read continuously, taking up at each service where one left off in the previous one, without recourse to a fixed order. As one looks at the indirect evidence below, therefore, it is necessary to bear in mind that there is no direct evidence of any lectionary in use in the first century.[13]

---

12. I am grateful to Professor Ed Sanders for this point.

13. Cf. Bowker, 'Speeches in Acts', p. 99: 'Obviously when there is no direct evidence either way, it is only possible to speak of probabilities, and in the present case the probability is extremely high that a lectionary existed before the destruction.'

D. *Goulder's Annual Cycle*

The Babylonian Talmud, *Megillah* 29b, refers in passing to 'the people of Palestine, who complete the reading of the Pentateuch in three years'[14] and the passage is usually taken as contrasting an assumed annual cycle in Babylonia with a triennial one in Palestine. As this is the first explicit mention of either annual or triennial cycles, it is necessary to ask how much earlier than the compilation of the Babylonian Talmud these practices can be dated.

Each cycle has two possible base dates: Nisan was the first Jewish month but there was also the old festival of New Year in Tishri.

Taking these considerations into mind, Goulder lists five possible theories about the lectionary system in the first-century Western synagogue (*EC*, p. 20):

1. Freedom and no system, the opinion of both Moore and Heinemann.
2. A triennial cycle beginning in Tishri, the opinion of Jacob Mann.[15]
3. A triennial cycle beginning in Nisan, the opinion of Adolf Büchler.[16]
4. An annual cycle beginning in Tishri, the system operating today.[17]
5. An annual cycle beginning in Nisan, Goulder's view.

A sixth possibility, not considered by Goulder, might be added to these: that there was no uniformity.[18]

What Goulder needs to show is that the fifth option here is the most likely. He is the only exponent of the view and a good deal of *EC* is devoted to this. His primary arguments (*EC*, chapter two) are these:

1. Redaction of the Pentateuch: Goulder finds clues in the Pentateuch itself of ancient reading practice. Leviticus 16, concerning the Day of Atonement, comes just over halfway

14. Quoted from M. Simon (ed.), *Tractate Megillah*, p. 180.
15. J. Mann, *Bible*.
16. A. Büchler, 'Reading'.
17. Moses Gaster thinks that this goes back very early: see 'Biblical Lessons'. Goulder does not refer to this though much of it, particularly the scathing comments about the possibility of a triennial cycle, is conducive to his case.
18. Cf. Heinemann, 'Triennial Lectionary Cycle', who claims that too much has been made of *b. Meg.* 29b; cf. also J.R. Porter, 'Pentateuch'.

through the Pentateuch. Atonement is on the 10th Tishri, just over halfway through a year beginning in Nisan, and the reading in the Mishnah and the Talmud is Leviticus 16. The Tabernacles reading, Leviticus 23, is also in the right place.[19]

2. The Chronicler: In *MLM*, chapter ten, Goulder argues that the Chronicler's history was composed as a series of second lessons to the Torah readings. The correspondences adduced are not only general but also detailed. For Goulder, this is evidence that the Law was read cyclically in fourth century BCE.

3. The Samaritan Annual Cycle: Goulder speculates that the Samaritans began reading the Torah in an annual cycle in the late Persian period and not in the Samaritan rennaissance period in the fourth century CE.

4. The Special Sabbaths: Of the four special readings for the sabbaths in Adar, three 'testify to the existence of an annual cycle in the BC period' (*EC*, p. 42).

   a. In the Mishnah the reading for sabbath Zakor, the second in Adar, is Deut. 25.17-19. *Sidrā* 49 in the annual cycle[20] is Deut. 21.10–25.19 end: if the cycle began in Nisan, these two readings would almost coincide.

   b. The last sabbath in Adar is Hahodesh, when Exod. 12.2 is read: 'This month shall be for you the beginning of months; it shall be the first month of the year for you...' Goulder says that the passage is 'aggressive' in tone because of 'the assertion of orthodoxy' which aimed at eclipsing the old Tishri annual cycle (*EC*, pp. 43-44).

   c. The Babylonian Tishri cycle is reflected in the reading for the first sabbath in Adar, Sheqalim, Exod. 30.11-16. In *b. Meg.* 29b-30a this reading is seen sometimes to coincide with the same reading in the annual cycle (*EC*, pp. 44-47).[21]

5. Philo: The divisions in *Questions on Genesis, Questions on Exodus* are held to reflect very closely the divisions of the

19. Guilding attempts something similar in *Fourth Gospel*; cf. Porter's criticism, 'Pentateuch', p. 165.

20. For the annual cycle *sidrôt*, Goulder uses the 'traditional' lections found in the Jewish Year Book and reprinted in *EC*, pp. 68-69.

21. Cf. M. Gaster, 'Biblical Lessons', pp. 531-32.

traditional *sidrôt* (*EC*, pp. 47-48).[22] Since Philo lived in first century Egypt, Goulder finds this evidence impressive.

6.   Matthew: Here a series of fulfilments of *sidrôt* is stressed
      a. The first *sidrā*, Gen. 1.1–6.8, features the Cain and Abel story. Matthew 23 falls opposite this in Goulder's scheme and it ends with: '...that upon you may come all the righteous blood shed on earth, from the blood of innocent Abel to the blood of Zechariah son of Barachiah' (v. 35).
      b. The second *sidrā* is Gen. 6.9–11.32, end, on Noah. Matthew 24 falls opposite, 'As were the days of Noah, so will be the coming of the Son of man...' (vv. 37ff.).
      c. Matthew 1 begins with the genealogy, traced back to Abraham, and *sidrā* 5 (Gen. 23.1–25.18) closes with a genealogy of Abraham's descendants (Gen. 25.1-18).
      d. In *sidrā* 6 (Gen. 25.19–28.9), Jacob is blessed, 'Let nations serve thee, and princes bow down to thee', and Esau (Edom) plans to kill him. Mt. 2.1-12 has Gentile magi bowing down and Herod, the Edomite king, planning to kill Jesus.
      e. *Sidrā* 7 (Gen. 28.10–32.2) features Rachel. Mt. 2.13-23 has the quotation from Jeremiah 31.15 which has often puzzled commentators: 'Rachel weeping for her children; she refused to be consoled because they were no more' (Mt. 2.18).

This is a point which can be tested: there are few references to figures from the Pentateuch in Matthew. The following list, with the exception of the names in the genealogy, is exhaustive:

Mt.	1.1, 2, 17	<u>Abraham</u>
	2.18	<u>Rachel</u>
	3.9	Abraham (as our father)
	8.4	Moses (commanded)
	8.11	Abraham, Isaac and Jacob
	17.3-4	Moses (and Elijah)
	19.7	Moses (commanded)
	22.24	Moses (said)
	22.32	Abraham, Isaac and Jacob
	23.35	<u>Abel</u>
	24.37-38	<u>Noah</u>

22.   The argument is from R. Marcus, *Quaestiones*, pp. xiii-xv. Morris refers to Marcus in *New Testament* (p. 16), against Guilding, but not in 'The Gospels'.

Those underlined are the ones which correspond with the appropriate *sidrôt*, to which Goulder draws attention. Of the remaining seven, two are the formulaic 'Abraham, Isaac and Jacob' and three are 'Moses commanded/said', another formulaic expression which could be applied to any statement from the Pentateuch. This leaves only Abraham (3.9) and Moses with Elijah on the mount of Transfiguration (17.3-4). In 3.9 the reference to Abraham is general—'children to Abraham'/'Abraham as our father' refers to Jewish identity. For 17.3-4, Moses occurs in the parallel *sidrā* from Numbers and, in any case, the Transfiguration in Matthew is in the Markan order.

This evidence is impressive but there are two difficulties with it. First, the names are not spread evenly over the Gospel—they are all in the 'Genesis' section. Second, the evidence is not, strictly speaking, a proof of Goulder's case. Rather it is something which would be explained if his thesis were shown on other grounds to be correct. Indeed most of Goulder's points are of the same nature. On Point 2 he says, 'the only satisfactory conclusion to this analysis is that the Chronicler was used to a *sidrā-haphtarah* system...' (*EC*, p. 39). On Point 3, the Samaritan cycle, Goulder says: 'At every step a simple continuous reading cycle from the beginning is the easiest solution' (*EC*, pp. 41-42). On Point 4, the special sabbaths, Goulder says: 'A solution to these problems is plain when the position of Deut. 25.17ff is noted in the proposed lectionary system...A second special reading whose institution is illuminated by the lectionary hypothesis is that on the last sabbath in Adar...' (*EC*, p. 43).

Point 5 (Philo) is strongest and it is free from this trait. However the evidence is not conclusive: whereas Goulder says Philo 'must have been following the *sidrā* divisions of his day for Genesis' (*EC*, p. 48), Marcus, on whom Goulder depends here, says 'there is room for doubt' that the hypothesis is sound.[23] It is worth noting, in particular, that there is no exact correspondence between the whole of a book and the whole of a *sidrā* on the list.[24]

The case, then, for an annual cycle beginning in Nisan established in the first century is patchy and if the idea 'explains numerous details which would otherwise remain puzzling', Goulder is over-stating the

---

23. *Quaestiones*, p. xv.

24. R. Marcus, *Quaestiones*, p. xiv. The nearest is Book VI on Gen. 25.20–28.9 and *sidrā* 6 on Gen. 25.19–28.9 but here the Book VI is Marcus's own reconstruction, corresponding to the last part of Book IV in the Armenian Version.

case to say that it 'rests, then, upon wide documentation' (*EC*, p. 48).

E. *A Festal Lectionary Cycle*

It could be said that a festal cycle is implicit from the earliest times. The best argument here is from common sense.[25] Moore says that it would be 'most natural' for relevant passages from the Pentateuch to be read at the festal seasons. In *b. Meg.* 32a, Moses ordained that the *halachah* should be studied in connection with the appropriate season, the laws of Passover at Passover and so on.[26] The only question here is whether or not, in the strict sense, one is talking about a lectionary: readings for the festivals cover, of course, only part of the year.

One of the advantages of appeal to a festal cycle is that it cuts through the problems found in discussion of annual and triennial cycles, as Goulder realised in *MLM*:

> It is irrelevant to our thesis which length of cycle was being followed, because the Jewish Festal year was invariable, and it is with this that Matthew shows strict agreement (*MLM*, p. 183).

It is this aspect of the thesis that is stressed for Mark and Luke too in the restatement in *LNP*:

> In the present state of knowledge the sabbath readings in the synagogue are speculative, and the correspondences with the Gospels are in any case patchy: so the sabbath hypothesis needs to be shelved, though it does not need to be abandoned. But the evidence of correspondence between all the Gospels and the main feasts and fasts of a (Jewish-) Christian Year is much stronger (*LNP*, p. 147).

Goulder avoids some of the severest criticisms of *EC* by means of this restatement but even so, an important problem remains. The discussion has concerned the reading of Scripture in lectionary cycles but in addition to this, it needs to be asked whether or not anyone actually composed books which were designed to be read as lectionaries. Sanders[27] says that Goulder is hard put to find good contemporary parallels for what he is proposing. Goulder offers in particular the example of the Chronicler but Harvey notes[28] that this requires a

25. Although see also H. St. John Thackeray, *Septuagint*.
26. *Judaism*, Vol. 1, p. 297; cf. Van Goudoever, *Biblical Calendars*, p. 147.
27. E.P. Sanders, Review of *MLM*, p. 454.
28. A.E. Harvey, Review of *MLM*, p. 192.

number of subsidiary hypotheses. It is the problem, once more, of hypothesis built on top of hypothesis. Sanders comments that:

> This is not necessarily a devastating criticism in view of the accidental nature of literary remains but it does place a question mark against the hypothesis.[29]

F. *Conclusion*

There is strong evidence that the Law and the Prophets were read regularly in at least some first century synagogues. It is less clear whether or not the scriptures were read according to a 'set order' in the New Testament period. Adequate evidence to make a judgment either way is lacking, but it is possible that lectionary cycles were employed in some places in the first century.

Goulder's reconstruction of an annual cycle beginning in Nisan is rather too hopeful, although there is probably enough in Goulder's case to warrant shelving it, as he recommends, rather than abandoning it. Particularly impressive are the correspondences he adduces between the *sidrôt* from Genesis and passages in Matthew. Nevertheless, most of Goulder's evidence for the reading of the Pentateuch in an annual cycle beginning in Nisan is indirect and at best suggestive rather than probative.

It is more reasonable to speak of a some kind of festal lectionary cycle as early as the first century and this is the basis of Goulder's restatement in *LNP*. There are, however, no parallels to festal lectionary books even if people did read the appropriate parts of Scripture at the right times. The Synoptic Gospels, then, will be books without clear parallel. This is an important weakness in Goulder's thesis and places all the more weight on the issue of correspondences between certain sections of the Gospels and the appropriate festal themes. We will turn finally, then, to the key question: how strong are the correspondences which Goulder adduces?

---

29. E.P. Sanders, Review of *MLM*, p. 454.

Chapter 21

THE STRENGTH OF THE CORRESPONDENCES

A. *Preliminary Comments*

Most of those who comment on Goulder's lectionary hypothesis do not look at the heart of the theory, the issue of correspondences. They concentrate on *a priori* questions and look at underlying difficulties like the nature of early Christian worship and the problem of Jewish lectionaries. This is, of course, quite legitimate since Goulder's theory, to remain plausible, needs to be shown to be consonant with the evidence we have of such matters. Nevertheless, if one looks purely at the general questions, one is in danger of missing Goulder's key argument and hence of distorting his thesis.

Goulder suggests that his lectionary hypothesis is not only plausible but also probable because of the correspondences between certain sections of the Gospels and themes of the Jewish festivals and fasts. The correspondences are simply too good not to be true. Only Evans really comments on this, when dealing with *EC*:

> Is this or that correspondence to be adjudged a bull's eye, an inner, an outer or a magpie? How many points are to be given for each, and what total or distribution of points would constitute plausibility approximating to proof? How many weak or forced correspondences may be admitted without the whole structure beginning to totter?[1]

Goulder claims that his restatement in *LNP* avoids the difficulties of the earlier weekly, sabbath case. The demand for correspondences every week is too great, whereas in a festal lectionary, Goulder is 'obliged to provide a bull's eye' for each festival (*LNP*, p. 173). He then suggests that the racecourse provides a better image than the shot because it allows one to 'compute probabilities, or odds, rather than awarding

---

1. C.F. Evans, 'Goulder and the Gospels', p. 431.

points'. The Passover/Easter positions suggested the theory, so they are fixed:

> But once they are fixed, all the other feasts have to be in their places, or the hypothesis fails. One black swan will kill it; and we need white swans in all the remaining ponds—four Matthean, three Markan and four Lukan ponds. That is a multiplication of eleven probabilities; and I should like to meet the bookmaker who will take money on that (*LNP*, p. 174).[2]

This sounds impressive and it ought to be enough to show the lectionary theory to be correct. It would only be enough, however, if Goulder is right to call each reading a 'bull's eye' or a 'white swan'. The aim of this chapter is to see whether or not these images are appropriate.

Clearly Goulder does not think that any of the eleven readings he finds are 'black swans'. It might be asked, however, whether the readings he proposes are the most appropriate ones that could be found for each occasion. If all the synoptists are writing their Gospels in accordance with the festal year, one will expect them to provide quite the most appropriate lesson imaginable for each festal occasion.

It is worth looking, therefore, to see whether Goulder's scheme provides the best possible reading from the Gospel in question for each liturgical occasion, or whether there are any other sections in any of the Gospels which would suit a given festival or fast as well as Goulder's sections do.

The eleven festal readings to which Goulder is referring are New Year, Atonement and Tabernacles for all three synoptics and Pentecost also for Matthew and Luke. These are the occasions found in Leviticus 23 and stressed in *LNP*. They will be taken in turn.

One difficulty is that there are no straightforward criteria for establishing what the most important themes of the feasts and fasts were to the synoptic writers. There are, however, ways out of the difficulty. First, it is worth noting that the themes to which Goulder draws attention are largely drawn, reliably, from the Bible and the Mishnah. Before looking at the correspondences in each section, then, we will look briefly at Goulder's presentation of themes for each festal occasion and attention will be drawn to any problems. Further, if we

---

2. Goulder uses the terms 'feasts', 'festivals' and 'festal' to cover liturgical occasions. I will avoid using 'feast' and 'festival' of Atonement, though it will sometimes be necessary to use 'festal' for ease of expression.

look primarily at the themes which Goulder claims to be important, then Goulder's theory will be able to be examined for its internal consistency. His theory will be being tested against the demands which Goulder himself makes on it in order to see whether or not the theory can be falsified.

B. *New Year*

1. *Goulder's Themes*

Goulder says that the New Year liturgy is marked in the Mishnah by the recital of three sequences of verses from scripture on three themes (*LNP*, p. 157; *MLM*, pp. 175, 312-13; *EC*, p. 84-85, 162-63, 245-46), Trumpet-blasts, *shôpārôt* (Lev. 23.24; Num. 29.1; Psa. 81.3, *m. Ro'sh Hash.* 1.3; 3; 4.5-6 etc.); God's sovereignty, *malkīyyôt* (*m. Ro'sh Hash.* 4.5-6; Pss. 93; 97; 99); and God's remembrance of Israel, *zikrônôt* (*m. Ro'sh Hash.* 4.5-6; cf. Lev. 23.24, 'a memorial').

Goulder adds that the festival is also characterized by two phenomena: first, 'sober rejoicing' and judgment (*m. Ro'sh Hash.* 1.2; psalms); and second, penitence, opening a season of penitence before Atonement (cf. the *'alēnû* prayer for the day; *b. Ro'sh Hash* 16b).

2. *Mark*

Goulder proposes that Mk 1.1-20 opens the Gospel at New Year, and he finds there, in some measure, all of the above themes. The trumpet-blasts, the *shôpār* theme, whereby 'the king's messengers would go out before him to summon his people to join in the annual pilgrimage feast' (*LNP*, p. 158), is present in John the Baptist's making the way ready. God's sovereignty, the *malkût* theme, 'is there verbally in the kingdom of God announced by Jesus' (Mk 1.15, *LNP*, p. 158). God's remembrance of Israel, the *zikrôn* theme, is implied 'in the time being fulfilled and the good news proclaimed' (*LNP*, p. 158).

Goulder adds that:

> The tone of sober joy is well reflected. God is inaugurating his final act of judgment/redemption, and his people repent for the forgiveness of their sins (*LNP*, p. 158).

In short, then, Goulder finds all the important themes of New Year present in the opening section of Mark's Gospel.

It is not possible to find any other section of Mark which features all these themes.

3. *Matthew*

Goulder proposes that Matthew 11 is the evangelist's reading for New Year,[3] thus Matthew 1–10 constitutes the 'new first half' which is prefixed to Mark (*LNP*, p. 159). Goulder is doubly impressed. First, he says:

> The remarkable thing about Matthew's treatment of John is that having described his ministry in the Markan context (Matthew 3), he returns to it in an extensive flashback in ch. 11 (*LNP*, p. 159).

Second, all the relevant New Year themes are again evident. The trumpet-blasts are there in reference to John again making the way ready, using the same Exod. 23.20–Mal. 3.1 quotation (Mt. 11.10 // Mk 1.2). God's sovereignty is there in the note that the kingdom suffers violence (Mt. 11.12, cf. 10.7-8 where the disciples proclaim the kingdom). Judgment is certainly a prominent theme with the mention of Sodom and 'the day of judgment' (Mt. 11.22 and 24). Likewise, repentance is implicit in the fact that John 'came to proclaim repentance to a hardened generation, who would play with neither him nor the Son of Man' (*LNP*, p. 160) and, further, 'Sodom and Gomorrah would have repented long ago in sackcloth and ashes' (Mt. 11.21).

Goulder does not draw attention to the theme of God's remembrance of Israel but he concludes confidently:

> So one after another, the themes of New Year are there in Matthew 11: the messenger, repentance, judgment to come, the kingdom. Matthew 11 seems to provide a very adequate, and extended, New Year lesson, and at just the right place: nearly half-way through Matthew 1-23 (*LNP*, p. 160).

Two other passages might also be adequate for New Year on the basis of Goulder's breakdown of the themes. The first is Matthew 3.1-17 which provides all the relevant themes. Since, however, it is the parallel to Mk 1.1-11, which *ex hypothesi* would have to be in this position in the Gospel, it is not a problem for Goulder's thesis. More serious is the fact that Mt. 24.1-51 (Eschatological Discourse)[4]

---

3. Cf. *MLM*, p. 314, 'For New Year itself Matthew provides two discourses, one in 10, one in 11'. In *LNP*, Goulder only deals with Matthew 11 for New Year. See further below, pp. 354-55 and 357-59 for difficulties with the division of the text.

4. This is actually two sections in *MLM*, both assigned to Passion week.

provides all the relevant themes. The trumpet-blasts, with the 'messenger' theme, are found literally in the prophecy that 'he will send out his angels with a loud trumpet-call' (24.31) on which Goulder comments:

> The Son of Man similarly ushers in the New Age by sending out his angels with a blast on the *shôpār* of heaven (*MLM*, p. 312).

A more appropriate fulfilment of New Year would be difficult to imagine and, further, God's sovereignty is implicit throughout (24.14, 'this gospel of the kingdom will be preached throughout the whole world'; 24.36, 'of that day and hour no one knows...but the Father only). Likewise, judgment is a key theme, particularly in 24.36-51, with Noah, the two women grinding at the mill and the wicked servant being punished with the hypocrites. One might say that the importance of penitence, then, is also an underlying theme. God's remembrance of Israel is explicit also—the angels 'gather his elect from the four winds' (24.31). This passage would, then, be as appropriate as Goulder's for New Year.

4. *Luke*

Goulder proposes that on a reasonable division of the text, Luke will have reached New Year by 7.18-35. This is Luke's parallel to Matthew 11.2-19 and the fact that Mt. 11.1 is the 316th verse in Matthew and Lk. 7.18 the 320th verse in Luke provides, Goulder suggests, a corroboration of the thesis. The New Year themes are, however, diminished a little. Mt. 11.12 (kingdom suffers violence) is paralleled in Lk. 16.16 and Mt. 11.20-24 (judgment on the cities of Galilee) is reproduced in Lk. 10.13-15. On the other hand, Goulder claims that 'Luke has stressed the messenger theme' (11.27) and, in addition, 'he distinguishes the impenitent Pharisees from the penitent people' (11.29-30; *LNP*, p. 160).

The correspondences in this section, then, with the themes of the New Year festival are not as strong as those for Matthew and Mark. All that remains is the messenger theme and an implied penitence theme. Goulder's case relies quite heavily, therefore, on the fact that Lk. 7.18-35 falls in the right place for the theory, that it deals with John the Baptist and that it is Luke's parallel to Matthew's New Year reading.

A handful of other passages have as many of the New Year themes. Lk. 3.1-20 (John the Baptist) would be quite appropriate but this is Luke's parallel to Mk 1.1-15 and one would expect it to feature the right themes (and the 'kingdom' saying in Mk 1.15 is omitted).

More seriously, Lk. 10.1-24 might be regarded as suitable for New Year. The messenger theme is present in that the seventy are sent out ahead of Jesus (Lk. 10.1) and they proclaim the gospel of the kingdom (10.9). God's sovereignty is also quite clear from 10.21-22 (Thanksgiving), a passage which is brought in, on Goulder's theory, from Matthew 11 (vv. 25-27), Matthew's New Year passage. Likewise, judgment is the theme of Lk. 10.13-15, brought forward again from Matthew 11 (vv. 21-23). There is a good deal here which, it could be argued, would be suitable for a Lukan New Year.

Perhaps also worth mentioning is Lk. 4.16-30 in which Jesus proclaims 'the acceptable year of the Lord' (v. 19). Themes like judgment and penitence are not a part of this section, but Jesus is God's messenger, the Spirit of the Lord having anointed him 'to preach good news to the poor' (v. 18).

5. *Summary*
Goulder's passage for Mark, 1.1-20, provides a suitable reading for New Year. No other passage turns up as many correspondences with the themes Goulder outlines for New Year.

Goulder's passage for Matthew, Chapter 11, is quite strong. Mt. 3.1-17 is as good a candidate, but this is the parallel to Mk 1.1-15. More problematic for Goulder is the fact that Mt. 24.1-51 would be a good reading for New Year, mentioning all the appropriate themes, and the *shôpār* explicitly.

Lk. 7.18-35 is the weakest. Although it falls in the right place for the theory, and is the parallel to Mt. 11.18-35, there are only a couple of themes appropriate for New Year, John the Baptist as messenger and penitence implied. Lk. 3.1-20 would be more appropriate, but this is the parallel to Mk 1.1-15. Also appropriate would be Lk. 10.1-24 which has most of the relevant themes, messenger, judgment, sovereignty and penitence. Perhaps also Lk. 4.16-30 would make a good New Year reading.

C. *Atonement*

1. *Goulder's Themes*
Goulder says that: 'We are not in doubt about the themes of Atonement' (*LNP*, p. 161; *MLM*, pp. 187, 200; *EC*, pp. 85-86, 178-79, 252-53):

> It is the Day (*Yoma'*) of the forgiveness of sins, and it is 'the Fast' *par*
> *excellence, Zoma' Rabba'*. Lev. 23.27-32 warns three times in the
> strongest terms that 'you are to afflict your souls' from evening to
> evening (*LNP*, p. 161).

Goulder adds:

> The *sidrā* was Leviticus 16 from early times (*m. Meg.* 3.4), with
> Leviticus 18 at the afternoon service (*minhah*) according to *b. Meg.* 31a:
> the prophetic readings at the two services according to the latter text
> were Isa. 57.15–58 (on the true fast), and the book of Jonah (on the
> preaching of repentance) (*LNP*, p. 161).[5]

Repentance is a theme also mentioned by Goulder for New Year and
so, perhaps, one cannot lay too much stress on it here. Forgiveness of
sins is a common theme in the Gospels, therefore one will expect to
find several readings appropriate for Atonement. Fasting, however, is
less common and a combination of forgiveness and fasting within a
Gospel passage will be impressive.

2. *Mark*

Mk 1.21-34 (Capernaum Day) and 1.35-45 (Preaching Tour; Leper)
provide a couple of lections for the one or two Sabbaths between New
Year on 1 Tishri and Atonement on the 10th.[6] Mark's Atonement
reading would then be 2.1-22, the Paralytic, the Call of Levi and the
Question about Fasting (*LNP*, pp. 161-62; *EC*, pp. 252-54). Goulder
asks: 'what story better epitomized' the notion that Jesus, as God's
vicegerent, 'brought forgiveness to the Church' (*EC*, p. 252) than the
Paralytic, in which Jesus pronounces: 'My son, your sins are forgiven'
(Mk 2.5) and Jesus is challenged: 'Who can forgive sins but God
alone?' (Mk 2.7)? In addition, the Call of Levi provides 'an especially
good' example of the 'many stories about Jesus' acceptance of sinners'
(*EC*, p. 252) and more remarkably, fasting is the theme of the
subsequent pericope.

Another appropriate section might be Mk 11.20-25 (v. 25: 'Whenever
you stand praying, forgive...'). Another possibility would be the
Beelzebul Controversy which concludes with the saying about

---

5.   The themes are also in the Mishnah, forgiveness in *m. Yoma* 3.7 etc. and
fasting in *m. Yoma* 8. For Goulder (*EC*, pp. 178-79), Jonah was designed for
Atonement.

6.   But contrast *MLM*, p. 200, where 1.21-28 is Mark's reading for Atonement.

forgiveness over blasphemy against the Holy Spirit (Mk 3.28-29). In neither of these passages, however, is there any mention of fasting, so Goulder's passage for Atonement, Mk 2.1-22, is an impressive one. No other passage in Mark features the two themes together.

3. *Matthew*

Goulder suggests that since Matthew 11 provides a suitable reading for New Year, Mt. 12.22-45 would fall at the right time for Atonement (*LNP*, pp. 162-63; *EC*, pp. 253-54; *MLM*, pp. 187-89).[7] For Matthew, though, there is not such a positive reading. He is 'the wise pastor' and 'the Day is rather an occasion to warn of the limits of Atonement' (*LNP*, p. 162). The healing dispute concludes with Jesus' words:

> Therefore I tell you, people will be forgiven for every sin and blasphemy, but blasphemy against the Spirit will not be forgiven. Whoever speaks a word against the Son of Man will be forgiven, but whoever speaks against the Holy Spirit will not be forgiven, either in this age or in the age to come (Mt. 12.31-32).

In addition to the forgiveness theme, Goulder sees Leviticus 16 reflected in Mt. 12.43-45 when the unclean spirit 'passes through waterless places seeking rest'. 'The purged sins', Goulder says, 'are repeatedly called ἀκαθαρσίαι' in Leviticus 16, 'and the scapegoat is let go in the wilderness' (*LNP*, p. 163; cf. *EC*, p. 254). More impressive still is the fact that Matthew also has here the material about the sign of Jonah (12.38-42).

Goulder's Atonement lesson for Matthew is, therefore, quite strong, but it is worth remembering that impressive as the reference to Jonah is, our authority for the Atonement *haptarôt*, the Babylonian Talmud, is relatively late. Also worth noting is that the fasting theme in Matthew is absent.

These points become serious when one bears in mind that forgiveness is a common theme in Matthew and that 18.23-35 (Unmerciful Servant) is, in many ways, the forgiveness parable *par excellence*. Further, Matthew's parallel to Mk 2.1-22, Mt. 9.1-17, would also be appropriate for Atonement, especially as here we have the fasting theme too (Mt. 9.14-15, Question about Fasting). For Goulder, the

---

7.   In *MLM*, the Beelzebul Controversy falls on the Sabbath before Atonement so Mt. 12.38-45 is the Atonement lesson proper. In *EC*, p. 252, 12.22-37 and 12.38-45 form the morning and afternoon readings respectively.

latter passage is Matthew's reading for 9th Ab (*MLM*, pp. 186-87 and 324-25; *EC*, p. 214).[8]

More seriously, Matthew has another passage with the twin themes, 6.7-18. The Lord's Prayer features the petition, 'Forgive us our debts...' and interprets:

> For if you forgive others their trespasses, your heavenly Father will also forgive you; but if you do not forgive others, neither will your Father forgive your trespasses' (Mt. 6.14-15).

The passage immediately following on from this gives advice on fasting (Mt. 6.16-19). In this connection it is also worth noting that there is a parallel[9] between Mt. 6.16 on looking dismal and disfiguring oneself when fasting and Isa. 58.5:

> Is such the fast that I choose,
> a day for a man to humble himself?
> Is it to bow down his head like a rush,
> and to spread sackcloth and ashes under him?

Since, then, an alternative reading not only has the two relevant themes, fasting and forgiveness, but also has an echo of one of the *haphtarôt*, the presence of this passage in Matthew diminishes the impressiveness of Goulder's case.

4. *Luke*

According to Goulder, Luke, like Mark, prefers a positive view of Atonement and his reading is 7.36-50, the Woman at Simon the Pharisee's house (*LNP*, pp. 163-64 and 397-99; *EC*, pp. 85-86, 254). For Luke, there is no intervening material between New Year and Atonement because Luke takes the relevant readings on the Sundays closest to the Festival or Fast. This pericope would indeed make a suitable lesson for a Christian Atonement. It is also telling, Goulder says, that several of the themes from Mark 2 recur in Luke.[10]

---

8.   This is criticized by Harvey, Review of *MLM*, p. 192; Goulder responds in *EC*, p. 214 n. 2. Because of the strictures of allotting Mt. 8–9 for the weeks between Pentecost and New Year, Mt. 9.9-17 actually falls on the Sabbath nearest to 9th Ab. See further on the difficulties over Mt. 8–9 below, pp. 354-55 and 357-59.

9.   Both RSV (1971) and UBS[3] note the parallel between Mt. 6.16 and Isa. 58.5.

10.   The same point is used in favour of Luke's use of Mt. 9 here. See above, pp. 258-59.

The fasting theme is not present. The only passage in Luke where fasting is mentioned is Lk. 5.17-39, parallel to Mk 2.1-22.

There are other passages in which the forgiveness of sins is prominent in Luke, perhaps most notably in the parables of ch. 15, but also in Zacchaeus (19.1-10). Nevertheless, if one were to choose a passage in which forgiveness of sins is explicitly expounded, 7.36-50 would probably be the best contender.

5. *Summary*

Goulder's Atonement reading for Mark, 2.1-22, turns up the twin themes of forgiveness and fasting, as required. In no other place in Mark do these themes occur together. Goulder's thesis is strong, therefore, on Mark. It is less strong on Matthew. Mt. 12.22-45 does not have the fasting theme in contrast to Mt. 9.1-17 (parallel to Mk 2.1-22) and Mt. 6.7-18 which both have the twin themes. Goulder's passage, 12.22-45, does clearly expound a Jonah theme and it features an echo of Leviticus 16, but this is at least half balanced by the fact that there is an allusion to Isa. 58.5 in Mt. 6.16. Further, there is other material on forgiveness in Matthew, like 18.23-35 (Unmerciful Servant).

Goulder's passage for Luke, 7.36-50, fully expounds the forgiveness theme. There is no reference to fasting here. Fasting is only found in Luke in 5.17-39, parallel to Mk 2.1-22. There are other places in Luke where one can find forgiveness, for example in ch. 15.

Goulder's thesis is, then, quite successful on Atonement. The case for Mark is impressive but there are greater difficulties for Matthew.

D. *Tabernacles*

1. *Goulder's Themes*

Goulder points to the fact that Leviticus 23, the *sidrā* for Tabernacles in the Mishnah and the Talmud, explains the name by the tabernacles in which people dwelt when they came out of Egypt (Lev. 23.43) but he adds:

> This seems to be an artificial idea, as it is not mentioned in the earlier calendars in Exodus and Deuteronomy, and has left no mark on the festal rites (*LNP*, p. 164).

Goulder continues:

> Originally, it will have been a harvest festival, the Feast of Ingathering of Exod. 13.16; 34.22; this aspect was primary in Deut. 16.13...and it

> was still stressed in Lev. 23.39...and symbolised in the *lûlāb* and *'etrôg*
> carried at the festival in NT times (*LNP*, p. 164).

Important rituals are the libation of water (*m. Suk.* 4.9) and the illumination of the Temple on the first night (*m. Suk.* 5.1-4) and another theme is the coming worship of all nations at Tabernacles in Zion, explicit in Zech. 14.16-19 and implied in Pss. 47, 96, etc. (cf. on Tabernacles, *EC*, pp. 31-35, 256-62 and *MLM*, pp. 187-88 and 364).[11]

There is a slightly defensive note in Goulder's presentation of the Tabernacles themes in *LNP* and this is, no doubt, because when it comes to looking at the Gospels, he is not going to be able to draw attention to a fulfilment of the dwelling in tabernacles theme. The festival is celebrated on 15-22 Tishri so the relevant reading in each Gospel will have to come just after the Atonement lections on 10 Tishri. Matthew, Mark and Luke all have the Harvest Parables sections nearby so Goulder stresses the 'ingathering' side of the Tabernacles festival.[12]

The idea of dwelling in Tabernacles should not, perhaps, be brushed aside so lightly. The matter is stressed in the Mishnah (*m. Suk.* 1–2) which legislates in detail, with references to Hillel and Shammai, for the right *sukkah* (booth), with no reference at all to harvest. Further, it is arguably the most important aspect of the festival in Leviticus 23 (vv. 42-43) and dwelling in booths is seen as the heart of the festival by Ezra in Nehemiah 8:

> And they found it written in the Law that the LORD had commanded by Moses that the people of Israel should dwell in booths during the feast of the seventh month, and that they should publish and proclaim in all their towns and in Jerusalem, 'Go out to the hills and bring branches of olive, wild olive, myrtle, palm and other leafy trees to make booths, as it is written' (Neh. 8.14-15).

This is not to deny that the harvest side of the festival was important but rather to note that it should not necessarily be seen as the heart of

---

11. Cf. *MLM*, p. 174, 'Tabernacles was both the feast of the Temple...and the Feast of Ingathering', but there is no Temple in Mt. 13 and Goulder is reduced to saying, 'It is in Chapter 12, in the readings for the first half of Tishri, [i.e. before Atonement] that the Temple-Solomon theme comes forward' (p. 188), and in *LNP*, the Temple aspect is not mentioned. Cf. *MLM*, pp. 364-65; *EC*, pp. 256-62.

12. To distinguish it from Pentecost, it is usually called 'Ingathering' rather than 'Harvest'; cf. Exod. 23.16 (RSV): 'You shall keep the feast of harvest [Pentecost]... You shall keep the feast of ingathering [Tabernacles].'

the festival. Goulder's contrasting claims about Pentecost should put one on guard:

> With the tendency to stress the historical rather than the agricultural side of the feasts, Pentecost has become the Lawgiving before the end of the era, both in orthodox Judaism and in some sectarian groups (*LNP*, p. 167).

In short, then, Goulder's usual stress on the evidence from Leviticus and the Mishnah, alongside the occasional emphasis on the 'historical' side of the festal occasions, here gives way to evidence from Exodus and Deuteronomy and an emphasis on the agricultural side of the festival.

2. *Mark*

Goulder proposes that if one allows Mk 2.23–3.6 as a reading, when necessary, for a Sabbath intervening between Atonement and Tabernacles, then one comes to a Markan Tabernacles in 3.7–4.34. This long section allows eight lections for the eight days of Tabernacles.[13] Mark 4 is appropriate, both the Sower (4.1-20) and the Seed Growing Secretly (4.26-29) being connected with harvest. Mark 3 is less obviously suitable, but Goulder stresses the links between chs. 3 and 4[14] and suggests also:

> The people who come from Galilee, Judaea, Jerusalem, Idumaea, Transjordan, Tyre and Sidon, are harbingers of the nations who will one day come with Israel to confess Jesus as the Son of God (*LNP*, p. 165; cf. *EC*, pp. 256-57).

Mark 3 is a little weak for Tabernacles, however, and Goulder attempts to show that this need not be a difficulty for his thesis by commenting:

> It is the second half of Mk 3.7–4.34 which appeals to us as the more effective Tabernacles sermon; and it was the second half which appealed to Matthew and Luke also (*LNP*, p. 166).

This is reminiscent of Goulder's claim that the six-and-a-half month

---

13. In *EC*, Goulder thinks that Mark's Church will have celebrated an eight day feast of Tabernacles (pp. 256-62) whereas in *LNP*, Goulder suggests that there might have been a long lesson on one day, but with a Palestinian history behind it (p. 194 n. 26).

14. For the links between Mark 3 and Mark 4, see also 'Those Outside'.

Mark is unsatisfactory to us and that it was unsatisfactory to Matthew
and Luke too (above, pp. 312-13).

Other Tabernacles themes like dwelling in booths, or the libation of
water, are not present though there is reference to light (under a bushel,
4.21-22). There is an obvious text which does feature a direct reference
to booths, Mk 9.2-13, the Transfiguration, when Peter says: 'let us
make three booths, one for you and one for Moses and one for Elijah'
(Mk 9.5).[15] Another reading which might be appropriate is Mk 13.1-37.
Although there are no references to tabernacles here, the discourse
several times refers to the Temple (vv. 1-2, 14). One might see
ingathering present in the prophecy that: 'he will send out the angels,
and gather his elect from the four winds, from the ends of the earth to
the ends of heaven' (v. 27). Similarly, the vision of all the nations
worshipping might be reflected in the statement that: 'the gospel must
first be preached to all nations' (v. 10).

Goulder's theory does not, then, have an easy ride through Mark 3–4
for Tabernacles.

3. *Matthew*

Shortly after Mt. 12.22-45 comes Matthew's parallel to the parable
chapter in Mark, Mt. 13.1-52. This, Goulder feels, would be quite
appropriate for a Matthean Tabernacles (*LNP*, p. 166; *EC*, pp. 256 and
261-62; *MLM*, pp. 187-88 and 364-76) and, like Mk 3.7–4.34, it is
amenable to division into eight sections to be taken one a day. If
anything, it is more appropriate than Mark 4 in its emphasis on the
harvest. The Seed Growing Secretly is expanded to the Wheat and the
Tares (vv. 24-30, 36-43) and there is also the Ingathering of Fish (vv.
47-50). θερισμός comes twice in v. 30 and once in v. 39. συλλέγω
comes in vv. 28, 29, 30, 40, 41 and 48 and συνάγω in vv. 30 and 47.

Other themes of Tabernacles are not present, except the worship of
nations which may be seen in the birds of the air in the Mustard Seed
parable (v. 32). Mt. 17.1-13, the Transfiguration, might, once more, be

---

15. For the Transfiguration against a Tabernacles background, cf. Plummer, *St
Matthew*, p. 240 and R. Finch, *Synagogue Lectionary*, pp. 41, 52, 66. Professor
Goulder responds (in correspondence, 15 May 1990) by saying that 'the harvest
was the background in people's lives, symbolised by the *lulav* etc.; and the
historical (imported) background is the desert / booths...The Transfiguration is
much less impressive than the Harvest Parables—the only primary reference is in
Peter's silly remark!'

thought to provide a good alternative reading. Perhaps one could see the light theme in Mt. 17.2: 'His face shone like the sun, and his garments became white as light'. Another appropriate reading would be Mt. 24.1-51, parallel to Mk 13.1-37 with the same relevant themes, temple, ingathering in v. 31 and worship of all nations in v. 14.

Even if one stayed with Goulder's harvest theme, however, another appropriate reading could be called to mind, Mt. 9.35–11.1, in which Jesus says:

> The harvest is plentiful, but the labourers are few; pray therefore the Lord of the harvest to send out labourers into his harvest (Mt. 9.37-38).

The 'harvest' image is insistent, three times in this logion, and the disciples are then called and sent to do the harvesting (Matthew 10).

In spite of such possible alternatives, however, Goulder's reading for Matthew's Tabernacles does stand out as particularly appropriate. Having taken 12.22-45 for Atonement, Matthew 13 is in the right place, the harvest theme is a repeated feature and the chapter is divisible into eight sections.

4. *Luke*

Goulder's Tabernacles reading for Luke is 8.1-21 which follows on from the Atonement reading in 7.36-50. It is parallel to Matthew 13 and Mark 4 and Goulder suggests that it is reduced in length because Luke does not celebrate the eight days of the festival but rather has the one lesson on a Sunday. The harvest theme is present in the Parable of the Sower (vv. 4-15), but there is no room for the worship of all nations since the Mustard Seed is moved to Luke 13. None of the other themes is present, unless one sees light in v. 16, light under a vessel or a bed.

An alternative reading might once more be seen in the Transfiguration in Lk. 9.28-36 with its reference to booths (v. 33). Another alternative reading could be Lk. 9.51–10.24.[16] Here the Sending out of the Seventy is prefaced with the logion about the plentiful harvest (10.2). The worship of all nations could, perhaps, be seen in the Seventy as the harbingers of the Gentile mission and dwelling in tabernacles might be seen reflected (at a push) in the logion in 9.58: 'Foxes have holes, and birds of the air have nests, but the Son of man has nowhere to lay his head.' Goulder's provision for Luke's Tabernacles is adequate, then, but not especially impressive.

---

16. Goulder's section 36, which brackets together three readings.

5. *Summary*

It is important for Goulder's thesis that harvest should be the central theme of Tabernacles since for all three synoptics the readings incorporate the Sower and associated parables. Matthew's reading, ch. 13, is the most appropriate since the harvest theme is insistent. There are difficulties with Mark's reading, the first half of which is Mark 3, where only vv. 7-8 are appropriate.

Appropriate alternatives might be imagined for all the Gospels. In particular, all have Peter's comment about the booths in the Transfiguration Story (Mk 9.2-8 // Mt. 17.1-8 // Lk. 9.28-36) and, since dwelling in booths does seem to have been a key part of the Festival, this explicit reference is interesting. Mk 13.1-37 might also be appropriate for Mark and Mt. 24.1-51 for Matthew, with references to the Temple, all the nations and ingathering. For Luke, 9.51–10.24 would be appropriate, with the harvest logion and the seventy as harbingers of the Gentile mission.

These results are mixed. Goulder's thesis is strongest on Matthew and weakest on Mark. The possible alternatives weaken the thesis and the question mark over the harvest theme casts further doubt on it.

E. *Pentecost*

1. *Goulder's Themes*

Goulder says that in early times Pentecost was the festival of the wheat-harvest (Exod. 23.16; 34.22; Deut. 16.9-12; Lev. 23.17) but the major theme became the giving of the Law. The *sidrā* was Exod. 19.1–20.23 (*b. Meg.* 31a), and Goulder suggests also that Psa. 119 was composed for Pentecost (*LNP*, p. 167; cf. *EC*, pp. 212-13 and *MLM*, pp. 174 and 184-86).

This is the opposite stress from that in Goulder's presentation of the Tabernacles themes. Here Goulder is not interested in the agricultural basis of the festival but rather in its secondary, historical side.

2. *Matthew*

Goulder points out that the Sermon on the Mount, Matthew 5–7, 'or the opening section of it' would be quite appropriate for Pentecost (*LNP*, p. 167). If Goulder is right about the Law-giving, this point is obvious and, furthermore, no passage is going to turn up as many correspodences with the Law theme. One passage would be relevant to the wheat-harvest, the Wheat and the Tares (Mt. 13.24-30, 36-43).

The only difficulty with the provision of the Sermon on the Mount for Pentecost is to know how to divide the chapter. Earlier, in *MLM*, Goulder suggested:

> The Sermon is far longer than a normal lection because it is the Church's Pentecostal lection. As a Jewish-Christian synagogue, the Matthean church celebrated Pentecost the day through. It required an octave of readings to expound the fulfilment of the Law in Christ's Torah, and that is precisely what the Sermon on the Mount supplied (*MLM*, p. 186).

In *LNP*, however, Goulder has dropped the case from the Alexandrinus *kephalaia* and is less sure how much of the sermon to assign to Pentecost.[17] Goulder is, here, in something of a 'no-win' situation. Both accepting and rejecting the Alexandrinus divisions cause problems for the thesis. The difficulty with the Alexandrinus divisions is that some of the sections, like the first part of the story of the Synagogue Ruler's Daughter (9.18-19), are too short for comfort.[18] Goulder requires the lections to be this short, though, in *MLM*, in order that enough weeks can be covered between Pentecost (Matthew 5–7) on Sivan 6 and New Year (Matthew 11) on Tishri 1, about sixteen weeks later. Even with the short Alexandrinus divisions, one reaches the New Year reading in Matthew 11 about a week too early (see *MLM*, p. 196 and cf. Table VIII in *EC*, facing p. 306).

If, however, one drops the Alexandrinus divisions in an attempt to release more space in the text for reading between Pentecost and New Year, a fresh problem arises. If one borrows into the latter part of the Sermon, using Matthew 6 and 7, for example, for the weeks following Pentecost, one is in danger of losing hold of the unity of the Sermon, an issue which was earlier vital to Goulder. The title of *MLM*, chapter 12, for example, is 'Pentecost, The Unity of the Sermon'.

17. *LNP*, p. 167, '5.1-?'. Professor Goulder suggests (in correspondence, 1 June 1988) that if one divides Mt. 1–4 into six sections, 'We could then *either* have 5.1-20 for Pentecost (the Fulfilling of the Mountain Law, introduced by eight blessings on the model of Pentecostal Ps. 119.1-2 [8]); *or* have 5-7 as a whole, with sections repeated through the following weeks'.

18. Goulder suggests amending the division into 9.18-22 and 9.23-26 (*MLM*, pp. 196 and 325-26) but this still means splitting in two an obvious unity.

3. *Luke*

Goulder feels that there are special conditions for Luke. Since in
Acts 2, the Holy Spirit descends on the church at Pentecost, one will
expect him to expound this theme in the relevant place in his Gospel.
Goulder's passage (*LNP*, p. 168; *EC*, p. 79; *MLM*, pp. 459-60) is
Lk. 3.1-20, John's preaching. At first this might not seem promising,
especially as the parallel forms part of Mark's New Year reading.
However at Lk. 3.16, we read: 'he will baptize you with the Holy Spirit
and with fire'. Goulder claims that this is 'the fire of Pentecostal
blessing' (*LNP*, p. 168) and adds that:

> He has developed the Mark 1/Matthew 3 tradition into the pattern of the
> Acts 2 scene (*LNP*, p. 168).

This 'pattern' is seen in Acts 2.37, 'What shall we do?' paralleled in
Lk. 3.10, 'What then shall we do?'

One difficulty with Goulder's theory is that Lk. 3.17 follows on the
supposed Pentecostal fire with an interpretation clearly about hell-fire:
'the chaff he will burn with an unquenchable fire'. Perhaps, though, it is
worth adding that the wheat gathered into the granary (3.17) would fit
in well with Pentecost.

Goulder's provision for Pentecost in Luke is possible, then, but not
strong. It relies almost entirely on the reading of one line in a twenty
verse piece, a reading compromised by the immediate context. Further,
other passages in the Gospel might draw out the theme of the giving of
the Holy Spirit for Pentecost like 'the Spirit of the Lord is upon me' in
Jesus' Nazareth sermon (4.18) or 'how much more will the Father give
the Holy Spirit to those who ask him' (11.13 QD).

4. *Summary*

It is difficult to imagine a more appropriate reading for Pentecost, if
Goulder is right to stress the giving of the Law as its theme, than
Matthew 5. This is one of the strongest links in Goulder's lectionary
theory. On the other hand, there are considerable difficulties over how
to divide the text in order to provide enough lections after Pentecost
and before Goulder's desired New Year lection in Matthew 11.

Luke's lesson, 3.1-20, fits in reasonably with the theme of the giving
of the Holy Spirit evidenced in Acts 2, but there are two problems: the
reference to fire is developed in Lk. 3.17, as in Mt. 3.12, as hell-fire,
and there are other lessons where the Holy Spirit theme appears.

F. *Conclusion*

Goulder claims that he is 'obliged to provide a bull's eye' for each of the high festivals. He says that 'no Matthean section would fit a Jewish-Christian Pentecost anything near as well as Matthew 5' (*LNP*, pp. 173-74) and that 'it would be difficult to find a more apposite story' for Atonement 'than the healing of the Paralytic in Mark 2' (*LNP*, p. 161). The question which naturally arises is whether or not Goulder is right that all of his proposed lections are the most appropriate reading in each Gospel for the given liturgical occasions.

Goulder's provision for New Year in the synoptics is quite strong. Mk 1.1-20 (John the Baptist etc.) fits better than does any other section in Mark. Matthew 11 (Messengers from John) does not fit quite as well as 3.1-17 (but this is parallel to Mk 1.1-15) or 24.1-51 (Eschatological Discourse). Lk. 7.18-35 (Messengers from John) does not fit as well as 3.1-20 (but this is the parallel to Mk 1.1-15) or 10.1-24 (Seventy, etc.) or 4.16-30 (Nazareth sermon).

Goulder's provision for Atonement is particularly strong for Mark since 2.1-22 (Paralytic; Levi; Question about Fasting) fits better than does any other section in Mark. The case for Luke is quite strong since Lk. 7.36-50 (Sinner) is at least as appropriate as any other section in Luke with the exception of 5.17-39, parallel to Mk 2.1-22. Mt. 12.22-45 (Beelzebub; Jonah; Unclean Spirit) is, perhaps, less appropriate for Atonement than is 9.1-17 (but this is parallel to Mk 2.1-22) or 6.7-18 (Lord's Prayer; Fasting).

With regard to Tabernacles, Mk 3.7–4.34 is problematic. Mk 9.2-8 (Transfiguration) or Mk 13.1-37 (Eschatological Discourse) might be as appropriate. Mt. 13.1-52 (Parables) is stronger, but again 24.1-51 (Eschatological Discourse) and 17.1-8 (Transfiguration) might be as appropriate. Lk. 8.1-21 (Sower, etc.) is at best only as good as 9.28-36 (Transfiguration) and 9.51–10.24 (Harvest logion; Seventy).

The provision for Pentecost is strong in Matthew (ch. 5, Sermon) but weaker in Luke (3.1-20, John's Preaching).

Goulder has, therefore, for several of the eleven festal occasions, provided a 'bull's eye' or a 'white swan'. Particularly strong are Mark's New Year and Atonement readings and Matthew's reading for Pentecost. On almost every occasion, though, one can find other sections of each Gospel which would be as appropriate as Goulder's reading. Particularly noteworthy is Mt. 6.7-18 as an alternative reading for Atonement, featuring both the forgiveness theme and the teaching about fasting and echoing the *haphtarah* for the day, Isaiah 58. Also noteworthy is Mt. 24.1-51 as an alternative for New Year, especially as explicit reference is made to trumpet-blowing.

The existence of the alternatives reduces the probability of Goulder's theory being correct. However, it is interesting that in many cases the best alternative reading to the one Goulder provides turns out to be the Matthean or Lukan parallel to a given Markan reading. This should not be surprising in that the evangelists would be free to write their own lesson and reproduce the Markan reading in its Markan sequence.

Furthermore, in no category is there a proliferation of possible alternative readings. One is pushed to find more than two in any section so that where Goulder fails to provide a bull's eye, he provides something quite close. The difficulty is, perhaps, that Goulder has overstated his case. To ask for a 'bull's eye' every time is, he says, 'a very large demand', but he does add, after all, that 'my family was more at home on the racecourse' (*LNP*, p. 173).

This is not the whole story, however. Other difficulties have arisen along the way. There is an incongruity between Goulder's discussion of Tabernacles where he stresses the agricultural side of the feast and his discussion of Pentecost where he stresses the historical side of the feast. In both cases, it could be argued, Goulder's stress results from the constraints imposed by the theory, the necessity to have a harvest theme for Tabernacles (for Mark 4 and parallels) and a Law-giving theme for Pentecost (for Matthew 5).

The most serious difficulty, perhaps, is the question of the division of the text. Here there are problems which are not purely peripheral. It is worth recalling Goulder's attempt to draw up the odds:

> Once Matthew is hypothesized as a year's readings, with Passover/Easter at the end of the Gospel, Pentecost must fall on the seventh unit from the beginning; and no Matthean section would fit a Jewish-Christian Pentecost anything near as well as Matthew 5. But there is no logical reason why the Matthean Sermon should fall there…There might be twenty positions Matthew could have chosen for his Matthew 5 material… And so with the Matthew 11/New Year matter; only that the probability of *both* passages falling on the right date will be the multiple of the two individual probabilities (*LNP*, pp. 173-74).

Goulder is right that the provision for Pentecost in Matthew 5 is impressive—one might reasonably count six sections in Matthew 1-4.

Goulder's provision for New Year is less impressive, however, in that one either has to take the Sermon as a unity, in which case there is not really enough material in Matthew 8–10 to cover the sixteen weeks between Pentecost and New Year, or one has to divide the Sermon.

Similarly, the provision of Mark 3 (in addition to Mark 4) for Tabernacles is a problem imposed by the necessity of having a Tabernacles lection following on from the appropriate Atonement one in Mark 2. The difficulties over division are limited primarily to these two places, Mark's Tabernacles and Matthew's Pentecost–New Year, but these two do help to undermine the impressiveness of Goulder's case. Once Passover/Easter is fixed, Goulder says, 'all the other feasts have to be in their places, or the hypothesis fails' (*LNP*, p. 174). Some of the feasts are not quite in their places so Goulder's hypothesis becomes less probable.

Goulder's lectionary theory is based on the unlikelihood that his festal features would occur in the right places in the Gospels by accident. Goulder says that he would like to meet the bookmaker who would take money on the odds he is offering (*LNP*, p. 174). The effect of this chapter has been to reduce the impressiveness of the odds substantially. Some of the relevant themes can be found not only in Goulder's festal readings but also elsewhere in the Gospels and on two occasions, the text has to be forced a little to bring the themes to the right place.

The strength of Goulder's lectionary theory, nevertheless, is that it takes Passover/Easter as fixed and then finds something approaching an appropriate reading for each festal occasion in or near the right place. Not once does Goulder find a pure 'dud' lection for the festal occasions. The overall odds are diminished, therefore, but not so much so that the theory is demolished.

Chapter 22

CONCLUSION TO PART III

Contrary to popular opinion, there are some strengths in Goulder's lectionary hypothesis. It has, to use Goulder's own phrase, 'explanatory power' at several points. If it is right, it explains the structure of Matthew's Gospel as 'Mark prefixed by a new first half' (*LNP*, p. 159); it explains Luke's long central section with its 'long Journey that never seems to advance' (*LNP*, p. 171); it sheds light on the development of the Gospel genre and it solves traditional problems over the chronology of the Passion story. Moreover, by postulating a lectionary origin for all three synoptics, Goulder provides a framework within which two form-critical problems might be answered: the *Sitz im Leben* for the creation and transmission of gospel stories is the church service and the gospel pericopae are reinterpreted as lections.

Goulder presses quite strongly the issue of the probability of his thesis being correct. The odds against the right themes occurring in the right places by accident are enormous. Our aim has been to see whether a thesis which explains so much and which apparently has odds so strongly in its favour can possibly be wrong.

There are some important difficulties. First, in *MLM* and *EC*, the creativity of the evangelists is expounded in terms of and by means of the lectionary theory and this imposes a strain on Goulder's overall thesis. Second, Goulder divides the text of Matthew in *MLM* and *EC* by using the Alexandrinus *kephalaia* and this can produce lections which are too short for comfort (like Mt. 9.18-19).

More seriously, the theory that Mark is a lectionary book designed for six and a half months lacks both precedent and plausibility. Further, the notion that Luke is a lectionary book but that Acts is not causes problems for the coherence of the overall thesis.

It is possible that Christians in the communities which produced the Gospels were, as Goulder suggests, keeping Jewish festivals and fasts.

Evidence from Paul, Acts and *1 Clement* points in this direction. However, Justin Martyr's statement in *1 Apol.* 67 about the reading of Scripture in church 'as long as time permits' tells against the idea that churches read the Gospels in lectionary sequence. Further, Goulder's proposal that a pre-baptismal catechesis lies behind both Mark and Luke is problematic, particularly in the light of the spontaneous baptisms in Acts.

Goulder has been most criticized over his reconstructions of lectionary cycles. It is certain that many synagogues as early as the first century read the Scriptures regularly. At least as early as the second century, some were reading the Law in continuous sequence, but it is not clear how early synagogues read in a lectionary order. The evidence which Goulder adduces in *EC* for an annual cycle of the reading of the Torah beginning in Nisan is not probative.

Goulder's restatement in *LNP* deals with several of these difficulties. Most importantly, his stress on the festal year dispenses with the need for a hypothetical reconstruction of a weekly lectionary cycle and makes sense of the evidence that early Christians were conservative in matters of worship. On the other hand, though, some problems remain. Goulder's dispensing with the Alexandrinus *kephalaia* only creates the fresh difficulty of how to divide the text in the 'common-sense' way which Goulder suggests. In particular, if one is to have enough material in Matthew to cover the sixteen or so weeks between Pentecost (Matthew 5) and New Year (Matthew 11), one has to borrow into the latter part of the Sermon (Matthew 6–7).

Further, although the pure stress on the festal year is welcome, it might mask the historical problem that there are no clear parallels to what Goulder is proposing, Christians (or Jews) composing books to be read round the year.

The onus in Goulder's thesis falls, then, on the question of correspondences. Some of them are strong, especially Mark's New Year and Atonement readings and Matthew's Pentecost reading. In these instances, no other section would suit the festal occasions as well. Further, all of Goulder's readings are at least adequate: never, having fixed the Passion narrative to Passover–Easter, does Goulder's thesis turn up a pure 'dud'.

The greatest difficulty with Goulder's correspondences is his provision for Tabernacles, for which Goulder stresses the 'harvest' theme over the 'booths' theme, and for which Mark's reading is ch. 3

as well as ch. 4. Overall, Goulder's odds are reduced sufficiently to cast doubt on but not to ruin the theory.

One feature of Goulder's lectionary stands out, the argument for a liturgical origin for the Passion narrative in the Gospels. Goulder explains the recurring three hour intervals by his theory of a twenty-four hour Paschal vigil at which portions of the Gospel story would be read.

This theory also faces difficulties, however. Much of our earliest evidence points to a Saturday night vigil and several of the relevant time-references in the Gospels have to be supplied, like 9 p.m. and midnight. This may suggest that Trocmé is right that the Passion narratives have a liturgical origin even if Goulder is wrong that the Passion narratives were designed by the evangelists to serve a liturgical purpose.

Goulder's restatement in *LNP* avoids several, but not all, of the difficulties of the earlier case and so the lectionary theory is still not totally convincing. If, though, one decides to shelve the restatement too, the odds and explanatory power in its favour will be enough to cause some regret and a few lingering hesitations.

Chapter 23

CONCLUSION

Michael Goulder has seized Austin Farrer's vision and made it his own, a vision 'for many days', of a world without Q. Building on his teacher's foundation, he has allowed the evangelists to become authors, writing as they are moved, without recourse to any complicating, dispensable and unevidenced lost documents. Adding also the theory of the liturgical origin of the Gospels, Goulder has attempted to initiate a revolution in New Testament studies. Sceptical of form-criticism, reforming source-criticism and inflating the role of redaction-criticism, Goulder wants to take the scholarly world by storm.

Although he has found allies along the way, the majority have remained sceptical or even ignorant of Goulder's ideas. Some question the point of challenging established, received truths like Q. Several, in the struggle to classify Goulder's work, relegate it to the lunatic fringe of Biblical Studies. Many think that Goulder is simply wrong.

Goulder makes, however, numerous criticisms of traditional approaches which his opponents will ignore at their peril and, further, his thesis has many strong points. One virtue is the simplicity of his solution to the Synoptic Problem. Another is the explanatory power of his thesis: frequently Goulder sheds new light on famous difficulties.

Both of these strengths, though, also lead us into difficulties. The simple solution to the Synoptic Problem, Matthew's knowledge of Mark alone and Luke's knowledge of Matthew and Mark alone, sometimes demands a degree of complexity in the application which partly undermines its credibility. Likewise, Goulder's thesis sometimes labours under the strain of attempting to explain too much. Rarely does Goulder admit to finding a difficulty and regularly, apparent weaknesses are read as strengths.

Goulder always asks the reader to judge his thesis on the basis of its plausibility. Sometimes he also asks for judgment on its probability.

One such key area is Goulder's claim that Q's vocabulary is indistinguishable from Matthew's vocabulary, a claim which can be tested by applying a control. My study in Chapter Two discovered Matthean and Lucan vocabulary in roughly equal proportions, a conclusion detrimental to Goulder's theory that Matthew composed the Q material and that Luke copied it from him. Especially problematic for Goulder's theory are the Lord's Prayer, the Messengers from John and the Lament over Jerusalem. In addition, Goulder's 'statistical proof' of the 'midrashic theory', at the conclusion of *MLM*, is circular.

The study of the Minor Agreements (MAs; Chapter Three) proved less disturbing for Goulder's thesis. Here Goulder has provided an important methodological contribution to the MA debate in his search for 'Mattheanisms' among them, the strongest among five separate, though overlapping, arguments on the MAs.

Once more, a control can be applied, with the result that confidence in Goulder's view ought to be shaken a little, but only a little, by the existence of a couple of 'Lukanisms' among the MAs (at Mk 6.44, ὡσεί + number, and 12.28, νομικός). By contrast, there are at least six MAs which feature Matthean language on stringently applied criteria, those at Mk 3.10 (πᾶς of the sick), 4.41 (ἄνεμος plural), 6.2 (αὐτῶν without antecedent, of 'the Jews'), 6.33 (οἱ ὄχλοι + ἀκολουθέω), 12.22 (ὕστερον) and 14.43 (ἰδού + genitive absolute).

Further, the question τίς ἐστιν ὁ παίσας σε; in the MA at Mk 14.65, which has defenders of the 2ST on the backfoot, actually features language which is at least as characteristic of Luke as it is of Matthew, problematic for the pure form of Goulder's argument, from Mattheanisms among the MAs.

Although they require revision, then, Goulder's arguments over the MAs still provide problems for a 'hardline' 2ST.

These two studies, on the QC words and the MAs, do not, of course, solve the Synoptic Problem but they should fuel the debate further. It is clear from them that, at least for the time being, there can be no hope of proving the thesis of Luke's knowledge of Matthew and defenders of the view might do well to rely on arguments about plausibility and dispensability, not probability.

In Part II the argument of *LNP*, chapter three was analysed, in an attempt to test Goulder's thesis that Luke was the author of the L material and that he had no substantial sources apart from Mark and Matthew. The features listed under Goulder's key heading 'The Lukan

Story' were seen to fall broadly into two groups, one covering features which occur in Luke in marked contrast with Matthew and Mark, the other covering Luke's compositional techniques.

The features in the first group were examined to see whether they are distinctive of Luke, asking also whether they occur in R and QD as well as L material. Often, the features are distinctive: notes of progress in the Infancy Narratives (§2.2); ἤρξατο used in a lively and pejorative sense (§3.2); soliloquy in parables (§4.1); interest in the details of work (§4.3); parties (§4.4); excuses (§4.5); illustration-stories (§7) and doubled visions (§14).

Sometimes the features are characteristic but not distinctive of Luke: foil questions and comments (§1.4); re-introduction in mid-pericope (§1.7); return home of characters at the end of pericopae (§2.1); promptitude and alacrity (§3); conversation in parables (§4.2); guillotine questions (§4.6); lower-class heroes (§4.7); middle-class setting (§5); hortatory parables (§8); oratio recta repetitions (§11) and fives and tens (§12).

Often, aspects of categories are distinctive of Luke: a particular audience addressed in the hearing of a wider audience (§1.2), a question asked by a specific speaker with Jesus' response to a wider audience (§1.4); foil questions of a 'cloying piety' (§1.5); controversial teaching set at a meal with a Pharisee (§1.6); characters rejoicing as they return home (§2.1); παραχρῆμα used of the fulfilment of a command of Jesus (§3); a parable told as the result of a foil question or comment (§4.2); guillotine questions with single opponents (§4.6); aspects of disreputable heroes (§4.7); and a master with a single servant (§5).

Sometimes, but not often, Goulder's features are neither distinctive nor characteristic of Luke: there are difficulties over the evangelist's comment (§1.3); controversial teaching set in a synagogue (part of §1.6); inclusio (§2.3); colourful details (§4.8) and the parable as lead-in (§10). In addition, some strengths, tempered with difficulties, were uncovered along the way. Goulder's stress on Luke's ability to write human characters into his Gospel (§4) is welcome and persuasive, but it relies too strongly on a comparison between the Two Sons in Matthew and the Prodigal Son in Luke, a comparison which assumes what is in the process of being demonstrated.

Also plausible is Goulder's case that Luke favours middle-class settings for his parables over against Matthew's aristocratic settings

(§5), but a difficulty here is that Goulder underestimates the extent to which a parable's 'doctrine' can determine its scale.

Goulder's criticism of the distinction between parable and allegory (§6) is healthy, but it carries with it, in Goulder's presentation, an unnecessary rider, the equation between 'colourful details' and 'non-allegorical details' (§4.8). In addition, Goulder's attempt to quantify the allegorical content of the parables is a useful but flawed experiment.

Goulder's distinction between 'hortatory' and 'indicative' parables (§8) is another fruitful aspect of the thesis. Goulder is right that Matthew and Mark prefer indicative parables and Luke hortatory parables, but Goulder overemphasises the difference between the evangelists.

Goulder has made strong general cases for the categories in his second group of Lucan compositional procedures, muddle (§9), inference of setting (§13), combination of sources (§15), splitting of sources (§16) and transfer of elements (§17). His suggestions vary between highly plausible and fairly strained, and muddle and inference probably do not occur on the kind of scale that Goulder is imagining.

Overall, the data suggest that in spite of some difficulties, Goulder is right that the L material is the substantial handiwork of the evangelist, especially as many of the features under discussion occur regularly not only in L but also in Luke's redaction of Mark and Q/Matthew. Goulder's work necessitates the abandonment of any theory on which the evangelist draws conservatively on a written L text.

The data do not so clearly demand the theory that Luke had no other substantial sources than Matthew and Mark for his L material. Indeed, elements of some of Goulder's features might suggest that Luke was creatively interacting with oral traditions in his L material. In particular, mismatches between content and context, under the 'muddle' heading (§9), make good sense on the assumption that Luke is attempting to apply parables which had slightly differing meanings in oral traditions. Similarly, given Luke's preference for hortatory parables (§8), underlying indicative forms may well point to sources in oral traditions. Likewise, underlying imperative forms in some of Matthew's parables may show sources in oral traditions for some of the parables in his Gospel.

Goulder's overarching conclusion that Luke had no substantial sources other than Mark or Matthew focuses on the parables and relies on the isolation of, and dispensing with, two alternatives, 'the selection hypothesis' and 'the standard view'. Goulder makes 'the selection hypothesis' his main opponent, but this is problematic because it involves the assumption that if the whole of a given parable is not from Jesus, then the whole of it is from Luke. It is problematic also because doctrinal interest can sometimes condition the details of a story. Further, Goulder does not deal with the important question of a parable's plot.

Goulder does not pay adequate attention to 'the standard view'. A nuanced redaction-critical viewpoint could incorporate, and make good sense of, aspects of both 'the selection hypothesis' and Goulder's thesis. In particular, to look at Luke's supposed treatment of Matthew's Talents and Banquet parables sheds light on his possible treatment of L parables.

In short, the conclusion of Part Two is that Luke undoubtedly plays a decisive role in the forming and framing of his material, but this does not necessitate the conclusion that Luke had no substantial sources other than Matthew and Mark.

The least popular aspect of Goulder's thesis, the lectionary theory, examined in Part Three, does not merit its poor reception, but, nevertheless, there are difficulties which may be insurmountable.

Goulder is wise to have shelved one aspect of the thesis, that the Gospels, and especially Luke, fulfil an order of Old Testament lections arranged according to an annual cycle beginning in Nisan. It is possible but not certain that synagogues read according to a set order in the first century, but Goulder's evidence for an annual cycle is far from probative.

Goulder has also dispensed with using the Alexandrinus *kephalaia* for Matthew, but this introduces a fresh difficulty of how to allot enough material to cover the sixteen or so weeks between Pentecost (Matthew 5) and New Year (Matthew 11). Also problematic is Goulder's provision of Mark 3 as well as Mark 4 for Tabernacles.

Although Christians in the communities behind the Gospels may have celebrated Jewish festivals and fasts, one difficulty for Goulder's theory stands out: Justin's statement that the Scriptures were read 'as long as time permits' (*1 Apol.* 67). Also problematic is the theory that pre-baptismal catechesis lies behind both Mark and Luke, especially in light of the evidence from Acts.

One general difficulty with the theory is the lack of any parallel for what Goulder is proposing: there is no direct evidence of anyone in this period composing a book as a lectionary. Further, the provision of six and a half months for the reading of Mark lacks both precedent and plausibility, and the idea that Luke is a lectionary book and that Acts is not is, at best, an oddity.

The greatest strength is the issue of correspondences. In an attempt to test Goulder's theory, one can search for other sections in each Gospel which would fit the themes of the festal occasions as well as the sections which Goulder allots. Several of Goulder's sections are 'bull's eyes'; all are at least adequate and there are few convincing alternative readings, impressive given the fact that Goulder 'pegs' the Passion story to Passover-Easter. A further difficulty, though, is Goulder's stress on a 'harvest' theme for Tabernacles.

Also impressive is Goulder's theory that a twenty-four hour Paschal vigil lies behind the Passion Narrative in all four Gospels. This theory explains the recurrence of the three-hourly feature and explains traditional difficulties like the rushed time-scale. Even here, however, there are difficulties. Much of our earliest evidence points to a Saturday-night vigil, not a 15 Nisan one, and some of the relevant time-references in the Gospels have to be supplied.

In short, the strengths of Goulder's lectionary theory are its explanatory power and the odds in its favour. The shelving of the annual, sabbath basis of the case of *The Evangelists' Calendar* is prudent but difficulties do remain with the restatement in *Luke—A New Paradigm*, most importantly Justin Martyr's 'as long as time permits', the lack of contemporary parallels for what Goulder is adducing and the problem of dividing the text successfully.

The lectionary theory has dwindled in importance in Goulder's work, and it is probably set to decline further still in scholarly opinion. The battle against Q, on the other hand, ought to intensify as more take cognizance of Goulder's offensive. Books are still appearing which take Q for granted, which make it the starting point rather than the goal of their enquiry, forgetting to use the word 'hypothesis'. As Goulder's ideas become more influential, many reconstructions of the life of the historical Jesus will have to be re-assessed, like the sage and cynic Jesus of many who believe in Q. Likewise, the degree of the evangelists' creativity will continue to be a pressing and necessary concern in Gospel studies, vital at several levels, and not only for those using literary-critical methods, but also for those delving into history.

At the conclusion of this study, it is worth noting that its presupposition, that one can break up Goulder's thesis into smaller, digestible units, each one capable of analysis on its own terms, actually does Goulder a slight disservice. Goulder's ideas are essentially intertwined and mutually supportive, cumulatively re-inforcing one another. Matthew is the church's liturgist and the church's poet, expanding Mark creatively, with no recourse to Q, partly by means of the lection. Luke is the great story-teller of the New Testament with the ability to weave and embroider material from Matthew and Mark, with a liturgical purpose.

Evans saw this 'all or nothing' character of the thesis as its great weakness. Yet Goulder's boldness is one of the great pleasures of British New Testament scholarship. On any pericope, on any subject, Goulder will always have something fresh or something interesting to say, the result of a virtue which above anything else commends Goulder's work, the extensive use of the imagination. It will always, in turn, stimulate the imagination of the reader and provide one with a clearer view of both the evangelists and the Gospels they wrote. It is a virtue which would profit from being much more widespread.

BIBLIOGRAPHY OF MICHAEL GOULDER

A. Books

Type and History in Acts (London: SPCK, 1964).
Midrash and Lection in Matthew (London: SPCK, 1974) (*MLM*).
The Evangelists' Calendar (London: SPCK, 1978) (*EC*).
The Psalms of the Sons of Korah (JSOTSup, 20; Sheffield: JSOT Press, 1982).
The Song of Fourteen Songs (JSOTSup, 36; Sheffield: JSOT Press, 1986).
Luke: A New Paradigm (2 vols.; JSNTSup, 20; Sheffield: JSOT Press, 1989) (*LNP*).
The Prayers of David (Psalms 51–72) (JSOTSup, 102; Sheffield: JSOT Press, 1990).
A Tale of Two Missions (London: SCM Press, 1994) (*TTM*).

with John Hick, *Why Believe in God?* (London: SCM Press, 1983).
(ed.), *Incarnation and Myth* (London: SCM Press, 1979).

B. Contributions to Multi-Author Works

'The Chiastic Structure of the Lucan Journey', in F.L. Cross (ed.), *Studia Evangelica*, II (Berlin: Akademie Verlag, 1964), pp. 195-202.
'Jesus, the Man of Universal Destiny', in John Hick (ed.), *The Myth of God Incarnate* (London: SCM, 1977), pp. 48-63.
'The Two Roots of the Christian Myth', in J. Hick (ed.), *Myth*, pp. 64-86.
'Paradox and Mystification', in M.D. Goulder (ed.), *Incarnation*, pp. 51-59.
'Incarnation or Eschatology?', in M.D. Goulder (ed.), *Incarnation*, pp. 142-46.
'The Samaritan Hypothesis', in M.D. Goulder (ed.), *Incarnation*, pp. 247-50 (replying to G. Stanton, 'Samaritan Incarnational Christology?', see below).
'The Liturgical Origin of St John's Gospel', in E.A. Livingstone (ed.), *Studia Evangelica*, VII (Berlin: Akademie Verlag, 1982), pp. 205-21.
'The Order of a Crank', in C.M. Tuckett (ed.), *Synoptic Studies: The Ampleforth Conferences of 1982 and 1983* (JSNTSup, 7; Sheffield: JSOT Press, 1984), pp. 111-30.
'Some Observations on Professor Farmer's "Certain Results..."', in C.M. Tuckett (ed.), *Synoptic Studies*, pp. 99-104 (commenting on W.R. Farmer, 'Certain Results...', see below).

'Farrer as a Biblical Scholar', Chapter 10 in Philip Curtis, *A Hawk among the Sparrows: A Biography of Austin Farrer* (London: SPCK, 1985).

'A House Built on Sand', in A.E. Harvey (ed.), *Alternative Approaches to New Testament Study* (London: SPCK, 1985), pp. 1-24.

'The Pauline Epistles', in R. Alter and F. Kermode (eds.), *The Literary Guide to the Bible* (London: Fontana, 1987), pp. 479-502.

'John 1.1–2.12 and the Synoptics, with Appendix: John 2.13–4.54 and the Synoptics', in A. Denaux (ed.), *John and the Synoptics* (BETL, 101; Louvain: Leuven University Press, 1992), pp. 201-37.

'A Pauline in a Jacobite Church', in F. Van Segbroeck *et al.* (eds.), *The Four Gospels*, II (Festschrift F. Neirynck; BETL, 100; Louvain: Leuven University Press, 1992), pp. 859-75.

'Luke's Knowledge of Matthew', in G. Strecker (ed.), *Minor Agreements: Symposium Göttingen, 1991* (Göttingen: Vandenhoeck & Ruprecht, 1993), pp. 143-60.

'Ruth: A Homily on Deut. 22–25?', in H.A. McKay and D.J.A. Clines (eds.), *Of Prophets' Visions and the Wisdom of Sages: Essays in Honour of R. Norman Whybray on his Seventieth Birthday* (JSOTSup, 162; Sheffield: JSOT Press, 1993), pp. 307-19.

'Did Jesus of Nazareth Rise from the Dead?', in J. Barton and G.N. Stanton (eds.), *Resurrection* (Festschrift Leslie Houlden; London: SPCK, 1994), pp. 58-68.

'Already?', in Thomas E. Schmidt and Moisés Silva (eds.), *To Tell the Mystery: Essays on New Testament Eschatology in Honor of Robert H. Gundry* (JSNTSup, 100; Sheffield: JSOT Press, 1994), pp. 21-33.

'The Phasing of the Future', in T. Fornberg and D. Hellholm (eds.), *Texts and Contexts* (Festschrift Lars Hartman; Oslo: Scandinavian University Press, 1995), pp. 391-408.

C. Articles

with M.L. Sanderson, 'St Luke's Genesis', *JTS* 8 (1957), pp. 12-30.

'The Composition of the Lord's Prayer', *JTS* 14 (1964), pp. 32-45.

'Characteristics of the Parables in the Several Gospels', *JTS* 19 (1968), pp. 51-69.

'The Bible and Extramural Teaching', *ScrB* 3 (1971), pp. 29-30.

'The Fourth Book of the Psalter', *JTS* 26 (1975), pp. 269-89.

'The Empty Tomb', *Theology* 79 (1976), pp. 206-14.

'On Putting Q to the Test', *NTS* 24 (1978), pp. 218-34.

'Mark XVI.1-8 and Parallels', *NTS* 24 (1978), pp. 235-40.

'Farrer on Q', *Theology* 83 (1980), pp. 190-95.

'The Apocalypse as an Annual Cycle of Prophecies', *NTS* 27 (1981), pp. 342-67.

with C.M. Tuckett, 'The Beatitudes: A Source-Critical Study', *NovT* 25 (1983), pp. 193-216.

'From Ministry to Passion in John and Luke', *NTS* 29 (1983), pp. 561-68.

'Did Luke Know any of the Pauline letters?', *PRS* 13 (1986), pp. 97-112.

Letter to the Editor (in response to A. Harvey, 'Rabbis, Evangelists—And Jesus'), *Theology* 92 (1989), p. 526.

'Σοφία in 1 Corinthians', *NTS* 37 (1991), pp. 516-34.

'The Visionaries of Laodicea', *JSNT* 43 (1991), pp. 15-39.

'Those Outside (Mark 4.10-12)', *NovT* 33 (1991), pp. 289-302.

'Nicodemus', *SJT* 44 (1991), pp. 153-68.

'Silas in Thessalonica', *JSNT* 48 (1992), pp. 87-106.

'An Old Friend Incognito', *SJT* 45 (1992), pp. 487-513.

'Exegesis of Gen. 1–3 in the New Testament', *JJS* 43 (1992), pp. 226-29.

'Translation and Exegesis: Some Reflections on the Swedish NT Translations of 1917 and 1981', *SEÅ* 57 (1992), pp. 102-14.

'Luke's Compositional Options', *NTS* 39 (1993), pp. 150-52.

'A Tale of Two Missions', an Inaugural Lecture delivered in the University of Birmingham, February 1993, School of Continuing Studies, University of Birmingham.

'2 Cor. 6.14–7.1 as an Integral Part of 2 Corinthians', *NovT* 36 (1994), pp. 47-57.

'Vision and Knowledge', *JSNT* 56 (1994), pp. 53-71.

'The Pre-Marcan Gospel', *SJT* 47 (1994), pp. 453-71.

'Colossians and Barbelo', *NTS* 41 (1995), pp. 601-19.

'Asaph's *History of Israel* (Elohist Press, Bethel, 725 BCE)', *JSOT* 65 (1995), pp. 71-81.

D. Book Reviews

René Laurentin, *Structure et Théologie de Luc I–II*, *JTS* 9 (1958), pp. 358-60.

Joachim Rohde, *Rediscovering the Teaching of the Evangelists*, *JTS* 20 (1969), pp. 596-99.

Hans-Theo Wrege, *Die Überlieferungsgeschichte der Bergpredigt*, *JTS* 20 (1969), pp. 599-602.

J.D. Kingsbury, *The Parables of Jesus in Matthew 13: A Study in Redaction Criticism*, *JTS* 21 (1970), pp. 164-66.

W.J. Harrington, *The Apocalypse of St John*, *ScrB* 2 (1970), pp. 21-22.

W.J. Harrington, *The Promise to Love*, *ScrB* 2 (1970), p. 51.

John Bligh, *Philippians*, *ScrB* 2 (1970), p. 57.

P. Pokorny, *Der Kern der Bergpredikt*, *JTS* 21 (1970), pp. 538-39.

M. Jack Suggs, *Wisdom, Christology, and Law in Matthew's Gospel*, *JTS* 22 (1971), pp. 568-69.

Albert Fuchs, *Sprachliche Untersuchungen zu Matthäus und Lukas: Ein Beitrag sur Quellenkritik*, *JTS* 23 (1972), pp. 197-200.

I. Howard Marshall, *Luke: Historian and Theologian*, *JTS* 23 (1972), pp. 201-202.

B. Vawter, *Biblical Inspiration*, *ScrB* 4 (1972), pp. 36-37.

R. Thysman, *Communauté et Directives Ethiques: La catéchèse de Matthieu*, *JTS* 26 (1975), p. 252.

R. Longenecker, *Biblical Exegesis in the Apostolic Period*, *JTS* 27 (1976), pp. 204-206.

H. Benedict Green, *The Gospel according to Matthew*, *JTS* 27 (1976), pp. 449-52.

R.J. Coggins, *The First and Second Books of Chronicles* and *The Books of Ezra and Nehemiah*, *Theology* 79 (1976), pp. 360-62.

Marie Isaacs, *The Concept of Spirit*, *ScrB* 8 (1977), p. 22.

Jack Dean Kingsbury, *Matthew: Structure, Christology, Kingdom*, *JTS* 28 (1977), pp. 144-46.

E. Schweizer, *The Good News according to Matthew*, *JTS* 28 (1977), p. 277.

John M. Rist, *On the Independence of Matthew and Mark*, *JTS* 30 (1979), pp. 265-67.

Ben F. Meyer, *The Aims of Jesus*, *Theology* 83 (1980), pp. 57-60.

K. Jones (ed.), *Living the Faith*, *Theology* 84 (1981), pp. 222-24.

G.B. Caird, *The Language and Imagery of the Bible*, *Theology* 86 (1983), pp. 223-24.

F. Neirynck, *Evangelica: Gospel Studies—Etudes d'Evangile. Collected Essays*, F. Van Segbroeck (ed.), *JTS* 35 (1984), pp. 194-99.

Acts and Letters of the Apostles: Newly Translated from the Greek (trans. R. Lattimore), *TLS* (Oct. 28, 1983), p. 1199.

A.T. Hanson, *The Living Utterances of God*, *Theology* 87 (1984), pp. 215-17.

G. Vermes, *Jesus and the World of Judaism*, *Theology* 87 (1984), pp. 456-57.

B. Chilton, *A Galilean Rabbi and his Bible*, *Theology* 88 (1985), pp. 304-306.

J. Drury, *The Parables in the Gospels*, *JTS* 37 (1986), pp. 172-74.

D.M. Paton, '*R. O.*': *The Life and Times of Bishop Ronald Hall of Hong Kong*, *Theology* 89 (1986), pp. 404-405

C. Rowland, *Christian Origins*, *Theology* 89 (1986), pp. 312-14.

H. Maccoby, *The Mythmaker: Paul and the Invention of Christianity*, *Theology* 90 (1987), pp. 227-29.

G.N. Stanton, *The Gospels and Jesus*, and E.P. Sanders and M. Davies, *Studying the Synoptic Gospels*, *TLS* (Oct. 20, 1989), p. 1166.

G. Strecker, *The Sermon on the Mount*, *Theology* 92 (1989), pp. 328-29.

A.T. Lincoln, *Ephesians*, *ScrB* 22 (1992), pp. 48-49.

J. Wenham, *Redating Matthew, Mark and Luke*, *Theology* 95 (1992), pp. 53-54.

C.F. Evans, *Saint Luke*, *SJT* 45 (1992), pp. 116-117.

J. Beutler and R.T. Fortna (eds.), *The Shepherd Discourse of John 10 and its Context*, *ScrB* 23 (1993), pp. 24-25.

R.E. Murphy, *The Song of Songs: A Commentary on the Book of Canticles*, *JTS* 44 (1993), pp. 206-208.

F. Neirynck, *Evangelica*. II. *1982–1991: Collected Essays* (ed. F. Van Segbroeck), *NovT* 35 (1993), pp. 199-202.

M. Casey, *From Jewish Prophet to Gentile God: The Origins and Development of New Testament Christology*, *SJT* 46 (1993), pp. 537-39.

A.E. Bernstein, *The Formation of Hell: Death and Retribution in the Ancient and Early Christian Worlds*, *Theology* 97 (1994), pp. 367-68.

D. Catchpole, *The Quest for Q*, *NovT* 36 (1994), pp. 205-207.

R. Schnackenburg, *The Epistle to the Ephesians: A Commentary*, *SJT* 47 (1994), pp. 386-88.

T.L. Brodie, *The Quest for the Origin of John's Gospel: A Source-Oriented Approach*, *SJT* 47 (1994), pp. 411-12.

S.E. Gillingham, *The Poems and Psalms of the Hebrew Bible*, *SJT* 48 (1995), pp. 263-64.

E. Reviews and Articles Dealing with Goulder

Only articles dealing directly and specifically with Goulder's work are listed here; for other relevant material, see the Select Bibliography, below. The following articles are all also listed in the Select Bibliography for ease of reference.

1) Reviews of *MLM*

A. Snell, *RTR* 33 (1974), pp. 84-86.

H. Wansbrough, *ScrB* 5 (1974–75), p. 49.

D.R. Catchpole, *EvQ* 47 (1975), pp. 239-94.

J.D.M. Derrett, 'Midrash in Matthew', *HeyJ* 16 (1975), pp. 51-56.

R. Crotty, *AusBR* 23 (1975), p. 44.

J.A. Sherlock, *TS* 36 (1975), pp. 338-40.

M. Smith, *JAAR* 53 (1975), pp. 604, 606.

R.E. Brown, *USQR* 31 (1976), pp. 297-99.

A.E. Harvey, *JTS* 27 (1976), pp. 188-95.

C.L. Mitton, *ExpTim* 86 (1976), pp. 97-99.

L. Sabourin, *BTB* 6 (1976), pp. 91-93.

J.A. Sanders, *Int* 30 (1976), pp. 91-92.

M. O'Connor, *RB* 83 (1976), pp. 304-305.

E.P. Sanders, *JBL* 96 (1977), pp. 453-55.

2) Reviews of *EC*

I.H. Marshall, *ExpTim* 90 (1979), p. 183.

J. Drury, *JSNT* 7 (1980), pp. 71-73.

M. Hooker, *EpRev* 7 (1980), pp. 91-93.

3) Reviews of *LNP*

J.-M. Roussée, *RB* 96 (1989), p. 475.

J. Drury, *EpRev* 17 (1990), pp. 89-91.

J. Fenton, *Theology* 93 (1990), pp. 67-68.

J.L. Houlden, 'Dispensing with Q', *TLS* (March 9, 1990), p. 260.

J. Nolland, *SJT* 43 (1990), pp. 269-72.

L. Cope, *RelSRev* 17 (1991), p. 261.

F.W. Danker, *JBL* 90 (1991), pp. 162-64.

F. Neirynck, *ETL* 67 (1991), pp. 434-36.

J. Muddiman, *JTS* 43 (1992), pp. 176-80.

4) Reviews of *TTM*

M. Davies, *ExpTim* 106 (1994), pp. 26-27.

F.G. Downing, *Theology* 97 (1994), pp. 465-66.

A.E. Harvey, 'Paulines v. Petrines', *TLS* (June 24, 1994), p. 31.

J. Carleton Paget, *RRT* 4 (1994), pp. 41-45.

5) Other Articles Dealing with Goulder

Thurmer, J., Letter to the Editor, *Theology* 79 (1976), pp. 355-56 (on 'The Empty Tomb').

C.F. Evans, 'Goulder and the Gospels', *Theology* 82 (1979), pp. 425-32.

G. Stanton, 'Samaritan Incarnational Christology?', in M.D. Goulder (ed.), *Incarnation*, pp. 243-46 (responding to 'The Two Roots of the Christian Myth').

C. Tuckett, 'On the Relationship between Matthew and Luke', *NTS* 30 (1984), pp. 130-42.

W.R. Farmer, 'Reply to Michael Goulder', in C.M. Tuckett (ed.), *Synoptic Studies*, pp. 105-109 (replying to 'Some Observations on Professor Farmer's "Certain Results..."').

F. Neirynck and T.A. Friedrichsen, 'Note on Luke 9.22: A Response to M.D. Goulder', *ETL* 65 (1989), pp. 390-94 = F. Neirynck, *L'Evangile de Luc— The Gospel of Luke* (BETL, 32; Louvain: Leuven University Press, 1989), pp. 393-98 = F. Neirynck, *Evangelica II: 1982–91. Collected Essays* (ed. F. Van Segbroeck; BETL, 99; Louvain: Leuven University Press, 1991), pp. 43-48.

F.G. Downing, 'A Paradigm Perplex: Luke, Matthew and Mark', *NTS* 38 (1992), pp. 15-36.

D.E. Nineham, 'Foreword: Michael Goulder—An Appreciation', in S.E. Porter *et al.* (eds.), *Crossing the Boundaries: Essays in Biblical Interpretation in Honour of Michael D. Goulder* (Leiden: Brill, 1994), pp. xi-xv.

F. Festschrift

S.E. Porter *et al.* (eds.), *Crossing the Boundaries: Essays in Biblical Interpretation in Honour of Michael D. Goulder* (Leiden: Brill, 1994).

SELECT BIBLIOGRAPHY

Abrahams, I., Review of *The Influence of the Triennial Cycle upon the Psalter*, by E.G. King, *JQR* 16 (1904), pp. 579-83.

Achtemeier, P.A., 'The Lukan Perspective on the Miracles of Jesus', in C.H. Talbert (ed.), *Perspectives on Luke–Acts*, pp. 153-67.

Adler, E.N., 'MS of Haftaras of the Triennial Cycle', *JQR* 8 (1896), pp. 528-29.

Aland, K., *Vollständige Konkordanz zum Griechischen Neuen Testament*, I.2-3, III (Berlin: de Gruyter, 1978, 1983).

—*Synopsis quattuor evangeliorum: Locis parallelis evangeliorum apocryphorum et patrum adhibitis* (Stuttgart: Deutsche Bibelgesellschaft, 13th edn, 1985).

Alexander, N. (ed.), *Time and Community: In Honor of Thomas Julian Talley* (Washington, DC: The Pastoral Press, 1990).

Alexander, P.S., 'Midrash and the Gospels', in C.M. Tuckett (ed.), *Synoptic Studies*, pp. 1-18.

—'Midrash', in *DBI*, pp. 452-59.

Allison, D.C., *The New Moses: A Matthean Typology* (Edinburgh: T. & T. Clark, 1993).

Anderson, J.C., *Matthew's Narrative Web—Over and Over and Over Again* (JSNTSup, 91; Sheffield: JSOT Press, 1994).

Argyle, A.W., 'Evidence for the View that St Luke Used St Matthew's Gospel', *JBL* 53 (1964), pp. 390-96.

Baasland, E., 'Zum Beispiel der Beispielerzählungen', *NovT* 28 (1986), pp. 193-219.

Ballard, 'Reasons for Refusing the Great Supper', *JTS* 23 (1972), pp. 341-50.

Bauckham, R., 'The Liber Antiquitatum Biblicarum of Pseudo-Philo and the Gospels as "Midrash"', in R.T. France and D. Wenham (eds.), *Gospel Perspectives*, III, pp. 33-76.

Beasley-Murray, G.R., Review of *According to Mark,* by P. Carrington, *BapQ* 19 (1961-62), pp. 255-57.

—*Baptism in the New Testament* (Exeter: Paternoster, 1972).

Beavis, M.A., *Mark's Audience: The Literary and Social Setting of Mark 4.11-12* (JSNTSup, 33; Sheffield: JSOT Press, 1989).

Bertram, G., *Die Leidensgeschichte Jesu und der Christuskult: Eine formgeschichtliche Untersuchung* (FRLANT, 32; Göttingen: Vandenhoeck & Ruprecht, 1922).

Billerbeck, P., 'Ein Synagogengottesdienst in Jesu Tagen', *ZNW* 55 (1964), pp. 143-61.

Black, C.C., *The Disciples according to Mark: Markan Redaction in Current Debate* (JSNTSup, 27; Sheffield: JSOT Press, 1988).

Black, M., 'The Parables as Allegory', *BJRL* 42 (1959–60), pp. 283-87.

Blair, H.A., 'The Gospel and the Jewish Lectionary' (Review of *Fourth Gospel*, by A. Guilding), *CQR* 162 (1961), pp. 365-66.

Blomberg, C. L., *Interpreting the Parables* (Leicester: Apollos, 1990).
—'Midrash, Chiasmus, and the Outline of Luke's Central Section', in R.T. France and D. Wenham (eds.), *Gospel Perspectives*, III, pp. 217-61.
Bock, D.L., *Proclamation from Prophecy and Pattern: Lucan Old Testament Christology* (JSNTSup, 12; Sheffield: JSOT Press, 1987).
Boismard, M.-E., 'The Two-Source Theory at an Impasse', *NTS* 26 (1979–80), pp. 1-17.
—'Introduction au premier récit de la multiplication des pains (Mt. 14.13-14; Mc 6.30-34; Lc 9.10-11)', in D.L. Dungan (ed.), *The Interrelations of the Gospels*, pp. 244-53.
—Review of *Fourth Gospel*, by A. Guilding, *RB* 68 (1961), pp. 599-602.
Bornkamm, G., G. Barth and H.J. Held, *Tradition and Interpretation in Matthew* (ET; London: SCM Press, 1963).
Bornkamm, G., 'The Stilling of the Storm in Matthew', in G. Bornkamm *et al.*, *Tradition and Interpretation in Matthew*, pp. 52-58.
Bowker, J.W., 'Speeches in Acts: A Study in Proem and Yelammedenu Form', *NTS* 14 (1967), pp. 96-111.
—*The Targums and Rabbinic Literature: An Introduction to Jewish Interpretations of Scripture* (Cambridge: Cambridge University Press, 1969).
Bowman, J., *The Gospel of Mark: The New Christian Jewish Passover Haggadah* (Studia Post-Biblica, 8; Leiden: Brill, 1965).
Brachman, A.J., Review of *Primitive Christian Calendar*, by P. Carrington, *JQR* 45 (1954–55), pp. 265-68.
Bradshaw, P.F. and L.A. Hoffman (eds.), *The Making of Jewish and Christian Worship* (Notre Dame: University of Notre Dame Press, 1991).
Bregman, M., 'The Triennial Haftarot and the Perorations of the Midrashic Homilies', *JJS* 32 (1981), pp. 74-84.
Brown, R.E., Review of *Fourth Gospel*, by A. Guilding, *CBQ* 22 (1960), pp. 459-61.
—'Parables and Allegory Reconsidered', *NovT* 5 (1962), pp. 36-45; reprinted in *idem*, *New Testament Essays* (Milwaukee: Bruce, 1965), pp. 254-64.
—*The Gospel according to John* (2 vols.; AB; New York: Doubleday, 1966).
—*The Birth of the Messiah: A Commentary on the Infancy Narratives in Matthew and Luke* (London: Chapman, rev. edn, 1993).
Browning, W.R.F., *The Gospel according to St Luke* (London: SCM Press, 1960).
Bruce, F.F., Review of *Fourth Gospel*, by A. Guilding, *JSS* 7 (1962), pp. 135-37.
—*The Acts of the Apostles* (Grand Rapids: Eerdmans, 3rd edn, 1990).
Büchler, A., 'The Reading of the Law and Prophets in a Triennial Cycle', *JQR* 5 (1893), pp. 420-68; 6 (1894), pp. 1-73.
Bultmann, R., *The History of the Synoptic Tradition* (ET; Oxford: Blackwell, rev. edn, 1972).
Burtchaell, J.T., *From Synagogue to Church: Public Services and Offices in the Earliest Christian Communities* (Cambridge: Cambridge University Press, 1992).
Burrows, E., 'The Use of Textual Theories to Explain the Agreements of Matthew and Luke against Mark', in J.K. Elliott (ed.), *Studies in New Testament Language and Text* (Leiden: Brill, 1976), pp. 87-89.
Cabaniss, A., *Pattern in Early Christian Worship* (Macon, GA: Mercer University Press, 1989).
Cadbury, H.J., *The Style and Literary Method of Luke* (Cambridge, MA: Harvard University Press, 1920).

—*The Making of Luke–Acts* (London: SPCK, 1958).

—'Four Features of Lucan Style', in L.E. Keck and J.L. Martyn (eds.), *Studies in Luke–Acts*, pp. 87-102.

Caird, G.B., *Saint Luke* (Pelican Gospel Commentaries; Harmondsworth: Penguin Books, 1963).

—*The Language and Imagery of the Bible* (London: Duckworth, 1980).

Carlston, C.E., *The Parables of the Triple Tradition* (Philadelphia: Fortress, 1975).

Carpenter, S.C., *Christianity according to St Luke* (London: SPCK, 1919).

Carrington, P., *The Primitive Christian Calendar: A Study in the Making of the Marcan Gospel* (Cambridge: Cambridge University Press, 1952).

—'St Mark and his Calendar', *CQR* 154 (1953), pp. 211-18.

—'The Ichthyology of the Gospels', *ATR* 37 (1955), pp. 50-55.

—'The Calendrical Hypothesis of the Origin of Mark', *ExpTim* 67 (1955–56), pp. 100-103.

—*According to Mark: A Running Commentary on the Oldest Gospel* (Cambridge: Cambridge University Press, 1960).

Casey, R.P., 'St Mark's Gospel' (Review of Carrington, Farrer and Taylor), *Theology* 55 (1952), pp. 362-70.

Catchpole, D.R., Review of *MLM*, *EvQ* 47 (1975), pp. 239-34.

—'The Anointed One in Nazareth', in M.C. de Boer (ed.), *From Jesus to John: Essays on Jesus and New Testament Christology in Honour of Marinus de Jonge* (JSNTSup, 84; Sheffield: JSOT Press, 1993), pp. 231-51.

—*The Quest for Q* (Edinburgh: T. & T. Clark, 1993).

Cave, C.H., 'The Sermon at Nazareth and the Beatitudes in the Light of the Synagogue Lectionary', in F.L. Cross (ed.), *Studia Evangelica*, III (Berlin: Akademie Verlag, 1964), pp. 231-35.

Chilton, B., 'Announcement in Nazara: An Analysis of Luke 4.16-21', in R.T. France and D. Wenham (eds.), *Gospel Perspectives*, II, pp. 147-72.

Cobb, P.G., 'The History of the Christian Year', in Cheslyn Jones *et al.* (eds.), *The Study of Liturgy* (London: SPCK, rev. edn, 1992), pp. 455-72.

Collison, J.G.F., 'Linguistic Usages in the Gospel of Luke', in W. Farmer (ed.), *New Synoptic Studies: The Cambridge Gospel Conference and beyond* (Macon, GA: Mercer University Press, 1983), pp. 245-60.

Connolly (trans.), H., *Didascalia Apostolorum* (Oxford: Clarendon, 1929).

Conzelmann, H., *The Theology of St Luke* (ET; London: Faber & Faber, 1960).

Cooper, J. and A.J. Maclean, *The Testament of the Lord* (Edinburgh: T. & T. Clark, 1902).

Cope, L., Review of *LNP*, *RelSRev* 17 (1991), p. 261.

Corley, B. (ed.), *Colloquy on New Testament Studies: A Time for Reappraisal and Fresh Approaches* (Macon, GA: Mercer University Press, 1983).

Cotterill, P. and M. Turner, *Linguistics and Biblical Interpretation* (London: SPCK, 1989).

Creed, J.M., *The Gospel according to St Luke* (London: Macmillan, 1930).

Crockett, L., 'Luke 4.16-30 and the Jewish Lectionary Cycle: A Word of Caution', *JJS* 17 (1966), pp. 13-46.

Cross, F.L., *1 Peter: A Paschal Liturgy* (London: A. R. Mowbray & Co., 1954).

Cross F.L. (ed.), *Studia Evangelica*, I (TU, 73; Berlin: Akademie Verlag, 1959).

Crossan, J.D., 'Parable and Example in the Teaching of Jesus', *NTS* 18 (1971–72), pp. 285-307; reprinted in *Semeia* 1 (1974), pp. 63-104.

—*In Parables: The Challenge of the Historical Jesus* (New York: Harper & Row, 1973).

—'Structuralist Analysis and the Parables of Jesus', *Semeia* 1 (1974), pp. 192-215.

—*Raid on the Articulate* (London: Harper & Row, 1976).

Crotty, R., Review of *MLM*, *AusBR* 23 (1975), p. 44.

Cullmann, O., *Early Christian Worship* (ET; London: SCM, 1959).

Dahl, N.A., 'Die Passiongeschichte bei Matthäus', *NTS* 2 (1955), pp. 17-32.

Danker, F.W., Review of *LNP*, *JBL* 90 (1991), pp. 162-64.

Daube, D., *The New Testament and Rabbinic Judaism* (London: Athlone, 1956).

—*The Sudden in the Scriptures* (Leiden: Brill, 1964).

Davies, J.G. (ed.), *A New Dictionary of Liturgy and Worship* (London: SCM Press, 1986).

Davies, M., Review of *TTM*, *ExpTim* 106 (1994), pp. 26-27.

Davies, W.D., 'Reflections on Archbishop Carrington's *The Primitive Christian Calendar*', in W.D. Davies and D. Daube (eds.), *The Background of the New Testament and Its Eschatology. Studies in Honour of C. H. Dodd* (Cambridge: Cambridge University Press, 1956), pp. 124-52; reprinted in W.D. Davies, *Christian Origins and Judaism* (London: Darton, Longman & Todd, 1962), pp. 67-95.

—*The Setting of the Sermon on the Mount* (Cambridge: Cambridge University Press, 1963).

—*Paul and Rabbinic Judaism: Some Rabbinic Elements in Pauline Theology* (Philadelphia: Fortress Press, 4th edn, 1980).

Davies, W.D. and D.C. Allison, *A Critical and Exegetical Commentary on the Gospel according to Matthew* (2 vols.; ICC; Edinburgh: T. & T. Clark, 1988, 1991).

Delling, D.G., *Worship in the New Testament* (ET; London: Darton, Longman & Todd, 1962).

Delobel, J. (ed.), *Logia: Les Paroles de Jésus—The Sayings of Jesus* (BETL, 59; Louvain: Leuven University Press, 1982).

—'La rédaction de Lc., IV, 14-16a et le «Bericht vom Anfang»', in F. Neirynck (ed.), *L'Evangile de Luc*, pp. 202-23.

Derrett, J.D.M., *Law in the New Testament* (London: Darton, Longman & Todd, 1970).

—'"Take thy Bond...and Write Fifty"', *JTS* 23 (1972), pp. 438-40.

—'Midrash in Matthew' (Review of *MLM*), *HeyJ* 16 (1975), pp. 51-56.

—*Studies in the New Testament* (5 vols.; Leiden: Brill, 1977–89).

Dibelius, M., *From Tradition to Gospel* (ET; Cambridge: J. Clarke, 1934).

Dodd, C.H., *The Parables of the Kingdom* (London: Nesbet & Co., rev. edn, 1961).

Donahue, J.R., *The Gospel in Parable: Metaphor, Narrative and Theology in the Synoptic Gospels* (Philadelphia: Fortress Press, 1988).

Doudna, J.C., *The Greek of the Gospel of Mark* (JBL Monograph Series, 12; Philadelphia, PA: Society of Biblical Literature and Exegesis, 1961).

Downing, F.G., 'Redaction Criticism: Josephus' *Antiquities* and the Synoptic Gospels', I, *JSNT* 8 (1980), pp. 46-65; II, *JSNT* 9 (1980), pp. 29-48.

—'A Paradigm Perplex: Luke, Matthew and Mark', *NTS* 38 (1992), pp. 15-36.

—Review of *TTM*, *Theology* 97 (1994), pp. 465-66.

Drury, J.H., 'The Sower and the Vineyard and the Place of Allegory in the Interpretation of Mark's Parables', *JTS* 24 (1973), pp. 367-79.

—'Midrash and Gospel', *Theology* 77 (1974), pp. 291-96.

—*Tradition and Design in Luke's Gospel: A Study in Early Christian Historiography* (London: Darton, Longman & Todd, 1976).

—Review of *EC*, *JSNT* 7 (1980), pp. 71-73.

—*The Parables in the Gospels: History and Allegory* (London: SPCK, 1985).

—Review of *LNP*, *EpRev* 17 (1990), pp. 89-91.

—'Luke, Gospel of', in *DBI*, pp. 410-14.

—'Parable', in *DBI*, pp. 509-11.

Dungan, D.L. (ed.), *The Interrelations of the Gospels: A Symposium Led by M.E. Boismard, W.R. Farmer, F. Neirynck, Jerusalem, 1984* (BETL, 95; Louvain: Leuven University Press, 1990).

Dunn, James D.G., *Unity and Diversity in the New Testament: An Enquiry into the Character of Earliest Christianity* (London: SCM Press, 1977).

—'Works of the Law and the Curse of the Law (Gal. 3.10-14)', *NTS* 31 (1985), pp. 523-42.

—*Christology in the Making: A New Testament Enquiry into the Origins of the Doctrine of the Incarnation* (London: SCM Press, 2nd edn, 1989 [1980]).

Easton, B.S., 'Linguistic Evidence for the Lucan Source "L"', *JBL* 29 (1910), pp. 139-80.

Elbogen, I., *Der jüdische Gottesdienst in seiner geschichtlichen Entwicklung* (Frankfurt: J. Kaufmann, 3rd edn, 1931; repr. Hildesheim: Georg Olms, 1962).

Elliott, J.K. (ed.), *The Language and Style of the Gospel of Mark: An Edition of C.H. Turner's "Notes on Marcan Usage" together with other Comparable Studies* (Leiden: Brill, 1993).

Ellis, E.E., 'New Directions in Form Criticism', *Prophecy and Hermeneutic in Early Christianity* (WUNT, 1.18; Tübingen: Mohr [Paul Siebeck], 1978), pp. 237-53.

—'Biblical Interpretation in the New Testament Church' in M.J. Mulder (ed.), *Mikra* (CRINT, II.2.1; Assen: Van Gorcum, 1988), pp. 691-725.

Evans, C.F., 'The Central Section of St Luke's Gospel', in D.E. Nineham (ed.), *Studies in the Gospels*, pp. 37-53.

—Review of *According to Mark*, by P. Carrington, *JTS* 14 (1963), pp. 140-46.

—'Goulder and the Gospels', *Theology* 82 (1979), pp. 425-32.

—*Saint Luke* (TPI New Testament Commentaries; London: SCM, 1990).

Fabricius, C., 'Zu *parachrema* bei Lukas', *Eranos* 83 (1985), pp. 62-66.

Farmer, W.R., 'Notes on a Literary and Form-Critical Analysis of Some of the Synoptic Material Peculiar to Luke', *NTS* 8 (1961–62), pp. 301-16.

—*Synopticon: The Verbal Agreements between the Greek Texts of Matthew, Mark and Luke Contextually Exhibited* (Cambridge: Cambridge University Press, 1969).

—*The Synoptic Problem: A Critical Review of the Problem of the Literary Relationships between Matthew, Mark and Luke* (New York: Macmillan, 1964; 2nd edn, Dillsboro, NC: Western North Carolina Press, 1976).

—'Certain Results Reached by Sir John C. Hawkins and C. F. Burney which Make More Sense if Luke Knew Matthew and Mark Knew Matthew and Luke', in C.M. Tuckett (ed.), *Synoptic Studies*, pp. 75-98.

—'Reply to Michael Goulder', in C.M. Tuckett (ed.), *Synoptic Studies*, pp. 105-109 (replying to 'Some Observations').

Farmer, W.R. (ed.), *New Synoptic Studies: The Cambridge Gospel Conference and beyond* (Macon, GA: Mercer University Press, 1983).

Farrer, A., *A Study in St Mark* (Westminster: Dacre, 1951).

—'A Liturgical Theory about St Mark's Gospel', Review of *Primitive Christian Calendar*, by P. Carrington, *CQR* 153 (1952), pp. 501-508.

—*St Matthew and St Mark* (Westminister: Dacre, 1954; 2nd edn, 1966).

—'On Dispensing with Q', in D.E. Nineham (ed.), *Studies in the Gospels*, pp. 55-88.

Farris, S., *The Hymns of Luke's Infancy Narrative: Their Origin, Meaning and Significance* (JSNTSup, 9; Sheffield: JSOT Press, 1985).

Fenton, J.C., 'Inclusio and Chiasmus in Matthew', in F.L. Cross (ed.), *Studia Evangelica*, I, pp. 174-79.

—*Saint Matthew* (Pelican Gospel Commentaries; Harmondsworth: Penguin, 1963).

—Review of *Tradition and Design*, by J.H. Drury, *Theology* 80 (1977), pp. 65-66.

—Review of *LNP*, *Theology* 93 (1990), pp. 67-68.

Finch, R.G., *The Synagogue Lectionary and the New Testament: A Study of the Three-Year Cycle of Readings from the Law and the Prophets as a Contribution to New Testament Chronology* (London: SPCK, 1939).

Fitzmyer, J.A., *The Gospel according to Luke I–IX and X–XXIV* (AB, 28 and 28A; New York: Doubleday, 1981, 1985).

—'The Priority of Mark and the "Q" Source in Luke', in *idem*, *To Advance the Gospel* (New York: Crossroad, 1981), pp. 3-40.

France, R.T., 'Scripture, Tradition and History in the Infancy Narratives of Matthew', in R.T. France and D. Wenham (eds.), *Gospel Perspectives*, II, pp. 239-66.

—'Jewish Historiography, Midrash and the Gospels', in R.T. France and D. Wenham (eds.), *Gospel Perspectives*, II, pp. 99-127.

—*Matthew* (TNTC; Leicester: Inter-Varsity Press, 1985).

—*Matthew: Evangelist and Teacher* (Exeter: Paternoster, 1989).

France, R.T. and D. Wenham (eds.), *Gospel Perspectives*. II. *Studies of History and Tradition in the Four Gospels* (Sheffield: JSOT Press, 1981).

—*Gospel Perspectives*. III. *Studies in Midrash and Historiography* (Sheffield: JSOT Press, 1983).

Franklin, E., *Christ the Lord: A Study in the Purpose and Theology of Luke–Acts* (London: SPCK, 1975).

—*Luke: Interpreter of Paul, Critic of Matthew* (JSNTSup, 92; Sheffield: JSOT Press, 1994).

Friedrichsen, T.A., 'The Matthew–Luke Agreements against Mark: A Survey of Recent Studies: 1974–1989', in F. Neirynck (ed.), *L'Evangile de Luc*, pp. 335-91 (= 'Survey').

—'New Dissertations on the Minor Agreements', *ETL* 67 (1991), pp. 373-94.

Fuchs, A., *Sprachliche Untersuchungen zu Matthäus und Lukas: Ein Beitrag zur Quellenkritik* (AnBib, 49; Rome: Biblical Institute Press, 1971).

—'Die „Seesturmperikope" Mark 4.35-41 parr im Wandel der urkirchlichen Verkündigung', in G. Strecker (ed.), *Symposium Göttingen 1991*, pp. 65-91.

Fuller, R.H., *The New Testament in Current Study* (New York: Charles Scribner's Sons, 1962).

Fuller, R.H., E. P. Sanders and T.R.W. Longstaff, 'The Current Debate on the Synoptic Problem', *PSTJ* 28 (1975), pp. 63-74.

Funk, F.X. (ed.), *Didascalia et Constitutiones Apostolorum* (Paderborn: In Libraria Ferdinandi Schoeningh, 1905).

Funk, R.W., *Language, Hermeneutic and the Word of God* (New York: Harper & Row, 1966).

—'The Good Samaritan as Metaphor', *Semeia* 2 (1974), pp. 74-81.

—*Parables and Presence: Forms of the New Testament Tradition* (Philadelphia: Fortress Press, 1982).

Frye, N., *Anatomy of Criticism* (London: Oxford University Press, 1957).

Gaster, M., 'The Biblical Lessons: A Chapter on Biblical Archeology', in *idem*, *Studies and Texts in Folklore, Magic, Medieval Romance, Hebrew Apocrypha and Samaritan Archeology* (3 vols.; London: Maggs Bros., 1925–28), I, pp. 503-99.

Gaston, L., *Horae Synopticae Electronicae: Word Statistics of the Synoptic Gospels* (Missoula, MT: SBL, 1973).

Gerhardsson, B., *The Good Samaritan—The Good Shepherd?* (ConBNT, 16; Lund: Gleerup, 1958).

—'The Parable of the Sower and its Interpretation', *NTS* 14 (1967–68), pp. 165-93.

—'The Narrative Meshalim in the Synoptic Gospels', *NTS* 34 (1988), pp. 339-63.

—'If we Do Not Cut the Parables out of their Frames', *NTS* 37 (1991), pp. 321-35.

—'Illuminating the Kingdom: Narrative Meshalim in the Synoptic Gospels', in H. Wansbrough (ed.), *Jesus and the Oral Gospel Tradition*, pp. 266-309.

Gingras, G.E. (trans. and ed.), *Egeria: Diary of a Pilgrimage* (Ancient Christian Writers, 38; New York: Newman Press, 1970).

Goodspeed, E.J., 'The Vocabulary of Luke & Acts', *JBL* 31 (1912), pp. 92-94.

Goudge, H.L. and P.P. Levertoff, 'The Gospel according to St. Matthew', in C. Gore *et al.* (eds.), *A New Commentary on Holy Scripture Including the Apocrypha* (London: SPCK, 1928), pp. 124-205.

Goudoever, J. Van, *Biblical Calendars* (Leiden: Brill, 1959).

Grabbe, L.L., 'Synagogues in Pre-70 Palestine', *JTS* 39 (1988), pp. 401-10.

Grant, F.C., 'A Critique of *The Style and Literary Method of Luke* by Cadbury', *ATR* 2 (1919–20), pp. 318-23.

—'Notice on Carrington, *Primitive Christian Calendar*', *ATR* 34 (1952), pp. 58-59.

Green, H.B., Review of *Der Weg der Gerechtigkeit*, by G. Strecker, *JTS* 16 (1964), pp. 361-65.

—*The Gospel according to Matthew* (Oxford: Clarendon, 1975).

—Review of *Tradition and Design*, by J.H. Drury, *ExpTim* 88 (1977), pp. 314-15.

—'The Credibility of Luke's Transformation of Matthew', in C.M. Tuckett (ed.), *Synoptic Studies*, pp. 131-56.

Guilding, A., 'Some Obscured Rubrics and Lectionary Allusions in the Psalter', *JTS* 3 (1952), pp. 41-55.

—*The Fourth Gospel and Jewish Worship: A Study of the Relation of St John's Gospel to the Ancient Jewish Lectionary System* (Oxford: Clarendon, 1960).

Gundry, R.H., *The Use of the Old Testament in St Matthew's Gospel* (NovTSup, 18; Leiden: Brill, 1967).

—*Matthew: A Commentary on his Literary and Theological Art* (Grand Rapids: Eerdmans, 1982).

—'Matthean Foreign Bodies in Agreements of Luke with Matthew against Mark: Evidence that Luke Used Matthew', in F. Van Segbroeck *et al.* (eds.), *The Four Gospels*, II, pp. 1467-95.

Haenchen, E., *Acts of the Apostles* (Philadelphia: Westminster, 1971).

Hagner, D.A., *Matthew 1–13* (WBC, 33A; Dallas, TX: Word Books, 1993).

Haire Forster, A., Review of *According to Mark*, by P. Carrington, *ATR* 44 (1962), pp. 90-93.

Harkins, P.W. (trans. and ed.), *Saint John Chrysostom: Discourses against Judaizing Christians* (The Fathers of the Church, 68; Washington, DC: Catholic University of America Press, 1979).

Harvey, A.E., *The New English Bible: Companion to the New Testament* (Cambridge: Cambridge University Press, 1970).

Harvey, A.E (ed.), Review of *MLM*, *JTS* 27 (1976), pp. 188-95.

—*Alternative Approaches to New Testament Study* (London: SPCK, 1985).

—'Rabbis, Evangelists—and Jesus', *Theology* 92 (1989), pp. 244-51.

—Review of *TTM*—'Paulines v. Petrines', *TLS* (June 24, 1994), p. 31.

Hawkins, J.C., *Horae Synopticae: Contributions to the Study of the Synoptic Problem* (Oxford: Clarendon, 2nd edn, 1909).

Heinemann, J., 'Preaching' (in the Talmudic Period), *EncJud*, XIII, pp. 994-98.

—'The Triennial Lectionary Cycle', *JJS* 19 (1968), pp. 41-48.

Herr, M.D., 'The Calendar', in S. Safrai and M. Stern (eds.), *The Jewish People in the First Century*, II, pp. 834-64.

Hick, J. (ed.), *The Myth of God Incarnate* (London: SCM, 1977).

Hoenig, S.B., 'The Suppositious Temple-Synagogue', *JQR* 54 (1963), pp. 115-31.

Honoré, A.M., 'A Statistical Study of the Synoptic Problem', *NovT* 10 (1968), pp. 95-147.

Hooke, S.H., 'Patterns in the Gospels', *CQR* 154 (1953), pp. 44-52.

Hooker, M., Review of *EC*, *EpRev* 7 (1980), pp. 91-93.

Houlden, J.L., 'Lectionary Interpretation (NT)', *DBI*, pp. 388-90.

—'Dispensing with Q' (Review of *LNP*), *TLS* (March 9, 1990), p. 260.

Huck, A., *Synopse der drei ersten Evangelien—Synopsis of the First Three Gospels* (rev. H. Greeven; Tübingen: Mohr [Paul Siebeck], 13th rev. edn, 1981).

Huggins, R.V., 'Matthean Posteriority: A Preliminary Proposal', *NovT* 34 (1992), pp. 1-22.

Hunkin, J.W., 'Pleonastic ἄρχομαι in the New Testament', *JTS* 25 (1924), pp. 390-42.

Idelsohn, I.Z., *Jewish Liturgy and its Development* (New York: Shocken Books, 1932).

Jacobs, J., 'Triennial Cycle', *Jewish Encyclopaedia*, VIII, pp. 254-57.

Jacobs, L., 'Liturgy', *EncJud*, XI, pp. 392-404.

Jameson, G. Hampden, *The Origin of the Synoptic Gospels: A Revision of the Synoptic Problem* (Oxford: Basil Blackwell, 1922).

Jeremias, J., *The Parables of Jesus* (ET; London: SCM Press, 6th edn, 1963).

—*The Eucharistic Words of Jesus* (ET; London: SCM Press, 3rd edn, 1966).

—'ΙΕΡΟΥΣΑΛΗΜ / ΙΕΡΟΣΟΛΥΜΑ', *ZNW* 65 (1974), pp. 273-76.

—*Die Sprache des Lukasevangeliums: Redaktion und Tradition im Nicht-Markusstoff des dritten Evangeliums* (Kritisch-exegetischer Kommentar über das Neue Testament Sonderband; Göttingen: Vandenhoeck & Ruprecht, 1980).

Johnson, L., *The Literary Function of Possessions in Luke–Acts* (SBLDS, 39; Missoula, MT: Scholars Press, 1977).

—*Sharing Possessions: Mandate and Symbol of Faith* (Philadelphia: Fortress Press, 1981).

Johnson, S.E., 'A New Theory of St Mark' (Review of *The Primitive Christian Calendar*, by P. Carrington), *ATR* 35 (1953), pp. 41-44.

—Review of *According to Mark*, by P. Carrington, *JBL* 80 (1961), pp. 177-80.

Jones, C. and G. Wainwright *et al.* (eds.), *The Study of Liturgy* (London: SPCK, rev. edn, 1992).

Jones, G.V., *The Art and Truth of the Parables* (London: SPCK, 1964).

Jülicher, A., *Die Gleichnisreden Jesu* (2 vols.; Tübingen: Mohr [Paul Siebeck], 2nd edn, 1910).

Karris, R.J., 'Poor and Rich: The Lukan *Sitz-im-Leben*', in C.H. Talbert (ed.), *Perspectives on Luke–Acts*, pp. 112-25.

Keck, L.E. and J.L. Martyn (eds.), *Studies in Luke–Acts* (London: SPCK, 1968).

Kenny, A., *A Stylometric Study of the New Testament* (Oxford: Oxford University Press, 1986).

Kilpatrick, G.D., *The Origins of the Gospel according to St Matthew* (Oxford: Clarendon, 1946).

—'Scribes, Lawyers and Lucan Origins', *JTS* 1 (1950), pp. 56-60.

Kimball, C.A., *Jesus' Exposition of the Old Testament in Luke's Gospel* (JSNTSup, 94; Sheffield: JSOT Press, 1994).

Kimelman, R., '*Birkat Ha-Minim* and the Lack of Evidence for an Anti-Christian Prayer in Late Antiquity', in E. P. Sanders *et al.* (eds.), *Jewish and Christian Self-Definition*. II. *Aspects of Judaism in the Graeco-Roman Period* (London: SCM, 1981), pp. 226-44.

King, E.G., 'The Influence of the Triennial Cycle upon the Psalter', *JTS* 5 (1904), pp. 203-13.

Klauck, H.-J., *Allegorie und Allegorese in synoptischen Gleichnistexten* (Münster: Aschendorff, 1978).

Klein, M., 'Four Notes on the Triennial Lectionary Cycle', *JJS* 32 (1981), pp. 65-73.

Kleist, J.A. (trans. and ed.), *The Didache; The Epistle of Barnabas & Martyrdom of St Polcarp; The Fragments of Papias; The Epistle of Diognitus* (Ancient Christian Writers, 6; Westminster, MD: Newman Press, 1948).

Knox, W.L., *Sources of the Synoptic Gospels* (2 vols.; Cambridge: Cambridge University Press, 1953, 1957).

Koet, B.Y., '"Today This Scripture Has Been Fulfilled in Your Ears": Jesus' Explanation of Scripture in Luke 4.16-30', in *idem*, *Five Studies on Interpretation of Scripture in Luke–Acts* (SNTA, 14; Leuven: Peeters, 1989), pp. 24-55 .

Lagrange, M.-J., *L'Evangile selon Saint Luc* (Paris: Librairie Lecoffre, 2nd edn, 1921).

—*L'Evangile selon Saint Matthieu* (Paris: Librairie Lecoffre, 3rd edn, 1927).

Lamb, J.A., 'The Place of the Bible in the Liturgy', in P. R. Ackroyd *et al.* (eds.), *The Cambridge History of the Bible* (Cambridge: Cambridge University Press, 1963–70), I, pp. 572-74.

Lane Fox, R., *The Unauthorised Version: Truth and Fiction in the Bible* (Harmondsworth: Penguin, 1991).

Lightfoot, R.H., *The Gospel Message of St. Mark* (Oxford: Oxford University Press, 1950).

Lindars, B., *The Gospel of John* (NCB; London: Oliphants, 1972).

Linnemann, E., *Parables of Jesus: Introduction and Exposition* (ET; London: SPCK, 1966).

Loisy, A., *Les evangiles synoptiques* (2 vols.; Ceffonds: Haute-Marne, 1907–1908).

Longstaff, T.R.W., 'The Minor Agreements: An Evaluation of the Basic Argument', *CBQ* 37 (1975), pp. 184-92.

—'The Women at the Tomb: Matthew 28.1 Re-Examined', *NTS* 27 (1981), pp. 277-82.

Lüdemann, G., *Jewish Opposition to Paul* (ET; Philadelphia: Fortress Press, 1989).

Lummis, E.W., *How Luke Was Written* (Cambridge: Cambridge University Press, 1915).

Luz, U., *Matthew 1–7: A Commentary* (ET; Edinburgh: T. & T. Clark, 1989).

Macrae, G.W., 'The Meaning and Evolution of the Feast of Tabernacles', *CBQ* 22 (1960), pp. 251-76.

Mann, C.S., *Mark: A New Translation with Introduction and Commentary* (AB, 27; New York: Doubleday, 1986).

Mann, J., 'The Observance of the Sabbath and the Festivals in the First Two Centuries of the Current Era according to Philo, Josephus, the New Testament and the Rabbinic Sources', *The Jewish Review* 4 (1914), pp. 433-56, 498-532.

—*The Bible as Read and Preached in the Old Synagogue*, I (Cincinnati: Jewish Publication Society, 1940); with Isaiah Sonne, II (Cincinnati: Jewish Publication Society, 1966).

Manson, T.W., Review of *Primitive Christian Calendar*, by P. Carrington, *JTS* 4 (1953), pp. 77-78.

Manson, W., *The Gospel of Luke* (MNTC; London: Hodder & Stoughton, 1930).

Marcus, R. (trans. and introduction), *Philo, Quaestiones in Genesim/Exodum* (LCL; London: Heinemann, 1953).

Marshall, I.H., *The Gospel of Luke: A Commentary on the Greek Text* (Exeter: Paternoster, 1978).

—Review of *EC*, *ExpTim* 90 (1979), p. 183.

Marxsen, W., *Introduction to the New Testament: An Approach to its Problems* (ET; Philadelphia: Fortress Press, 1968).

Martin, B., 'The Indispensability of Q', *Theology* 59 (1956), pp. 182-88.

Martin, R.P., *Mark: Evangelist and Theologian* (Exeter: Paternoster, 1972).

—'Patterns of Worship in New Testament Churches', *JSNT* 37 (1989), pp. 59-85.

Martyn, L., Review of *Fourth Gospel*, by A. Guilding, *USQR* 17 (1962), pp. 170-71.

McLoughlin, S., 'Les accords mineurs Mt–Lc contre Mc et le problème synoptique: Vers la théorie des deux sources', in I. de La Potterie (ed.), *De Jésus aux évangiles: Tradition et rédaction dans les évangiles synoptiques: Donum natalicium Iosepho Coppens...*, II (Gembloux: Duculot, 1967), pp. 17-40.

McNeil, B., 'Midrash in Luke?', *HeyJ* 19 (1978), pp. 399-404.

Mealand, D., *Poverty and Expectation in the Gospels* (London: SPCK, 1980).

Meier, J.P., *Law and History in Matthew's Gospel: A Redactional Study of Matt. 5.17-48* (Rome: Biblical Institute Press, 1976).

Metzger, B.M., *The Text of the New Testament: Its Transmission, Corruption and Restoration* (Oxford: Clarendon, 1964).

—*A Textual Commentary on the Greek New Testament: A Companion Volume to the United Bible Societies' Greek New Testament* (London: United Bible Societies, 1971).

Minear, P.S., 'Jesus' Audiences according to Luke', *NovT* 16 (1974), pp. 81-109.

Mitton, C.L., Review of *MLM*, *ExpTim* 86 (1976), pp. 97-99.

Miyoshi, M., *Der Anfang des Reiseberichts Lk 9.51–10.24* (AnBib, 60; Rome: Biblical Institute Press, 1974).

Montefiore, H., 'Does L Hold Water?', *JTS* 12 (1961), pp. 59-60.

Moore, G.F., *Judaism in the First Centuries of the Christian Era: The Age of the Tannaim* (3 vols.; Cambridge, MA: Harvard University Press, 1927).

Morgenthaler, R, *Die lukanische Geschichtsschreibung als Zeugnis* (ATANT, 15; Zürich: Gotthelf Verlag, 1948).

—*Statistische Synopse* (Zürich: Gotthelf Verlag, 1971).

—*Statistik des neutestamentlichen Wortschatzes* (Zürich: Gotthelf Verlag, 1973).

Morris, L., *The New Testament and the Jewish Lectionaries* (London: Tyndale, 1964).

—'The Gospels and the Jewish Lectionaries', in R. T. France and D. Wenham (eds.), *Gospel Perspectives*, III, pp. 129-56.

—'The Saints and the Synagogue', in M. J. Wilkins and T. Paige (eds.), *Worship, Theology and Ministry in the Early Church: Essays in Honor of Ralph P. Martin* (JSNTSup, 87; Sheffield: JSOT Press, 1992), pp. 39-52.

Moule, C.F.D., Review of *The Parables of Jesus*, by J. Jeremias, *ExpTim* 66 (1954–55), pp. 46-48.

—*An Idiom-Book of New Testament Greek* (Cambridge: Cambridge University Press, 2nd edn, 1959).

—'Mark 4.1-20 Yet Once More', E.E. Ellis and M. Wilcox (eds.), *Neotestamentica et Semitica: Essays for Matthew Black* (Edinburgh: Alec R. Allenson, 1969).

—*Birth of the New Testament* (London: Black, 3rd edn, 1981).

Moulton, W.F., A.S. Geden and H.K. Moulton, *A Concordance to the Greek Testament* (Edinburgh: T. & T. Clark, 5th edn, 1978).

Muddiman, J., Review of *LNP*, *JTS* 43 (1992), pp. 176-80.

Naegele, T., 'Translation of *talanton*, "talent"', *BT* 37 (1986), pp. 441-43.

Navone, J., 'Lucan Joy', *Scr* 20 (1968), pp. 49-62.

—*Themes of St Luke* (Rome: Gregorian University Press, 1970).

—'The Dynamic of Question in the Gospel Narrative', *MillSt* 17 (1986), pp. 75-111.

Neill, S., *The Interpretation of the New Testament, 1861–1961: The Firth Lectures, 1962* (London: Oxford University Press, 1964).

Neirynck, F., 'Hawkins's Additional Notes to his *Horae Synopticae*', *ETL* 46 (1970), pp. 78-111.

—*The Minor Agreements of Matthew and Luke against Mark, with a Cumulative List* (BETL, 37; Louvain: Leuven University Press, 1974).

—*Evangelica: Gospel Studies—Etudes d'évangile: Collected Essays* (ed. F. Van Segbroeck; BETL, 60; Louvain: Leuven University Press, 1982).

—'Recent Developments in the Study of Q', in J. Delobel (ed.), *Logia*, pp. 29-75.

—'The Matthew–Luke Agreements in Matt. 14.13-14/Luke 9.10-11 (par. Mark 6.30-44): The Two-Source Theory beyond an Impasse', *ETL* 60 (1984), pp. 25-43.

—'ΤΙΣ ΕΣΤΙΝ Ο ΠΑΙΣΑΣ ΣΕ, Matt. 26.68 / Luke 22.64 (diff. Mark 14.65)', *ETL* 63 (1987), pp. 5-47; reprinted in *Evangelica*, II, pp. 95-138.

—*Duality in Mark: Contributions to the Study of the Markan Redaction* (BETL, 31; Louvain: Leuven University Press, 2nd edn, 1988).

—*L'Evangile de Luc—The Gospel of Luke* (BETL, 32; Louvain: Leuven University Press, 1989).

—'The Two-Source Theory: Introduction', in D.L. Dungan (ed.), *The Interrelations of the Gospels*, pp. 3-22.

—'Response to the Multiple Stage Hypothesis: The Introduction of the Feeding Story. Mt. 14.13-14; Mk 6.30-34; Lk 9.10-11', in D.L. Dungan (ed.), *The Interrelations of the Gospels*, pp. 81-93.

—Review of *LNP*, *ETL* 67 (1991), pp. 434-36.

—'A Symposium on the Minor Agreements', *ETL* 67 (1991), pp. 361-72.

—*Evangelica*. II. *1982–91 Collected Essays* (ed. F. Van Segbroeck; BETL, 99; Louvain: Leuven University Press, 1991).

—'The Minor Agreements and the Two-Source Theory', in *Evangelica*, II, pp. 3-42; reprinted in G. Strecker (ed.), *Symposium Göttingen 1991*, pp. 25-62.

—'Q', in *IDBSup*, pp. 715-16.

—'The Synoptic Problem', in *IDBSup*, pp. 845-48.

Neirynck, F.C. (ed.), *L'Evangile de Luc: Problèmes littéraires et théologiques: Mémorial Lucien .Cerfaux* (BETL, 32; Louvain: Leuven University Press, 1973).

Neirynck, F. and T.A. Friedrichsen, 'Note on Luke 9.22, A Response to M. D. Goulder', *ETL* 65 (1989), pp. 390-94 = F. Neirynck, *L'Evangile de Luc —The Gospel of Luke* (BETL, 32; Louvain: Leuven University Press, 1989), pp. 393-8 = F. Neirynck, *Evangelica*, II, pp. 43-8.

Neirynck, F. and F. Van Segbroeck, *New Testament Vocabulary: A Companion Volume to the Concordance* (BETL, 65; Louvain: Leuven University Press, 1984).

Newport, K., 'The Sources and *"Sitz im Leben"* of Matt. 23' (DPhil dissertation, Oxford, 1988).

Nineham, D.E., 'Eye Witness Testimony and the Gospel Tradition', *JTS* 9 (1958), I, pp. 13-25; II, pp. 243-52.

—*Saint Mark* (Pelican Gospel Commentaries; Harmondsworth: Penguin, 1963).

—'Foreword: Michael Goulder—An Appreciation', in S. E. Porter *et al.* (eds.), *Crossing the Boundaries*, pp. xi-xv.

Nineham, D.E. (ed.), *Studies in the Gospels: Essays in Memory of R. H. Lightfoot* (Oxford: Blackwell, 1955).

Nineham, D.E. *et al.*, *History and Chronology in the New Testament* (Theolog. Collecs., 6; London: SPCK, 1965).

Nolland, J., *Luke 1–9.20* (WBC, 35A; Dallas: Word Books, 1989).

—Review of *LNP*, *SJT* 43 (1990), pp. 269-72.

O'Connor, M., Review of *MLM*, *RB* 83 (1976), pp. 304-305.

Oesterley, W.O.E., *The Jewish Background of the Christian Liturgy* (Oxford: Clarendon, 1925).

Orchard, B., *A Synopsis of the Four Gospels in Greek Arranged according to the Two Gospel Hypothesis* (Edinburgh: T. & T. Clark, 1983).

Orton, D.E., *The Understanding Scribe: Matthew and the Apocalyptic Ideal* (JSNTSup, 25; Sheffield: JSOT Press, 1989).

Paget, J. Carleton, Review of *TTM*, *RRT* 4 (1994), pp. 41-45.

Perrin, N., *Rediscovering the Teaching of Jesus* (London: SCM, 1967).

—'The Modern Interpretation of the Parables and the Problem of Hermeneutics', *Int* 25 (1971).

—*Jesus and the Language of the Kingdom* (London: SCM, 1976).

Pilgrim, W.E., *Good News to the Poor: Wealth and Poverty in Luke–Acts* (Minneapolis: Augsburg, 1981).

Piper, R.A., *Wisdom in the Q-Tradition: The Aphoristic Teaching of Jesus* (Cambridge: Cambridge University Press, 1989).

Plummer, A., *The Gospel according to St Luke* (ICC; Edinburgh: T. & T. Clark, 1896).

Porter, J.R., 'The Pentateuch and the Triennial Lectionary Cycle: An Examination of a Recent Theory', in F.F. Bruce (ed.), *Promise and Fulfilment: Essays Presented to Professor S.H. Hooke* (Edinburgh: T. & T. Clark, 1963), pp. 163-74.

Porter, S.E. *et al.* (eds.), *Crossing the Boundaries: Essays in Biblical Interpretation in Honour of Michael D. Goulder* (Leiden: Brill, 1994).

Potterie, I. de la, 'Les deux noms de Jérusalem dans l'évangile de Luc', *RSR* 69 (1981), pp. 57-70.

Prior, M., 'Revisiting Luke', *ScrB* 10 (1979), pp. 2-11.

Pryke, E.J., *Redactional Style in the Marcan Gospel: A Study of Syntax and Vocabulary as Guides to Redaction in Mark* (Cambridge: Cambridge University Press, 1978).

Rehkopf, F., *Die lukanische Sonderquelle—Ihr Umfang und Sprachgebrauch* (WUNT, 5; Tübingen: Mohr, 1959).

Reicke, B., *The Gospel of Luke* (ET; Richmond, VA: John Knox Press, 1964).

—'Der barmherzige Samariter', in O. Böcher and K. Haacker (eds.), *Verborum Veritas* (Festschrift G. Stählin; Wuppertal: Theologischer Verlag R. Brockhaus, 1970), pp. 103-109.

Reumann, J., 'A History of Lectionaries: From the Synagogue at Nazareth to Post-Vatican II', *Int* 31 (1977), pp. 116-30.

Richard, E., *Acts 6.1–8.4: The Author's Method of Composition* (SBLDS, 41; Missoula, MT: Scholars Press, 1978).

Roberts, B.J., *The Old Testament Text and Versions: The Hebrew Text in Transmission and the History of the Ancient Versions* (Cardiff: University of Wales Press, 1951).

Robinson, J.A.T., *The Priority of John* (ed. J. Coakley; London: SCM Press, 1985).

Ropes, J.H., *The Synoptic Gospels* (Cambridge, MA: Harvard University Press, 1934).

—'An Observation on the Style of St Luke', *Harvard Studies in Classical Philology* 12, pp. 299-305.

Rordorf, W., *Sunday: The History of the Day of Rest and Worship in the Earliest Centuries of the Christian Church* (ET; London: SCM Press, 1968).

Rosenblatt, S., Review of *The Bible as Read and Preached in the Old Synagogue*, by J. Mann, *JBL* 60 (1941), pp. 194-97.

Ross, J.M., 'The Use of Evidence in New Testament Studies', *Theology* 79 (1976), pp. 214-21.

Roussée, J.-M., Review of *LNP*, *RB* 96 (1989), p. 475.

Sabourin, L., Review of *MLM*, *BTB* 6 (1976), pp. 91-39.

Safrai, S., 'The Synagogue', in S. Safrai and M. Stern (eds.), *The Jewish People in the First Century*, II, pp. 908-44.

Safrai, S. and M. Stern (eds.), *The Jewish People in the First Century: Historical Geography, Political History, Social, Cultural and Religious Life and Institutions* (2 vols.; CRINT; Assen: Van Gorcum, 1974–76).

Sanday, W. (ed.), *Studies in the Synoptic Problem by Members of the University of Oxford* (Oxford: Clarendon Press, 1911).

Sanders, E.P., 'The Argument from Order and the Relationship between Matthew and Luke', *NTS* 15 (1968–69), pp. 249-61.

—*The Tendencies of the Synoptic Tradition* (SNTSMS, 9; Cambridge: Cambridge University Press, 1969).

—'The Overlaps of Mark and Q and the Synoptic Problem', *NTS* 12 (1972–73), pp. 453-65.

—Review of *MLM*, *JBL* 96 (1977), pp. 453-55.

—'New Testament Studies Today', in B. Corley (ed.), *Colloquy on New Testament Studies*, pp. 11-28.

—*Paul, the Law and the Jewish People* (London: SCM Press, 1983).

Sanders, E.P. and M. Davies, *Studying the Synoptic Gospels* (London: SCM Press, 1989).

Sanders, J.A., Review of *MLM*, *Int* 30 (1976), pp. 91-92.

Sanders, J.T., *The Jews in Luke–Acts* (London: SCM Press, 1987).

Schille, G., 'Das Leiden des Herrn. Die evangelische Passions-tradition und ihr "Sitz im Leben"', *ZTK* 52 (1955), pp. 161-205.

Schmidt, T.E., *Hostility to Wealth in the Synoptic Gospels* (JSNTSup, 15; Sheffield: JSOT Press, 1987).

Schneider, G., *Die Apostelgeschichte* (HTKNT, 5.2; Freiburg: Herder, 1982).

Schmid, J., *Matthäus und Lukas: Eine Untersuchung Des Verhältnisses Ihrer Evangelien* (Freiburg: Herder, 1930).

Scholes, R. and R. Kellogg, *The Nature of Narrative* (London: Oxford University Press, 1966).

Schürmann, H., 'Der "Bericht von Anfang": Ein Rekonstruktionsversuch auf Grund von Lk 4.14-16', in *Studia Evangelica*, II (TU, 87; Berlin: Akademie Verlag, 1964), pp. 242-58.

—*Das Lukasevangelium* (HTKNT, 3.1; Freiburg: Herder, 1969).

Schütz, R., ''Ιερουσαλημ und 'Ιεροσολυμα im NT', *ZNW* 11 (1910), pp. 169-87.

Schweizer, E., *The Good News according to Matthew* (ET; London: SPCK, 1976).

Scott, B.B., *Hear Then the Parable: A Commentary on the Parables of Jesus* (Minneapolis: Fortress, 1989).

Seccombe, D.P., *Possessions and the Poor in Luke–Acts* (SNTU, 6; Linz: SNTU, 1982).

Seidel, H., 'The Prayers of David (Psalms 51–72)', *Theologische Literaturzeitug* 117 (1992), 348–50.

Sellew, P., 'Interior Monologue as a Narrative Device in the Parables of Luke', *JBL* 111 (1992), pp. 239-53.

Sellin, G., 'Lucas als Gleichniserzähler', *ZNW* 65 (1974), pp. 166-89; 66 (1975), pp. 19-60.

—'Komposition, Quellen und Funktion des lukanischen Reiseberichts (Lk ix.51–xix.28)', *NovT* 20 (1978), pp. 100-35.

Senior, D., *The Passion of Jesus in the Gospel of Luke* (Wilmington, DE: Michael Glazier, 1989).

Sheeley, S.M., *Narrative Asides in Luke–Acts* (JSNTSup, 72; Sheffield: JSOT Press, 1992).

Sherlock, J.A., Review of *MLM*, *TS* 36 (1975), pp. 338-40.

Sider, J.W., 'Proportional Analogy in the Gospel Parables', *NTS* 31 (1985), pp. 1-23.

Simon, M., *Tractate Megillah* (ET with Notes, Glossary and Indices), in I. Epstein (ed.), *The Babylonian Talmud, Seder Mo'ed* (8 vols.; London, 1938).

Simons, E., *Hat der dritte Evangelist den kanonischen Matthäus benutzt?* (Bonn, 1880).

Simpson, R.T., 'The Major Agreements of Matthew and Luke Against Mark', *NTS* 12 (1965-66), pp. 273-84; repr. in A.J. Bellinzoni, J.B. Tyson and W.O. Walker (eds.), *The Two Source Hypothesis: A Critical Appraisal* (Macon, GA: Mercer University Press, 1985), pp. 381-95.

Smith, D.E., 'Table Fellowship as a Literary Motif in the Gospel of Luke', *JBL* 106 (1987), pp. 613-38.

Smith, M., Review of *MLM*, *JAAR* 53 (1975), pp. 604, 606.

Snaith, N.H., Review of *Fourth Gospel*, by A. Guilding, *JTS* 12 (1961), pp. 322-24.

—Review of *New Testament*, by L. Morris, *JTS* 17 (1966), pp. 129-31.

Snell, A., Review of *MLM*, *RTR* 33 (1974), pp. 84-86.

Soards, M., *The Passion according to Luke: The Special Material of Luke 22* (JSNTSup, 14; Sheffield: JSOT Press, 1987).

Sonne, I., 'Synagogue', in *IDB*, IV, pp. 479-80.

Sparks, H.D.F., *A Synopsis of the Gospels: The Synoptic Gospels with the Johannine Parallels* (London: Black, 1964).

Spong, J.S., *Born of a Woman: A Bishop Rethinks the Birth of Jesus* (San Francisco: Harper & Row, 1992).

Srawley, J.H., *The Early History of the Liturgy* (Cambridge: Cambridge University Press, 2nd edn, 1947).

Stanley, D.M., 'Liturgical Influences on the Formation of the Four Gospels', *CBQ* 21 (1959), pp. 24-38.

Stanton, G., 'Samaritan Incarnational Christology?', in M.D. Goulder (ed.), *Incarnation and Myth*, pp. 243-46 .

—'The Origin and Purpose of Matthew's Gospel: Matthean Scholarship from 1945–1980', in W. Haase (ed.), *Aufstieg und Niedergang der römischen Welt*, II (Principat, 25.3; Berlin: de Gruyter, 1985), pp. 1889–1951.

—*A Gospel for a New People: Studies in Matthew* (Edinburgh: T. & T. Clark, 1992).

—'Matthew, Gospel of', in *DBI*, pp. 432-35.

Stegemann, W., *The Gospel to the Poor* (Philadelphia: Fortress Press, 1984).

Stein, R.H., 'The Matthew–Luke Agreements against Mark: Insight from John', *CBQ* 54 (1992), pp. 482-502.

Stern, D., *Parables in Midrash: Narrative and Exegesis in Rabbinic Literature* (Cambridge, MA: Harvard University Press, 1991).

Stevenson, J. (ed.), *A New Eusebius: Documents Illustrative of the Hstory of the Church to A.D. 337* (London: SPCK, 1957).

Stewart, J.S., Review of *According to Mark*, by P. Carrington, *SJT* 15 (1962), pp. 428-31.

Strecker, G. (ed.), *Minor Agreements: Symposium Göttingen 1991* (Göttingen: Vandenhoeck & Ruprecht, 1993).

Streeter, B.H., *The Four Gospels: A Study of Origins* (London: Macmillan, 1924).

Sukenik, E.L., *Ancient Synagogues in Palestine and Greece: The Schweich Lectures, 1930* (London: Oxford University Press, 1934).

Styler, G.M., 'Excursus 4', in C.F.D. Moule, *The Birth of the New Testament*, pp. 285-316.

Sylva, D.D., '*Ierousalem* and *Hierosoluma* in Luke–Acts', *ZNW* 74 (1983), pp. 207-21.

Talbert, C.H., *Literary Patterns, Theological Themes and the Genre of Luke–Acts* (SBLDS, 20; Missoula, MT: Scholars Press, 1974).

—*What is a Gospel? The Genre of the Canonical Gospels* (London: SPCK, 1977).

—*Perspectives on Luke–Acts* (Edinburgh: T. & T. Clark, 1978).

Taylor, V., *Behind the Third Gospel: A Study of the Proto-Luke Hypothesis* (Oxford: Clarendon, 1926).

—'Commentaries on St Mark', *ExpTim* 72 (1960–61), pp. 169-70.

—'Rehkopf's List of Words and Phrases Illustrative of Pre-Lukan Speech Usage', *JTS* 15 (1964), pp. 59-62.

—*The Passion Narrative of St Luke* (Cambridge: Cambridge University Press, 1972).

Thackeray, H. St John, *The Septuagint and Jewish Worship: A Study in Origins, The Schweich Lectures 1920* (London: Oxford University Press, 1921).

Thomas, R.L., 'An Investigation of the Agreements between Matthew and Luke against Mark', *JETS* 19 (1976), pp. 103-12.

Thurmer, J., Letter to the Editor, *Theology* 79 (1976), pp. 355-56 (on 'The Empty Tomb').

Tolbert, M.A., *Sowing the Gospel: Mark's World in Literary-Historical Perspective* (Minneapolis: Fortress Press, 1989).

Trocmé, E., *The Formation of the Gospel according to St Mark* (London: SPCK, 1975).

—*The Passion As Liturgy: A Study in the Origin of the Passion Narratives* (London: SCM Press, 1983).

Tuckett, C.M., 'Luke 4.16-30, Isaiah and Q', in J. Delobel (ed.), *Logia*, pp. 343-54.

—*The Revival of the Griesbach Hypothesis* (Cambridge: Cambridge University Press, 1983).

—'On the Relationship between Matthew and Luke', *NTS* 30 (1984), pp. 130-42.

—'Arguments from Order: Definition and Evaluation', in *idem* (ed.), *Synoptic Studies*, pp. 197-219.

—*Reading the New Testament: Methods of Interpretation* (London: SPCK, 1987).

—Review of *Studying*, by E.P. Sanders and M. Davies, *SJT* 44 (1991), pp. 242-45.

—'The Minor Agreements and Textual Criticism', in G. Strecker (ed.), *Symposium Göttingen 1991*, pp. 119-41.

—'Synoptic Problem, the', in *DBI*, pp. 659-61.

—'Q (Gospel Source)', in *ABD*, V, pp. 567-72.

—'Synoptic Problem, the', in *ABD*, VI, pp. 263-70.

Tuckett, C.M. (ed.), *Synoptic Studies: The Ampleforth Conferences of 1982 and 1983* (JSNTSup, 7; Sheffield: JSOT Press, 1984).

Turner, C.H., *The Study of the New Testament 1883 and 1920* (Oxford: Clarendon, 1920; 2nd edn, 1924).

—'The Use of Numbers in Mark's Gospel', *JTS* (o.s.) 26 (1925), pp. 337-46; repr. in Elliott (ed.), *Language and Style*, pp. 53-62.

Turner, N., 'The Minor Verbal Agreements of Matthew and Luke against Mark', in F.L. Cross (ed.), *Studia Evangelica*, I, pp. 223-34.

—'The Style of Luke–Acts', in J.H. Moulton, *A Grammar of the Greek New Testament*, IV (Edinburgh: T. & T. Clark, 1976), pp. 45-63.

Van Segbroeck, F., *The Gospel of Luke: A Cumulative Bibliography, 1973–88* (BETL, 88; Louvain: Leuven University Press, 1989).

Van Segbroeck, F. *et al.* (eds.), *The Four Gospels* (Festschrift F. Neirynck; 3 vols.; BETL, 100; Louvain: Leuven University Press, 1992).

Via, D.O., *The Parables: Their Literary and Existential Dimension* (Philadelphia: Fortress Press, 1967).

—'Parable and Example Story: A Literary-Structuralist Approach', *Semeia* 1 (1974), pp. 105-33.

—'A Response to Crossan, Funk and Petersen', *Semeia* 1 (1974), pp. 222-35.

Wansbrough, H., Review of *MLM*, *ScrB* 5 (1974–75), p. 49.

Wansbrough, H. (ed.), *Jesus and the Oral Gospel Tradition* (JSNTSup, 64; Sheffield: JSOT Press, 1991).

Wenham, J., *Redating Matthew, Mark and Luke: A Fresh Assault on the Synoptic Problem* (London: Hodder & Stoughton, 1991).

Werner, E., *The Sacred Bridge: The Interdependence of Liturgy and Music in Synagogue and Church during the First Millennium* (vol. I; New York: Columbia University Press, 1959; vol. II; New York: Ktav, 1984).

Wilson, A.N., *Jesus* (London: Flamingo, 1993).

Wilson, R.M., 'Farrer and Streeter on the Minor Agreements of Matthew and Luke against Mark', in F.L. Cross (ed.), *Studia Evangelica*, I, pp. 254-57.

Wilson, S.G., *The Gentiles and the Gentile Mission in Luke–Acts* (Cambridge: Cambridge University Press, 1973).

Winter, P., *On the Trial of Jesus* (Berlin: de Gruyter, 1961).

Witherup, R.D., 'Cornelius Over and Over and Over Again: "Functional Redundancy" in the Acts of the Apostles', *JSNT* 39 (1993), pp. 45-66.

Wright, A., *The Gospel according to St Luke in Greek* (London: Macmillan, 1900).

Wright, N.T., *Who Was Jesus?* (London: SPCK, 1992).

Yoon, Victor Seung-Ku, 'Did the Evangelist Luke Use the Canonical Gospel of Matthew?' (PhD dissertation, Graduate Theological Union, Berkeley, CA, 1986).

Young, F., 'Two Roots or a Tangled Mass?', in J. Hick (ed.), *Myth*, pp. 87-121.

Zuntz, G., 'The Centurion of Capernaum', *JTS* 46 (1945), pp. 183-90.

INDEXES

INDEX OF REFERENCES

OLD TESTAMENT

OTHER ANCIENT LITERATURE

INDEX OF AUTHORS